Daniel Henry Haigh

The Conquest of Britain by the Saxons

A Harmony of the historia britonum, the Writings of Gildas, the Brut and the Saxon Chronicle

Daniel Henry Haigh

The Conquest of Britain by the Saxons
A Harmony of the historia britonum, the Writings of Gildas, the Brut and the Saxon Chronicle

ISBN/EAN: 9783337091453

Printed in Europe, USA, Canada, Australia, Japan

Cover: Foto ©ninafisch / pixelio.de

More available books at **www.hansebooks.com**

THE

CONQUEST OF BRITAIN

BY THE SAXONS;

A HARMONY OF THE "HISTORIA BRITONUM," THE WRITINGS OF
GILDAS, THE "BRUT," AND THE SAXON CHRONICLE,
WITH REFERENCE TO THE EVENTS OF THE
FIFTH AND SIXTH CENTURIES.

BY DANIEL H. HAIGH.

"Hic reges populosque vides, quos alea fati
"Extulit et pressit, sed ab his metire futura.
"Aspice——quo devenere potentes:
"Aspice quam nihili sit honor, lux, gloria mundi."
HENRY OF HUNTINGDON.

LONDON:
JOHN RUSSELL SMITH,
36, SOHO SQUARE.
1861.

TO JOSEPH MAYER.

MY DEAR SIR,

I VENTURE to hope that these results of my researches will be acceptable, not only to you, but to many others, who, with myself, have believed in Hencgest and Arthur from our childhood, and whose faith has not wavered in maturer years, even though criticism has seemed to controvert the possibility of the details of their history, and scholars, (whose names must always be held in the highest respect), have altogether denied their personality; that your having encouraged and assisted me to publish them, will be esteemed not the least of the services you have rendered to antiquarian science. For, surely, if the elucidation of a single doubtful point of history be a matter worthy of the attention of every student of antiquity, the importance of the object proposed, and attained, in the following pages, cannot be denied. The history of a century, and that one of the most eventful in our annals, is now for the first time truly set forth; the hidden links of the chain, which connects the Anglo-Saxon Octarchy with the Roman Province of Britain, are discovered; the separate narratives of our early chroniclers are harmonized; and their authority as historians is established. The subject, however, is far from being exhausted; although I have carefully made use of every authority within my reach, I am satisfied that our National and University Libraries contain treasures in print and in manuscript, which would have supplied additional and important matter; and the Bardic poems also, though chronologically useless, would have been valuable in the way of illustration, if I had had access to them. I have done little more than lay the foundation of the history of the fifth century; still, this is something, and may justify a plea for indulgence, for faults of style, of which I am only too sensible; and I willingly leave the completion of the work to abler hands than mine. With no other object than that of ascertaining the truth, I am not conscious of having avoided any difficulty, or suppressed anything that seemed to militate with my conclusions; and if I have inadvertently been betrayed into error, if I have advanced anything in the way of conjecture, which may prove to be at variance with facts of history (related by authors whose works I have not had the opportunity of consulting), to no one will the discovery and refutation of such errors be more welcome, than to

Yours most truly,

DANIEL H. HAIGH.

Erdington, July 22, 1861.

CONTENTS.

CHAPTER I.

Page

OBSCURITY in which the history of the Conquest of Britain is involved 1
This has arisen from the adoption of erroneous dates 3
The general trustworthiness of Gildas, the History of the Britons, and the Brut, asserted . . . *ib.*
The History and the Epistle of Gildas shown, by internal evidence, to be distinct works . . . . *ib.*
The Cambridge MS., F. f. i. 27, presents them in this form . . 4
Another, D. d. i. 27, presents them incorporated together . . *ib.*
The History must have been written in A.D. 471, and is therefore entitled to implicit confidence 5
The Epistle, written in A.D. 492 or 493, is also a cotemporary document . . . . *ib.*
The History of the Britons, ascribed to Nennius, but more probably compiled by S. Gildas 6
An edition of this History, written in Kent, in A.D. 675, represented by the Paris and Vatican MSS. 8
Other editions of A.D. 831, 857, 907, and 976 . . . . . 10, 11
Extracts from a larger work by S. Gildas, probably incorporated in the Chronicle of Henry of Huntingdon 12
Geoffrey of Monmouth, the first editor or translator of the Brut in England 13
Layamon furnishes a clue to its author . . . . *ib.*
He was probably S. Albinus, Bishop of Angers 15
Hector Boece made use of a Chronicle, written in the eleventh century, by Veremund, Archdeacon of S. Andrews 16
His information valuable, but to be used with caution 17
Scheme of the Chronology of the Conquest of Britain, from the revolt of Maximus, A.D. 385, to the accession of Cyneric, A.D. 534 18

CHAPTER II.

[1] I have omitted to notice in connection with this ring, that its inscription, DORPNAR, gives the name of Woden's magic ring *Draupner*.

---

[2] If the evidence of Nunez de Vega be cited correctly, for I have not access to the work itself, this Votan may have been an ancestor of the Votan who colonized America. The latter was the third of his name. He certainly came from the east, and says, that after his coming to America he made voyages to the country whence he came; that in the first of these he visited a town where men were building a great temple to God; that thence he proceeded to visit the great building which men had erected by order of their common grandfather, thereby to reach heaven, and that he was told that it was the spot whence God had given to each family of mankind a special language. (ABBÉ DOMENECH'S *Seven Years' Residence in the Great Deserts of North America*, I. 12.)

If the temple that men were building were the Temple of Solomon, the æra of this Votan would be, as it has been thought to have been, about one thousand years before Christ.

	Page
Taaut, and others, invented phonetic writing for their families	104
Plato's story of Theuth and Thamus	105
Evidence of the common origin of the Phœnician alphabet, and the futhorc	106
Sir H. C. Rawlinson's remarks on the origin of the cuneiform systems of writing	108
The art of writing part of the primitive tradition, common to all races of mankind	109
Original[3] and derivative significations of the word *rún*	*ib.*

CHAPTER III.

The Anglo-Saxon genealogies are substantially genuine historic documents	115
Geat or Gaut, the common ancestor of the Gothic and Anglo-Saxon royal dynasties, flourished probably about A.D. 100	116
Ostrogotha, his fifth descendant, died A.D. 251	117
The Goths defeated by Constantine in A.D. 323 and 332	*ib.*
Geberic, fourth in descent from Ostrogotha, flourished about A.D. 335	*ib.*
Hermanaric, his successor, died A.D. 375	118
The successors of Hermanaric	*ib.*
The Gothic genealogy intrinsically probable, and consistent with history	*ib.*
The Anglo-Saxon genealogies correspond with it as nearly as could be expected	120
Woden's æra determined to have been the third century ending, and the fourth commencing	121
Woden regarded as a historic personage by all our Chroniclers	*ib.*
His history, deduced from northern tradition	122
His expedition, probably consequent on the defeat of his nation by Constantine, commenced about A.D. 325	123
The Longobardic[4] tradition confirms this conjecture	124
" genealogy consistent with the Gothic	125

[3] I have supposed the existence of a primitive word, *ru* or *run*, designating a "sword," "knife," or other weapon. The Welsh language supplies such a word, *ron* a "spear."

Mr. George Stephens of Copenhagen has a work ready for the press, which promises to be one of the most important that has yet appeared, on the subject of Runes. It will contain illustrations of upwards of one hundred inscriptions of the class which I have noticed, from page 52 to 65 of this chapter. The publisher of this work is authorized to receive the names of subscribers.

[4] I have preferred the authority of Paul Warnefrid for the history of the Longobards, because he was of their race. I must not, however, omit noticing that Procopius makes Hildigisl the great grandson of a brother of Tato, not the son of Tato. My argument, even admitting this, will not be affected; for Tato was strictly the cotemporary of Ossa, the father of Eormanric, whose name appears in the same line with his in the genealogies, p. 135. Ossa began to reign A.D. 491, Tato, A.D. 493.

CHAPTER IV.

CHAPTER V.

	Page
The "Littus Saxonicum per Britannias," several local, and some personal names, indicate Teutonic settlements in this island, during the time of its occupation by the Romans . . .	161
Dion Cassius, Zosimus, Aurelius Victor, and Ammianus Marcellinus, bear witness to the fact of such settlements having been made	162
The History of the Britons records the reception of a body of Saxons by Vortigern, in A.D. 375[5]	163

CHAPTER VI.

The date of the accession of Vortigern, A.D. 425, and that of the coming of the Angles, A.D. 428, established by the Chronological Notes, appended to four MSS. of the History of the Britons	167
and supported by statements in the History itself . . .	169
by Osbern, in his Life of S. Dunstan, and by the genealogies of Vortigern's descendants	172
The false date of the coming of the Angles, A.D. 449, originated in a misunderstanding, on the part of Bæda, of one of the above passages in the History of the Britons	174

CHAPTER VII.

Maximus invades Gaul, kills Gratian, makes a treaty with Valentinian	176
Britain, left defenceless by the withdrawal of her militia, is invaded by the Picts and Huns, commanded by Guanis and Melga .	177
Maximus sends Gratian Municeps from Italy to oppose them; he expels them from the island	179
Maximus is defeated and slain at Aquileia	177
Chrysanthus, Vicar of the British Isles	180
The Picts, Scots, and Huns, invade Britain again; the Britons send an embassy to Rome imploring aid; an expedition commanded by Stilicho, assisted by Marcus and Victorinus, comes to their assistance and defeats their enemies; Marcus, stationed in the South, fortifies the Saxon shore; and Victorinus, in the North, repairs the rampart of Antonine	*ib.*
Britain revolts; Marcus and Gratian Municeps successively raised to the sovereignty, and slain	184

---

[5] "In Britain," should be added to the note [9]. As Prosper says, "iidem con- "sules permansere," and Gratian and Æquitius actually discharged the functions of the consulate in A.D. 375, I have supposed that in Britain this year might be marked "Gratiano IIII. et Æquitio II. coss.," whilst at Rome, where it was known that there was no fresh election, it was "Post consulatum, &c."

CHAPTER VIII.

CHAPTER IX.

CHAPTER X.

CHAPTER XI.

CHAPTER XII.

CHAPTER XIII.

CHAPTER XIV.

CHAPTER XV.

CHAPTER XVI.

CHAPTER XVII.

CHAPTER I.

The Authenticity of the Histories of the Conquest of Britain.

IN entering upon the task I have imposed upon myself, the investigation of the history of the establishment of the Teutonic race in Britain, I cannot do better than quote the words of one of the most indefatigable and judicious labourers of our day in the field of antiquity; for nowhere else have I found the interest of the subject, and the obscurity in which it has been hitherto involved, so well represented.

"If there be an epoch in the early history of our country, "which, above all, excites the curiosity and raises the in- "terest, it will probably be acknowledged by all historical "inquirers to be, that period which intervenes between the "withdrawal of the lights supplied by the Roman writers, and "the evidence afforded by the Saxon historians. The great "events, (for great they must have been, though we cannot "picture but in the imagination, even the outlines of their "forms), accompanying the relaxation of the grasp of imperial "Rome, which for centuries held Britain in subjugation, "would have furnished stirring themes to a Tacitus, or a "Marcellinus, or even to the most feeble pen of the lowest "writers, whose names are written on the roll of fame; had "not inexorable fate decreed otherwise, and deprived those "times of a chronicler. For that epoch of transitions the "steady torch of history burns no longer; and the glimmer-"ings, which here and there supply its place, are like the "flashes of lightning to the benighted and road-lost wanderer, "which reveal more sensibly the gloom around him, without "directing his footsteps.

"When the light of history dawns again upon the mys-"terious drama, it is fitful and uncertain; but when the "curtain, or shroud rather, is raised, we see upon the stage a "mighty change. A new people has occupied the land; and "the inauguration of new governments, soon to merge into "one grand and lasting kingdom, has commenced. These "new possessors of Roman Britain were not, in earlier times, "unknown to history. They had, long before, explored the "coasts of Gaul and Britain;—*per tractum Belgicæ et Armoricæ* "*pacandum mare accepisset* (*Carausius*), *quod Franci et Saxones* "*infestabant*—says Eutropius (lib. XII. cap. XXI.); and Am-"mianus Marcellinus describes, more circumstantially, their "growing power in the reign of Valentinian and Valens, "which caused greater apprehension to the declining empire, "than the hostile incursions of any other enemy; *præ cæteris* "*hostibus Saxones timebantur*. They are represented as pirates "by sea, and invaders by land; yielding up their young "warriors, when conquered, to serve as auxiliaries in the "Roman armies; and we find a long line of maritime district, "both in Gaul and Britain, actually taking its appellation "from their descents and invasions as enemies, or, as some "suppose, from their visits as friends and traffickers; and "once at least, we find a body of them located in Britain, "and siding with the provincial against the imperial army. "These were the people whom we now recognize seated in "security upon the shores of Britain; in one view we see "them as warlike adventurers, breaking in upon the Roman "provinces in all directions; in another as conquerors, with "laws of their own, and all the elements of civilization. But "of the precise time when the great advent commenced, how "continued, and when completed, the traditions, which, under "the name of history, have descended to us, leave us in doubt."[1]

This passage may serve as a fitting introduction to an inquiry, the result of which will be found to throw the light of the torch of history over the whole period between the revolt of Maximus and the inauguration of the new governments, to show that it is not absolutely deprived of chronicles, to fix positively the date of the great advent, and to give a clear and consistent account how the struggle was continued, and when completed.

The difficulties, which have hitherto beset the investigation of the history, have arisen, for the most part, from the adoption of erroneous dates. These, more than anything else, have tended to throw the imputation of falsehood, on authorities as trustworthy as any of those on whom we are obliged to depend for the history of the middle ages, Gildas, and the authors of the "History of the Britons," and the "Brut;" and we have been deprived of the benefit of their evidence, because, as false witnesses, they have been put out of court. Their character will be sufficiently vindicated in the following pages; but I cannot avail myself of their assistance without premising a few words, as to the authorship of the works which bear these names, and the grounds of my reliance on their testimony.

I. We have two distinct works which bear the name of Gildas; the first entitled "Historia Gildæ," the second, "Epistola Gildæ." That they are distinct works, although by the same author, we need no other proof than the internal evidence, which each supplies, of their having been written at different times; the former recording, as a recent event, the siege of Bath-hill; the latter mentioning the murder of the sons of Modred by Constantine, as having been perpe-

[1] C. Roach Smith. Preface to "Inventorium Sepulchrale."

trated in the very year in which it was written. To my mind, a milder spirit seems to have dictated the former, than that which is manifested in the latter; the one lamenting the vices of the British nation, and the calamities which had befallen them; the other indignantly rebuking the vices of their rulers. The different circumstances under which they were written sufficiently account for this; and, although the tone in which the vices of the Britons are censured, especially in the Epistle, has been made the ground of an argument against their genuineness, I think no one can rise from the perusal of the "Gododin"[2] without the conviction, that the morality of the British nation, professedly Christian though it was, was deplorably corrupt. The whole course of the history tends to strengthen this conviction; there was unhappily much in the lives of the Britons, princes and people, for a good man to lament, much for a priest to censure.

The original form of the History appears to be represented by a MS. in the Cambridge Public Library (F. f. i. 27), more nearly than by any other. It has a short preface, concluding with a summary of the subjects to be treated of, and, at the end, a recapitulation, the difference between which and the summary will be fully noticed hereafter. The original colophon, "Explicit Liber Gildæ Sapientis de Excidio "Britanniæ et Britonum Exulatione," follows this, and then three lines by some early copyist alluding to the authorship of the treatise. This MS., therefore, is evidence of the existence of the History, distinct from the Epistle which commences, "Reges habet Britannia."

Eventually the two were incorporated together, and of this incorporation another MS. in the same Library (D. d. i. 17)

[2] I say nothing of the abundant evidence to the same effect, which the "Lives of the Saints" supply; but in this poem we have a bard of no mean repute, and, in this case, an unimpeachable witness, telling us, how not even the sense of danger, nor the presence of the foe, could curb the infatuated sottishness of the Britons.

presents the earliest form; others, now lost, having had variations at the commencement of the Epistle, resulting from a desire to connect it with the conclusion of the History.[3]

The early date, A. D. 471, at which, (as I shall have an opportunity of showing), the History must have been written, entitles it to be regarded as a trustworthy epitome of the annals of Britain at the close of the fourth, and during the greater part of the fifth century. The events it relates may be considered as established facts; yet it would scarcely have been available as history, had not other documents supplied the names of persons and places, which it most commonly omits. Yet these omissions do really vindicate the genuineness of the work, showing that it must have been issued at a time, when the circumstances of which it treats were fresh in the minds of men, and when the allusions it contains would be readily understood.

The Epistle is valuable, inasmuch as it affords cotemporary evidence of the fact of the murder of the sons of Modred, related in the "Brut;" and of the cotemporaneity of certain kings in different districts, who are said in the "Brut" to have reigned in succession over all Britain;[4] and some details, of the authenticity of which their very nature is the best guarantee, of the personal history of the princes, whose vices are the object of its unsparing censure.

S. Gildas, however, wrote the "Histories of the Kings of

---

3 "Habet etenim Britannia reges," or "Enimvero habet Britannia reges." That which was used by Josselin has adopted the "sed ante promissum" of the recapitulation, which there has a meaning, (referring to the promise at the end of the preface), but here has none, at the end of a longer preface; as well as the "curabo" of the same for the "conamur" of the original preface. The two quotations from this combined work, in the "Life "of S. Gildas of Rhys," seem to be interpolations in the text; this Life being evidently an amplification of a much earlier original.

4 It has been intimated that the author of the "Brut" borrowed their names from this work; but that he did not appears from the fact that he does not notice Cuneglas, who, alone of the five to whom the Epistle is addressed, did not succeed to the sovereignty of Britain.

"the Britons" at Glastonbury, and it is on these chiefly that his claim to the title "Historiographus Britonum" rests. No such work has been preserved under his name; but I suspect that an epitome of such a history, or the rough notes from which it was compiled, exist in the "History of the Britons" ascribed to Nennius; and that extracts from the work itself are to be found in the pages of Bæda, and of Henry of Huntingdon.

II. The earliest extant form of this "History of the Britons" seems to be preserved in a MS. in the Bibliothèque Impériale at Paris, (Suppt. Latin, 165^{16}).[5] The Vatican MS. generally resembles it, but has two additions; one at the beginning, some chronological data "Ab Adam usque ad diluvium," &c; the other at the end, a biographical notice of S. Patrick. Three Cottonian MSS. (Vespasian, B. xxv. and D. xxi. and Vitellius, A. xii), of the twelfth, thirteenth, and fourteenth centuries respectively, agree with the Paris MS. in commencing with "Britannia insula a quodam Bruto," &c. but have the notice of S. Patrick inserted in the body of the history, after the genealogy of Vortigern; so also has the Harleian MS. 3859, which, in common with many others, is prefaced by chronological notes, "A principio mundi usque "ad diluvium," &c.

Now seventeen MSS., out of twenty-seven collated by Mr. Petrie, agree in ascribing this work to S. Gildas; William of Malmsbury, Geoffrey of Monmouth, and Henry of Huntingdon cite it as his, and Giraldus Cambrensis appears to have regarded it in the same light. If, then, in addition to these testimonies, we take into consideration the remarkable similarity between certain passages and their correspondents in

---

[5] The names of the cities of Britain (evidently a marginal note introduced into the text), the notices of the third year of Mervyn, of S. Patrick, S. Brigid, and S. Columcille, of the fifth year of Eadmund, of Vortigern's genealogy, and of Ida, seem to be the only additions to the original work in this MS.

S. Gildas' "History,"[6] which are just such as the same person may readily be believed to have written at different periods of his life, the probability that this work was compiled by S. Gildas appears to be very great; and the differences between them are no more than the different circumstances, under which they were written, will readily account for; the one at Armagh, "ex transmarinâ relatione," where he had not access to written documents, the other at Glastonbury, where he had those documents at hand. If this probability be admitted, the ascription of the History and Epistle to S. Gildas of Glastonbury is confirmed, for he, not S. Gildas of Rhys, is the "Historiographus Britonum," as not only his "Life," but William of Malmsbury[7] also, testifies. The notice, in the Paris and Vatican MSS., of S. Faustus the son of Vortigern, as still living,[8] shows that this work must have been originally composed in the fifth century; and the catalogue of Arthur's first twelve battles is certainly the work of a cotemporary; facts which go far to confirm its ascription to S. Gildas. But it passed through several editions, indicated by notices in the

---

6 "Britannia—ab Africo boreali "propensius tensa axi, octingen-"torum in longo millium ducento-"rum in lato spatium—duorum "ostiis nobilium Thamesis et Sa-"brinæ fluminum, velut brachiis "per quæ eidem olim transmarinæ "deliciæ vehebantur ratibus, alio-"rumque minorum meliorata, bis "denis bisque quaternis fulget ci-"vitatibus, ac nonnullis castellis "decoratur."—*Hist.* GILDÆ, 3.

"(Britannia) consurgit ab Africo "boreali ad occidentem versus, oc-"tingentorum in longitudine mil-"lium, ducentorum in latitudine "spatium habet. In ea sunt viginti "octo civitates et innumerabilia "promontoria cum innumeris cas-"tellis."—*Hist. Brit.* 7.

"Sunt in ea multa flumina—sed "tamen duo flumina præclariora "cæteris fluminibus, Tamesis ac "Sabrina, quasi duo brachia Bri-"tanniæ, per quas olim rates vehe-"bantur ad portandas divitias."—*Ibid.* 9.

7 "Gildas, neque insulsus neque infacetus historicus, cui Britones de-"bent si quid notitiæ inter cæteras gentes habent."

8 "Quartus fuit Faustus—et ædificato monasterio non parvo super ri-"pam fluminis nomine Renis sibi consecravit, ibique perseverat usque in "hodiernum diem."

various MSS.,[9] and one of these must have been issued in A.D. 675.

1. This is represented by the Paris and Vatican MSS. Passing over the blundering date in the preface to the latter, that as well as the former contains the following passages:—

"Saxones autem ('vero,' V.) a Gurthergirno suscepti sunt "anno CCCXLVII post passionem Christi. A tempore quo "advenerunt primo ad Britanniam Saxones usque ad primum "imperii annum regis Eadmundi DCXLII, adhuc ('ad hunc,' "V.) in quo nos scribimus annos DCXLVII didicimus, quippe "quia iste imperii quintus ann ('ante,' V.) dicti regis est "annus."

"Saxones a Guortegerno anno post domini passione "CCCXLVII suscepti sunt, ad hunc in quo nos scribimus "annum DCXLVII numeramus."

It is clear that the meaning cannot be that 647 years had passed since A.D.P. 347=A.D. 375, because that would carry us beyond the reign of Eadmund, to A.D. 1022. Doubtless the second passage gives the more correct reading, and the computation of these years is not from the coming of the Saxons, but from the Passion of our Lord. This history, therefore, must have been transcribed in A.D.P. 647=A.D. 675; and the two MSS. which supply this date furnish also a notice, (apparently one of the many additions to the original work), which precisely confirms it. After saying,—"Mortuo "autem Hencgesto, Ottha ('Ochta,' V.) filius ejus advenit de "sinistrali parte Britanniæ ad regnum Cantuariorum;" they add,—"Et de ipso omnes reges Cantuariorum ('Cantpariorum,' "V.) usque in hodiernum diem."

Now this statement would be strictly true in A.D. 675, but not after A.D. 685; for in the latter year Cædwealha, King of the West Saxons, conquered Kent, and after his

[9] As Mr. Hardy has shown in the introduction to the "Monumenta "Historica."

death it was governed by others who were not of the royal line, until A.D. 694, when Wihtræd recovered the kingdom. So the succession of the descendants of Octa was interrupted in A.D. 685; their line failed soon after A.D. 760; and long before another edition of this History appeared, the Kentish monarchy had ceased altogether.

The expression "advenit" in these two MSS. indicates that the original from which they were transcribed was written in Kent; all other copies having "transivit" instead, and "reges illius patriæ," instead of "reges Cantuariorum;" and suggests the probability that Eadmund was a King of Kent in A.D. 675. The history of the seventh century is very imperfect, and altogether silent with regard to several kings, whose names are preserved in charters,[10] or incidentally mentioned in the "Lives of the Saints;" and as it further appears that Kent comprised more kingdoms than one, it is very possible that Eadmund was a son of Eormenræd, or Earconberht, and a cotemporary of Ecgberht. The original of the Paris MS. was, undoubtedly, a transcript of this history by an Anglo-Saxon hand, for it alone gives the names of the ancestors of Hencgest, spelt with the Anglo-Saxon *Wen*, "Wictgils, "Wicta, Wecta, and Woden." The Vatican MS., which seems to have been written on the Continent, also presents a trace of this original in the word "Cantpariorum."

It is, therefore, very probable that this History was originally written in the fifth century, and that it was transcribed in Kent, in A.D. 675, the fifth year of the reign of a King, otherwise unknown to history, Eadmund. These circumstances completely set aside the claims of Nennius to be considered its author; for he tells us, (if we may trust the prologues), that he was a disciple of S. Elbod, who became Bishop of Bangor in A.D. 762, and died early in the ninth

---

[10] Ex. gr. Sigiræd and Eardwulf, Kings of Kent; Nothhelm, Nunna, Waltus, and Æthelberht, Kings of the South Saxons.

century. He may, indeed, have transcribed it; for during the ninth century we have indications of two distinct editions; but the prologues, which are found in only five MSS., are so different from the history in their style as to preclude the supposition of his having been the author, even if their genuineness, (which is very doubtful), were admitted.

2. The earlier of these editions appears to have been issued in A.D.P. 796, or A.D. 831.[11]

3. The latter, in A.D. 857. The fourth year of Mervyn, mentioned in the chapter which indicates this date, has been supposed to mark A.D. 823, this prince being identified with Mervyn Vrych, who reigned in Powys from A.D. 819 to A.D. 844. But the number of years from the coming of the Saxons joined to this date forbid this supposition; whilst the actual date of their arrival, A.D. 428, shows that the fourth year of Mervyn is really the year which is determined by the decemnovenal calculation at the end of the same paragraph,[12] viz. A.D. 857, in which Mervin, son of Rotri, whose death the "Annals of Cambria" record in A.D. 903, may have been reigning.

---

[11] These may, indeed, be the dates of two distinct copies; for they do not agree with the usual relation of the æra of the Passion to that of the Incarnation.

[12] "A primo anno quo Saxones venerunt in Britanniam, usque ad an-" num quartum Meruini regis, supputantur anni ccccxxix. Initium" compoti xxiii cycli decemnovales ab Incarnatione Domini usque ad" adventum Patricii in Hiberniam et ipsi annos efficiunt ccccxxxvii. Et" ab adventu Patricii ad cyclum decemnovalem in quo sumus xxii cycli" sunt, id est ccccxx unus sunt, duo anni in ogdoade usque in hunc an-" num in quo sumus."

For "unus" we must read "anni," as the computation shows:—

$23 \times 19 = 437$, the date assigned for S. Patrick's advent;

$22 \times 19 + 2 = 420$, the interval between it and the year in question, which, therefore, is 857.

And $857 - 429 = 428$, the date of the coming of the Saxons.

A.D. 854 must be the year of Mervyn's accession, which will give him a reign of forty-nine years, if he be the same as Mervyn son of Rotri, and the date in the "Annals of Cambria" be correct.

4. Another edition appeared in A.D. 907, the thirtieth year of Anaraut, King of Gwynedd.

5. Another, in A.D. 976. This is represented in the preface to the Vatican MS. alone, in which the history is ascribed to Mark the Anchorite, a Briton by birth, who received his education and was raised to the episcopate in Ireland, made a pilgrimage to Rome, and died at Soissons before A.D. 977. Mr. Stevenson's conjecture appears sufficiently to account for the introduction of his name in the MS., viz. that the scribe ventured to attribute it to him, because he found the miracles of S. Germanus, which Heric of Auxerre had recorded on Mark's authority, in the MS. which he copied.

This work will be cited in the following pages as the "History of the Britons;" for I will not venture to quote it under the name of S. Gildas, though I regard him as its author, and am convinced that it was originally compiled in his time. I shall follow almost exclusively the Paris and Vatican text,[13]

---

[13] The more important variations of the Paris MS. are here given:—

Vatican MS. (Gunn.)	Paris.
"Et filius esset omnium Hytalorum, fortissimus amabilis omnibus hominibus," p. 49.	"Et filius mortis erit, quia occidet patrem suum et matrem, et erit exosus omnibus hominibus."
"Omnes superabat, ut omnium dominus videretur, idcirco autem invidia expulsus est ab Italiâ, et armilis fuit," *ib.*	"Ictu sagittæ occidit patrem suum, non de industriâ sed casu, et pro hoc expulsus est ab Italiâ et armiger fuit."
"Et implevit," to "Bryttania," p. 50.	Omitted.
"Advenerat, et cum omnibus ducibus Romanæ gentis qui erant cum eo Bryttaniam verberavit, ac omnes regulos ducesque Bryttonum, et vindicavit in illis Severum et purpuram Bryttaniæ devastavit," pp. 57, 58.	"Cum omnibus regulis ac ducibus suis verberavit, et vindicavit in illis Severum et purpuram Britanniæ devastavit."
"Ipse est Catel Drunluc," p. 64.	Omitted.
"Morati," p. 65.	"Metati."
"Quærebant qualiter pacem rumperent."	"Quærentes qualiter pacem haberent, abierunt."
"Brittones mixti Saxonibus vir ad inimicum sederunt," p. 75.	"Brittones mixti Saxonibus discubuerunt."

which represents the earliest editions, and appears to have preserved the history in its purest form; for the scribes, to whom we owe the other MSS., appear to have collated different copies, and to have introduced gradually into the text —sometimes even to the prejudice of its consistency—what had been originally marginal notes. It is interesting to remark, that Henry of Huntingdon must have used a copy of this work, which had several of the peculiar readings of the Paris MS.

III. A larger work, bearing the name of Gildas, was certainly in existence in the twelfth century. Geoffrey of Monmouth refers to it as containing the Molmutian laws, the acts of the missionaries who were sent from Rome at the invitation of Lucius, and a narrative of the victory of Aurelius Ambrosius; and Gaimar, as containing notices of the kings whom he connects with his story of Havelok. Extracts from this work appear to be incorporated in Henry of Huntingdon's Chronicle; for whilst in the earlier parts he has some passages so closely resembling their correspondents in Bæda's Ecclesiastical History that he has been thought to be quoting from him, the fact, that these passages appear to extend to greater length in the former than in the latter, seems rather to suggest the probability that both made use, the former more largely than the latter, of an earlier work; and the passage which introduces the notice of the coming of Ælle is evidently Gildasian, though the words are differently arranged from those of the corresponding passage in the "History" of Gildas.[14] If, then, as it seems probable, Henry of Huntingdon, in these instances, quoted from a work of S. Gildas, which was extant in his days, he must have used it elsewhere; and possibly he has extracted from it all that it con-

[14] It is true that the style of these passages is less involved and obscure than that of the works above mentioned, but in writing a chronicle he would naturally adopt a simpler form of language than in treatises of a declamatory character such as these.

tained relative to the wars of the Angles; and his detailed accounts of several battles, from that at Stamford, A.D. 428, to that of Charford, A.D. 498, which are all dated according to one computation, "from the coming of the Angles," have been derived from this source. The fact that these notices contain, like the works ascribed to S. Gildas, numerous applications of the words of Holy Scripture,—not from the Vulgate (which alone Henry of Huntingdon would have quoted), but probably from the version it superseded, the "Vetus Itala"—seems to confirm this conjecture; nor do I think the apparent continuation of the same series of notices beyond the date of S. Gildas'-death, A.D. 512, fatal to it; for nothing is more likely, than that a Chronicle commenced by him should be continued by his disciples at Glastonbury after his death.

IV. To Geoffrey of Monmouth the credit is due of having first made his countrymen acquainted with the "Brut," a precious ancient Chronicle, which his friend Walter, Archdeacon of Oxford, brought to him out of Bretagne. I cannot see how his statement respecting this document, and the manner in which it came into his possession, can be questioned. His own high character entitles him to be believed on his word; and such a statement, if false, would never have been published whilst the individual who could have contradicted it,—himself an ardent student of antiquity, a diligent searcher into old libraries, and the author of an edition of this very work,—was living. The only question, therefore, can be, what is the value of the work itself? And here Lappenberg remarks, that "those who in later times have "concurred in rejecting it have failed to observe, that many "of his accounts are supported by narratives, to be found "in writers wholly unconnected with, and independent of, "Geoffrey."

Fortunately we are furnished with a clue to its origin, which will give us great confidence in availing ourselves of it as an authority for the history of the fourth and fifth centuries, in the metrical version which Layamon composed, about the beginning of the thirteenth century.

Layamon tells us in his preface, that the sources from which he compiled his history, (for he certainly regarded it as such, and wrote in good faith), were three, viz. a book in English by S. Bæda, another in Latin by S. Albin and S. Austin, and a third by a French clerk named Wace. By the first King Ælfræd's translation of Bæda's Ecclesiastical History cannot be intended; for when Layamon refers to the "English book," it is for matter which is not to be found there, but only in the "Brut." It was probably an English version of a work now lost, of which the commencement only is preserved in a Cottonian MS. (Vespasian, D. IIII.), bearing the title,—

"Incipit quidam libellus de Bruto et Britanniâ secundum "Bedam."

It begins with the same words as the "History of the Bri-"tons," and relates the story of Brutus in not very different terms. Two Welsh poems, also,—"The Chair of Ceridwen," and "The Song of the Months,"—refer to the books of Bæda, as relating events of British history which are not in Bæda's great work. It appears, therefore, that there was really a British Chronicle written by a person of this name; and it is no improbable supposition, that one whose literary labours were continued to the last hour of his life, who even on his deathbed had two works in hand, might have applied himself, during the four years which elapsed between the completion of his great work and his death, to a history of the times and events which it did not embrace, and drawn more largely from sources of which he had already availed himself when treating of the ecclesiastical affairs of his country. However this may have been, the fact that such a work, ascribed to him, did exist, prepares us to receive Layamon's statement as to the authorship of the second book from which he derived the materials of his history, with greater confidence.

He says it was written by S. Albin and S. Austin, identifying the latter with the Apostle of the English nation, by adding, "who brought baptism in hither." Who, then, was the former? Certainly not Bæda's friend Albinus, for he was never regarded as a saint; but very probably S. Albinus, who was born A.D. 469, of British ancestry, in Armorica, and died Bishop of Angers, March 1, A.D. 549. He might very well have compiled a history from the traditions of his forefathers, or even from those writings which S. Gildas testifies were conveyed to Armorica; and the history, as we have it in Layamon, is just such as he might have written, and S. Augustine translated or transcribed. For it is very remarkable that the connected narrative ends with the notice of Gurmund, who must have lived early in the sixth century; and then a sentence follows just such as S. Augustine might have written in closing a translation or transcription of a book by S. Albinus; "The Angles dwelt here for one hundred "and five years,[15] so that never Christendom came to be "known in this land, nor bell rung, nor mass sung, nor "church was there hallowed, nor child baptized." This work might have been used by some of the editors of Wace, who mention a period of one hundred years and more of the cessation of Christianity in Britain; and Geoffrey's Breton MS. was probably a copy in the vernacular of the work of S. Albinus, the original conclusion of which is distinctly marked by the ninth chapter of his eleventh book, which is evidently the effusion of a writer cotemporary with the events of which he treats, indignant at the wickedness of the Britons, yet deploring their misfortunes. After this chapter, Geoffrey

[15] This period is probably computed from A.D. 492, the date of the battle of Camlann, and the fall of Arthur, "when the might of the Britons "was scattered, for God had cast them off." There is exactly this interval between it and the advent of S. Augustine, A.D. 597.

proceeds to speak of the flight of the Britons, with their three Archbishops, into Cornwall and Wales; and then, after promising a translation of a book about their banishment, (which promise, unfortunately, he did not fulfil), passes on to the time of S. Augustine's mission.

As far, then, as this chapter, I regard the "Brut" as being in substance the compilation of S. Albinus; and to the circumstances of its author having been an Armorican Briton, and a cotemporary of Arthur, as S. Albinus certainly was, and an eye-witness of some of the scenes he describes, as S. Albinus might well have been, I attribute the minuteness of detail with which the stories of Arthur's Gallic campaigns, and of the festival at Caerleon, (at the date of which he was about twenty-one years of age), are related. With this conviction, I have no hesitation in accepting the "Brut" as an authority for the history of the fifth century, but particularly of the reign of Arthur, and of those events with regard to which it is most likely that an Armorican would have the best information. The sequel will be found fully to justify the value I set upon it. Those editions, of course, which appear most free from interpolation must be preferred; yet Layamon's has a peculiar value, inasmuch as he constantly gives names of persons and places, and relates circumstances which are not to be found elsewhere, which, doubtless, he found either in the authorities he especially mentions, or in others to which he appears to have had access, which frequently confirm what we find recorded by others, and sometimes help us in identifying the scenes of the events he relates.[16]

V. Hector Boece says, that through the influence of John Campbell, treasurer to the King of Scotland, he received from Iona a Chronicle, written by Veremund, Archdeacon of S. Andrews in the eleventh century, and that this was one of

---

[16] We cannot suppose he invented them, for he evidently intended to write a true history.

the chief authorities he made use of in the compilation of his history. The love of truth which characterized Boece, as his friend Erasmus testifies, and which, indeed, appears in every chapter of his history, justifies us in crediting this statement. It was uttered, be it remembered, whilst Campbell, Bishop Elphinstone, (who is also said to have made use of it), and the monks of Iona, were living to contradict it if it had been false; and possibly much of what he relates may yet be confirmed by an examination of Bishop Elphinstone's MSS. in the Bodleian Library. To this Chronicle of Veremund, probably, we owe the circumstantial accounts of the times of Vortigern and his successors, which as yet have appeared only in the pages of Boece. These, in several instances, strikingly illustrate the narrative in the Brut, and confirm its general truthfulness; detailing, as they do occasionally, events which there are only mentioned cursorily, and supplying notices of others which there are wanting, but are necessary to the completeness of the story. Those, in particular, which relate to the wars of Hencgest are so minute in their descriptions of the scenes in which his battles were fought, and so vividly pourtray his character, that I am convinced they must have been derived originally from Anglo-Saxon poems in which his exploits were celebrated, whilst his memory was yet fresh in Northumbria, in which province most of the scenes are laid. The narratives are evidently those of one friendly to his memory, although Hencgest was the adversary of the Picts and Scots, and (as we now have them) they are presented to us by one who was writing Scottish history, and who, in common with the British historians, elsewhere attributes treachery to him.

But if Boece was truthful, he was sadly uncritical. In the earlier part of his history he appears to have had two distinct narratives before him, and, not perceiving that they relate to the same personages, has given their transactions in duplicate. These errors are palpable; but it is not always easy to ascertain how much of the context may be affected by them. At any rate they serve to show how carefully he followed his authorities, whatever we may think of his want of discrimination in the use of them; and whilst we may avail ourselves of his aid in illustration of the history of the fifth century, it is only with the greatest caution we can make use of the information he affords where he is wholly unsupported, directly or indirectly, by other authorities.

It is from these sources, and from others better appreciated and more relied on, that I propose to deduce the history of our country during the great epoch of transitions. A collation of Gildas, the History of the Britons, the Brut, and Boece, furnishes us with a connected history of the gradual encroachments of the Teutonic race, from their arrival, as allies of Vortigern, to their establishment in the sovereignty of the greater part of the island, under Garmund, at the beginning of the sixth century.

It is obvious that the computation from the æra of the Incarnation could not have been introduced amongst our forefathers before their conversion to Christianity; whilst that "from the coming of the Angles" is free from all objection: A. D. 428 will be established as the date of their coming, and on this basis the following scheme of the chronology of the period, from the revolt of Maximus to the accession of Cyneric to the West Saxon kingdom, will be vindicated in the following pages:—

A.D.

385. Maximus leads an army into Gaul; defeats and kills Gratian; makes peace with Valentinian.

386. Guanis and Melga invade Britain.

387. Maximus marches into Italy; compels Valentinian to seek refuge with Theodosius; sends Gratian Municeps to the relief of the Britons.

388. Maximus is defeated and slain at Aquileia.

393. Chrysanthus vicar of the British Isles.

A.D.

397. Stilicho leads an expedition to Britain to repel the Picts and Scots; defeats them, repairs the rampart of Antonine, and fortifies the Saxon shore. Victorinus stationed in the North, Marcus in the South (Boece).

407. Marcus raised to the throne of Britain, deposed and slain. Gratian Municeps succeeds him, and is slain in his turn. Constantine follows, rebels against Honorius, and invades Gaul and Spain. Another invasion of the Picts and Scots compels the Britons to seek aid from Rome, and Severus Æquitius is sent. He defeats the Picts and Scots, and connects the stations of the rampart of Hadrian with a stone wall. Victorinus usurps the sovereignty, is deposed by Heraclius; Placidus left as governor in Britain, defeated by the Picts and Scots, dies.

410. Castius, his successor, is slain in battle, and the Picts and Scots overrun Britain. The Britons send a letter to Severus Æquitius requesting aid. Honorius replies, exhorting them to defend themselves.

411. Constantine of Armorica, comes to the assistance of the Britons.

412. Many battles with their enemies, whom eventually he completely overcomes; is chosen king, and reigns peaceably for twelve years; assassinated by a Pict.

424. Constantius, his son, raised to the throne; is assassinated after a short reign by his Pictish guards.

425. Vortigern usurps the throne. His army defeated by the Picts. He invites the aid of the Saxons.

428. Horsa and Hencgest arrive casually, and are enlisted in the service of Vortigern; fight with the Picts near Stamford; are reinforced from Germany; fight again with the Picts in Yorkshire and Northumberland.

429. Fresh forces of Angles arrive; another battle is fought in Northumberland; Horsa is appointed to the defence of the south-eastern coasts; Hencgest entertains

A.D.

Vortigern at a banquet, and gives him in marriage his daughter Rumwen; Kent is ceded to the Angles; Hencgest murders the Bishop of London; Octa and Ebissa are invited to Britain, and arrive with Childeric; war with Ambrosius; S. Germanus comes for the first time to Britain.

433. Vortigern is deposed, and Vortimer is raised to the throne; he defeats the Angles on the Derwent.

434. Vortimer defeats the Angles again at Aylesthorpe.

435. The Alleluia victory, followed by the battle of Episford; Horsa is slain; Hencgest succeeds as King of Kent; continues the war with Vortimer; eventually is defeated at Stonar, and expelled from Britain.

436. Vortimer dies; Vortigern is restored; invites Hencgest to return; on his arrival the Britons are resolved to expel him, advance into Kent, and are defeated at Crayford.

437. Feud between Guitolin and Ambrosius. Massacre of the British nobles at Ambresbury; Essex and other provinces ceded to Hencgest.

441. Hencgest completes the subjugation of Britain; Vortigern retires to Ganerew.

443. Ambrosius returns and is invested with the sovereignty of Britain. S. Germanus comes for the second time; Ambrosius besieges Vortigern's castle and destroys it by fire; defeats Hencgest at Maes Beli and Conisbrough; captures him and puts him to death; makes peace with Octa, Ebissa, and Ossa; orders the restoration of the churches; expels the Saxons from London; gives his sister in marriage to Loth.

444. Ambrosius fights Hencgest II. at Wippedesfleet; mutual cessation of hostilities; the laws revived, estates restored to their owners, and cities rebuilt.

445. Stonehenge erected about this time.

447. (At the latest) S. Germanus returns to Gaul.

A. D.

449. Octa and Ebissa, allied with Pascent, break the peace; Ambrosius defeats them; comet observed, Dec. 11th, (Chinese Records.)

450. Octa, Ebissa, and Pascent land at Menevia; Ambrosius sends Uther to oppose them; dies by poison; Uther succeeds him and defeats the invaders; Octa and Ebissa escape to Northumbria, and are pursued by Uther, who again defeats them, and takes them prisoners. After some time they escape, and, in

452, in conjunction with Hencgest II. and Æsc-Octa, defeat the forces of Uther commanded by Gorlois; a peace is concluded, which lasts until nearly the close of Uther's reign; Uther puts Gorlois to death, and marries Igerna; and about the close of this year, or the beginning of

453, Arthur is born.

457. Ælle and his sons arrive, and settle on the coast of Sussex.

465. They advance into a distant region, and defeat the forces of Uther at Mearcredes-burn; send to their countrymen, inviting aid.

466. Octa and Ebissa, in conjunction with Ælle, occupy Verulam; Uther marches against them, and a battle is fought, in which Octa and Ebissa are slain; the Northumbrians elect Æsc-Octa as Octa's successor.

467. Uther dies and is succeeded by Arthur in the fifteenth year of his age; Hencgest II. dies, and his son Æsc-Octa gives Northumbria to Colgrim, and succeeds him in Kent; enters into alliance with Loth, King of the Picts; Arthur defeats him on the Glem, and afterwards, being reinforced by Hoel, Prince of Armorica, defeats Colgrim in four battles on the Douglas, and another on the Bassas, pursues him to York and besieges him; is obliged to retire on the arrival of fresh forces under Childeric and Æsc-

A.D.

Octa, but leaves a garrison in Caer-Loit-coit; the Saxons besiege it; Hoel escapes, and, in

468, brings fresh forces from Armorica to the aid of Arthur; they return to the North, take York, raise the siege of Caer-Loit-coit, defeat Colgrim in the wood of Caledon, and force him to leave the country. Rhiotimus is defeated at Bourges by Euric, King of the Visigoths.

469. Arthur defeats the Saxons, Picts, and Scots at Guinnion castle; Loth, hitherto opposed to Arthur, now enters into an alliance with him.

470. Arthur fights several battles with Hueil, and defeats him at Chester and Trefdraeth in Anglesey; returns to the North, and gains a victory at Edinburgh; the Saxon fugitives return, and, in conjunction with Ælle, take Andredes-ceaster, overrun the neighbouring districts, and lay siege to Bath.

471. Arthur raises the siege of Bath; Colgrim is slain; Arthur prosecutes his war with the Picts.

472. Arthur returns to York, rebuilds churches, restores estates to their owners.

473. Arthur proceeds to London; repels a fresh invasion of Saxons, marries Guennuuar, and spends the rest of the year in Cornwall.

474. Arthur undertakes his first foreign expedition; receives the submission of the Kings of Ireland, Isoland, the Orkneys, Gothland, and Winetland; Cerdic and Cyneric arrive, and settle on the coast of Dorsetshire.

475. Arthur returns to Britain; many battles with Cerdic during the following years.

479. Cerdic circumnavigates Wessex.

480. Port and his sons land at Portsmouth.

483. Feud between Arthur and Meluas.

486. Arthur makes peace with Cerdic, ceding to him Hampshire and Somersetshire.

A.D.

487. Arthur undertakes his second foreign expedition; subdues part of Denmark, &c; during his absence Natanleod attacks Cerdic, who defeats him with the assistance of Æsc-Octa, Ælle, and Port.

490. Arthur invades Gaul, takes Boulogne, defeats Frollo, besieges and takes Paris; subdues Lorraine and Burgundy, assisting Gundebald against Chilperic, and enabling him to ascend the throne.

491. Arthur returns to Paris, and thence to Britain; holds a festival at Caerleon; invades Gaul a second time; a skirmish on the river Aube, and then a decisive battle on the Secy; he subdues the Cisalpine provinces. Æsc-Octa dies and is succeeded by Ossa.

492. Arthur prepares, in conjunction with Gundebald, to invade Italy; Modred makes an alliance with Cerdic against Arthur; Arthur is compelled to abandon his enterprise, and Gundebald prosecutes it alone; he returns to Britain, defeats Modred in two battles; Modred receives assistance from Germany, and engages with Arthur's forces at Camlann; he falls in the battle, and Arthur is mortally wounded.

493. Arthur dies; Constantine succeeds, continues the war with the Saxons; murders the sons of Modred.

495. Constantine murdered by Conan, who usurps the throne.

496. Vortipore succeeds Conan.

498. Cerdic fights with the Britons; the West Saxon kingdom begins.

500. Maglocun succeeds Vortipore.

502. Caredig succeeds Maglocun.

506. Garmund arrives in Britain; a battle is fought at Charley; Cirencester taken; Caredig escapes; Muircheartach Mac Erc succeeds him, and reigns seven years.

513. Muircheartach goes to Ireland.

514. Cerdic conquers Wight.

A. D.
515. Creoda succeeds Cerdic.
534. Cyneric succeeds Creoda.

After preparing these sheets for the press, I have had an opportunity of consulting the additions to the Chronicles of Sigebert of Gemblours, by an anonymous monk of Orcamp, of which Vincent of Beauvais made use. I find that he follows a chronology nearly the same as mine. He dates the victory of Constantine of Armorica, A. D. 413, and his death, A. D. 424; the victory of Uther at Verulam, A. D. 466, and Arthur's return to York after his Scottish campaign, A. D. 472.

CHAPTER II.

The Antiquity of Phonetic Writing, as practised by the Teutonic Races.

WE shall have no difficulty in admitting the probability that our forefathers had records before their conversion to Christianity, by means of which they preserved their genealogies, and in which they noted the events of their kings' reigns under successive regnal years; that the scattered notices of their transactions in Britain during the fifth and sixth centuries may be fragments of such records; that they supplied Bæda, for instance, with matter for his notices of the reign of Æthelfrith; and that the stories of Havelok, Horn, and Beowulf, may be representatives of very early poems in which the deeds of those worthies were celebrated—if we can establish the fact that they had a system of writing at the time of their coming to Britain. This we can do most satisfactorily; we can show that they had such a system, the only one with which they were acquainted, before missionaries from Rome introduced amongst them the *abecedarium;* we can prove that the Teutonic nations possessed the art from the earliest periods of their history; we can even trace the system to its origin, and identify its author. No department of research in the field of Teutonic antiquities possesses a higher value, is invested with a deeper interest, than this; for it not only tends to ennoble our forefathers, but it brings us to the very feet of the great patriarch of our race.

The first step in this investigation must necessarily be an examination of the various systems which were in use amongst the several branches of the Teutonic stock, and which, whilst they present some variations, have at the same time a general family likeness, and have evidently been derived from a common original. Their most striking features are, an order altogether distinct from that of every other system with which we are acquainted, and a nomenclature essentially Teutonic. In the order, on account of which we claim for our system the name *futhorc*, (for the same reason as the Greek, Latin, and Irish systems are called *alphabet, abecedarium*, and *beithluisnion*), all its varieties — Anglo-Saxon, German, and Norse—are accordant up to a certain point; for, although the last contains fewer characters than the others, it preserves the same relative sequences after each interval, with only one exception, and the differences in the names of the characters are, for the most part, merely dialectic.

In the accompanying table (Pl. I.), the 1st column gives the Anglo-Saxon futhorc, derived from the following MSS.

I. Cotton: Otho, B. 10. In this the 20th, and 22nd characters are confounded; but, as all other authorities are agreed as to their forms, we have no difficulty in correcting this error, and another, which makes *Oethel* the 23rd instead of the 24th. *Ior*, the 29th, is placed before *Ear;* and this also I venture to correct on the authority of the following.

II. Domitian, A. 9. In this there are some blunders in the names of the characters. *Sigel* is written erroneously over *Eóh; Eolhx* is without a name, but its name is written over *Calc*, and another character is given at the end, with the name *Calc*, which is really *Eolhx; Ethel* is written over *Eh*, and is wanting over that to which it really belongs; the

Pl. I.

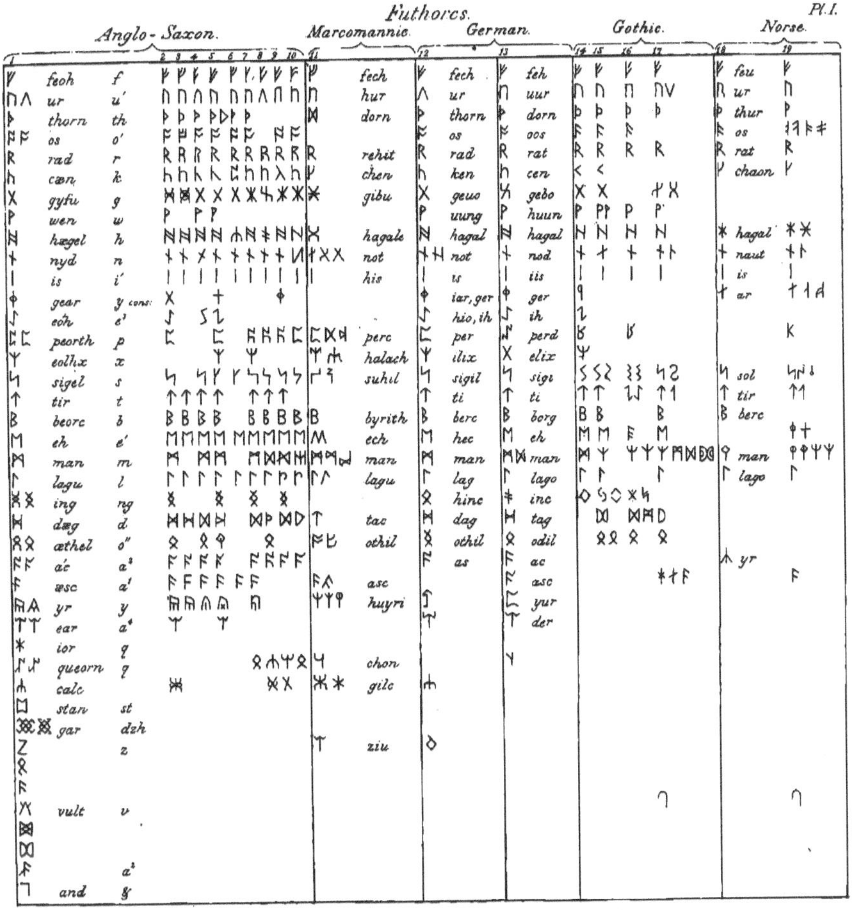
Futhorcs.
Anglo-Saxon.
Marcomannic.
German.
Gothic.
Norse.
feoh f
ur u'
thorn th
os o'
rad r
cæn k
gyfu g
wen w
hægel h
nyd n
is i'
gear y cons:
eoh e³
peorth p
eolhx x
sigel s
tir t
beorc b
eh e'
man m
lagu l
ing ng
dæg d
æthel o"
ác a³
æsc a'
yr y
ear a⁴
ior q
queorn q
calc
stan st
gar dzh
z
vult v
a²
and &
fech
hur
dorn
rehit
chen
gibu
hagale
not
his
perc
halach
suhil
byrith
ech
man
lagu
tac
othil
asc
huyri
chon
gilc
ziu
fech
ur
thorn
os
rad
ken
geuo
uung
hagal
not
is
iar, ger
hio, ih
per
ilix
sigil
ti
berc
hec
man
lag
hinc
dag
othil
as
feh
uur
dorn
oos
rat
cen
gebo
huun
hagal
nod
iis
ger
ih
perd
elix
sigi
ti
borg
eh
man
lago
inc
tag
odil
ac
asc
yur
der
feu
ur
thur
os
rat
chaon
hagal
naut
is
ar
sol
tir
berc
man
lago
yr

names of *Dæg* and *Man* are exchanged; *Tir* is given erroneously for *Ear*. The characters, however, appear to be in their true order, except that a second *Ræd* takes the place of *Sigel*, and the values are correctly given.

III. Galba, A. 2. This is the most correct, giving the forms of the characters accurately, and particularly that of *Queorn*, which in the two preceding is indistinguishable from *Ear*. *Calc* and *Ior*, however, are made to change places.

IV. S. John's, Oxford, 27. The order is correct as far as the 23rd character; then *Ior* is inserted before a character which resembles *Oethel;* the next five are in the usual sequence; then *Gar*, and another resembling *Gifu*, *Stan*, *Calc*, *Oethel* (of the usual form), and five others. *Gifu* appears to be the only character which is repeated; in its place I venture to substitute z, which in many of these futhorcs follows *Gar*. The character which occupies the place of *Oethel*, but is distinguished from it by a mark attached to it, represents a modification of sound, and is not to be discarded. The 38th differs from *Stan*, and may be intended for one which occurs in some alphabets with *Ecce* written over it.

V. S. Gallen, No. 878. It is called *Anguliscum*, to distinguish it from one of German runes which precedes it. It has twenty-nine characters in the same order as II. and III.

VI. Vienna, Salisbury, 140. From the spelling of the names[1] this appears to be of Northumbrian origin, and as early as the eighth century. It gives twenty-eight characters, but places *Ior* before *Yr*.

In the 12th column we have a futhorc from MSS. of Isidore at Brussels and Paris. The order is as usual as far as the 25th character, after which there is a blank.

---

[1] Fech, Ur, Thorn, Os, Raeda, Cen, Geofu, Uyn, Haegil, Naed, Is, Gaer, Ih, Peord, Ilcs, Sygil, Ti, Berc, Eh, Mon, Lagu, Ing, Daeg, Oedil, Ac, Aes, Yr, Eor.

In the 5th is one, inlaid in a sword or knife, found in the Thames. It gives twenty-eight characters in the same order as II. III. and V., except that *Man* and *Lagu*, instead of following *Eh*, are placed after *Dæg*, and transposed.

In the 14th is one impressed on a bracteate of gold found at Wadstena in Sweden. It seems to have contained twenty-four characters; but the last, and part of the last but one, are destroyed by the loop which has been attached to it. We cannot be sure whether the 23rd was *Dæg* or *Oethel*, but the rest are in the same order as before.

In the 13th is a German futhorc, from a MS. at S. Gallen, No. 270. The same runes are given in No. 878, but as an alphabet. Here we have twenty-eight characters in the same sequence as II. III. and V.

In the 18th is a Norse futhorc, entitled *Abecidarium Nord* in the S. Gallen MS. No. 878.[2] It is the most ancient copy we possess, being of the ninth century, and therefore older than the earliest existing inscriptions in these characters. The first six have the same order as the foregoing; the next five correspond to the 9th, 10th, 11th, 12th, and 16th; and the last five to the 17th, 18th, 21st, 20th, and 24th (*Lagu* and *Madr* changing places).

Now all these different copies of the futhorc agree as to the sequence of most of the characters. As far as the 29th, there can be no doubt that it was as given in the 1st column; I. II. and III. agree as to the places of the 30th, 32nd, and 33rd. Several authorities extend this system to thirty-three, and one to forty, distinct characters; and the latter is probably the correct number; for we have evidence that it was divided into classes, as we see it on the bracteate, each containing eight characters; and as these were regulated by the sacred number eight, we may well presume that another

---

[2] The usual Norse names of the characters are Fe, Ur, Thurs, Os, Ridr, Kaun, Hagl, Naud, Is, Ar, Sol, Tyr, Biarkan, Laugr, Madr, Yr.

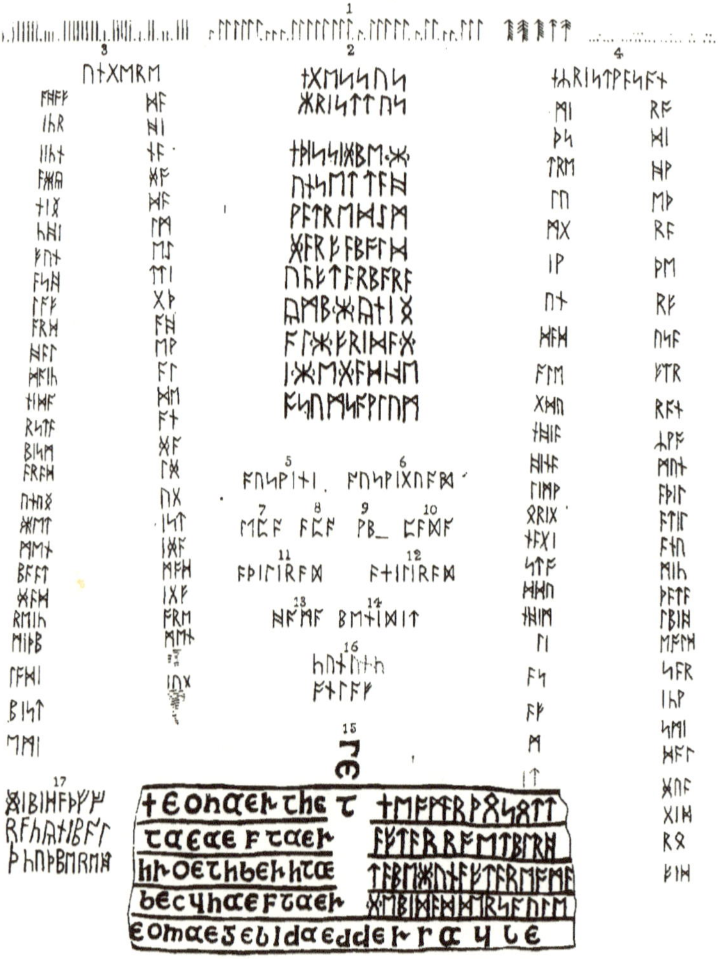

sacred number, forty, determined the extent of the futhorc, and completed the fifth class.

This evidence is contained in the S. Gallen MS. No. 270, which gives us several varieties of secret runes, viz.:—

Iis-Runa, which are simple repetitions of the rune *Is,* the number of shorter ones in each group denoting the class to which the character intended belonged, and that of the longer ones its position in the class;

Lago-Runa, differing only in the use of *Lago* for *Is;*

Hahal-Runa, consisting of branching stems, in which the branches to the left denoted the class, and that to the right the letter; and

Stof-Runa, in which the class is indicated by points placed above, and the letter by others below, or *vice versâ.*

As an example the word *Corvi* is given (Pl. II. fig. 1); and it appears that *Cæn* is I. 6, *Othil,* (these being German runes), III. 8, *Rad,* I. 5, *Ur,* I. 2, and *Is,* II. 3.

This notice, therefore, of secret runes vindicates the order of the futhorc as far as the 24th character, and reveals the fact that it consisted of classes of eight letters each. At Hackness, in Yorkshire, an inscription in *Hahal-Runa* exists, but is unfortunately too much defaced to be read satisfactorily. In Scandinavia some examples both of this and *Iis-Runa* have been found; and Liljegren, in his notice of this kind of writing, says that the futhorc (Norse) comprised three divisions; that *Fe* led the first, *Hagl* the second, and *Tir* the third; and that the classes to which the characters belonged, and their places therein, were denoted in the same way as they were in Germany and in England.

It is obvious that writing such as this would be too laborious to be much used; and it could not be very secret, for this very principle suggested itself as the key to the Hackness inscription, before I was aware of the existence of evidence that such a system had ever prevailed. Such, however, as it was, we find that it was in use amongst distinct and remote branches of the Teutonic stock,—a fact which is itself a proof of the great antiquity of the system, and of the order and arrangement of the futhorc, on which it was founded; an order and arrangement which, in its turn, proves most clearly that the Teutonic race were not indebted for the art of writing to any of the nations of antiquity, the order of whose phonetic systems is known.

Again, each character of the futhorc was distinguished by a name, expressive of some object; and instances are not unfrequent in Anglo-Saxon MSS. of the use of the symbol for the word which designated it. This nomenclature prevailed, as far as we know, amongst all the Teutonic tribes, as the variations, mostly dialectic, in the accompanying table show.

The Cotton MS. Otho, B. 10, now unfortunately lost, contained a poem explanatory of the names of the Anglo-Saxon runes; and a similar explanation of those of the Norse runes is given in a MS. in the University Library at Copenhagen. These explanations are not to be relied on in every instance; difference of opinion appears to have existed as to the meanings of some of these names; and we can but take them as the conjectures of Christian authors, who lived at a period when the futhorc was rather an antiquarian curiosity than a living system.

1. *Feoh* (*fech*, &c.) is explained as "money." Such was its secondary meaning, Latin *pecunia;* its primary sense was "cattle," *pecus*, perhaps even an individual "ox."
2. *Ur*, a "bull."
3. *Thorn*, the "tree." Its Norse correspondent is *thurs*, a "giant;" and we have also the variations *dour* and *thur*, a "door."
4. *Os*, a "mouth." The Norse poem explains it a "door," or "entrance."
5. *Rad*, a "saddle."
6. *Cæn*, a "torch," or the firtree whereof torches were

made. In the poem it is a log of wood on the fire; in the Exeter book the meaning "bold" is attached to it; in the Norse poem it is an "ulcer."

7. *Gifu*, a "gift."
8. *Wen*, "hope." In the Exeter book it is *wæn*, a "waggon;" the Vienna MS. gives *wyn*, the "vine," "wine," or "joy."
9. *Hægl*, "hail."
10. *Nyd*, "necessity." The original meaning was probably a bond or knot; for it was an ancient Teutonic custom, when a man espoused a woman, to write this rune on her nail; and we still talk of tying the marriage knot. The form of the rune may be the symbol of a knot, and its secondary meaning would easily follow.
11. *Is*, "ice."
12. *Gear*, a "year."[3] The Norse futhorc has *ar* with the same sense; and here we see how the name kept its place in the system, though both the form and the value were changed.
13. *Eóh*, or *éh*, is interpreted the "yew" tree; but that would be *eow*, or *iw*. All authorities agree in giving *h* as the final letter; and it is very possible that its meaning is nearly the same as the following, which in the German futhorc has a very similar form. It represents, however, the long *e*.
14. *Peorth*. In the poem the word is certainly a "chess-pawn;" but the Icelandic *ped*, the Persian *piadeh*, and the Italian *pedone*, all want the *r*. It is more probably a "horse;" O. G. *perd*, M. G. *pferd*.
15. *Eolhx*, "sedge."
16. *Sigel* is certainly the "sun;" and so *sol* is interpreted in

[3] I know of but one instance of the occurrence of this rune, and that is in the dialogue of Solomon and Saturn, where it is the correspondent of G in *regnum*, in the passage which gives the letters of which the Lord's prayer is composed. *Regnum* is the Anglo-Saxon *regen*, our reign; so here the character has the same value as in the word *gear*, "year."

the Norse poem; but in the Anglo-Saxon it is treated as if it were *segel*, a "sail."

17. *Tir.* In the poem it is said to be a constellation, always visible, and moving at night; that is, certainly, six stars of Ceorl's or Woden's wain, lines connecting which would give the form of this character.
18. *Beorc*, a "birch" tree.
19. *Eh*, a "horse."
20. *Man*, a "man." The Norse *madr* is the same. The resemblance of this rune to *Dæg* suggests that it was also the symbol of a measure of time — a moon or month.
21. *Lagu*, "water."
22. *Ing.* Unable to explain this word, the author of the poem has introduced a valuable notice of a hero of this name. Its resemblance to *Oethel* suggests that its meaning may be *ing*, a "field," a word of provincial use.
23. *Dæg*, "day."
24. *Oethel*, "patrimonial land." It is the symbol of an enclosure.
25. *A'c*, an "oak" tree.
26. *Æsc*, an "ash" tree.
27. *Yr*, a "bow."
28. *Ear.* In the poem it is spoken of as an instrument of death; perhaps *earh*, an "arrow."
29. *Ior.* Said to be a "water-fish," but our glossaries give no such word.
30. *Queorth* should be *queorn*, a "mill," as *quirun* of the Vienna MS. shows.
31. *Calc.* 32. *Stan.* 33. *Gar.* No explanation.

34, 35, 36. Names unknown.

37. *Vult.* In the dialogue of Solomon and Saturn, a rune is mentioned after D which can only correspond to V in *adveniat*. Its form is not given, but instead thereof

the word *fýr*. I have no doubt but that this is the character intended, and that *Vult* is the lost root of the Anglo-Saxon *wuldor* (Goth. *wulthus*), "glory."

We observe, then, that one uniform nomenclature was applied by different Teutonic nations to the characters of their futhorc; and although the meaning of some of the words may be doubtful, and that of others have changed since the original arrangement of the system, it is as evident that all belong to the language which the system was designed to express as it is that the *Alpha*, *Beta*, &c. of the Greeks were exotic; and it can no longer be doubted that the futhorc originated with the Teutonic race themselves. But when? Clearly in times of primitive antiquity. The nomenclature of the Phœnician-Hebrew alphabet[4] is admitted to indicate its having originated in a primitive state of society, and that of the futhorc has precisely the same character; indeed, it is remarkable how many of the objects named are common to both, how identical was the feeling which dictated in each case the choice of the symbols. We shall see this more clearly in the sequel; at present we are but on the threshhold of our inquiry, and can do no more than advert to the fact, and call attention to the remarkable coincidence in both systems, commencing with the names of domestic cattle.

In the examination of the different futhorcs we shall commence with that which longest maintained its ground in this country, of which, as we have seen, we have many copies more or less complete; to which all the Runic inscriptions in Northumbria, and all the runes introduced into the text of the Exeter book and other MSS. belong; and which I believe represents the system most nearly in its primitive form.

[4] *Aleph*, an ox; *Beth*, a house or tent; *Gimel*, a camel; *Daleth*, a door; *He*, a lattice or window; *Vau*, a hook; *Zain*, a weapon; *Cheth*, an enclosure; *Teth*, a serpent; *Iod*, a hand; *Coph*, the palm of the hand; *Lamed*, a whip or goad; *Mem*, water; *Nun*, a fish; *Samech*, a prop; *Ain*, an eye; *Pe*, a mouth; *Ssade*, a scythe or reapinghook; *Koph*, the back of the head; *Resh*, a head; *Schin*, the teeth; *Tau*, a mark or sign.

There is very little difference in the forms of the characters given in the several MSS. from which the first futhorc in the accompanying table is taken. The MS. Otho, B. 10, gives us, besides the usual Anglo-Saxon form of *Hægel*, a second, which belongs to another, probably German (Pl. I. fig. 8), and a third, which will be noticed as occurring on the gold bracteate, and in inscriptions in Kent and Norway; also, as a second form of *Eóh*, a character which in other MSS. follows *Gar*, and possibly had the same value as in the Greek and Latin alphabets. The MS. Galba, A. 2, gives a second form of *Oethel*, identical with that on the sword found in the Thames. In the Northumbrian inscriptions we have not only the rune *Cæn*, but another, identical in form with the Marcomannic *Chilch*, *Gilc*, or *Kalk*; and in some instances *Gifu* assumes an ornamental form approaching *Gar*, but not identical with it; for the characteristic mark of the latter is the recurving of the ends of the diagonal strokes. Nothing certain can be determined with regard to the characters of the fifth division, since, with the exception of two, their names are lost, until inscriptions be discovered containing them. The 37th occurs in two MSS. at Oxford, and its power no doubt was *v*; the 38th in one of these MSS., and in Cotton, Galba, A. 2; the 39th in three distinct alphabets, always with the value of *e*, and in one of these where *Eóh* and *Eoh* are also given; yet, from its resemblance to *Dæg*, I suspect its value was rather đ (*dh*); the 40th has the value *æ* assigned to it, and was perhaps a modification of *Æsc*, expressing the sound of the vowel in *æcer*, "acre."

Now this futhorc approves itself as indigenous to our language by its capability of expressing all the sounds thereof, which the Roman abecedarium does not. The uncertainty of Anglo-Saxon orthography, the confusion of sounds attached to different letters, and the irregular pronunciation of our modern English, are all attributable to the circumstance that our forefathers accepted from the missionaries of the Christian faith, in place of their ancient futhorc, an abecedarium by no means suited to their tongue. Long ago this was observed by Mr. Sheridan, with the fact that nine letters at least are required besides those we have, in order that each may be expressive of a single determinate sound. His scheme of the sounds which our language embraces is nearly as follows:—

13 vowels.	a^1 a^2 a^3 a^4 e^1 e^2 i^1 i^2 hat, hate, hall, harm, bet, beet, fit, fight, o^1 o^2 o^3 u^1 u^2 not, note, noose, cub, cube.	
2 ,,	w y short oo, short ee.	
19 consonants,	4 labials, eb, ef, ep, ev. 8 dentals, ed, et, edh, eth, ess, ez, esh, ezh. 4 palatals, eg, ek, el, er. 3 nasals, em, en, eng.	
	1 aspirate, h.	
	2 superfluous,	c, equivalent to ek or ess. q, ,, ek before u.
	3 compound,	j, ,, edzh. ch, ,, etsh. x, ,, eks.

Nearly forty characters, therefore, are necessary to express the sounds of our language; and we may believe that the futhorc did actually express these sounds, since, as far as our knowledge of its powers extends, we find that it included many which the abecedarium does not.

The names of the runes themselves, their occurrence in ancient inscriptions, and a comparison of the words in which they occur, with the same words in their modern form, are, of course, our only criteria as to their value; and these are not always certain, since words might be differently pronounced, as the runes had different powers amongst different tribes. The inscriptions discovered as yet are very few, yet they have supplied twenty-six characters, and amongst these nearly all the vowels, which may be arranged as follows:—

Æsc, "ash,"	a^1	At Ruthwell, double i	
A'c, "oak,"	a^3 or o^2	expresses	i^2
Ear, "arrow,"[5]	a^4	*Os*,	o^1
Eoh,	e^1	*Oethel*,	oe or o^2
Eóh,	e^3	*Ur*,	u^1
I's,	i^1	*Yr*,	y

The 40th character, which is distinguished from *Æsc* by a stroke to the left of the stem, may have expressed a^2. *Wen* sometimes makes a diphthong with another vowel, as in modern use. *Yr* is always a vowel, the quasi-consonant sound of *y* being represented by *Gear*.

The consonants, of which the value is known from inscriptions and MSS., supply all the sounds required but six, and we can account for nearly all these. *Gar* must represent *edzh*, a sound which in Roman letters was expressed by *cg*, or *dg;* it cannot be *gar*, a "spear," since that sound is already supplied by *Gifu*, a "gift." *Vult*, and the 34th and 39th characters, I have already supposed to represent *ev*, *ez*, and *edh*. For *esh*, which in Roman letters was expressed by *sc* (as in *sceaf*, a "sheaf"), and *etsh*, expressed by *c* (as in *cild*, a "child"), we have two characters unappropriated: the 36th, resembling *Cæn*, and the 38th. And besides these we have *Stan*, representing the compound *st*.

Thus we find in the futhorc, so far as its powers are known, nearly all the sounds of our language; and those which have not occurred may be represented by the unknown characters of the fifth division. It was, therefore, perfectly calculated for the expression of our language, and, as such, presents the strongest evidence of its indigenous origin. Its invention and arrangement belong to the race who spoke the language.

---

[5] It occurs also in the word *fearran*, "from afar."

To this system most of the Northumbrian inscriptions belong. Two of them are of particular interest, as being of greater length than others, and presenting us with specimens of the Anglian dialect, as spoken in Northumbria in the seventh century. The first, on the western face of the cross at Bewcastle in Cumberland, is simply a memorial of Alcfrid, who was associated by his father Oswiu with himself in the kingdom of Northumbria, and died probably in A.D. 664. It gives us (Pl. I. fig. 2) three couplets of alliterative verse, thus:—

✠ THIS SIGBECUN	This memorial
SETTÆ HWÆTRED	Hwætred set
EM GÆRFÆ BOLDU	and carved this monument
ÆFTÆR BARÆ	after the prince,
YMB CYNING ALCFRIDÆ	after the King Alcfrid,
GICEGÆD HEOSUM SAWLUM	pray for their souls.

Other inscriptions on the same monument present merely names of some of Alcfrid's kindred, in which, however, some additional characters occur.

The second inscription, on two sides of a similar cross at Ruthwell, in Annandale, which may possibly have been brought from Bewcastle, and once have stood at the other end of Alcfrid's grave, consists of fragments of a poem[6] on

[6] A later version of this poem was discovered by the late Mr. Kemble in a MS. from Vercelli. For the sake of comparison, the passages which correspond to these fragments are here extracted.

Ongyrede hine thá geong hæleth,	Then the young hero prepared himself,
thæt wæs God Ælmihtig,	that was God Almighty,
strang and stíthmód.	strong and firm of mood.
Gestáh he on gealgan heanne,	He mounted the lofty cross,
módig on manigra gesíhthe,	courageously in sight of many,
thá he wolde mancyn lýsan.	when he would redeem mankind.
Bifode ic thá me se beorn ymbclypte,	I trembled when the hero embraced me,
ne dorste ic hwæthre búgan to eorthan,	yet dared I not bow down to earth,

the crucifixion of our Lord, supposed to be uttered by the cross itself. It reads (Pl. II. fig. 3) commencing at the top, and proceeding down the right margin of one side:—

UNGEREDÆ HINÆ GOD ÆLMEETTIG	God Almighty prepared himself,
THA HE WALDE'AN GALGU GISTIGA	when he would to the cross ascend,
MODIG FORE MEN	courageously before men,
an maNYGra	in sight of many.

Then (Pl. II. fig. 4) returning to the left margin:—

AHOF IC RIICNÆ CYNINGC	I raised the mighty King,
HIFUNÆS HLAFARD	heaven's lord.
HÆLDA IC NI DARSTÆ	I durst not fall down.
BISMÆRÆDUN UNGCET MEN	They reviled us two
BÆ ÆTGÆDRE	both together,
IC MITH BLODI BISTEMID	I stained with blood.

---

feallan to foldan sceatum,	fall to the bosom of the ground,
ac ic sceolde fæste standan.	but I should stand fast.
Ród wæs ic arǽred.	A cross was I reared.
Ahóf ic rícne cyning,	I raised the mighty King,
heofona hláford,	heaven's lord,
hyldan me ne dorste.	I durst not fall down.
Bysmeredon hie unc butu æt gædere.	They reviled us both together.
Eal ic wæs mid blóde bestémed,	I was all stained with blood,
begoten of thæs guman sídan.	poured from the man's side.
Crist wæs on róde,	Christ was on the cross,
hwæthre thær fusæ,	yet thither hastening,
feorran cwomon,	men came from afar,
to thám æthelinge.	to the noble one.
Ic thæt eal beheóld,	I beheld that all,
sáre ic wæs mid gedréfed.	with sorrow I was afflicted.
Eal ic wæs mid strælum forwundod.	I was all wounded with nails.
Aledon hic thær limwérigne,	They laid him down limb-weary,
gestódon him æt his lices heafdum.	they stood by him at his corpse's head.

Commencing again at the top of the other side, and proceeding down the right margin:—

✠ CRIST WÆS AN RODI	Christ was on the cross.
HWETHRÆ THER FUSÆ	Lo! thither hastening,
FEARRAN CWOMUN	come from afar
ÆTHILÆ TI LÆNUM	nobles to him in misery.
IC THÆT ÆL BIHEOLD	I all that beheld,
SÆR IC WÆS mith dALGUÆ GIDRŒFID	Sore was I with pain vexed.

Then returning to the left margin:—

MITH STRELUM GIWUNDÆD	Wounded with nails,
ALEGDUN HIÆ HINÆ LIMWŒRIGNÆ	they laid him down limb-weary;
GISTODDUN HIM æt LICÆS hÆFduM	they stood by him at his corpse's head.

The poem of which these are fragments was probably one of those which Cædmon, who was living at the time when these monuments were erected, composed. That they belong to the seventh century cannot be doubted; they contain forms of the language which are evidently earlier even than those which occur in the cotemporary version of Bæda's verses in a MS. at S. Gallen, and the copy of Cædmon's first song at the end of the MS. of the "Historia Ecclesiastica," which was completed two years after its author's death.[7] Thus *hifun* (ana-

[7] It seems desirable to subjoin the original and later versions of these venerable documents, as they will be occasionally referred to in the sequel.

VEN. BÆDA.

For the neidfæræ,	For thám neódfere,	Before the needful journey,
nænig uuiurthit	nenig wyrtheth	no one is
thonc snotturra	thances snottra	wiser
than him tharf sie,	thonne him thearf sý,	than he need be,
to ymbhycgannæ,	to gehiggenne,	to consider,
ær his hiniongæ,	ær his heonengange,	before his departure,

logous to the Gothic *sibun* for *seofen*) is certainly an earlier form than *hefaen* and *heben*, which we find in the latter of these little poems. *Em* in the Bewcastle inscription is *efen* contracted. *Boldu, galgu,* and *dalgu,* present a form of nouns which later would be monosyllabic. *Heosum,* the dative plural of the possessive pronoun of the third person, regularly formed, like *ůsum*, from the genitive of the personal, (*hire, úre*), occurs only in the Bewcastle inscription; *ungcet,* the dual of the first personal pronoun, only in that at Ruthwell. *Gærfæ* is a strange instance of a strong verb taking

---

huæt his gastæ,	hwæt his gáste,	what to his soul,
godæs æththa yflæs,	godes oththe yfeles,	of good or evil,
æfter deothdæge,	æfter deathe heonen,	after the death day,
dœmid unieorthæ.	démed wurthe.	shall be decreed.

CÆDMON.

Nu scylun herga*	Nu we sceolon herigean	Now we shall praise
hefaen-ricaes uard,	heofon-ríces weard,	heaven-kingdom's guardian,
metudaes mæcti,	metodes mihte,	the Creator's might,
end his mod-gidanc,	and his mód-gethanc,	and His counsel,
uerc-uuldur fadur.	weorc wuldor fæder.	the work-glorious Father.
Sue he uundra gihuaes	Swá he wundra gehwæs	As He of every wonder
eci dryctin	éce drihten	the æternal Lord
or astelidæ.	ord onsteald.	formed the beginning.
He aerist scopa	He ærest scóp	He first created
elda barnum	eorthan bearnum	for the children of men (or, of earth)
heben til hrofe,	heofon to rófe,	heaven as a roof,
haleg scepen;	hálig scippend;	the holy Creator;
tha middungeard,	tha middangeard,	then mid-earth,
moncynnæs uard,	moncynnes weard,	mankind's guardian,
eci dryctin,	éce drihten,	the æternal Lord,
æfter tiadæ,	æfter teode,	afterwards produced,
firum foldu	firum foldan,	earth for men,
frea allmectig.	freá ælmihtig.	the Lord Almighty.

---

* The word is *hergen* in the MS., with a mark to indicate an error, and *a* written above. With the abundant evidence we possess of the Northumbrian form of the infinitive, we have no difficulty in making this correction. This copy is transcribed from a tracing of the original.

an additional syllable in the præterite; but it seems to be warranted by *scopa* in Cædmon's song, and even by *ahofe* in the Durham ritual; and the analogy of the Sanscrit præterite (*tutôpa, tutôpa*), and the Greek (τέτυφα, τέτυφε), shows that such forms as these, not only for the third person, but for the first also, are more ancient than *cearf*, *scóp*, and *ahóf*.

A cross at Collingham in Yorkshire, on which the name (Pl. II. fig. 5) AUSWINI occurs, and which is probably the monument of King Oswine, who perished in A. D. 651; a coin in the possession of Mr. Lindsay, which has the legend (Pl. II. fig. 6) (AU)SWIGUARD, "Oswiu the chief," and may be assigned to King Oswiu, A. D. 642 to 670; others of similar type, presenting the name (Pl. II. figs. 7, 8) EPA or ÆPA, referred to the brother of the Mercian Peada, who fell in the battle of Maserfield, A. D. 642; others, with the names (Pl. II. fig. 9) WB, (fig. 10) PÆDA, and (figs. 11, 12) ÆTHILIRÆD, almost certainly belonging to Wibba, Peada, and Æthelræd, Kings of Mercia; a gold coin, an imitation of those of Theodosius, found at Harlingen, with the name (Pl. II. fig. 13) HAMA, for which I can find no more probable claimant than Hama of the "Traveller's Tale," a Mercian prince of the sixth century; and another, found at Dorchester in Oxfordshire, with the name (Pl. II. fig. 14) BENIDIT, are additional evidences of the use of these characters in Northumbria and Mercia about the time when Christianity was first preached to our forefathers. Somewhat later is the following inscription (Pl. II. fig. 15), written first in runes, and then in Romanesque characters, on a fragment found at Falstone in Northumberland, and now in the Museum of the Society of Antiquaries at Newcastle-on-Tyne:—

✠ EOMÆR THŒ SŒTTÆ	Eomær set that,
ÆFTÆR HROETHBERHTÆ	after Hroethberht,
BECUN ÆFTÆR EOMÆ	a memorial after his uncle,
GEBIDÆD DER SAULE	pray for his soul.

Here, as in Venerable Bæda's song, we have the indeclinable *the*—here used for *thæt*, there for *thám*.

These runes continued to be used in inscriptions in Northumbria as late as the middle of the tenth century; for the name (Pl. II. fig. 16) of CUN(UNC) ONLAF, "King Onlaf," was written on one of the fragments of crosses which were discovered during the demolition of the old parish church at Leeds. The only differences between the characters in these inscriptions and those of the usual futhorc are in the forms of *Gifu* and *Calc*. A character the same as the usual *Gifu* occurs at the commencement of the word GESSUS, "Jesus," on the Bewcastle cross, and therefore must represent *Gear*.

In the Manchester Museum a cross is preserved which was found at Lancaster, on which is an inscription (Pl. II. fig. 17) in characters slightly differing from these, GIBIDÆTH FORÆ CYNIBALTH CUTHBEREHT, "Pray for Cynibalth and Cuthbereht." The difference in the spelling of these names is merely dialectic, (the former has its parallel in Aethilbalth, in a Mercian charter, the latter in Eatbereht, on a tombstone at Wensley in Yorkshire), and I regard this monument as one of the eighth century.

A casket of whalebone, the subject of a memoir communicated by Mr. Franks to the Archæological Institute at their Carlisle meeting, presents a series of inscriptions in characters nearly identical with those in the Vienna MS. They are as follows:—

1. Around a representation of the myth of Romulus and Remus (Pl. III. fig. 1):—

OTHLÆUN NEG ROMWALUS END REUMWALUS TWŒGENI GIBROTHÆRÆ

FŒDDÆ HIÆ WYLIF IN ROMÆCÆSTRI.

"Romwalus and Reumwalus, twin brothers, lay out near "(together): a wolf fed them in Rome city."

2. Titus storming Jerusalem, and the Jews taking to flight.

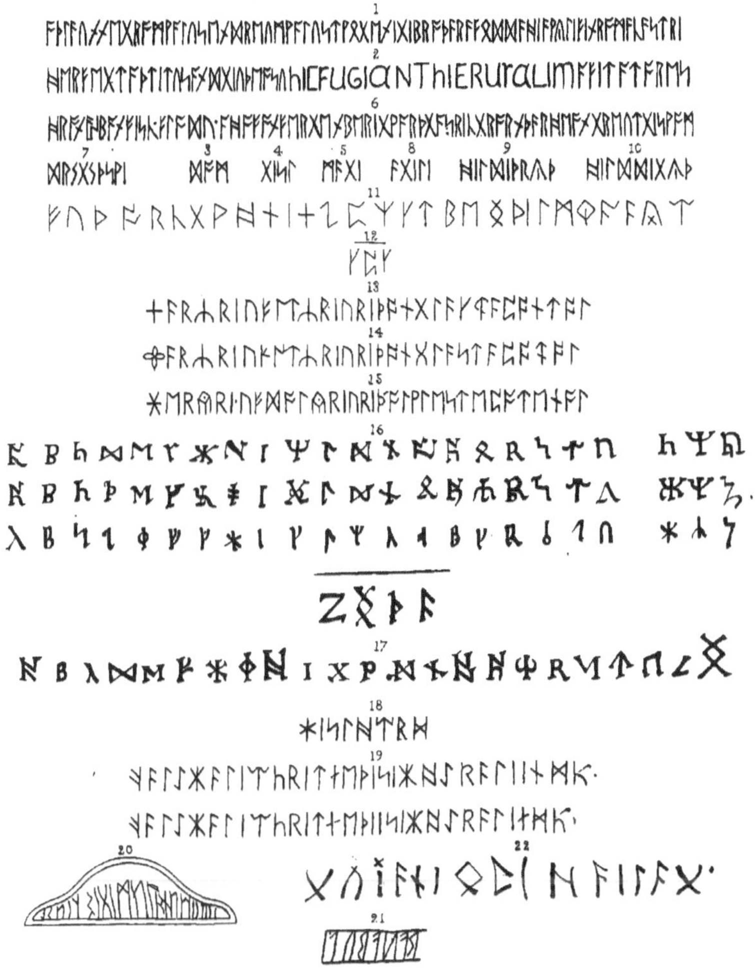

The inscription is partly in runes (Pl. III. fig. 2), HER FEGTATH TITUS END GIUTHEOSU, "Here Titus and the Jews "fight." The rest is in Latin and, with the exception of the last word, which is in runes, in Romanesque characters, HIC FUGIANT HIERUSALIM AFITATORES (*habitatores*). Beneath these is a representation of a tribunal, with the word (Pl. III. fig. 3) DOM, and another of a person led off to prison, with the word (Pl. III. fig. 4) GISL; the two, perhaps, forming a rebus of the name of the maker of this casket,—DOMGISL.

3. The front represents the delivery of the head of St. John the Baptist to Herodias and her daughter, and the offering of the (Pl. III. fig. 5) MÆGI. Around the whole the artist has inscribed, in verse, a memorial of the capture of the whale whose bone furnished the material wherewith to make the casket (Pl. III. fig. 6):—

HRONÆS BAN FISC FLODU	The whale's bone from the fish-flood
AHOF ON FERGEN BERIG	I raised on the high hill;
WARTH GASRIC GRORN	his hazy sovereignty was overthrown
THÆR HE ON GREUT GISWOM	where he swam ashore.

The jaws of the whale are frequently to be seen doing duty as gate-posts—trophies, probably, of whaling expeditions—in the northern coast counties. These verses appear to allude to something of the kind.

4. Nothing remains of the fourth side but part of the letters (Pl. III. fig. 7) DREGETH SWIClíce, "oppresseth trea-"cherously;" referring, perhaps, to a representation of the slaughter of the Holy Innocents.

5. On the top there is a scene from the history of one of the Ægels, whose name (Pl. III. fig. 8), ÆGILI, is written above him.

It was probably a common name. Ammianus Marcellinus and Zosimus mention a Teutonic chief Agilo; we have also Ægel the brother of Weland, and another of the name is mentioned in the Ynglinga Saga.

These inscriptions appear to be in a Northumbrian dialect, differing, however, in some respects, from that of the Ruthwell and Bewcastle monuments. The characteristic differences between these and the later forms of the language appear to be in the frequent use of *Gifu* for *Hægl*, as in *neg* for *neáh*, *fegtath* for *feohtath*, *gas-ric* for *haso-ric*, *grorn* for *hroren*; in additional syllables (a mark of early date), as in *gibrothæræ* for *gebrothra*, *wylif* for *wylf*, *berig*, (cf. *pereg* in the Weissenbrun hymn), for *beorh*. *Othlæun* later would have been *othlægon*, and *giswom*, *geswam*.

The third inscription indicates that the district in which it was written was on the coast; and the identity of the forms of the characters with those on two of the tombstones found at Hartlepool may warrant the conjecture that it was the eastern rather than the western coast of Northumbria. These bear respectively the names HILDITHRYTH and HILDDIGYTH, and the eighth century, at the latest, must be assigned for their date, as for that of the casket.

The use of these runes, as far as at present appears, was confined to the Anglian race who occupied Northumbria, Mercia, and East Anglia. Beyond the limits of those kingdoms no inscription in these characters has yet been found; whilst within them, and particularly in the first, we have them of various dates, from the middle of the seventh to the middle of the tenth century.

The retention of the Runic system in Northumbria, long after it had fallen into disuse in the southern kingdoms, will account for the fact, that nearly all the runes in the Exeter book and in other MS. belong to the Northumbrian futhorc; and that, although we have other runes in MSS., they are arranged in the abecedarium rather than in the futhorc order.

But how is the circumstance of its having so long maintained its ground in Northumbria to be explained? I believe by the peculiar circumstances under which Northumbria received the Christian faith.

The first missionaries, S. Augustine and his brethren, used all their endeavours to destroy every monument of Runic antiquity, because runes had been the medium of pagan augury, and of preserving the memory of pagan hymns and incantations; for, knowing how prone the common people were to their ancient superstitions, (of which even after the lapse of twelve centuries many vestiges still remain), and how difficult it would be to teach them to distinguish the use of a thing from its abuse, they feared that their labours would be in vain so long as the monuments of ancient superstition remained. So every Runic writing disappeared; and we may well believe, that records which to us would be invaluable perished in the general destruction of ancient monuments.

In the first instance, S. Gregory had commanded that everything connected with paganism should be destroyed; but afterwards, in a letter to S. Mellitus, he recommended that the symbols only of paganism should be done away with, but that the sanctuaries should be consecrated and used as churches. These instructions were in force when S. Paulinus evangelized Northumbria; and we cannot doubt that the work of destruction would be effectually done under the auspices of a prince whose police was so vigorous as we are informed that Eadwine's was. But after his death and the flight of S. Paulinus, the restoration of Christianity in Northumbria was effected by missionaries of the Irish school, whose fathers in Ireland had pursued from the first a different policy, by allowing the memorials of antiquity to remain, and contenting themselves with consecrating the monuments of paganism, by marking them with the symbols of Christianity. Under their auspices Runic writing was permitted, for we can trace its use in Northumbria to the very times of S. Oswald, whilst every vestige has disappeared of the Runic records of an earlier period. Mercia received its Christianity from the Irish school of Lindisfarne, and we have runes on the coins of its first Christian kings Peada and Æthelræd.

We are not entirely deprived of the means of knowing what were the characters which other Teutonic tribes, settled in Britain, used in writing, for they are preserved on monuments which might be lost at the time of the coming of S. Augustine, and so escaped the general destruction. The most precious relic of this kind that has come to light is the sword found in the Thames, now in the British Museum, in which is inlaid in gold and silver a futhorc of twenty-eight runes (Pl. III. fig. 11), followed by the name BEAGNOTH. In this futhorc there are some important differences in the forms of the characters; *Thorn* is of the usual form, but in the name it has that of D in the colophon of Harl. MS. 1772, (written in German runes); *Gear* is a simple cross, but this, as well as the usual form, is used to express E in some Norse inscriptions; *Eóh* is inverted; *Sigel* is a peculiar form, instances of the occurrence of which elsewhere we shall have occasion to notice, (and here we see the original type of the minuscule used in later Anglo-Saxon writing); *Dæg, Oethel,* and *Yr* are also curious varieties; something like the first will be noticed on a gold ring in the sequel, and the second occurs in the Cott. MS. Galba, A. 2.

Traces remain of the use, in Northumbria, of a futhorc distinct from all the foregoing. Three characters occurred on one of the fragments of the coffin of S. Cuthbert, with the mark of contraction over them (Pl. III. fig. 12), and there can be no doubt that they must be read $\overline{\text{scs}}$ for *Sanctus.* The s is the same as that just noticed on the sword, and the c occurs in the curious alphabet attributed to Nemnivus. Now both these characters appear in the inscription on a ring which was found at Kingsmoor near Carlisle (Pl. III. fig. 13), whilst in the same legend on another found at Bramham in

Yorkshire (fig. 14), the usual *Sigel* represents the former. The attempts that have been made to interpret this inscription have not been successful: and the late Mr. Kemble was even willing to admit that these rings might be of Celtic origin. Yet the localities in which they were found will warrant us in regarding them as Teutonic, and seeking their interpretation in the Teutonic language; whilst the fact that the same legend occurs on two rings, and what is evidently intended for the same on a third, suggests that it is nothing more than a magical spell in common use; and such, (analogous to some which have been published by Grimm and Kemble), we shall find it to be. Indeed, the only difficulty in deciphering it arises from the fact that it belongs to a futhorc in which the runes which represent C, H, and S had different forms from those which usually occur. C and S we have found on S. Cuthbert's coffin, and H appears in a Runic bethluisnion preserved in a MS. at Trinity College, Dublin, to be noticed in the sequel. The inscription is simply, AR HRIUF EL HRIURITHON GLAS TACON TOL.

Hriurithon is undoubtedly a Teutonic word, the 3rd pers. plur. præt. of a verb in *ian*, analogous to the sing. *astelidæ* in Cædmon's song, and to the usual Gothic form, examples of which in other inscriptions will be noticed presently. The collation of the original copy of Venerable Bæda's verses with the later version shows that words were spelt in later times with *y*, of which the earlier form would be *iu;* consequently *hriurithon* is the ancient form of *hrýrodon* from *hrýrian*, to "overthrow." *Tacon* similarly appears to represent *tócon*, "took." *Tol* is "toll," or "tribute." The nominative to *hriurithon* and *tacon* must of course be plural; and I think we have here the names of three mythological personages: *Ar* (Ares), a name of the Teutonic god of war, and implying "war" itself; *Hriuf*, equivalent to *hrýf*, *hreáf*, "spoil," or "plunder," perhaps also personified; *El* or *Hel*, the infernal goddess, also "hell," and the "grave." In this view *Glas*, which means "glass," or anything bright or clear, might also personify some mythological being; and the whole sense of this mysterious legend would be " Ar, Hriuf, and El (or war, rapine, and the grave) have vanquished Glas (or glory) taken tribute."

These rings being too large to have been worn on the finger, Mr. Franks has suggested that they were attached to hilts of swords. In this opinion I fully acquiesce; and I believe that in these inscriptions we have examples of the *Sigrúna*[8] which were supposed to ensure victory to the possessor. The ancient forms of the words, as well as the localities in which these rings have been found, seem to refer them to the age of the Teutonic conquest of Britain.

The inscription on the fourth ring (Pl. III. fig. 15) seems to be a copy by a person who did not understand the spell, took the character which I have read H for the Norse *Yr*, and substituted for it the corresponding Anglo-Saxon rune. With this and other blunders he has converted the inscription into perfect gibberish.

The Cottonian MS. Vitellius, A. 12, gives two alphabets of runes, resembling the Anglo-Saxon, followed by one of Norse runes (Pl. III. fig. 16). An Exeter MS., cited by Hickes, gives two copies of the first of these and one of the second. In the first F has only a single branch attached to the stem; G has the form of the Marcomannic *Gilch;* K is the same as X; Q has the form of the usual *Oethel* C is repeated before X. This alphabet gives us a futhorc, imperfect of course, somewhat different from those we have noticed, which is supported as to the form of G by the inscription (Pl. III. fig. 18) GISLHEARD on a tombstone at Dover.

---

[8] Sigrunar thu skalt kunna	Thou shalt know the runes of victory
ef thu vilt sigr hafa,	if thou wilt have victory,
ok rista á hialti hiors.	and cut them on the hilt of the sword.—Brynhildr Quida, I 6.

The second in giving the form of *Thorn* for D, that of the German *Hinc* for H, that of *Oethel* for O, and in the German form of G, seems nearly allied to the German futhorc. An Anglo-Saxon *Gifu* appears in the place of K, the usual form of which stands under the second C of the preceding alphabet, and before X. Y has a peculiar form, resembling one which will be noticed hereafter. In both MSS. the runes Z, *Ing*, *Thorn*, and *Æsc* follow.

Hickes (Gramm. Island. Tab. III.) has given an alphabet (Pl. III. fig. 17), from a MS. without reference, in which the names of the characters are written in Greek letters. In this *Gear* is given as a second form of G, the usual form of which appears as K; L has a singular form, and Q resembles that in Otho, B. 10 and Domitian, A. 9. *Ing* follows. These may be regarded as varieties of the usual futhorc, belonging to different tribes; and the peculiar forms of G in the first and third, of L in the third, and of Q in the first, occur in an inscription in the Harleian MS. 1772, an early Latin bible written in Germany, in which also we have some other German forms, and two, N and M, which occur in no other Runic series.

I give (Pl. III. fig. 19) an inscription on a box in the museum at Brunswick. The first character is new, and I know not what value to assign to it; the ninth would be *Eor* if this were an Anglo-Saxon inscription; in the German futhorc it is called *Der*, and in the Marcomannic, *Ziu*. CRITNETHI may be equivalent to *grithneátas*, "enjoyers of protection;" SIGHERÆ is clear, a proper name in the oblique case; and LINDC' may be *lind-cempæ*, "shield warrior." With some hesitation, on account of the uncertainty of the value of the two characters above noticed, I venture to translate the whole, WALE GALIA CRITNETHI SIGHERÆ LINDCEMPÆ, "Weal! joy! a retinue! to Sighere the shield warrior."

Here we must notice a remarkable alphabet, copied by Hickes from a Bodleian MS. NE. D. II. 19. In the words by which it is introduced no claim is made for a British origin, except that it is said to have been invented by Nemnivus;[9] and that it is not British is clear, from the fact that this alphabet contains four letters, K, Q, X, Z, which do not occur in the Coelbren y Beird. In fact, Nemnivus would appear to have palmed off on his Saxon acquaintances an alphabet which he had derived from some Teutonic source, and to have given to its characters names very much resembling those of the futhorc.[10] His alphabet is nearly identical with one which is preserved in two MSS., Cotton. Galba A. 2, and C. 27 in S. John's Library, Oxford; and, although the latter presents some curious varieties, its connection with the Anglo-Saxon and German futhorcs is evident.

We have several copies of the system which prevailed among the Marcomanni in the ninth century, long after this kind of writing had become obsolete in the south of England. One of these Hrabanus Maurus introduces with the information that they were employed by those who still remained pagans, for charms, incantations, and divinations.[11] In the other copies there are no essential differences; but all being written in the Roman order, we have fewer characters than in the futhorc. Of those it contains, F, R, I, P, B, M, L, A, and K, are identical with the corresponding Anglo-Saxon

---

9 "Nemnivus istas reperit literas vituperante quodam scolastico Saxonici "generis, quia Brittones non haberent rudimentum; et ipse subito ex "machinatione mentis suæ formavit eas ut vituperationem et hebetu-"dinem dejiceret gentis suæ."

10 Of the names he has given, the following are interpreted:—*Estiaul*, "sitting;" *alar*, "grief;" *guichr*, "brave;" *muin*, "a gift;" *rat*, "free;" *aur*, "gold;" *braut*, "judgment;" *huil*, "a wheel;" *nulin*, "a mist;" *surg*, "filth;" *cuic*, "expanse;" *cusil*, "counsel;" *iechuit*, "health;" *or*, "a border;" *traus*, "angry;" *hinc*, "threshold;" *dexu*, "to lurk;" *ham*, "crooked;" *parth*, "a part;" *uir*, "a grandson;" *ud*, "lord;" *egui*, "a "plague;" *louber*, "light;" *guith*, "wrong;" *arm*, "a weapon."

11 "Litteras quippe quibus utuntur Marcomanni, quos nos Nord-"mannos vocamus, infrascriptas habemus; a quibus originem qui Theo-"discam loquuntur linguam trahunt; cum quibus carmina sua, incan-"tationesque, ac divinationes significare procurant, qui adhuc paganis "ritibus involvuntur."

runes; C is the same as its Norse equivalent; U and Q resemble the Gothic and German forms of the same letters; D, T, and O have names corresponding to *Thorn*, *Dæg*, and *Oethel*, but the forms respectively of *Dæg*, *Tír*, and *Os*. G, H, X, and Y differ from all other forms of these characters.

Besides these, we have evidence of the use of two other systems in Germany. One, contained in two MSS. of Isidor, differs from the usual Anglo-Saxon futhorc, only in the interchange of the characters *Ing* and *Oethel*, and in the peculiar forms of *Yr* and *Ear*. That it is German is evident, from the dialect in which the names of the characters are written. Of the other we have two copies; one, in the Roman order, in a MS. of the ninth century, at S. Gall (No. 878), the other, in the Runic order, in another MS. at S. Gall (No. 270). These are certainly German runes, not Anglo-Saxon; for the first copy is followed by the usual Anglo-Saxon futhorc, marked for distinction *Anguliscum*, and by the Norse marked *Abecidarium Nord*; and four characters differ in their forms, and six in their names and powers, from their Anglo-Saxon correspondents.

A single instance only has occurred of the use of runes such as these in England; the inscription on the pommel of a sword found in the Anglo-Saxon cemetery at Gilton, now in the possession of Mr. Mayer (Pl. III. fig. 20). The characters at the beginning and end are not so distinct as we could wish, owing to the wearing away of the edges of the instrument; in fact the distinctive marks of those at the end are gone. The first character is the lower part of the 13th rune, equivalent to E long; the second is C, of a form which occurs on the golden bracteates, and golden horn; the fifth is the Marcomannic *Chon*, and is therefore equivalent to CH or K; the sixteenth is M, of which the upper part is worn away; the rest is clear, and the whole must be read, ECU IK SIGI MUARNUM, (which, in later Anglo-Saxon, would be, *Eáce ic sige mǽrnum*), "I eke victory to great deeds."

The first person singular present indicative of the verb, ending in *u* or *o*, characterizes the gloss to the Cottonian Psalter, Vespasian, A. 1; a MS. identified with one which was traditionally believed in the fifteenth century to have belonged to S. Augustine of Canterbury, and evidently of Italian origin. Under these circumstances we may believe that the gloss represents a Kentish rather than a Northumbrian dialect, from which, (as exemplified in the Durham Ritual), it differs in certain forms of the conjugation of verbs, whilst it agrees with it in the particular form in question. Otfrid, the Heljand, &c. have also the same; as well as the spelling *ua* for *a*, *uo* for *o*, which thus, in the word *muarnum* for *mǽrnum*, connects this inscription with the old German dialects. The dative plural in *um* belongs to the Anglo-Saxon and the Gothic. *Muarnum* for *mǽrnum* supposes a noun *mǽren* connected with *mær*, "great," or "illustrious," as *mægen*, "might," with *mæg*, "mighty." This inscription may be regarded as having been intended to ensure victory to the owner of the sword,—another instance of the *Sigrúna.* Its character, the ancient forms of the language, and the presumed antiquity of most of the interments in the Gilton cemetery, will warrant us in regarding this pommel as a relic of the sixth century, possibly even of the fifth. As such it presents an early and very interesting example, of the runes which were in use amongst the race which occupied Kent, that is, probably the Jutes.

A monumental stone found near Canterbury, and now in the museum of that city, presents an interesting trace of the use in this country of a futhorc distinct from all the foregoing, in which, as in the MS. Otho, B. 10, *Hægl* had a single transverse bar. It gives us merely a name (Pl. III. fig. 21) RAHABUL, of a form unusual indeed, but supported as to both its elements by Rahulf (C. D. 1367), and Theabul (C. D. 43. 47).

On the continent, and especially in the Scandinavian kingdoms, most interesting monuments of Teutonic palæo-

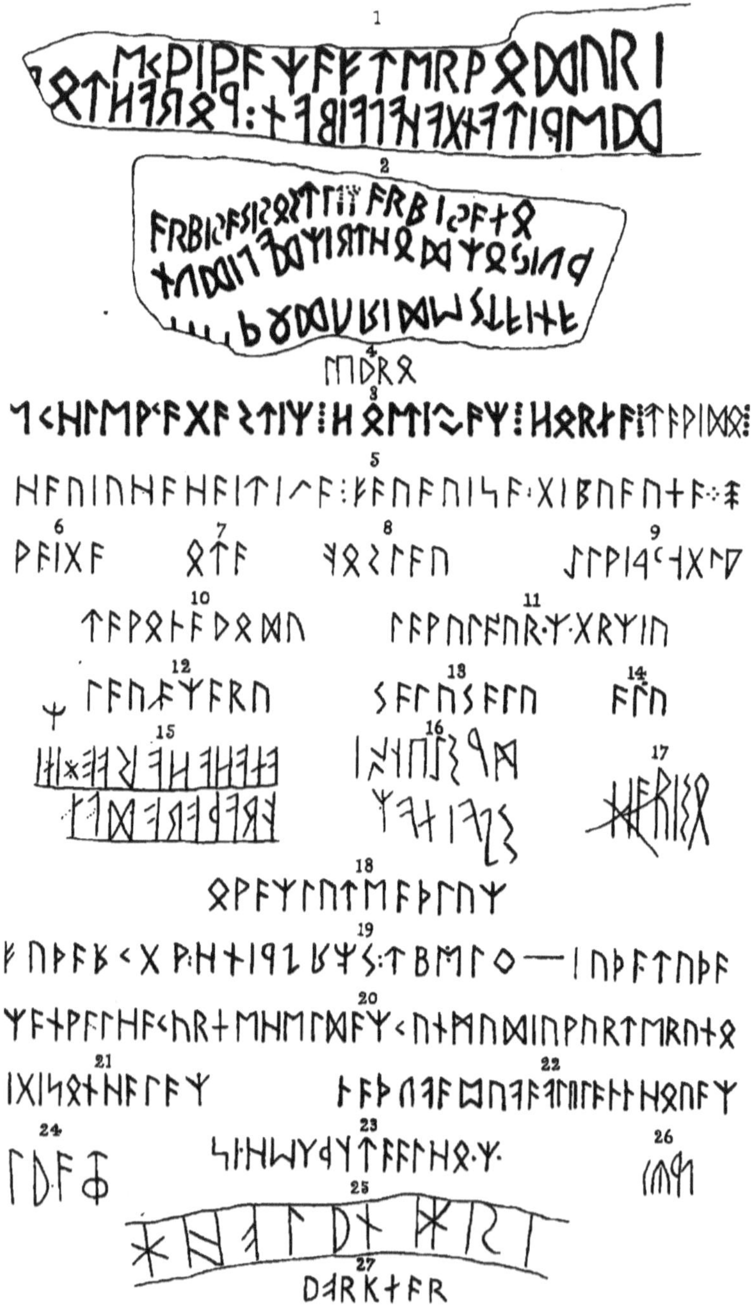
1
2
4
3
5
6
7
8
9
10
11
12
13
14
15
16
17
18
19
20
21
22
24
23
26
25
27

graphy have been discovered. Of these, the inscription on a gold bracelet found at Buzeu in Wallachia, and now in the museum at Bucharest, claims our first attention, because it is probably the most ancient Runic relic in existence (Pl. III. fig. 22). All the characters in this inscription are plain, except the third and eighth. The latter, however, is certainly *Dæg*, of the form which this character has in the futhorc on the Anglo-Saxon knife; the latter has been read TH, (and this I prefer), and T. I propose to divide the whole thus:—

GUTH ANIOD HAILAG, " God only holy," or, " One only " holy God." *Aniod* I take to be an adjective, related to the Anglo-Saxon *ánod*, Old Saxon *enódi*, " solitude," (the *i* being warranted by the form *anga*). The place of the discovery of this bracelet, within the limits of the ancient territory of the Goths, and the dialectic forms of the words of this inscription, leave no doubt as to its origin; it is a monument of Gothic Christianity, of the third or fourth century, probably anterior to the time of Ulfilas.

The inscriptions on a rude stone pillar at Tun, in the district of Christiania in Norway, have long exercised the ingenuity of the students of Runic literature, and at length have met with a successful interpreter in Professor Münch. They are as usual in verse, written *bustrophedon*, and appear to read as follows. On one side (Pl. IV. fig. 1):—

EC WIWA Markido	I Wiwa marked
AFTER WODURIDE	after Wodurid,
WITAN GAHALAIBAN	my counsellor and companion,
WORAHTO Runos	wrought runes.

On the other (fig. 2):—

ARBINGA SINGOST	Singost of the Arbings,
EM ARBINGA NO—	and No— of the Arbings,
mit THUINGOM DOHTRIM	with his orphan daughters,
DALIDUN for WODURIDE STAINA	quarried the stone for Wodurid.

In the first inscription the last letter is imperfect, but appears to have been R, and in Wormius' copies there are other letters in a lower line which may have completed the word RUNOS. In the second, Wormius gives UM after SINGOST, and the traces of letters which remain in Professor Münch's copy will allow of this or EM, which I prefer; and the injuries which the monument has suffered have occasioned two blanks in the remainder of the inscription, which I have ventured to supply in part.

The dialect in which these inscriptions are written, bears, as Professor Münch has observed, a great resemblance to the Gothic; but he has overlooked the fact that it corresponds even more nearly with that of the Weissenbrun hymn. Even the prefix *ga,* in *gahalaiban,* which seems peculiar to the Gothic, appears in that document, although it has been misread *chi,* on account of its being represented by the rune which stands for G in the Dover inscription. For it is evident that it is equivalent to *ga,* because it is used in *for*pi,* the second person singular præterite of the verb, of which the imperative *forgip* immediately follows, which therefore must be read *forgapi;* and the words to which this rune is prefixed are therefore *ga-fregin, ga-uuorahtos, ga-uurchanne.*[12] The second of these presents the same form as

---

[12] A copy of this hymn is subjoined:—

Dat gafregin ih mit firahim	That I have heard from men
firiuuizzo meista,	of most wisdom,
dat ero ni uuas	that before was not
noh ufhimil,	nĕither heaven above
noh paum noh pereg ni uuas,	nor tree nor hill was there,
ni (prunno) * noh heinig,	nor any spring,
noh sunna ni scein,	nor did sun shine,
(noh sterron ——)	nor stars——
noh mano ni liuhta,	nor moon give light,

* A word of this kind seems necessary to the alliteration. So also a line in which stars were mentioned seems wanting after the next; indeed the poem appears to be defective in other places as well.

worahto of the inscription, equivalent to the Gothic *waurhta*, Anglo-Saxon *worhte*. In this word, and in *ga-halaiban*, as well as in *firahim*, *ganada*, and *galaupa* of the hymn, we observe the peculiarity—of which instances have been noticed in the inscription on the whalebone casket, and others will be noticed in the sequel—of a freer use of vowels than in later dialects, and even than in the Gothic, and a disinclination to allow two consonants to stand together. *Ec* is the Norse and modern Dutch form of the pronoun, which in other dialects is spelt with *i*, as *ic*, *ih*, *ik*. *Gahalaiban*, Gothic *gahlaiban*, is a "companion" (*cum-panis*), one who eats "bread," *hlaibs*, at the same table. The Anglo-Saxon word *gehláf* has not yet appeared; but instead thereof we have *geneát*, and its compounds *beod-geneát* and *heorth-geneát*, the "enjoyer of the same bed or hearth," and *gesíth*, the "comrade" or associate in an expedition, all denoting the *comes* of a prince, who was himself *hláf-ord*, the "bread chief,"

noh der mareo seo.	nor the broad sea.
do dar ni nuiht ni uuas	Then there was nothing
enteo ni uuenteo;	from end to end;
enti do uuas der eino	and then was the one
almahtico cot,	Almighty God,
manno miltisto;	most merciful of beings,
enti dar uuarun auh manake mit inan,	and there were also with Him many,
cootlihhe geista,	godlike spirits,
enti cot heilac.	and Holy God.
Cot almahtico!	God Almighty!
du himil enti erda gauuorahtos,	who heaven and earth hast wrought,
enti du mannun	and who to men
so manac coot forgapi,	so much good hast granted,
forgip mir in dino ganada	grant to me in Thy grace
rehta galaupa	right faith
enti cotan uuilleon	and good will,
uuistom enti spahida	wisdom and knowledge
enti craft tiuflun za uuidarstantaune,	and craft to withstand devils,
enti arc za piuuisanne,	and prudence to be wise,
enti dinan uuilleon	and Thy will
za gauurchanne.	to do.

and whose wife was *hláf-dige*, the "bread distributor." *Em*, as in the Bewcastle inscription, is *efen* contracted. *Gethuing* is "affliction" in the Heljand, and in Anglo-Saxon *thwingan* is to "afflict;" here *thuingom* appears to be an adjective agreeing with *dohtrim*. *Dal* is a "pit" or "hole;" *dalidun*, therefore, the third person plural præterite of *dalian* can only have the sense I have given to it. In this, as in other inscriptions, *m* appears to be an abbreviation for *markido*, A. S. *mearcode*. *Staina* answers to the Gothic *stain*.

Professor Münch considers this monument as belonging to the beginning of the sixth century; a conjecture which the following attempt to identify the person who erected it tends to establish. Wiwa, to whom Wodurid stood in the relation of *wita* and *gehláf*, must have been a prince. The fact of his having inscribed this monument to the memory of his friend, is an illustration of the intimate bond of affection and devotion which united Teutonic chieftains and their *gesíthas*, and perfectly consistent with what we learn from other sources, that the art of writing was one of the accomplishments of kings, however limited its use may have been amongst their people, and that men of high rank did not disdain to employ their leisure in handicraft. So, four centuries later, King Gorm himself made the memorial for Queen Thyre. The fact, therefore, that Wiwa wrote this inscription in memory of Wodurid, is by no means derogatory to the rank which is proved to have been his, by the titles ascribed to his friend. Precisely at the time to which Professor Münch refers this monument, a prince of this name was living. Florence of Worcester calls him Wewa or Wehha, and the Cambrian genealogist says "he first reigned in Britain over the nation "of the East-Angles." His great grandfather, Hrothmund, probably accompanied Horsa and Hencgest, but may have remained abroad after the reverses which his kindred sustained. Thus Wewa and his people may have been settled on the coast of Norway in the earlier years of the sixth century, and thence have come to occupy East Anglia, where Wiveton near the coast of Norfolk, and Wivenhoe in Essex, bear his name, as Erpingham, not far from Wiveton, does that of the Arbings.

This identification of Wiwa is important, for, as he appears to have spoken a dialect akin to the Gothic, it confirms the probability, which will appear in the next chapter, that Woden, his ancestor, was of the Gothic race. According to the traditions of the North, the sons of Woden were of a different stock from the tribes they ruled. Most probably, therefore, they would use a different form of speech, just as at the present day the peasantry have their provincial dialects, distinct from the language of the highly-educated classes; and so we find, in Sweden and Denmark, inscriptions in the same characters, and in the same dialect as this at Tun, collateral with others which differ in the forms of the language, as well as of the characters. It is, moreover, highly important to have an inscription like this, of which the antiquity is determined, as it suggests the possible identity of persons whose names will be noticed in others; for these names are for the most part those of persons who are mentioned either in the genealogies, or in the history of the fifth and sixth centuries.

Indeed, the history of the Teutonic colonization of this island is remarkably illustrated by the identity of the types of weapons and ornaments discovered in Norway, Sweden, and Denmark, and in Anglo-Saxon barrows in this country.[13]

---

[13] It cannot be doubted, for instance, that such objects as the following, figured in Worsaae's "Afbildninger,"—the head of an axe, p. 96; end of a sword-sheath, p. 66; boss of shield, p. 96; keys, p. 93; tweezers and spoon, p. 51; brooches, pp. 85, 82, 75, 76, 77; glasses, pp. 63 and 65; belonged to the same races as similar objects engraved in the "Collec-" tanea Antiqua," "Inventorium Sepulchrale," &c. Their age must, therefore, be referred to that in which these races established themselves in Britain. In the same work, p. 81, we have a beautiful necklace chiefly formed of Roman coins, adapted to be so worn by the addition of a loop,

This identity, it seems, is best accounted for by the theory that these objects belong to the period, when the Teutonic tribes were alternately invading Britain, and, when repulsed, seeking refuge in Denmark and Norway, there recruiting their strength, and thence returning to renew the conflict.

Two horns of gold were found at Gallehus, near Tondern in Schleswig, one in 1639, the other in 1734. They were apparently the production of one hand, covered with barbarous figures, some of which had been moulded separately and attached to the gold plates of which the horns were composed, others engraved on the metal itself. These figures strikingly resembled certain rude sculptures which have been found at Caerleon, York, and Ilkley, and those on a stone tablet from Monk-Wearmouth, in the Cathedral library at Durham. The horn last discovered had this inscription round the rim (Pl. IV. fig. 3):—

EC HLEWAGAST IM HOLTINGAM	I Hlewagast among the Holdings
HORNA TAWIDO	prepared horns.

Hlewagast is a proper name like Arbogast, Liudegast, &c. *Im* is a contraction for *in thaim*, like the modern German *im* for *in dem*. *Haurn* in Gothic, being neuter, has its plural *haurna*, and I have translated *horna* in the plural; but I suspect that it is singular, and refers merely to the horn in question. *Tawido* is the first person singular præterite of *dawian*, but spelt like the Gothic *tauida* with the hard consonant.

These horns, of course, belong to the same race as those who

and in the "Atlas de l'Archéologie du Nord," coins of the Constantines, Crispus, Julius Nepos, and Mauritius Tiberius, similarly treated, are figured; evidences that, from the fourth century downwards, it was customary amongst these people to convert foreign coins into personal ornaments. Roman and Merovingian coins, applied to the same purpose, have been found in this country; amongst others, a remarkable instance may be mentioned, in which seven coins, Roman and Merovingian, and a Roman gem, all looped, were found together in the churchyard of S. Martin, Canterbury.

erected the monument at Tun, and equally with that monument must be referred to the sixth century at the latest. Holdingham in Lincolnshire bears the name of the Holdings, and may possibly have been the place where these horns were made.

A head circlet of gold, found at Starup in Schleswig, is inscribed LUTHRO (Pl. IV. fig. 4). This appears to be a proper name.

The most interesting relics of antiquity discovered in the Scandinavian kingdoms are the golden bracteates, of which nearly two hundred varieties are figured in the "Atlas de "l'Archéologie du Nord." Some of these are copies of Roman coins, others have types of presumed Teutonic origin, and on many of the latter we have legends in Runic characters.

The type which is most common presents a head or bust, and occasionally, (as on Nos. 77, 79, 221), a half figure of a man above a quadruped. On one of this class (No. 239), found in Sjælland, we have the following legend (Pl. IV. fig. 5) in small and very neatly executed runes:—

HAUIUHAH AITILA : FAUAUISA : GIBUAUNA

or, HAUIUHA HAITILA, &c.

Of the meaning of the two last words there can be no doubt. *Fauauisa* is certainly an adjective, in the genitive plural feminine, corresponding to the Gothic *faúaizô* (from *faús*, "few"), and *gibuauna* represents a Gothic *gibônô*: for, although the strong form *gibô* alone has occurred in the extant remains of the Gothic, other dialects, (O. H. G. *kepônô*, O. S. *gebônô*, A. S. *gifena*), agree in retaining the more ancient form, (closely resembling the Sanscrit *ânâm*, and the Zend *anaṅm*), for the genitive plural of feminine nouns of this class, and would warrant the expectation — which is fulfilled by the appearance of this *gibuauna*—of the same in the Gothic. *Fauauisa gibuauna*, then, is "of the few gifts;" and as a want of generosity was one of the greatest defects a Teuton could conceive in a prince's character,[14] it is not without a lively interest that we read, immediately preceding these words, the name of *Aitila*, the enemy of the Goths, who checked his victorious career on the plains of Chalons. The remaining word, *hauiuhah*, is extraordinary. It appears to be derived from a verb represented by the Gothic *hahan*, to "hang;" and I believe that it is the first appearance, in any Teutonic dialect, of the passive imperative, since it seems to bear the same relation to the active *hauah*, (which the analogy of the other words would lead us to expect in this dialect as the representative of the Gothic *hah*), that the Sanscrit and Zend passive forms, (and particularly that discovered by Sir H. C. Rawlinson in the Behistun inscription, *patipayuwâ*, "be prepared," or, "hold thyself prepared"), do to their corresponding actives. The syllable *iuha*, I conceive, answers to the Sanscrit *ya*, the characteristic of the passive, (of which Bopp has detected the trace in the Latin *fio* and *morior*, and in *veneo* as contrasted with *vendo*). In these words, then, we appear to have a malediction on the great king of the Huns, uttered by a Gothic cotemporary in the middle of the fifth century:—"Be hanged! Attila of the few gifts."

Another bracteate (No. 113), found in North Germany, has the name of WAIGA (Pl. IV. fig. 6), which was borne by the grandfather of Wærmund, ancestor of the Kings of Mercia; others (Nos. 118 and 234), found at Carlskrona, and in Skänen, have OTA (Pl. IV. fig. 7), the name of a son of Hencgest. These are of the same type as the first. On another (No. 76), found in the neighbourhood of Faxö, we have a bust, and a small human figure before it; in the legend the F is turned in a different direction from the rest, as if the artist in engraving the die had written this first, and then altered his intention; the name is clearly OSLAUF (Pl. IV.

[14] As instanced in these lines from Beowulf:—

nallas beágas geaf	he gave no rings
Denum æfter dóme.	to the Danes after judgment.

fig. 8), and it is that of an associate of Hencgest at the battle of Finnesham.

Four bracteates (Nos. 69 to 72) are evident imitations of the reverse of a Roman coin, representing an emperor, and a soldier who follows him, met by victory; and one of these (No. 69), found in Denmark, bears distinctly the name ELWIG (the last letter being *Gear*), and other letters which may be intended for CUNUNG (Pl. IV. fig. 9). This is the name of Offa's antagonist mentioned in the "Traveller's Tale;" and in connection with this piece we may mention a leaden brooch, exactly in the taste and style of these bracteates, on which we have the name and title of Witta, the King of the Swæfs, mentioned also in that document VIT CONU(ng) in Roman letters.[15]

On another (No. 111), found at Troedhætten in Sweden, we have a bust, apparently copied from a coin of Arcadius, and the legend TAWOLA THODU (Pl. IV. fig. 10). *Thodu* is probably intended for *théodu*, for although the usual form of the word is *thiudans*, *théodan*, or *theoden*, the Heljand gives us in one instance *thiodo*, a "king" or "ruler." *Tawola*, then, will be a proper name, corresponding to the Anglo-Saxon *Teol*. But the character which I have read L may possibly be S, and if so, it must be read TAWOS ATHODU, "two" (make) "a league," or confederacy; *tawos* corresponding to the Gothic (feminine) *twôs*.

Another type (Nos. 84 to 88) presents a man kneeling before a quadruped and a bird. One of these (No. 84), from Skänen, is inscribed LAWULAUR . M . GRMIU (Pl. IV. fig. 11), in which we observe, besides the usual *Æsc*, the Anglo-Saxon *A'c*. As there is certainly a vowel wanted between G and R, or between R and M, the simplest mode of correcting the blunder seems to be to transpose M and I, and read

---

[15] In the possession of Mr. Nightingale; figured in the "Proceedings of Numismatic Society," 1844, p. 28.

LAWUL AUR . M . GRIMU, which in Anglo-Saxon forms would be *Læwel ar macath grim*, "a false envoy maketh hatred." Another (No. 88), from Haderslev, has simply the initials of these words LA . G. Another (No. 83) has a man, hawk, hound, and stag, with the legend LAUAM . ARU (fig. 12), which seems intended to convey the same sense, *aru*, "war," taking the place of *grimu*. Another (No. 85), from Sjælland, has SALU SALU (fig. 13), "luck! luck!" and another (No. 219) has ALU (fig. 14), which may be for *salu* or *halu*, "health!"

We must take leave of these bracteates for a time, in order to notice a monument in the parish of Hagby, in the Swedish Upland, figured in Goransson's Bautil, No. 361. It presents a rude design of a warrior on horseback, very similar to the type of one of the bracteates (No. 75), and above it two lines of an inscription (Pl. IV. fig. 15). The characters are large and distinct; but in the two last, which are both consonants, and follow D, there must be an error, which I propose to correct, by supposing a line omitted in the first, which restored would change L into A, and, producing the diagonal line in the second across the vertical stroke, thus making it N. The tenth and eleventh characters are strange; but, guided by the analogy of other systems of writing, I assign to them conjecturally the values E and NG. Some uncertainty, of course, must attach to the reading, so far as it depends on these values, but I believe it to be,—

ANA HAHAPA	Eana raised
ENGINIM FRATHA RADAN	in grief for Frode this pillar.

Ana is a proper name, corresponding to the Anglo-Saxon *Eana;* and as the Gothic dialect has *frathjis*, (as well as *frôths*), for the Anglo-Saxon *frod*, so *Fratha* will be the Gothic equivalent, in the dative, of the Anglo-Saxon proper name *Frod*. *Hahapa* is the reduplicated præterite tense of a verb corresponding to the Anglo-Saxon *hefan*, (as *forgapi* and *forgip* in the hymn to *forgafe* and *forgif*), and apparently an instance of the ancient unabbreviated form, already alluded to; *enginim*, the dative plural of *engin*, equivalent to the Gothic *aggweins*, employed adverbially;[16] and *rada* represents the old Saxon *roda*, a "rod," which, (by the analogy of στήλη, and our provincial "stale"), may signify a "pillar," such as this monument.

On another Upland monument, in the parish of Tuna, we have a still ruder attempt to portray a human figure, and an inscription on two of its sides (Pl. IV. fig. 16), in which there are three strange characters; for, although one of them has the form of the Anglo-Saxon rune *E'h*, it cannot have the corresponding value here. The first on the second side must be S, of a form which occurs in some ancient alphabets; and the juxtaposition of the other characters suggests that the second must be T. The seventh on the first side appears to represent the rune *Ing*, similar to that on the Tun pillar, and the horn. Thus read, the inscription is very simple:—

D— with STUINGI	D— with a point
STAINA Markido	marked the stone—

the alliterating words only being written in full. *Stuingi* answers to the Anglo-Saxon *stincg*, any sharp-pointed instrument. The peculiar S occurs also on a silver fibula from Himlingó, in Sjælland, of a type which has been found in England, and also in the tombs at Kertch. We have, however, here only a name, DARISO (Pl. IV. fig. 17), as on the Starup diadem; and this, perhaps, is the ancient form of Theresa.

The above are in a dialect akin to the Gothic; the next is in one much nearer to the Anglo-Saxon. On a bracteate

16 The Heljand gives the adjective *engi*, answering to the Gothic *aggwus*, represented by the modern German *enge*, and related to our *anguish*.

(No. 218), from Bolbro in Fyen, we have a kneeling figure, and the legend, OWA MLUT EATHLUM (Pl. IV. fig. 18). Here L and U are transposed. The reading is, *Owa mult eathlum*, i. e. *Owa myld æthelum*, "Owa gracious to his nobles." Owa is a common Anglo-Saxon name.

A bracteate, found at Wadstena in Sweden, of the same type as those first noticed, presents us with three nearly complete divisions of the futhorc (Pl. IV. fig. 19), in groups of eight, and after them the name TUTHA twice. The order of the characters is correct as far as the twenty-second; the twenty-third, and last, may have been *Dæg*, but looks more like the lower part of *Oethel;* the *Ræd* is reversed; the *Peorth* of the form we have noticed in the Upland monument; the *Man* is of the usual Anglo-Saxon form; and this character distinguishes this futhorc from those to which the above-noticed inscriptions belong, in which M has the form of the Norse *Madr*, and Anglo-Saxon *Eolhx*. As, then, this M occurs on a bracteate (No. 102) found in the district of Carlskrona, we must assign to the other character a different value, and that I take to be CH or K, which it has in some Anglo-Saxon futhorcs, and in the Phrygian inscription.

In the legend on this piece (Pl. IV. fig. 20) we have two LL between two consonants. One of these must be A, from which it differs by a single stroke; and the twelfth character must be G (Gear), as on the sword. With this correction we obtain,—

KANWALHA CUR GEHELD,	Kanwalha chose thaneship,
AK CUNIMUDD IU WURTE RUNO	but Cunimund indeed wrought runes.

Kanwalha has its counterparts in Kannabaudes, (a Gothic chief in the days of the Emperor Aurelian), Kanegneub, (on one of the Hartlepool tombstones), and Kanebad, (in the letters of S. Boniface), Coenwealha and Cædwealha; *wurte* shows that this inscription belongs to a dialect akin to the

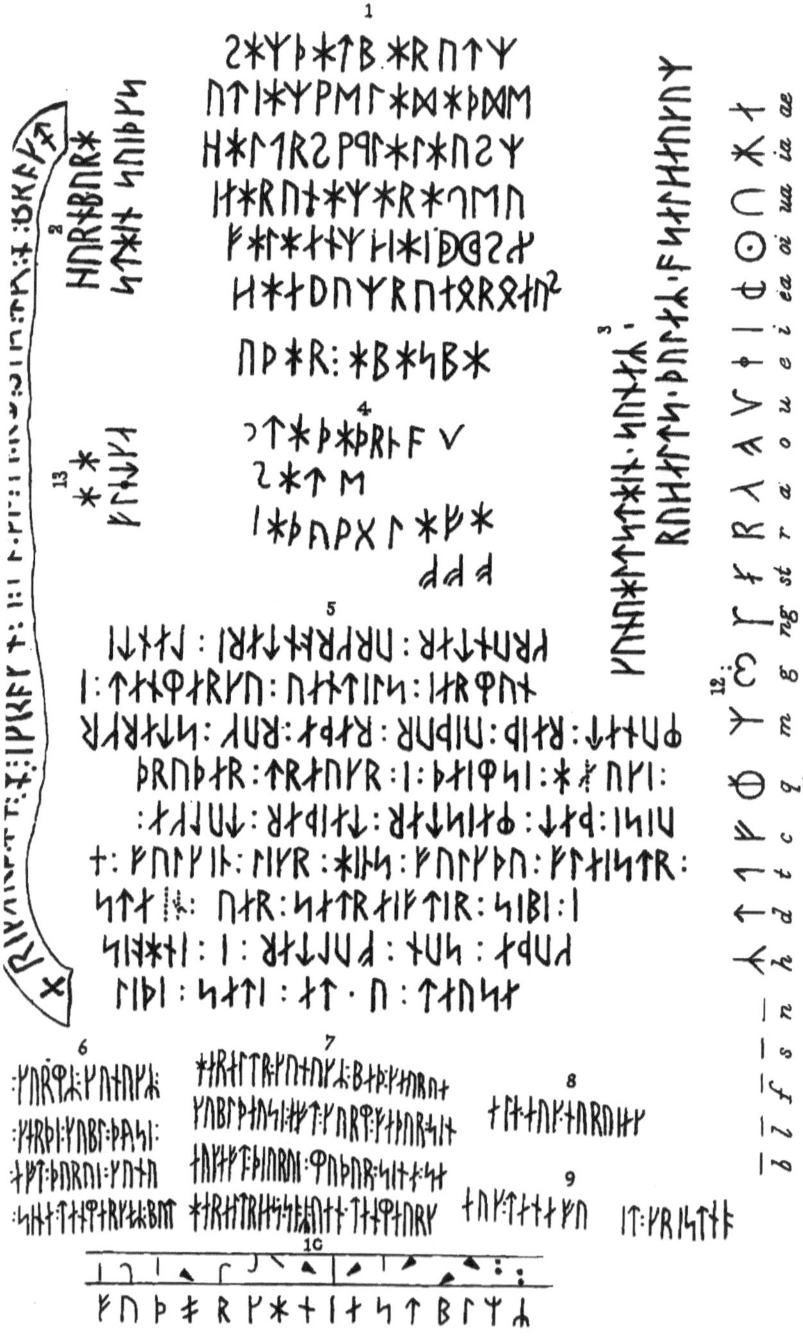
b l f s n h d t c q m g ng st r a o u e i ea oi ua ia ae

Anglo-Saxon; and *cur* presents a trace of the old præterite which gave place to *ceás*, *cure* being still retained in the second person singular, and *curon* in the plural.

An inscription (Pl. IV. fig. 21), on a monumental stone at Thelemark, appears to belong to the same futhorc. It is INGI SON HALAK, and is particularly interesting, for it contains names which occur, and in the same succession, in the genealogy of the ancestors of Ida.

Unfortunately, the futhorc on the bracteate is imperfect, and the occurrence of characters of unknown value on other pieces, opposes an obstacle to the satisfactory interpretation of their legends. One from Fyen (No. 101), and another from Sjælland (No. 226), appear to be the work of the same artist; for the former has, under the head of the animal, HOUA . M ., "Houa marked," and the latter HO . M; on the former, and perhaps on the latter also, we observe the form of the Anglo-Saxon *Stan*, and both inscriptions end with the same characters (Pl. IV. figs. 22, 23). Inscriptions on a stone axe (fig. 24), on a stone hammer (fig. 25), on a clasp (fig. 26), and on a gold ring, deserve notice, on account of the peculiarities of some of their characters; but I will not venture to interpret them.

On two monuments, in the district of Blekingen in Sweden, we observe a great change in the writing, and some forms of the Norse dialect mingled with others akin to the Gothic. The more remarkable of these, situate between the villages of Leerager, Birketorp, and Listerby, consists of three pillar-stones, standing in a triangle, on the largest of which, on the sides which face the other two, is the following inscription, which is completed by a single line on the other side (Pl. V. fig. 1):—

SAM THAT BAR UT-MUTI	As that bar without toll
AM WELA-MATHME HALTR	holds for (*i. e.* symbolizes) free gifts,

SAMALAUS MINA RUN AM ARAVE	so my rune for honours
UF ALANAM HAIMS-GAHANDUM	to the brave home-associates
RUNOR ONUS UTHAR	runes freely gives.
ABA SBA	May Aba speed!

Prof. Lauth, (Das Germanische Runen-Fudark), has for the first time explained this inscription, and there can be no doubt that he has happily seized the general sense. We have here two sentences exactly parallel. *Sam*, "as" (Gothic *sama*), in the first, answers to *samalaus*, "so also" (Gothic *samalauds*), in the second. *Am*, "for" (ἀμφὶ, Gothic *amb*, A. S. *emb, em*, Norse *om*), is followed in each by a noun in the genitive plural. *Wela-mathme* (Gothic *maithmé*) is "well" (*i.e.* "free") "gifts," and *arave*, "honours;" (the Gothic genitive plural of the noun corresponding to the A. S. *ár* would be *arivé*). *Haltr* answers to *uthar;* the former is certainly "holds," and here has the sense of "symbolizes," "signifies;" the latter presents a trace of the original present of the Anglo-Saxon *uthe*, which, though not in the præterite form, stands in our glossaries for the præterite of *unnan*, to "give." *Bar* is the word we retain to this day for the gates of our cities, and for toll-gates; and *ut-muti* (Gothic *mota*, O. H. G. *muta*) is "without toll;" *that bar ut-muti* referring to the open gate, formed by the two stones which stand in front of that which bears this inscription. *Onus*, which corresponds to *ut-muti*, is an adverb, meaning "without pay," akin to Gr. ἄνευ, O. S. *áno*, M. G. *ohne;* and this is exactly parallel to the derivative sense of the Latin verb *sinere*, from *sine*. *Alanam* is an adjective, related to Gothic *aljan*, O. S. *ellan*, A. S. *ellen*, "strength," "vigour;" *gahandum*, a word for "companions," additional to those noticed above. *Run* has obviously a different sense from *runor;* the latter means, as usual, letters; the former, I believe, expresses the instrument with which the letters were formed. *Aba* I take to be a proper name—probably that of the writer's feudal lord—answering to the Anglo-Saxon *Eaba;* and *sba* the subjunctive, or imperative, of a verb equivalent to *spówan*, to "prosper."[17]

The dialect of this inscription seems to be intermediate between the Gothic and the Norse. The writer has borrowed from other futhorcs besides his own, giving us no less than four varieties of *Man*, two of *Tir*, two of *Sigel*, and two of *Æsc*. We have also the Anglo-Saxon *Wen*, the German *Gibu*, and a peculiar V, of which we have another instance in an inscription at Berrig in Norway. The most remarkable characteristic of this inscription is the frequent recurrence of a character, which in the usual Anglo-Saxon futhorc is named *Ior*, in the Norse *Hagal*, and has occasionally the value of G: here it is A, and with this value it occurs in an inscription at Kallerup in Sjælland (Pl. V. fig. 2):—

HURNBURA STAIN SUITHGS The stone of Hornburu the prudent:

and in another at Snoldelev (Pl. V. fig. 3):—

CUNUALT STAIN SUNAR RUHALTS THULAR A SALHAUGUM

"The stone of Cunualt son of Ruhalt the orator in Salhaug:"

where we have also the Norse form, and another, expressing perhaps different powers.

The other Bleking monument has an inscription on each of its four sides in similar characters (Pl. V. fig. 4). Prof. Lauth has furnished an explanation of these also, based on

---

17 The points on which I have ventured to differ from Prof. Lauth are these. *Smalaus* he reads *swalaus*, regarding the second character as *Wen* doubled; it is certainly *Man*, and *smalaus* agrees very well with the Gothic *samalauds*. *Alanam* he suggests as equivalent to the Gothic *allaim*, "all," but with much hesitation. The last words he divides *Abas ba*, taking the latter as the præterite of a strong verb, meaning "condidit," or that of a weak verb abbreviated.

sound principles; but I think he has slightly misconceived their object. They are:—

STATH A THaRNAU SATE IATHU Wang GaLAFA Frithu Frithu Frithu

"The place of (those who are) set in the shades. Survivors gave the field. Peace! Peace! Peace!"

Stath (Gothic *staths*, A. S. *stede*) is a "place." *Tharnau*,[18] a noun in the dative singular, governed by *a*, is akin to the A. S. verb *dyrnan*, to "hide," the adjective *dearn*, "dark," and the O. H. D. verb *kitarnan*; like *hel*, therefore, and *helan*, it is applied to the state of souls departed. *Iathu* Prof. Lauth supposes the reduplicate præterite of *utha*, which occurs in the inscription above, (analogous to *iok* from *auka*, and *ios* from *ausa*), in the third person plural; *galafa* he interprets "companions," "dwellers in the same bower" (Germ. *laub*, Fris. *láf*); I prefer "survivors," "relict," A. S. (*læfan*, to "leave.") Possibly F F F may be the initials of these companions or survivors; but *frithu*, twice repeated, seems a suitable termination to such an inscription as this, which commemorates, as it seems, the appropriation of a plot of land for a cemetery. The runes, though they simply record the fact, would be supposed to have the effect of consecrating the spot, and securing it from profanation.

The existence of these inscriptions in Scandinavia is an important fact, for they are certainly of greater antiquity than the earliest copy we possess of the Norse futhorc of sixteen runes.

This, with the title *Abecidarium Nord*, occurs in the S. Gall. MS. No. 878, of the ninth century. It gives the runes, named as follow: *Feu*, *Ur*, *Thur*, *Os*, *Rat*, *Chaon*, *Hagal*,

---

[18] Prof. Lauth supposes the last letter of *tharnau* an *m* imperfectly copied. It may be so; but he was not aware of the fact that it occurs in an early Scandinavian inscription with the value *u*, and that I believe it has here. *Tharnam* would be the dative plural.

Naut, Is, Ar, Sol, Tir, Brita, Man, Lago, Yr, in a series of verses in an Old High German dialect, with some mixture of Anglo-Saxon forms. Above *Feu, Hagal, Naut, Ar,* and *Yr,* are equivalent runes, more resembling the Anglo-Saxon; and beneath *Feu,* the word WREAD, (A. S. *wrǽd,* a “flock), is written, apparently as a synonym or explanation of it.

I know of but one inscription in Norse runes which can claim equal antiquity with this copy of the futhorc, and that is on a monument at Karlevi in Öland (Pl. V. fig. 5):—

✠ FULCIN LICR HINS FULC-THU	Buried lies, whom followed,
FLAISTR UISI THAT MAISTAR	most know that, as master,
TAITHAR TULCA-THRUTHAR	the fierce spirits of death,
TRAUCR I THAIMSI HAUCI	the hero in this howe.
MUNAT RAITH-UITHUR RA-THA	May not a prince rule,
RUC-STARCR I TANMARCU	more mighty in Denmark,
UANTILS IARMUN-CRUNTAR	of the Wendels' territory
URCRONTARI LANTI	in the spacious land.
STAIN UAR SATR AIFTIR SIBI I CUTHA	The stone was set after Sibi the good,
SUN FULTAR I INHOIS LITHI	the son of Fulda in Inho's army,
SATI AT U TAUSI	placed (buried) in this isle.

In this inscription, which is partly in verse and partly in prose, we have all the characters of the futhorc given above, except *Yr;* and, what is very remarkable, the ordinary form of R occurs at the end of words throughout, and the words are written in full, without the elision of certain letters, which is so usual in later inscriptions, and of which the following, the latest Pagan, and the earliest Christian inscriptions, supply examples. These are, the epitaph which Gorm the Old, who died in A.D. 935, wrote, during her lifetime, for Thyre his queen, who survived him four years (Pl. V. fig. 6), and that which Harald caused to be written for Gorm and Thyre (Pl. V. figs. 7, 8, 9):—

CURMR CUNUDCR CARTHI CUMBL THAUSI	King Gorm made this memorial
AFT THURUI CUNU SINA	after Thyre his queen,
TANMARCAR BUT	Denmark's blessing.

HARALTR CUNUDCR BATH CAURUA	King Harald bade carve
CUMBL THAUSI AFT CURM FATHUR SIN	this memorial, after Gorm his father,
AUC AFT THIURUI MUTHUR SINA	and after Thyre his mother;
SA HARALTR IAS SAR UAN TANMAURC ALA AUC	that Harald who conquered Denmark all and
NURUIAC	Norway
AUC TANA(FULC A)T CRISTNO	and the Danish folk to christen.

Now, although I think it probable that these runes are of great antiquity, notwithstanding the absence of any evidence of their use earlier than the ninth century, I cannot admit their claim to be the parents of the Anglo-Saxon and German runes, nor can I regard the Norse futhorc of sixteen characters as anything but an abridgment of an earlier system. The futhorc which those tribes of the Goths used, whose language is represented by the Ulfilan fragments, must indeed have resembled this; but on the other hand, as we have seen, we have inscriptions nearly reaching to the antiquity of those fragments, in a language approaching more nearly to the Gothic than to any other Teutonic dialect, the characters of which are almost identical with the Anglo-Saxon; and we shall be able to trace many symbols of the Anglo-Saxon futhorc to the very fountain-head of all phonetic writing. If either system were derived from the other, it would be more natural to regard the single-stroke Norse runes as a simplification of the double-stroke Anglo-Saxon, than the latter as a development of the former; and this would agree not only with the primitive derivation of phonetic characters from symbolic signs, but with the later phases of the Norse system, in which even these simple characters were still farther simplified, and in one district, (that of Helsing), reduced, by the omission of the vertical strokes, to a series of mere points and lines (see Pl. V. fig. 10).

Again, this system of sixteen characters is evidently imperfect. It wants the vowel *e*, the hard consonant *p*, and the soft *d* and *g*, besides others; and the inconvenience and confusion, which must have resulted from the want of these, are only too evident in the inscriptions given above, and much more so in others. Eventually it was found necessary to remedy this defect by the invention of pointed runes; but earlier than this we have occasional traces of the existence of these characters, though discarded from common use. We find E, for instance, under the form of a simple cross; P occurs in Snorre's Edda, and on a gold ring (Pl. IV. fig. 27), under a form nearly resembling that on the gold bracteate and the Upland monument; we have an additional character for C on a monument at Flekkevik (Pl. V. fig. 13), and V we have already noticed. The inscription on the Bridekirk font, although its language is English of the twelfth century, is so evidently in Norse runes, that we cannot suppose the characters it contains, over and above those in the usual Norse sixteen-rune futhorc, anything but those which are wanting to its completeness, and which it did originally comprise. It is (Pl. V. fig. 14):—

RICARD HE ME IWROCTE	Richard he me wrought,
& TO DIS MERTH GERNAR	and to this beauty carefully
ME BROCTE	me brought:

and here we have E, W, TH (hard), G (*Gear*), whilst the ordinary form of *Thorn* or *Thurs* has the power of D, as in some futhorcs. The Runic beithluisnion, which Mr. Curry discovered in a fragment of a MS. in Trinity College, Dublin, had, of course, twenty-five characters, for it is arranged, (by the Irish copyist no doubt), in the Ogham order, and the first five are wanting (see Pl. V. fig. 12). It is genuine, I am convinced; for, although we know of no system which corresponds with it, rune for rune, many of its peculiar characters are found in other systems. H, for instance, we have noticed on the rings; D has the usual form of *Tir*, and T, the later Scandinavian form of the same character; M is Gothic and Norse; G resembles that in the Bridekirk inscription; R, A, O, E, and I are Norse; U occurs on one of the Bleking monuments; OI (=WI or W) is the Gothic HW; IA is the character to which in other systems the value IO, H, G, or A is given. The verses which accompany this curious document tell us:—

"Hither was brought in the swordsheath of Lochlann's King
"The Ogham from across the sea. It was his own hand that cut it."

The futhorc on the knife above noticed presents a striking analogy to this statement, and we need not hesitate in receiving these runes as Scandinavian, whether the values are correctly assigned to them, (and particularly to the last five), or not. But this is certainly not the system which the Scandinavian invaders of Ireland in the ninth century used; and for the time it was written we seem to be referred to the fifth century, when Fionn MacCumhaill, and his Lochlannaigh, were playing their part on the stage of Irish history.

These facts are proofs that systems of phonetic writing once were in use, allied to the Scandinavian, but more complete; and, in addition to these, the irregularity of the divisions of the Norse futhorc, six, five, and five, as contrasted with the regularity of the Anglo-Saxon, recurrences of the sacred number eight, would of itself suggest the suspicion that this irregularity is a departure from the primitive system, even were it not confirmed, as it is, by the occurrence on one monument, (Goransson, 646), of the sixth character of the third division in an inscription in *Iis-Runa,* and of the sixth of the fourth on another (816) in *Hahal-Runa.*

The inscriptions which remain to us ascend no higher than the fourth century of our æra; but whilst the differences we have observed in the systems of writing, which were in use in England, Germany, and Scandinavia, are sufficiently accounted for by the diversity of tribes which composed the Teutonic people, their resemblances distinctly prove that they had a common origin in a much earlier period, when Angles, Saxons, Jutes, and Frisians, with the other tribes who peopled Germany, formed one nation.

The internal evidence, therefore, of the futhorc clearly vindicates for it an indigenous and remotely ancient origin. Let us now turn to the external.

Hrabanus Maurus has acquainted us with the fact, that the Pagan Marcomanni, in the ninth century, used runes nearly identical with the Anglo-Saxon, not only for incantations and divinations, but also for the preservation of the memory of their songs.

About the beginning of the seventh century, when the greatest part of Germany was still Pagan, Venantius Fortunatus wrote to his friend Flavus, complaining of his neglect, and suggesting a variety of expedients to take away all excuse for not writing; in default of paper, beech bark or ashen tablets might be employed, and if it were distasteful to write in the Roman character, he might make choice of Hebrew, Persian, or Greek, or of the Barbaric rune.[19] Of the exact

---

19 An tibi charta parum peregrinâ merce rotatur?
  Non amor extorquet quod neque tempus habet?
Scribere quo possis discingat fascia fagum,
  Cortice dicta legi fit mihi dulce tui.
An tua Romuleum fastidit lingua susurrum?
  Quæso vel Hebraicis reddito verba notis.

sense of his words there can be no doubt. *Pingere* was applied to writing of every kind, even to inscriptions on stone. The context, which speaks of four different kinds of writing, Roman, Greek, Hebrew, and Persian, shows clearly that the Barbaric rune was a system equally recognized; and *Barbarus* in Venantius' writings always means German, for he constantly uses it in speaking of Germany, and in concord with words such as *leudus* a "song," *harpa* a "harp," which, like *rhuna*, are certainly Teutonic. The rune, therefore, as a system of writing, was in use at the close of the sixth century, amongst the tribes who still remained Pagans.

Other branches of the Teutonic stock, who had embraced Christianity, the Franks and the Goths, had received in its stead the letters as well as the faith of their teachers; and just as the Anglo-Saxons later were obliged to introduce into the abecedarium, the *Thorn* and *Wen* of their discarded futhorc, so the inadequacy of the Greek and Roman systems to express the vocal sounds of the Teutonic language compelled both Franks and Goths to introduce into them other characters.

With regard to the former, Gregory of Tours says of Chilperic, King of the Franks, "He added also letters to our "letters, that is ω as the Greeks have it, *æ*, *the*, *uui*, of which "we have underwritten the forms ω, Ψ, Z, Δ, and sent letters "to all the cities of his kingdom, that boys should be thus "taught, and that books written in old times should be "scoured with pumice-stone, and re-written." The new characters are given with much variety in different MSS., so that it is impossible now to determine what their precise forms were.

Doctus Achæmeniis quævis præscribito signis;
Aut magis Argolico pange canora sopho.
Barbara fraxineis pingatur rhuna tabellis,
Quodque papyrus agit virgula plana valet. vi. 18.

The "Achæmenia signa" can only be the cuneiform writing which Mr. Loftus says was practised as late as 200 B.C. It would appear from these words that it was a recognized, though obsolete, system in the seventh century.

By *our letters* Gregory certainly means those of the abecedarium, and as certainly Chilperic's intention was to add to it certain letters, expressing Germanic sounds which it did not contain. Of these sounds the futhorc does supply representatives, and it is most probable that the letters, which Chilperic introduced, resembled their correspondents in the old system of the Franks, as the runes which expressed the sounds *w, th, dh,* were added to the abecedarium in this country, when the want of them began to be felt; the earliest monuments of our language, written in Roman letters, (the hymn of Cædmon, and Venerable Bæda's verses), being without them.

More important, however, is the fact which this passage reveals, that there existed at the time books written in old times, for these books could not have been in Latin; if they had, there would have been no occasion to erase the writing in them, and re-write them, with the addition of characters which had no value in the Latin language. They were in the language of the Franks, and written in Teutonic characters; they were to be re-written in the same language, but in Roman characters; and these additional signs were employed to express the vocal sounds, which had no corresponding symbols in the abecedarium. Had books of the period been preserved, no doubt we should have had something like what we observe in Anglo-Saxon and Gothic writing, some Teutonic characters occurring amongst the Latin or Greek; but Chilperic's work was an unavailing attempt, to arrest in his dominions the progress of the Latin literature—a surrender of the old system of writing for the sake of preserving the language. The first part of his injunctions, which related to the erasure of the old writing, may have been fulfilled; but probably there was not sufficient interest felt, to secure the transcription of the old books, generally, into Latin characters; and Latin literature advanced, and in the end prevailed, to the utter extinction of the primitive Frank language. So the old books of the Franks have disappeared. Some remains of them may yet be discovered in the form of palimpsests; but their only memorial as yet is in this passage of Gregory of Tours; and the only relic of the futhorc, in Frank literature, is the *Wen* in the fragment of the "Lay of Hildibrand." The time referred to was about A.D. 580.

The Longobards established themselves in Italy in A.D. 568, and we are informed that they used for writing at the time very thin and smooth tablets of wood; some of which, inscribed with their peculiar characters, Pancirolo, (in the sixteenth century), testifies that he had seen.

The Goths received Christianity in the fourth century, and Ulfilas, or Wulfila, is said to have invented letters for one division of their nation, the Little Goths, who occupied Mæsia in the time of Jordanis. Yet the letters referred to in this story, (see Pl. VI.), cannot be said to have been invented. Nearly one half of their number, B, G, E, I, K, M, N, P, T, CH, and Z, are adopted from the Greek alphabet; S in some MSS. has the Greek, in others the Latin form; but in one MS., discovered by Cardinal Mai in the Ambrosian Library (G. 82), it is undoubtedly Runic; A more nearly resembles its Scandinavian than its Greek equivalent; F, U, O, R, L, W, and Q, are Runic. Four characters remain; the second, G or J, corresponding to the Runic *Gear*, appears to resemble the form of that character on the gold bracteate; H has the form of the Roman minuscule, the antiquity of which, however, cannot be traced higher than this alphabet; TH, in the Ambrosian palimpsest (G. 82), has the form of the Greek *Phi*, and this is one of the forms of T in the Celtiberian alphabet, the resemblance of which to the Runic system will be noticed presently; HW is also found in the Celtiberian alphabet, and, (as already noticed), in Mr. Curry's Runic beithluisnion.

The Greek alphabet, then, was the basis of Ulfilas' system; yet he retained some Runic characters for which he could easily have found Greek or Latin equivalents, and others expressing vocal sounds of the Gothic language which the alphabet did not supply. There are, in fact, only eight letters in the system which are not Runic, although some of the rest are Greek also; and this is a clear proof of the existence of a futhorc, amongst the Goths, different from that to which the inscription on the gold ring belongs, and more nearly allied to Mr. Curry's, and to the Norse; whilst it is equally clear that the alphabet was the basis of Ulfilas' modification of this ancient system, and that Greek writing was the model on which he formed his text of the Holy Scripture.

Before the fourth century, our notices of the Teutonic tribes are only such as were occasioned by their conflicts with the forces of the Roman Empire, and we should have known very little about them had not their polity and social virtues interested Tacitus, and prompted him to write his valuable treatise "De Moribus Germanorum." In this we have indications of the practice of the art of writing amongst them.

It is highly probable that the inscriptions of which he speaks,[20] on monuments on the borders of Germany and Rhætia, were in runes, misunderstood by the persons from whom his information, (evidently not very precise), was derived; and it has been conjectured that they also mistook the name, or a representation of Woden for that of Odysseys or Ulixes.

Where he speaks of the Germans' veneration of Aurinia,[21] it is certain that it is not a proper name, but *alruna*, a "witch" or "prophetess," Jordanis' *alioruna*.[22] The word still remains in German, *alraun* a "mandrake," (originally a charm made therefrom); in old German it was *helliruna*, and in Anglo-Saxon *helrún*, both signifying "divination," from *hel*, "hidden"

---

20 "Quidam opinantur aram Ulixi consecratam, monumentaque et "tumulos quosdam, Græcis literis insculptos, in confinio Germaniæ "Rhætiæque adhuc extare." *Germ.* 3.

21 "Sed et olim Auriniam, et complures alias venerati sunt, non adu-"latione, nec tanquam facerent deas." *Germ.* 8.

22 "Quasdam mulieres magas, quas patrio sermone Aliorumnas cog-"nominant." *De Rebus Geticis*, VIII.

and *rún*, a "letter." It is evident that *rún* was in use in Tacitus' days, since they had its derivative, *alruna;* and it cannot be doubted that it is of runes, used in divination, that he speaks in the following passage:—"They divide into slips a "rod cut from a fruit-bearing tree, and these, distinguished "by certain marks, they scatter at random on a white gar- "ment; then, the priest of the city, if the augury be in public, "the father of the family, if in private, praying to the gods, "and looking up to heaven, thrice takes them up one by one, "and interprets them according to the mark previously im- "pressed upon them."[23]

Thus we can trace the use of runes distinctly to the first century of our æra; and a comparison of the futhorc with other primitive systems of writing will enable us to refer its origin to a period many centuries earlier still.

Of all these, the Iberian, as we find it on the autonomous coins of Spain, presents the greatest analogy to it, in the forms and values of its characters. Strabo testifies that the Iberians had records and poems in writing, and that by this means they had preserved their metrical laws, for which, (not, of course, for their copies of them), they claimed an antiquity of six thousand years. All these, as well as the early writings of most nations, have disappeared, on account of the perishable nature of the vehicle to which they were committed; but their coins remain to show that they had alphabetic writing some centuries before the Christian æra.

It appears to have been of a very mixed kind. Some of

---

[23] "Virgam frugiferæ arbori decisam in surculos amputant, eosque, "notis quibusdam discretos, super vestem candidam temere ac fortuito "spargunt; mox, si publice consulatur sacerdos civitatis, sin privatim, "paterfamilias, precatus deos, cœlumque suspiciens, ter singulos tollit, "sublatos secundum impressam ante notam interpretatur." *Germ.* 10.

The tree of which he speaks is probably the mountain-ash, rown, or witch, the magical uses of which are not obsolete even in this nineteenth century. In Yorkshire, for instance, small pieces of it are worn as charms against witchcraft, and in Warwickshire a necklace partly composed of it has been mentioned to me as a charm for the cure of whooping-cough.

Alphabets.

Pl: VI.

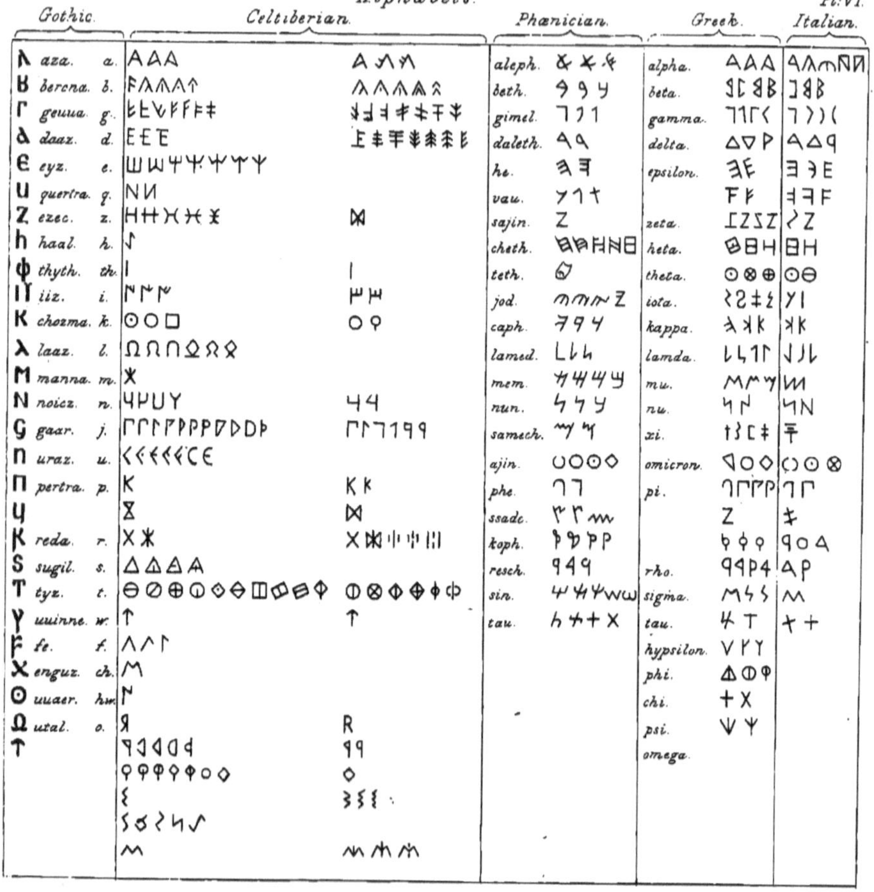

the characters correspond with those of the Phœnician and Greek alphabets, whilst the rest not only resemble those of the futhorc, but are admitted to have had nearly, if not quite, the same values.

In the accompanying table I have attempted a classification of the different forms which occur on the coins of Tarraconensis and Bætica, generally following M. de Saulcy, who has done more than any one else to illustrate this series. Still, it must be admitted that our acquaintance with their precise values is at present imperfect; future discoveries may yet show that some of those which are now regarded as homophonous, represented distinct sounds (Pl. VI).

1. A. We have here the Greek, Lycian, and Samaritan forms.

2. A. The first is the rune *Æsc* or *Asc*. The last occurs in the Lycian inscriptions, most frequently with the power of A, sometimes with that of E.

3, 4, 5. These are considered to represent the Phœnician *He*, and the Greek *Epsilon*. Some of the last may have the power of A, and amongst them we observe the form of the rune *Ear*.

6, 7, 8. These are equivalent to the Phœnician *Cheth*, Greek *Heta*, and perhaps represent not only the vocal sound, as in the latter, but also the aspirate, as in the former. The sixth may be compared with the form of the rune *Hægel;* the last of the seventh class has the form of another rune, which sometimes has the power of H, sometimes that of E; and the eighth is the rune *Eh*.

9. This is Greek, Latin, Lycian, and Runic.

10. These appear to be related to the Phœnician and Hebrew *Iod*.

12. These connect the Greek *Omega* with the rune *Oethel* or *Othil*.

15 and 27. B, P, R. B, R, and D are easily confounded, as in the Phœnician and early Greek alphabets, and R and D are sometimes exchanged one for the other. M. de Saulcy re-

marks that in the modern Basque language R has a sound very similar to that of D. This may account for the occurrence of the form of the rune *Thorn, Thur*, or *Dour*, amongst these, and of one which seems to belong to the twenty-first class, TH, amongst the representatives of R in the twenty-eighth.

16. The first of these occurs in the Lycian alphabet, in the Tun inscription, on the horn, the bracteates, and the Gilton sword-pommel. The other varieties in this and the Lycian alphabet may represent modifications of sound.

21. Amongst these characters, which correspond to *Teth* or *Theta*, are two which are identical with the Gothic.

The other classes of this series contain the runes *Tir, Lago, Rad*, and *Sigel*, and the Lycian S.

This alphabet is certainly one of very great antiquity; and whilst the Phœnician and Greek colonizations of Spain may account for the many characters it contains, either identical with, or closely resembling, letters of the Phœnician and Greek alphabets, the rest must assuredly be regarded as belonging to the original alphabet which the Iberians brought with them from Asia; and thus we can account for the resemblances between it and the Lycian. But the identity of many of these Iberian characters with the equivalent runes, decisively establishes for them a community of origin, and that origin must be referred to an epoch of very remote antiquity, anterior to the migration of the Iberians from Asia. This conclusion will be confirmed by an examination of the systems of writing, which were in use in the earliest times in Greece and Italy, and a comparison between them and the early Phœnician; and we shall be able at the same time to determine more nearly the true age of the futhorc.

In the Greek and Roman alphabets we have two characters, B and I, and in the latter a third, R, identical with the corresponding runes; besides these, Σ in some early inscriptions was the same as *Sigel;* the Iberian inscriptions indicate the identity of the primitive form of Ω with that of *Oethel;* the *Digamma* and the Roman F had occasionally the form of *Feóh;* and the rune *Eolhx,* which had sometimes the power of K, or the Greek X, occurs with this value in a Phrygian inscription. Nor must we overlook the facts that the form of the Greek X, which in the futhorc generally represents the cognate sound of G, occurs in one instance with the power of K; and that in Greek orthography, the sound *Ing* is expressed by ΓΓ, as if the Greeks had once a character, which, like the Runic *Ing* in several different systems, resembled the duplication of C or G. In fact the origin of this sound for ΓΓ is unintelligible, until we turn to the Runic inscriptions, and see in the Anglo-Saxon *Ing,* as it were, a double *Gifu,* and in the Gothic a double *Cæn.*

The order of the Greek alphabet, and the names of the characters which compose it, fully bear out the tradition that Cadmus brought it from Phœnicia. The first nineteen names are exactly in the order of the Phœnician alphabet. *Vau, Ssade,* and *Koph,* indeed, are wanting, but these also once belonged to it; and as it is not likely that Cadmus would have introduced an incomplete system, nor that, (on the supposition that the Phœnician alphabet had only sixteen characters in his day), *Zeta, Heta,* and *Theta* should have been inserted at a later period in the exact places of *Zain, Cheth* and *Teth,* it seems to follow, that his alphabet was really the same as the Phœnician and Hebrew of twenty-two sounds; that *Vau, Ssade,* and *Koph* fell into disuse; and that *Hypsilon, Phi, Chi,* and *Omega* were added from some other source.

Further, this alphabet, in the primitive forms of its characters, presents indisputable tokens of its Cadmæan origin. *Alpha, Beta, Gamma, Delta, Epsilon, Zeta, Heta, Theta, Lamda, Nu, Omicron, Pi, Koph, Rho,* and one form of *Tau,* will be observed, on comparison with their equivalents in the Phœnician, Hebrew, and Samaritan alphabets, to be essentially the same; but other forms of *Beta, Vau, Iota, Kappa,* the more usual form of *Lamda, Mu, Sigma,* and *Tau,* indicate the elements of a distinct, and that probably the original alphabet. Such at least seems the most satisfactory way of accounting for their presence, in the company of a greater number of Phœnician characters. Whence, then, shall we suppose these to have come? Were these eight letters, which are certainly not Phœnician, but all more or less resemble the Runic, invented in Greece, or introduced from some other country? Will the theory of derivation from the Greeks, or that of a common origin, best account for the appearance of some of them, in the equally Phœnician primitive alphabets of Italy? The solution of these questions is very easy.

The Greeks had their language before they received an alphabet from Phœnicia, and what their primitive language was cannot now be doubted. Plato represents Socrates asserting, as an unquestionable fact, that words which the Greeks had in common with the Barbarians were of Barbarian origin; such, for example, as πῦρ, ὕδωρ, ἀὴρ. Modern research has established the fact, that the Greek and Latin languages are closely allied to the Teutonic; that these simple words which Socrates instanced, and an immense number of others, are common to the three languages; that the Teutonic contains roots which the Greeks had, but not the Latins, others which the Latins had, but not the Greeks, in the classical days of their literature, and others which may be traced in the Greek and Latin languages, only under the form of derivatives. If, then, their languages point so distinctly to a community of origin with the Teutonic race, it seems that we may also refer those characters in their alphabets, which are rather Runic than Phœnician, to a more ancient alphabet substantially identical with the futhorc.[24]

---

[24] Mr. Rawlinson, on account of the similarity of the Greek, Lycian, Phrygian, Etruscan, and Umbrian alphabets, admits the possibility of one anterior to the Phœnician, as their common original. Herodotus, I. 264.

Perhaps we have a record of such a system, in the story which Plutarch tells, of a brazen tablet found in the tomb of Alcmena near Thebes. It was inscribed with many wonderful and very ancient letters, which could not be read, though perfectly distinct. Their forms were peculiar and barbaric; yet, as it was thought that they bore some resemblance to Ægyptian characters, copies were sent to Ægypt to be deciphered by the priests. One most learned priest, named Cnouphis, after spending three days in collecting from ancient books the forms of various letters, declared that they belonged to the system, which Hercules the son of Amphitryon had learned in the days of King Proteus, and that they signified that a festival must be celebrated in honour of the Muses. It is evident that Cnouphis was at fault; the three days that he spent in trying to decipher the inscription, and the unlikely interpretation which he gave of it, are proofs of his failure; and we may conclude that it was an inscription in alphabetic characters, differing from those which were in use at the time of its discovery. Whatever their character may have been, we seem to be referred, for the common origin of the Greek, Latin, and Teutonic systems of writing, beyond that remote epoch, when the Japhetic division of the human family migrated eastward and westward from their Asiatic home. Even in that pre-historic age the art must have been known and practised, for nearly all the words, which Greeks and Latins used in reference to it, are found in the Teutonic language; and this alone possesses many of the roots whence they are derived, besides other words connected with the art, peculiar to itself. Our forefathers did not learn to write from Greeks or Latins; the art of writing was a part of the tradition, which descended to them from the time when the human race was still one family.

The bark and leaves of trees, and smooth tablets of close-grained wood, were the most ancient vehicles of writing. Our forefathers seem to have preferred the bark of the beech-tree, and hence in their language one word, *bóc,* denotes equally the tree, and the volume or roll which was formed from its bark; as in modern German *buche* is the tree, and *buch* a "book." The Latins had *liber* for "bark," and a "book;" and probably we had a word corresponding to this; for *lib* means "witchcraft," and we shall see that most of the words connected with writing have come to have a similar application. *Beacon* was one of these. Its root is certainly *béce,* or *bóc,* whence *bécen,* or *bócen,* signified originally a writing on a roll "made of beech" bark. In the sense of a writing or inscription, it is used in the Northumbrian Runic epitaphs; thence it came to signify a "sign," or "token," and, because applied to soothsaying, an "omen," (in which sense *bocan* in the Heljand, and *boken* in the Codex Bernensis, are used); and its derivative verb, *beacnian,* with us meant simply to "beckon," "indicate," &c., whilst among the Old Saxons *bócnian* was to "portend."

Leaves suitable for writing would not be found by our forefathers in Germany, yet they had *hleaf-gewrit* for a "document," a memorial, perhaps, of their eastern home; and we still speak of the leaves of a tree and of a book, as the Germans use the word *blätter,* and the Latins *folia.*

Words derived from the use of tablets of wood for writing are very common, although our *tæfel,* identical with the Latin *tabella,* was exclusively used, (as far as we know), to denote the board on which games were played. *Stæfas,* originally the smooth staves (Tacitus' *surculi*) on which runes were engraven, was generally used to signify the characters themselves, either alone, or compounded with *rún,* or *bóc,* (*rún-stafas, bóc-stafas*); thence it was applied to a "tale," or an "epistle." *Beám* occurs with reference to the same subject in one of the fragments of Anglo-Saxon poetry in the Exeter book. A messenger, who has brought a letter to a lady from her lover, says,—

Hwæt. Thec thonne biddan het,	Yes! Then bade me beseech thee,
se thisne beám agróf.	(he) who inscribed this beam.

Thomas of Ercildoune, in the thirteenth century, represents Tristrem communicating with Ysoude, by writing on *spón*, *i. e.* "chips:"—

bi water he sent adoun
light linden spon,
he wrote em al with roun.

Spell had, and still has, the same meaning as *spón;* it was applied also to whatever was written upon it, and came to signify a "story," "message," "intelligence;" the act of reading from it was "spelling," or "instruction;" but it now most commonly conveys the idea of a "charm," or "witchcraft," because it was also used for magical purposes.

Tácen, with its correspondents in the different dialects of our language, is a "letter," "mark," "inscription," "standard," "wonder," "omen;" its verb *tácnian* is to "draw," "demonstrate," "predict;" its root *tác,* which no longer appears in our glossaries, is found in the Greek δοκὸς and Latin *docus,* a "beam," from the writing on which these various senses are derived; and, because such beams were made the medium of instruction, we have from the same root the Latin *docere,* and our *tæcan,* to "teach."

The instruments used in writing were of iron, of different forms. One was called *græf,* whence the verb *græfan,* (which we have seen applied to writing in the passage above quoted), and the Greek γράφειν. But whilst the Greek verb designated equally the latest and the earliest forms of the art, ours was restricted to the earliest, to inscriptions on wood, stone, or metal; and *groove,* from its præterite *gróf,* aptly expresses the character of primitive writing.

Otfrid has *scríban,* to "write," the Heljand *scrífan,* the Old Norse *scrífa,* ancient forms of the modern German *schreiben.*

These words are not derived from the Latin *scribere;* we must claim them for our own, for we have the root, a "scribe," or "scrive," in our language. It denotes a tool used by carpenters, coopers, and woodmen, for scoring timber, and the marks made by it are said to be "scribed." This, doubtless, was the sense of the Anglo-Saxon *scrîban,* or *scrífan,* derived (with the old and modern German forms, and the Latin verb) from the root, which is still applied amongst us to the instrument originally so called, one peculiarly fitted for its purpose of scoring wood; and its other meanings, to "pass sentence," (such sentences being anciently committed to writing), and to "impose penance," and "absolve" after confession, (the priest being regarded as a spiritual judge), are later applications.

Mearc denotes "letters;" but it was an iron instrument, the same as the scribe, which in Holland is still called *merk;* and in Beowulf, *gemearcod* is applied to *rún-stafas.* Its derivative meanings are, a "boundary mark," "marches," and a "sum of money," akin to the Latin *merx, merces,* and *mercari.*

The knife, *seax* or *secg,* was also used for writing on wood.[25] A passage to be cited hereafter will best exemplify the use of the former, and many terms connected with writing are derived from the latter. *Segen*[26] was a "sign," or "standard;"

---

[25] Diminutive knives have been found in some Kentish barrows. These may have been the kind used for writing.

[26] In illustration of the formation of these words, we may instance the exactly parallel derivations from the roots, *ríc,* "wealth," and *mece,* a "sword." From the former, *rîces,* a "ruler," Latin *rex; regen* (a word only fonnd in Anglo-Saxon in composition with an intensitive force, but its Gothic correspondent *ragin* means "authority"), Latin *regnum; regol,* a "law," (found also under the form Ricule in the name of Æthelberht's sister), Latin *regula; recan,* to "rule," Latin *regere.* From the latter, *mæcg,* (applied like *secg*), a "man," a "warrior;" *mægen,* "strength," or "power," Latin *magnus; macian,* or *mæcgan,* to "make," originally to "cut," (*maecte eene wide score,* Jac. v. Mærl.); and *mægan,* to "have "power;" whence *mæht,* "might," and the Latin *mactus; meagol* and *micel* great. *Regen* is the authority of wealth, or "right;" *mægen,* that acquired by the sword, or "might."

its Latin relative, *signum*, was primarily equivalent to *nota*, (as Cicero says), and in this sense Venantius uses it, in the passage above quoted; thence, in the plural, it became "writings" in general, "signatures" to a document, a "standard," an "omen;" thus passing through precisely the same process of various application as *bécen* and *tácen*. The Anglo-Saxon correspondent to the Latin *secare* has not appeared, but it may be traced in the provincial word *segg*, (applied to emasculated animals); and *sæcgan* (*sægan, secgan, seggan*), to "say," "tell," "narrate," seems so closely related to *sæcg*, or *secg*, that it is not improbable, its primitive meaning was to convey intelligence by means of writing with the knife.

We still use the word *scur*, a "score," in a limited sense with reference to writing; it must, therefore, have had this sense in ancient times. In Anglo-Saxon literature it occurs but once, and once in Old German,[27] and in both instances it denotes the wound inflicted by a sword; whence we see its relation to other words of this class, to which *wrítan* itself belongs. *Wrítan* is used in Beowulf to express the gash made by a *seax*, for which *writ* itself may have been another name. Hence its usual meaning, and from its past participle we have *writ*, a "letter."

Mál, or *mæl*, is a "mark," "sign," "character," "writing," "picture." Ulfilas uses the verb *mêljan*, to "write;" but its primitive meaning, as we have it in the Heljand, was to "wound" with the sword; thence, from the use of the knife in writing, it acquired its secondary meanings; and, because such writing was the medium of secret conversation, we have the Anglo-Saxon *mælan*, to "converse," an exact parallel to *secgan*.

From all these facts, but especially from the occurrence in our language of the roots of γράφειν and *scribere*, it is clear that the art of writing was practised by the common ances-

---

[27] "Mece scurum heard," Beowulf; "scrítan scarpen scurim," Hildebrand.

tors of the Teutons, Greeks, and Latins, before the separation of the peoples; and, consequently, that the characters of the Greek and Latin alphabets, which are not Phœnician, but akin to runes, are the remnants of a primitive system, which was in use amongst them before their migration from their original home in Asia. Words essentially the same in the languages, characters common to the futhorc and the alphabet, writing from right to left and *bustrophedon,* found equally on Runic monuments in Norway and Sweden, and on those of Greece and Phrygia, point distinctly to the one origin of the races, and show that the invention of the futhorc must be sought, not in the classical time of Greece and Italy, but in the dark ages of pre-historic antiquity. These correspondences in the systems of writing, no less than those of the languages they were employed to express, refer us for their origin to the epoch of the dispersion of the children of Japhet, whom (as Iapetus) the Greeks regarded as the common father of mankind.

Tradition tells us the name of the inventor of runes, and tradition must never be altogether disregarded; for, even when most corrupted, it always contains the germ of truth. If, then, he can be identified, and the identification supported by intrinsic and extrinsic probabilities, our task will be fully accomplished; and, even if our conclusions with regard to their inventor be rejected, the claim we have established for their primitive antiquity can scarcely be disputed.

In the Icelandic Runa Capitul, Odin is represented saying, "I invented runes;" and in the Anglo-Saxon prose dialogue of Salomon and Saturn, the answer to the question, "Who "invented letters?" is, "Mercurius the giant." Now not only does Tacitus imply the identity of Woden and Mercury, when he says of the Germans, "they worship chiefly the god Mer-"cury," but Jonas of Bobbio and Paul Warnefrid expressly assert it; and accordingly the Latins consecrated to Mercury the day we call Wednesday. Indeed, we can easily understand how Mercurius is a name of Woden, on account of his having invented letters, (as it were *mearcere*, or *merkari*, the "writer"); nor is this inconsistent with the usual derivation of his name *a mercibus*, for *merx* is represented by the Anglo-Saxon *mearc*, of which "money" is a secondary sense. So the tradition, which the Teutonic nations cherished, may have been carried to Italy by its first colonists. Mercury has much in common with Woden, the wanderer, the guardian of boundaries, and the undoubted owner of a similar name, Mearcwulf; even the two serpents of Mercury's caduceus correspond to Woden's Ofnir and Sfænir, as we see them, sometimes intertwined, sometimes forming together a sort of garland, on the coins of the Mercian Offa.

Hermes is the name of the Greek Mercury, and ἑρμήνευς, with other derivatives, seem to show that it was identical with Eormen, a word which the late Mr. Kemble conjectured was originally the name of a god, although the positive proof of the fact was hidden at the time beneath the ruins of the palaces of Assyria. The mythological tablets from Kouyunjik tell us that Armannu was the tutelar god of Susa, and Goransson's Edda calls the son of Woden, (who is called Heremod in other copies), by this name Herman. He, too, in Scandinavian mythology, has many of the characteristics of Mercury. Armenia, the land of Armen, is regarded as the cradle of the Indo-Germanic races; and Armen, as a name, was borne, not only by Teutonic chiefs,[28] but by a Trojan, (if we may regard Virgil's notice of a person of this name as derived from tradition[29]), and by a Roman, the associate of Horatius Cocles.[30] It entered into the composition

---

[28] Hermin, the ancestor of the Herminones, who was a son of Mannus, and grandson of Tuisco, according to a tradition quoted by Tacitus; Arminius and Herminius of historic fame, and the progenitor of the Eormenings in England.

[29] Æneid, XI. 642.

[30] Livy, II. 10.

of many other names,[31] and, like *regen* and *mægen*, it had the sense of power, and gave an intensitive force to words with which it was united. Eormen, I believe, was the Hermes of the Greeks; and if they gave this name to the Ægyptian Thoth, it was only because tradition connected him also with the invention of letters.

Woden, then, identified with Mercury, and perhaps the father of Hermes, seems to be connected with the primitive races which colonized Italy and Greece, as well as with our own. If so, he must have lived about the time of the migration of the children of Japhet. So, remembered by his descendants as the patriarch who conducted the fathers of their race, and from whom they received such knowledge as they possessed, he was deified in after times like the ancestors of other races, and regarded as discharging those offices towards mankind as a god, which, as a patriarch, he had really discharged towards his children. Now, of the sons of Japhet, Javan was the ancestor of the Greeks, whom Homer calls Ἰάονες, and the Persian, Assyrian, and Ægyptian records *Yavan*, or *Yuna*. It is thought that he sojourned for a time in Thessaly, and thence passed over into Italy, of which country, as Janus, he was always regarded as the first colonist, and the inaugurator of the golden age. Italian tradition farther relates, (and it is important to notice it, as additional evidence of the community of origin and tradition of that primitive race and our own), that Saturn, fleeing from the vengeance of Jove, came to Italy during his reign, was kindly received by him, and associated with him in the kingdom; and that Latium (*a latendo*) was so called because it was the place of his concealment. This is exactly expressed by the Hebrew סָתוּר, and Saturn is doubtless the Teutonic Saetere, the Roman *dies Saturni* being our Saturday.

Javan, then, belongs to the Greeks and Romans; he is

[31] Airmanareik, Eormenric, Hermenefrid, Irminfrid, &c.

unknown to the traditions of our forefathers; but in Ezechiel xxvii. 19 he is associated with Woden in a very remarkable way:—

ודן ויון

"Wodan and Javan:"[32]

and we may believe that they, whose names are thus associated, were connected by ties of kindred; such belief being warranted by the whole context of the chapter in which these names occur. For in v. 13 Javan is associated with his brothers Meshech and Tubal, and these two occur again in company in c. xxxviii. v. 2, 3; in v. 17 we have Judah and Israel; in v. 22, Sheba and Raamah; and so also in c. xxxviii. v. 6, Gomer and Togarmah. Thus Woden may be inferred to have been related to Javan, and this inference will be found to receive confirmation in the sequel; more than this, we shall perhaps be enabled to ascertain the exact degree of their relationship.

Javan, we believe, settled first in Thessaly, and then in Italy. In the district to the north, extending from the Adriatic to the Euxine, Tiras, one of his brothers, is generally regarded as having occupied Thrace, and may have given

---

[32] This is translated "Dan also and Javan;" but Michaelis has observed, (and he is followed by Gesenius and Simonis), that the ו at the commencement is not a copulative, but belongs to the word, which is therefore ודן, not דן. Whether this word should be pointed so as to read *Wĕdan* or *Wadan*, Hebrew scholars are not agreed; but it is very doubtful whether the comparatively modern system of pointing does convey the ancient pronunciation of words. Where we have an opportunity of comparing proper names occurring in the Hebrew Scriptures with the same in other authorities, we find that the pronunciation frequently differs from that which the Hebrew points require; and even many of the names in the Scriptures themselves are very differently read in different versions. Thus Manetho's Sesonchis is Shishak in Hebrew, Osorkon is Zerach, Sevechus is So, and Uaphris Hophra; and Meshach—Mash, Homam—Hemau, Shimma—Shammah, are instances of variations resulting from the uncertainty of the pointing. So, in the instance before us, the *Cholem* point would give to the word the pronunciation *Wodan*.

name to the Trausi, one of the chief tribes of that country. Possibly, also, we can identify amongst the Thracians their father Japhet; for their chief god, their original preceptor and lawgiver, to whom they believed that their souls went after death, (in the same spirit as the Israelites spoke of Abraham's bosom), was Zalmoxis; and Mr. Rawlinson has doubtless divined the truth, when he hints that he is the same as Selm, to whom his father Feridun gave the western third of the world. Feridun certainly represents Noah, and Selm Japhet. Salmo is also the name of a fish; and in Assyrian mythology Hea, who represents Japhet, in reference to the identity of his functions with those of the antediluvian Oannes, is called the "lord of understanding," and the "intelligent "fish;" and amongst the names of gods which the tablets supply, Zalmu is one, (whether he be identical with Hea or not).

The Teutonic character of many of the Thracian tribes cannot be doubted. The Getæ are the Goths; the Briggi, (whom the Greeks connected with the Asiatic Phrygians, and whose name, Hesychius tells us, signified "freemen"), the Brysi (Frysas), the Pæti (Peohtas), the Elethi (Hælethas), the Mædi, (Mæth, or Matha, enters into the composition of Anglo-Saxon and Gothic names), have all names of Teutonic character, and the Satræ seem to bear the name of Saetere. *Gebeleizis*, a title of Zalmoxis, as the receiver of souls after death, may be rendered in Anglo-Saxon *gifa-lisse*, the "giver of release or happiness." The Thracian Diana was Bendis, whom not only her name, but the torchlight race which characterized her festival, identifies with Abonde, or Habundia, of German superstition. So, when Herodotus tells us that, besides her, the Thracians worshipped Mars and Bacchus, we can at once identify them with Ear, or Tíw, the Teutonic god of war, and with Fricco; and when he proceeds to say that their kings, unlike the rest of the nation, worshipped Mercury more than any other god, always swearing by him, and proclaiming themselves his descendants, we recognize Woden at once. His descendants, therefore, were a distinct race or tribe; and this may well have been the Budini, (B in Greek representing our W), who appear to have been settled on the Don, and whose physical characteristics—tall stature, light-blue eyes, and bright red hair—exactly accord with those of our forefathers. Thus we seem to have the descendants of Woden, as a royal family, amongst those of Javan's brother, (a race who paid divine honours to one who appears to be identical with their common father Japhet), and probably, as a nation, located near them; consistently with our inference, (drawn from the occurrence of his name in connection with that of Javan), that Woden was of Javan's kindred; and confirming the tradition which was cherished by Greeks, Latins, and Teutons, that he, (who, as the collateral ancestor of the former, and the direct ancestor of our race in particular, would necessarily be the first preceptor of the latter in arts and sciences in patriarchal times), taught them the use of phonetic writing.

Now it is most remarkable that the traditions of the New World should be found not only to corroborate what has been here advanced, but even to indicate Woden's precise position in the patriarchal family. According to Nunez de Vega and Humboldt, the people of Teochiapan in Guatimala say that the first leader of their race was Votan, who co-operated in the raising of the tower which was intended to reach the skies, a grandson of the old man who was saved on a raft, when the rest of mankind perished by the deluge. The Crees also preserved a traditional remembrance of the land of their origin, for they say that the first land seen above the water was Nunih Waiya, and they had a Nunih Waiya of their own, an artificial mound, supposed to represent the mountain of the ark. The name, however, seems to point to Nineveh, and the records of Assyria and Babylonia, as interpreted by Sir H. C. Rawlinson, not only confirm what we have deduced from other sources, even from the Chiapanese tradition, but indicate that Woden's associates in the Teutonic mythology, equally with himself, belong to the first generations after the Flood.

This accomplished scholar has shown that a mythological system originated in Babylonia, and was afterwards corrupted in Assyria, resembling that which prevailed in Greece and Italy, presenting the same general grouping, not unfrequently the same genealogical succession, and occasional explanations of the names and titles of classical deities; hence he infers that a Scytho-Arian race existed amongst the tribes who dwelt on the Tigris and Euphrates in times of primitive antiquity, who afterwards migrated to Europe, and carried with them the traditions of their ancient home; and he remarks that, in addition to the Arian element which forms the basis of the Greek and Latin mythological systems, there is a prevailing Semitic or Assyrian character in the former, and a Scythic or Babylonian character in the latter. But the banks of the Tigris and Euphrates are, in truth, what they are represented to be in Genesis, the *morgenland*, the region wherein the fathers of all nations dwelt together in the "morning of "time;" and the Teutonic mythology proves to be, as might be expected, derived from the same source as the Greek and Latin; and, like the Latin, corresponds more nearly with the primitive Babylonian, than with the later Assyrian.

We must not, however, look for exact correspondence between the systems; although derived from a common origin, they would be varied by different races springing from the parent stock, who, whilst they deified the patriarchs generally, would be inclined to raise to the highest rank those who were their direct progenitors. Thus, individuals who seem to be identified by similarity of names or attributes, do not always hold the same rank in each system; thus Asshur, who is undoubtedly the son of Shem, was elevated in Assyria to the rank of the supreme god, and has titles assigned to him which belong more properly to the second divinity of the first triad, *i.e.* the individual whom Sir H. C. Rawlinson identifies with Shem himself. And thus also Woden, whose true place we shall be enabled to determine, was sometimes identified in Teutonic superstition with the Supreme Being Himself, most inconsistently with what was otherwise believed of him, and with his position as indicated by the order of the days of the week.[33]

The supreme god in Babylon, as in Ægypt, was Ra; but it does not appear that in Babylon he was identified with the sun, as he was in Ægypt. The Semitic equivalent of this name was Il (אֵל), which appears to be the root of Ἥλιος, an indication of the original pre-eminence of the sun-god, who was afterwards identified with Apollo, amongst the Greeks. The name of the supreme æternal God, the All-Father of the Teutons, has been withheld from us; it was a mystery which the author of the Edda dared not reveal.

Next in order was the triad, named by Damascius Ἀνὸς, Ἴλλινος, and Ἀὸς, whose Babylonian names were probably Anna, Il-Enu, and Hea; answering to the patriarchal triad Ham, Shem, and Japhet. In Greece, Ἀΐδης, Ζεῦς, and Ποσειδῶν: in Italy, Dis, Jupiter, and Neptunus, correspond to these, though not invested with precisely the same attributes.

The identity of Dis and Anna, at least, is certain. Many

---

[33] In his Essay on the Mythology of Babylonia and Assyria, to which I am indebted for the substance of what follows, Sir H. C. Rawlinson has noticed the illustrations which the Greek and Latin mythological systems derive from this source. In one instance only, (in the identity of the names Armannu and Herman), he has indicated a connecting link between these early Asiatic systems and the Teutonic; but he remarks that no discovery of Arian analogies in the former need excite surprise. I believe that the subject is capable of further and most important illustrations, and hope it will not be long before he undertakes to communicate more fully to the world the results of his interesting researches. It is probable that the Scandinavian mythology is substantially the system which was introduced into the North by the great conqueror Woden, and his original country was not very remote from Assyria.

of the names of Anna can only be explained by the supposition that they refer to the infernal regions; he is the "King "of the lower world," "Lord of darkness" or "death," "Ruler "of the far-off city;" and the symbol of his sacred number, 60, has not only the power of *Ana*, but also that of *Dis*. His sacred city was אֶרֶךְ, 'Ὀρὲχ, or *Urka*, the necropolis of Babylonia; so that his identity with Dis, the King of Orcus, is clear. Our ancient language had *Orc* for "hell," and *Orc* for a "goblin."

A second triad was composed of Hurki, San, and Iva, the "moon," "sun," and "æther;" and, although distinct from the former, it is not improbable that it may have been originally the same, (that is, representing the same personages, deified under different forms). This appears clearly in the case of San, less so in that of Hurki. San's Assyrian name was Shamas, Hebrew שֶׁמֶשׁ, afterwards corrupted in Babylonia to Savas, or Saōs. Now the old Babylonian name corresponds to the old Greek from Ζᾶν or Ζῆν, and the more recent one to the later Ζεῦς: Ζεῦς, we have seen, is represented by the second person of the first triad, himself the representative of the patriarch Shem; and the Semitic name of the sun is that of Shem, with the addition of אֵשׁ, "fire" or "splendour." Diespiter, the name of Zeus, Sir G. Wilkinson has remarked, is the Indian Diuspiter, "Sun-father;" Jupiter answers to Diupiter, "Heaven" or "Air-father." San, again, is the original form of the Teutonic Summi, Sunno, &c., the name of the god to whom the first day of the week was consecrated. In like manner the moon-god may have been originally the same as Anna the "Lord "of darkness;" they have equally the attribute of priority, (as might be expected in Hamite Babylonia), and antiquity; and the name of Anna seems to be an element in all the titles which were applied to the moon-god or goddess, σελάνα or σελήνη, Luna, Diana, Mano, and Mona. Erce, the "mother "of earth," a goddess invoked by our forefathers in incantations, possibly represents the female form of Hurki, and

Eorcan, (with the addition of *an*, "god"), the male form; for, from the way in which it enters into the composition of proper names, it seems to have been the name of a god.

The third person of the first triad, Hea, who represents the patriarch Japhet, and answers to Ποσειδῶν, or Neptunus, (though not a god of the sea), was regarded as the source of knowledge; had the titles, "Lord of understanding," and "teacher of mankind," amongst others; and answers exactly to the Oannes of Berosus, Oe of Helladius. His sacred city is thought to have been the modern Hit, called Is by Herodotus, Ihi originally, Ihidakira, (with reference to its bitumen springs), in the Talmud, and Ἀείπολις by Isidor of Charax. His symbol, the "wedge," or "arrow-head," the essential element of cuneiform writing, indicates that he was regarded as the inventor of the Babylonian alphabet. Amongst the stars he was known by the name of Kimmut.

The name of the third person of the second triad, Sir H. C. Rawlinson feels inclined to read as Iva, but admits that it may probably be Aír, and says that one of the phonetic values of the symbol of his sacred number, 6, is *ar*, or *er*. There is one indication of his original identity with Hea in the fact that on some tablets he has the title *Misharu*, evidently the same as Μυσαρὸς, which Berosus applies to Oannes, and which certainly belongs to Hea, if, (as is probable), it means "king;" for *Hea* has constantly the sign denoting "king" attached to his name. Now, as the sun-god has given name to the first day of the week, and the moon-god to the second, we may expect to find that the third, to complete the triad, bears a name of *Hea*, or *Iva*. Accordingly Aír, or Ar, is an element in the name which, in some parts of South Germany, is given to this day,—Ertag or Eritag; and the identity of a god named Ear, with Tíw, Tiig, or Ziu,—in honour of whom other Teutonic races called the day Tiwesdæg, Tijsdag, or Zistag,—is indicated by the fact, that the rune which in our futhorc was called *Ear*, and in the German *Aer*, (as W. Grimm suggests, instead of

Der), was *Ziu* in that of the Marcomanni; and this rune may be compared with the weapon with forked points, which symbolizes Iva, or Aïr, in the groups of divine emblems. Wíg, or Wíh, was another name of this god, the Teutonic Mars; and here we have a close approximation to the name of Hea, with its variations indicated above. Ear, of course, is the Greek Ἄρης.

It appears, then, that the gods of the first three days of the week are the same as those of the second triad; and these, I believe, are but other forms of those of the first, whom Sir H. C. Rawlinson identifies with Shem, Ham, and Japhet. Iva, indeed, is said to have been a son of Anna, but his name does not occur in the list of Anna's sons.

One of Hea's sons was Nabiu, or Nebo. This is rather a title than a name, equivalent to נָבִיא, a "prophet." As an inventor or patron of writing, he has the same symbol as his father. In the heavens he was represented by the planet Mercury, and the fourth day of the week was named after him Nebuk, in the Mendæan and Sabæan calendars. One of his best authenticated names was Tir; a name which the Persians gave to the planet, and which, in their language, signifies an "arrow." The French verb *tirer*, to "draw out," to "shoot," indicates the former existence of a Teutonic word of the same import, and *Tir* in our futhorc has the form of an arrow. Tir-Nebo, then, the son of Hea, may be identified with Tiras, the son of Japhet.

Nin, *i.e.* "Lord," a god worshipped at Calah, is called the son of Kimmut, or Hea, in all the invocations to him there. Two remarkable figures, with inscriptions in his honour, from the temple of Zira in that city, are now in the British Museum. One of these is a human figure, clothed with the skin of a fish, and agrees exactly with Helladius' description of Oannes; it may, therefore, represent Hea, his father. The other is a four-winged divinity with a horned helmet, who chases with a thunderbolt a griffin or satyr; and this, perhaps, is the god himself. It was the god of war who was honoured in this temple, and he has the titles "Lord of the brave," "champion," "whose sword is good," "who strengthens the hearts of "his followers." One of his earlier Babylonian titles was Vadana; and thus, by identity of name and attributes, we recognize in him our Woden, whom other sources of information have indicated to have been of the family of Japhet. If the figure of the fish-god really represents him, we may believe that he shared the attributes of his father, as Tir-Nebo did; and this will still farther illustrate our subject, for he was to the West and North, what Tir-Nebo was to the East—the inventor of writing, the god of the planet Mercury, and of the fourth day of the week. The fact that Woden was also a sea-god, and as such had the name of Hnikuthr, or Nikus, must not be overlooked.

Elsewhere, Nin is said to have been the son of Bel-Nifra. The evidence of the inscriptions in the temple at Calah can scarcely be questioned, and we must either suppose that there were two gods to whom this title was applied, or that Bel-Nifra in this case stands for Hea, who is sometimes called the lesser Bel-Nifra.

The god who comes next in order is Bel-Merodach. He is called the son of Hea and Daukina, and thus corresponds to Belus of Assyrian tradition, who is said, by Damascius, to have been the son Ἀοῦ καὶ Δαύκης. Of the identity of Bel and Merodach there cannot be a doubt. Sir H. C. Rawlinson regards the latter as a qualificative epithet, originally attached to the name Bel, and afterwards used instead of it. The Mendæans give the name Bel to the planet Jupiter; the Sabæans of Harran called the fifth day of the week after him; and Gesenius has adduced many arguments to prove that the planet Jupiter was the object of Phœnician idolatry under the name of בַּעַל. According to one of the values which the vocabularies give, for the initial sign of an old Hamite name by which he was distinguished, that name must be read Zur-ut, and this may confirm his identity with the Phœnician divinity, whose most ancient temple was in the city of צור, or Τῦρος, (now Sûr), which may have been named after him; and perhaps also, (as in the Aramæan ט is occasionally put for צ, and even in Hebrew these letters are interchanged), connect him with Thor, or Thur, after whom our forefathers named the same day Thuresdæg. The other value of this sign, Amar, supplies another indication of this connection, for Hamar was a name by which the same god was known in Germany. It may be merely a coincidence, that *gates* were regarded as being especially under Bel-Merodach's protection, and that the meaning of the name of the third rune of the futhorc, which was sacred to Thor, is almost certainly a "door," or "gate," as the sequel will show; but, even without it, we have sufficient ground for identifying our Thor with the primitive Belus of Babylonian tradition.

The wife of Nin, said to have been a daughter of Anna, who was worshipped with her husband in the temple of Zira at Calah, in honour of whom the sixth day of the week was called Beltis in the Sabæan calendar, had the title of Rí; whence probably the Greek Ῥέα, and the Teutonic Fríg, or Freya, the name of Woden's wife, the mother of the gods.

Saetere has been already noticed as the cotemporary of Javàn or Jànus in Italy, a fugitive from the arms of Jove.

Ishtar, the goddess of war and of the chace, answers to Eoster, to whom, as the goddess of the opening year, our forefathers dedicated the month of April. Her Babylonian name was Nana; to this day Nana is the Syrian, as Ashtar is the Mendæan, name of the planet Venus, which represented her in the heavens; and Nanna in Scandinavian mythology is the wife of the god Baldr. The untimely death of Thammuz, and the lament for him of all the gods in Babylon, has its counterpart in that of the death of Baldr, and of all creation weeping for him; and the name of Thammuz, which is said to mean "hidden," aptly describes the state of Baldr detained in Hel's kingdom of darkness. But Thammuz or Adonis is recognized as the lover of Astarte or Venus, so that we can identify unhesitatingly Eoster and Nanna, with Ishtar and Nana, as names of the same goddess.

Allata, a goddess of high rank, is probably the same as Herodotus' Alytta; if so, she corresponds to Diana, and to the German Holda. Diodorus says she was worshipped in Babylon under the name of Hera, and this name also she had in Germany.

Here, then, we have a series of correspondences, which scarcely leaves room for doubt, that the gods of the Anglo-Saxons, and other kindred races, were the deified patriarchs of Babylonian and Assyrian mythology; and we may well believe that it is no mere fancy, but a remnant of primitive tradition, which, (in the dialogue of Salomon and Saturn), represents Woden "the wandering wolf" as the "friend of "Nebrond," or Nimrod; other traditions, as independent as it is possible to conceive, concur to show that he was the grandson of Noah, and so one of the great founders of nations; and his character, as inventor of writing, is remarkably illustrated by the fact, that his father Japhet, and his brother Tiras, were also regarded in Assyria as gods of learning and letters.

The mythology of Ægypt supplies most interesting confirmation of this theory that the gods of heathenism were deified patriarchs, and shows the system extended still farther, so as to embrace even their forefathers who lived before the Flood.[34]

Thus Atum, "King of the gods," "Lord of the worlds," "god of the setting sun," and "of the lower world," the judge of souls departed, whom he calls children, whilst they call him father, is evidently Adam.

Seti, who shares with *Atum* the highest veneration at Kar-

---

[34] Mr. Osburn's works have drawn my attention to this. I do not know how far the statements in the text may be affected by the recently announced discoveries of Simonides. If true, they serve to illustrate my argument; if erroneous, it loses, indeed, the benefit of this illustration, but none of its force.

nak, and pours blessings on the great Sesertesen, appears to be Adam's son, Seth. Sothis or Sirius was his star in the heavens, and the 19th dynasty, whose accession to power seems to have been nearly coincident with the commencement of the Sothiac cycle, B.C. 1322, paid him peculiar honour. Now, as Josephus records the tradition that astronomical observations were begun by Seth's children, it is not improbable that Sirius was connected with his memory, and was made the basis of those observations even in the antediluvian age. If Sothiac cycles were computed before that which commenced B.C. 1322, one would commence B.C. 4244, very near to the times of Seth, if not actually during his life.

Nuh seems identical with Noah. His name is certainly Nuh, (not Num), for in the name of Nuh-otp it is spelt with the ram and twisted cord, and with the Nile-jug and twisted cord; and the latter symbol is acknowledged to have the power of *h*. Now the name of Noah, נוֹח, means "rest," derived from נוּחַ, to "rest," to "settle." The original idea is to "draw breath," to "sigh," to "breathe." And with regard to Nuh, Plutarch, (who calls him Knéph), and Diodorus, say that the name of the Ægyptian Zeus signified "spirit;" and in the hieroglyphic writings of ancient Ægypt, *nif* is "breath," and to "blow." Nuh is the "lord of the inundations," who presided over the rising of the Nile, the "sculptor of all men," said "to have made mankind on his wheel, and fashioned the gods;" and he was, like Atum, a god of the lower world; as Noah was the patriarch of the flood, and the ancestor of the post-diluvian race of mankind.

Amen corresponds to Ham, and is occasionally represented by the criomorphite figure which usually represents Nuh.

The god who is generally called Khem is perhaps Shem, for his name is never written phonetically, but only with the bolt, which is the well-known phonetic s. He is represented as phallic, enveloped in swathes, one arm protruded and upraised, brandishing a scourge, the other holding the priapus.

Ptah appears to correspond to Japhet. The name of Japhet, יֶפֶת, is derived from פָּתָה, to "spread," "open," "expand," and so also is believed to be that of Ptah. He is sometimes represented wearing a scull-cap, enveloped in swathes, holding with both hands the Tet, the sign of life, and the kukufa sceptre; sometimes as phallic, holding the priapus, and raising his hand; and sometimes as a child, which recalls another sense of פָּתָה, to "be open," "ingenuous," like children, and פֹּתֶה, "simple."

The rest of the gods of Ægypt probably belong also to the patriarchal age, and to the family of Ham.

Sanconiatho attributes the invention of letters among the Phœnicians to Taaut, the son of Misor, and grandson of Hamyn, and says that he afterwards passed into other countries and eventually became King of Ægypt. His story is quite consistent with one which Plato learned from the Ægyptians, in which Theuth is represented coming to King Thamus in Ægypt, and explaining to him the utility of the sciences he had invented, that of phonetic writing amongst the rest; and which in itself contains nothing improbable.

Accepting, then, the traditions of distinct races, we find that about the same time, the epoch of the dispersion of the family of Noah, Tiras-Nebo and Woden, sons of Japhet, and Taaut, the grandson of Ham, invented alphabetic writing for their children in the countries in which they settled. The separate traditions corroborate one another, and warrant the probability that other patriarchs did the same.

Instead of regarding phonetic writing as the property of any race in particular, we must rather believe that different races received it at the same time nearly, from the one primitive source. Symbolic writing was the first stage of the art, the next was attaching a phonetic value to the symbols. This Josephus, relying on ancient tradition, believed was invented by Seth, and practised before the Flood; and certainly the title and contents of the fifth chapter of Genesis, seem to indicate that there were written records in that age. Enoch also was the author of a book of prophecies, cited by S. Jude, Clement of Alexandria, Tertullian, and Origen. Berosus says that in the days of Alorus, King of Babylonia before the Flood, an intelligent being, named Oannes, taught the people of that country the use of letters, and wrote a book on the origin of things; and speaks of antediluvian records hidden in the city of Zippara: so that it is certain that Babylonian tradition spoke of the practice of writing of some kind, in the age before the Flood. This, I believe, was the very system which we find in full vigour in Ægypt in the twenty-fifth century, B.C.; for nothing can account for the fact, of a system so complete having prevailed in that country almost from the very beginning of its history, without the least trace of one less perfect having preceded it, but acquiescence in these traditions, so far at least as to regard it as one which had descended to the Ægyptians from antediluvian times. If, then, the art of writing was practised before the Flood, the children of Shem and Japhet would be acquainted with it, as well as the children of Ham.

But the inconveniences attached to such a system would be very great; the multiplicity of the symbols would limit the number of those who could master it, and their forms would be a hindrance to quick writing. Hence, I suppose, Taaut invented in Phœnicia, and Woden and others elsewhere, systems which would facilitate the acquisition of learning, and expedite writing; systems, which consisted in the selection of a single symbol out of many that were previously in use, to represent each sound, and in the reduction of its form to a simple outline. Thus Lucan distinguishes alphabetic writing from the hieroglyphic; and whilst he attributes the invention of the former to the Phœnicians, asserts the prior existence of the latter. He says:—"If we may trust tradi- "tion, the Phœnicians first ventured to devote by rude "figures an expression which was to be fixed. Not yet had

"Memphis learned to join together the bibli of her river; "and only birds, beasts, and animals, engraven on stones, "preserved mysterious language."[35]

This view is completely borne out by Plato's story. He represents Theuth recommending his system of writing to King Thamus in these words:—

"Great King! this science will increase the wisdom of the "Ægyptians, and will give them a more faithful memory; it "is a remedy against the difficulty of acquiring and retaining "knowledge."

When the number of distinct characters, phonetic, determinative, and symbolic, in the Ægyptian hieroglyphic system is considered, we can better appreciate the facilities for the acquisition of knowledge which Theuth's simple alphabet afforded. The memory must have been well trained which could read off an inscription in such characters, and Thamus seems to have thought that Theuth's alphabet would put an end to such discipline of the memory, if it facilitated reading. He is said to have replied:—

"Wise Theuth! some persons are more apt at discovering "arts, and others in judging how far they may be useful or "injurious. Thou, father of letters, hast allowed thyself to "be blinded by thine inclinations, till thou seest them dif-"ferent from what they are. Those who learn them, will "leave to these strange characters, the care of recalling to "them all they should have committed to memory, and they "will preserve no actual recollection of them. Thus thou "hast discovered a means of reminiscence, not of memory. "Thou givest to thy disciples the means of appearing wise, "without being really so, for they will read without the in-

[35] Phœnices primi, famæ si creditur, ausi
Mansuram rudibus vocem signare figuris;
Nondum flumineas Memphis contexere biblos
Noverat, et saxis tantum volucresque, feræque,
Sculptaque servabant magicas animalia linguas. III. 220. 4.

"struction of masters, and will think themselves wise in "many things, when in fact they will be ignorant, and their "intercourse will be insupportable."[36]

It is quite evident that all this applies to simple alphabetic writing, as distinguished from symbolo-phonetic. Such was Theuth's system, a series of simple forms each adapted to the expression of a single sound, selected out of a multitude of symbols, and such also was the Runic; for although we cannot trace the precise symbolism of each particular form, we can identify so many of the characters of which the futhorc is composed, with known symbols, that we may well believe that a definite symbolic meaning originally belonged to each. We have already noticed some of these; we are now in a position to identify others, and in this identification shall discover fresh traces of the primitive Asiatic origin of the Anglo-Saxon futhorc.

Aleph, the first character of the Hebrew and Phœnician alphabet, was the head of an ox with its horns; *Feoh,* the first letter of the Runic, with the same meaning, is but a variant of the same symbol, and corresponds very nearly with the Samaritan character. *Ur,* which means a "bull," the animal sacred to the god of the firmament, meant also the firmament itself; and the connection between its form and the symbol of the firmament, is obvious. *Thorn,* the third rune, is certainly allied to *Daleth,* and as the latter is a "door," so we may regard the former, (of which *Thur* is one of the variants), as *thuru* or *duru* with the same signification. The Phœnician-Hebrew letters, *Koph* and *Resch,* signify and symbolize the "head;" the Greek *Rho* is identical with the primitive *Resch;* the Latin R and the Runic *Ræd* differ from it only in the addition of a beard; whilst the Runic *Wæn* again has the primitive form. It cannot be accidental that *Ræd* means "knowledge," and *Wén,* "thought," "hope," "expectation;"

---

[36] Phædrus.

the head being the recognized seat of these faculties would fitly be their symbol; and most fitly the beardless head, *Wén*, is "hope," the bearded, *Ræd*, "counsel," or "knowledge." The Phœnician *Cheth* or *Heth*, has sometimes exactly the form of the Anglo-Saxon *Hægel;* it means and represents an "enclosure," or "park," and it is very probable that *Hægel* means the same, for *hæge* is a "hedge," and *hægian* to "hedge" would admit of a derivative noun *hægel*, like *gyrdel* from *gyrdan;* and our modern name for this character confirms this view. We have noticed the fact, that in the cuneiform system the primary element, the single wedge, was the symbol of *Hea*, and of his son *Nebo* or *Tir*. Now the sacred city of *Hea* was called *Is*, *Ihi*, or *I*, (the two last with the addition of Dakira, on account of its bitumen pits), and by a remarkable coincidence, which we cannot now precisely explain, the primary element of the futhorc, the letter I, has the name *Is*. Probably the original meaning of these symbols was the same, and that *ís*, *ísen*, "iron;" they may represent a wedge or bar of the metal. The forms of S, in all the alphabets which have passed in review before us, seem to be but variants of an original type, representing the serpent; whilst the Doric *San* is the name of the Babylonian sun-god, and the Runic *Sigel*, *Suil* or *Sol*, signifies the "sun." *Tir* in Persian has the meaning, and in the futhorc the form, of an "arrow." The Runic *Eh* has the form of the Greek *Mu* and the Latin M; the Phœnician word *Mu*, and the Hebrew *Mem* mean "water;" and although we cannot discern this symbol in the Phœnician or Hebrew forms of the letter, as distinctly as in the Samaritan, it is clear in the Greek and Latin; and as *éh* in our language has the same meaning, it was perhaps the original name, rather than *eh*. The Phœnician-Hebrew *Lamed* is a "whip," "rod," or "goad;" the Runic *Lagu* has the form of a "whip," the symbol of authority in Ægyptian hieroglyphics, and there cannot be a doubt that its meaning is "law." *Calc* has precisely the form of the thunderbolt, which characterizes Nin in the Assyrian sculptures, and when his title *Khalkhalla,* "brother of the lightning," and the name of his father's sacred city Khalkha, are considered, we cannot doubt that the word signified what the form of the character denotes. *Stan* has the form in which the Phœnicians cast their pigs of tin, and is stamped as a symbol on one so formed, found in Cornwall and now in the Truro Museum; it is, therefore, extremely probable that the word, like the Latin *stannum,* means "tin." *Vult* meaning "fire," was, perhaps, the symbol of that element. Lastly, the Runic copulative sign, which occurs even in the late inscriptions at Kirkdale and Bridekirk, has precisely the ancient form of *Vau,* which means a "hook," and, as such, became in Hebrew the copulative conjunction.

Thus we see that the Phœnician alphabet and the Anglo-Saxon futhorc are derived from a common source; that the same feeling dictated the choice of the symbols which were to be used as letters in each case; and that each letter represents the initial sound of the name of the corresponding symbol. This is somewhat similar to what Sir H. C. Rawlinson has observed with regard to the Babylonian and Assyrian cuneiform systems. He says that the Babylonian Scyths first employed rude pictures of objects, afterwards fashioned them into letters, and then gave to each letter a phonetic power, corresponding with the name of the original object. This system was in full vigour twenty-two centuries before our æra. More than a thousand years later, the Assyrians attempted to apply this system to their own language, retaining all the old Scythic values of the letters, obtained from terms in the Scythic language, and, moreover, assigning to each character a fresh equivalent power in their own language; that is, the power belonging to the Semitic equivalent of the original Scythic term; and this double function applied not merely to individual letters, but also to words formed of several letters, or rather of several syllables. So whilst several characters of the alphabet and futhorc represent the same symbols, their powers differ, because the names of the symbols differ in the languages.

Again, therefore, by a different path we arrive at the same end. Their own internal evidence, and external evidence besides, have led us through a long series of ages, to seek the origin of the Anglo-Saxon and kindred futhorcs, at the epoch of the dispersion of the human race. There we have found, not only the individual whom tradition declares to have been their inventor, but many members of his family, who were afterwards deified with him. We have discovered that the Anglo-Saxon futhorc was not derived from any other system of phonetic writing, but directly from the symbolic system which preceded it, which the whole human race had originally in common, and which Ægypt retained even when the simpler system was offered to her; that, equally with the Phœnician, and more nearly than any other, even than the most ancient cuneiform, it represents the original character of phonetic writing; that it is the parent, rather than the offspring, of the systems which prevailed amongst other divisions of the Teutonic race. The art of writing originated with no nation in particular, but is a part of the primitive tradition, which was common to all.

The Bleking inscription seems clearly to speak of *run* as an instrument with which runes were written, and the Hebrew verb רוּן, to "overcome," (a sense naturally derivative from that which signified the instrument of victory, like our Anglo-Saxon *mægen* from *mece*), with its kindred verb רוּם, to "exalt," and the Greek words *ῥωννύειν*, to "strengthen," and *ῥώμη*, "strength," may indicate the existence of a primitive word *ru* or *run* designating a "sword," "knife," or other weapon. To such a word the sense of a "letter" or "writing" would naturally be applied when the knife was used for writing; and I am satisfied that its other senses, a "whisper," "mystery," "charm," are all derivative from this. The analogy of *becen, tácen, segen,* and *spel,* passing from their primitive senses into others connected with magic, affords a fair presumption that *rún* has passed through the same process, rather than the inverse.

In our language the oldest sense that can be traced is that of phonetic writing. Of this Venantius speaks when he alludes to the *barbara rhuna;* the words *literæ solutoriæ* in Venerable Bæda, (IV. 22), are translated by Ælfræd *alýsendlíce rúne,* showing that *rúne* is the equivalent of *literæ;* when the invention of writing is ascribed to Woden in the Runa Capitul, and in the dialogue of Salomon and Saturn, *runar* in the former is the equivalent of *bócstafas* in the latter; and *runar* constantly occurs in the Norse inscriptions, for "letters" used in simple records and epitaphs, as *becun* does in those of Northumbria for epitaphs. So also Hrabanus calls the runes, of which he gives us the forms, simply *literæ.*

It is certain that they were used for correspondence amongst those who could read, and for committing matters to writing. In the following passage of one of the riddles in the Exeter book:—

thrý sind on naman	in its name are three
rýhte rún-stafas,	right letters,
thára is Rad furum—	whereof Rad is—

rún stafas evidently means nothing more than letters; nor does it in Beowulf (f. 167):—

swá wæs on thǽm scenne	so was on the hilt
scíran goldes,	of bright gold,
thurh rúnstafas	through letters
ríhte gemearcod—	rightly marked—

where an inscription, not magical but narrative, is the subject.

A passage has been already quoted from the Exeter book, which speaks of runes used in correspondence, as also one from Thomas of Ercildoune, containing probably the latest instance of the use of the word in this sense. Layamon has not only the word *runen* for "letters," but *writ-runen*, *boc-runen*, *run-staven*, and *boc-staven*.

Fortunately we are not left to conjecture how *rún* a "letter" came to signify a "whisper," "council," "secresy," &c. A curious riddle in the Exeter book (p. 471) illustrates the process exactly. Its subject is clearly a writing tablet, made of timber which had once formed part of a pier or jetty, abandoned and allowed to go to ruin:—

Ic wæs be sande,	I was by the sand,
sǽ-wealle neáh,	nigh the sea-wall,
æt mere-farothe.	at the ocean-shore.
Mínum gewunade	I dwelt in my
frum-stathole fæst.	first station fast.
Feá ǽnig wæs	Scarce any was there
monna cynnes,	of mankind,
thæt mínne thær	that there
on ánæde,	in the loneliness,
eard beheold.	my dwelling beheld.
Ac mec, uhtna gehwám,	For me, each early morn,
ýth sio brúne	the brown wave
lagu-fæthme beleolc.	locked in its watery bosom.
Lyt ic wénde	Little I weened
thæt ic, ǽr oththe síth,	that I, early or late,
æfre sceolde,	should ever,
ófer meodu,	over mead,
múthleas sprecan,	mouthless speak,
wordum wrixlan.	converse with words.
Thæt is wundres dǽl,	That is a deal of wonder,
on sefan gearolíc,	curious in the mind,
thám the swylc ne conn,	to those who such a thing understand not,
hú mec seaxes ord,	how me the knife's point,

and seó swíthre hond,	and the right hand,
eorles ingethonc,	man's sagacity,
and ord somod,	and the point together,
thingum gethydan,	purposely associate,
thæt ic with the sceolde,	that I with thee should,
for unc ánum twám,	for us two alone,
ærend-sprǽce	a speech-errand
abeódan bealdlíce;	boldly announce;
swá hit beorna má	so that it more men
uncre word-cwidas	our word-sayings
widder ne mænden.	further imagined not.

The old story of the slave, who fancied that the letters, of which he was the bearer, held secret converse with his master's correspondent, is familiar to us all; and so those who, unable to read and write themselves, witnessed a scholar scribing his runes on a spell, might easily imagine he was confiding his secrets to it in whispers, and those in turn, who beheld the receiver of the mysterious spell poring over its strange characters, and perhaps pronouncing them to himself, would think, as this riddle tells us, that they were whispering secrets, holding mute converse together. It is precisely this sense which Venantius' expression, *Romuleus susurrus,* applied to private correspondence, conveys.

To the lower classes, to the rude spear-men, whom Ælian represents as despising the art of writing, runes were indeed mysterious, yet they were not so to warriors of higher rank, nor to priests, nor to ladies. Ignorance of letters was general, not universal. Tacitus represents the paterfamilias as interpreting runes: Hrothgar read the inscription on the sword-hilt; Wiwa wrote the epitaph for his comrade Woduridi; and, (at a later period indeed, but still one in which ancient customs were in full force in Denmark), Gorm the epitaph for his queen Thyre. Runes were certainly the medium of correspondence amongst those who could read and write, and those who could do neither would think it strange, that a man could communicate with his friend in words they could not hear, by means of the point of his knife, and others would wonder what the spell was saying to its recipient, when it came to hand. Hence *rún*, a simple "letter," as the medium of correspondence, which was understood but by few, became the symbol of a "whisper," or secret communication, then of consultation, plotting, and mystery in general; (just as one whose education had not proceeded so far, would say of anything he could not understand, "It is all Greek to me"); because it was also used in divination, it became the expression of a "portent," "charm," or "incantation;" and the feeling of mystery with which it was regarded became a deeper one of superstitious awe. This at least seems to me to have been the process by which these secondary meanings have been developed from the primary; it is precisely the same as that by which "stave" has become the expression of an oral recitation or song; and other words, "beacon," "beckon," "sign," "token," which we can trace to equally simple primitive meanings, connected with the act of writing, convey to modern ears ideas the most remote therefrom.

The inscriptions on stone, metal, and ivory, which have been noticed in the foregoing pages, have presented us with many forms of our language, more regular than those which we have derived from MSS. less ancient far than they are. This is no more than might be expected; it is exactly what the most ancient inscriptions in the Latin language have afforded with regard to its primitive forms. The higher we can ascend in tracing the antiquity of the speech of our fathers, the more nearly shall we find its declensional and conjugational forms approaching to those of the age, when the ancestors of nations were one family; and should some fortunate discovery put us in possession of old records on tablets, (which certainly once existed), of the days of paganism, we might expect that the assistance they would afford to the study of our language, would be of even greater importance than that which these brief inscriptions supply.

NOTE *to p.* 47.

IT seems necessary to say a few words relative to *tacon*, for although I have said that it corresponds to *tócon*, (which is its only representative in our language), I have omitted to account for the difference in its vowel sound. I believe that, besides *tacan*, of which the præterite is *tóc*, there once existed a verb *tǽcan*, with præterite *tec*, which would answer to this *tac*. For in the Gothic we have five verbs, *flêkan*, *grêtan*, *lêtan*, *rêdan*, and *têkan*, which should retain in the reduplicated præterite the vowel of the present, (as *slêpan saizlêp* actually does), according to the analogy of all other verbs of this kind, but of which the existing præterites are *faiflôk*, *gaigrôt*, *lailôt*, *rairôth*, *taitôk*. Now, with regard to four of these, our language preserves the contracted forms of præterites, which analogy would lead us to expect in the Gothic; *grǽtan*, *lǽtan*, *rǽdan*, and *slǽpan*, give us *gret*, *let*, *red*, and *slep;* whilst, to correspond with *têkan*, we have, not *tǽcan tec*, but *tacan tóc*. So also in Old Saxon we have *lâtan lêt*, *râdan rêd*, and *slâpan slêp;* but, instead of *grâtan grêt*, *greotan greot*, with which the Anglo-Saxon *greótan*, (Beowulf, 2684), exactly agrees. I conclude, therefore, that there were in early times two forms, (or more), of each of these verbs, differing in their vowel sounds; that we had once a verb *tǽcan*, corresponding to *têkan*, as *slǽpan* to *slêpan*, and that *tac* in this inscription represents its præterite *tec;* that *flêkan*, &c., have lost their regular præterites, and that *faiflôk*, &c., were regularly formed from presents, which have also disappeared. To these anomalous præterites *rodun*, which occurs once in the Heljand instead of *redun*, and *loot*, which has remained amongst us in provincial use, for *let*, exactly correspond; and *hwépan* and *wópan* may be mentioned, as instances of verbs in our language, different in sound, (for which we have only *hwôpan* in the Gothic, and *wôpan* in Old Saxon), signifying equally to "lament" and to "shout;" whilst their modern representatives, to "weep" and to "whoop," warrant the inference that these duplicate forms of verbs were each originally distinguished by slight modifications of one sense. So the Anglo-Saxon *flocan* to "revile," (or express contempt with a gesture of the hands), and the Old Saxon *flocan* to "curse," may represent a Gothic *flôkan*, of which we have the præterite *faiflôk*, "I lamented."

CHAPTER III.

The Anglo-Saxon Genealogies.

THE genealogies of the Teutonic royal dynasties are substantially genuine historic documents. That they ascend much higher than the annals, and even than the distinct traditions of our forefathers, is no more than might be expected; for, (like the title-deeds of an estate), records, by which the succession to the throne would sometimes be determined on the failure of elder lines, would be preserved, even when others were allowed to perish, because the interest of the events they related was eclipsed by that of succeeding events. So the Anglo-Saxons may well have had records of the ancestry of their kings, beginning with Sceaf, which writers of Christian times have disfigured, by giving us their own uncritical conjecture as a historic fact, and calling Sceaf the son of Noe, born in the ark, or even identifying him with the patriarch Shem.

Now, if on examining the genealogies as they have been handed down to us, we find them to be intrinsically probable, and consistent, not only with one another, but with history, in the later portion which comprises twenty-five generations, we shall more readily acquiesce in the statement which presents to us the first nine, although we are unable to submit it to the same tests. These we shall pass over, because we have no independent authorities by the aid of which we might have formed a judgment as to their accuracy, nor dates wherewith we might have verified their chronological succession, and shall commence our inquiry with Geat.

His identity with Gaut[1] of the Ostrogothic line is admitted, and, indeed, will be found to acquire confirmation from what we shall have to advance in the sequel, and his æra is satisfactorily ascertained. For Jordanis tells us, that the Goths regarded the chiefs,[2] to whose valour and generalship they were indebted for the victory they gained over the forces of Domitian, A.D. 86, as something more than human, and called them *Anses*, i. e. "demigods." Some centuries earlier, indeed, we know that their kings were so regarded, for Herodotus tells us that they were a distinct race who claimed descent from Mercury; but Jordanis evidently intended to mark the period, when the line of the Anses, as he states it, commenced. His silence as to Geat's ancestry may be accounted for by a statement, in a genealogy given by Langhorne, that Geat was the first of his family who settled in the district, whence his descendant Woden emigrated to Scandinavia. He would, therefore, be regarded in the East as the founder of the fortunes of his family; and probably the distinguished part which he played on the occasion in question, was the first step of their advancement to the sovereignty of the Ostrogoths, which was completed in the person of his

---

[1] *Gaut* is certainly the correct reading, which inaccurate scribes, (mistaking *Wen* for P), have transformed into *Gapt*. *Gáut* is the Gothic equivalent of the Anglo-Saxon *Geát*, as Procopius' Γαῦτοι are the *Geátas*. The analogy of the Gothic verb *giutan*, *gáut*, *gutans*, Anglo-Saxon *géotan*, *geát*, *goten*, to "pour," (in which Mr. Kemble discerned the etymology of the name), further illustrates this identity; for as the names just given correspond to the præterite of this verb, so do the Gothic *Gutans* and the Anglo-Saxon *Gotas*, "the Goths," correspond to the participle.

[2] De Rebus Geticis, v.

great grandson Amal. Thus we may assume the beginning of the second century as the period when Geat flourished, and with this date the genealogy of his descendants is consistent throughout.

For, in the middle of the third century, we overtake his fifth descendant Ostrogotha, far advanced in years, (as we may infer from an examination of the genealogies), at the close of his career. He had passed the Danube in the fifth year of the Emperor Philip; Decius was sent against him, but on his being saluted Emperor made peace with him, and returned to Italy. Cniva, his successor, and probably his son, renewed the war after his death, and it was in opposing him that Decius lost his life, A. D. 251. During the reign of Constantine, Aoric and Araric are mentioned as Kings of the Goths; they probably belonged to a line, elder than that through which the genealogy is traced. So also did Geberic their successor, the fourth in descent from Ostrogotha, if, (as is not improbable), we may identify Cnivida with Cniva. In A. D. 323, during the reign of Aoric and Araric, Constantine defeated the Goths in several engagements, drove them out of Illyricum, and carried the war into Dacia with such success, that he was enabled to boast that he had recovered that province, which Aurelian had relinquished to them half a century before. The Goths, however, were merely checked, not subdued; for, in A. D. 331, the Sarmatians sought the assistance of Constantine against them, and when it was known that he had espoused their cause, Araric passed the Danube, ravaged Mæsia, and routed the Roman forces commanded by the Emperor in person. In the following year, under the generalship of the younger Constantine, the Romans retrieved their honour, expelled the Goths from Mæsia, pursued them into Sarmatia, and reduced them to submission, exacting from Araric his eldest son as a hostage. About this time Geberic succeeded to the throne. Jordanis tells us, that, desiring to mark the commencement of his reign by some deed of glory, he made war upon the Vandals, who had recently migrated from the shores of the Western Ocean, and settled upon the borders of Dacia; and that, after an obstinate conflict on the banks of the river Marosk, he so completely defeated them, that the remnant of their army, with all who were unfit for war, emigrated to Pannonia, and were allowed to settle there by Constantine. The great Hermanaric, after some interval, succeeded Geberic. He subjected to his authority Southern Russia, Lithuania, Poland, and great part of Germany, and carried his arms even to the shores of the Western Ocean. After a long and prosperous reign, he died by his own hand, in A.D. 375, because he despaired of being able to resist the Huns successfully.[3] Withemir and Witheric followed successively; their relation to this line does not appear. Winithari, grandson of Hermanaric's elder brother Wulduf, was the next; then Hermanaric's son Hunimund; then his son Thorismund, whose death, in the flower of his age, and the second year of his reign, so afflicted the Goths, that for forty years they allowed no one to occupy his throne; and his son Berimund, disdaining the supremacy of the Huns, as it is said, but probably disgusted at being debarred of his rights, fled to the Visigoths. These five reigns must have occupied a short period, for after this interregnum of forty years, Winithari's grandsons, Walamir, Theodemir, and Withemir, appear reigning conjointly, and confederate with Attila. Theodemir survived his brothers until A.D. 475, and then was succeeded by his son Theodoric, who died in A.D. 526. Eutharic, of the younger line, married Theodoric's daughter, Amalasuinth, and their son, Athalaric, died in infancy, the last male representative of his race.

Here, then, we have a genealogical descent, which is not only intrinsically probable, but consistent at every point of contact with cotemporary history. We cannot, indeed, allow

---

[3] Ammianus Marcellinus, XXXI. 3.

to Hermanaric the extraordinary age of one hundred and ten years, which Jordanis assigns to him, and which would make him upwards of seventy years old at the date of his accession to the throne; but from the death of Ostrogotha to that of Hermanaric, we have an average of thirty-one years for the generations; and if we suppose Ostrogotha to have been born about A.D. 180, from that date to the date of Theodoric's birth, A.D. 455, we obtain an average of thirty years and a half; and this, notwithstanding that from Ostrogotha downwards, the succession appears to be continued in the line of a younger son; for Hermanaric appears to have been the first of Hunnuil's family who occupied the throne, and there are traces of two elder lines.[4] So this genealogy, in the facts it presents,

---

[4] It is certain that a number much less than the usually estimated average will suffice for the genealogies of these early times. The Barbarians married sooner than is usual now. We may well believe that Goths and Anglo-Saxons in the fourth and fifth centuries, followed much the same customs as Danes and Swedes in the eleventh and twelfth; and it is no uncommon thing to meet with notices in the Sagas, of warriors on the field of battle at the early age at which Arthur commenced his victorious career. Eric Blödoxe even in his thirteenth year received the command of a fleet, and sailed on his first expedition. Magnus Barfod was the father of Eystein at the age of sixteen, and some of the Merovingian princes were fathers at fifteen. The Anglo-Saxon genealogies, in purely historic times, prove that early marriage was the rule with our forefathers. Thus Eadwine was certainly married before he was twenty-one to Quœnburh, and was a grandfather when he died, at the age of forty-seven. But, not to multiply instances, we will take the West-Saxon genealogy, of which we know more than of any of the others. We find that five generations from the death of Cyneric, A.D. 560, to that of Æscwine, A.D. 676, give an average of about twenty-three years; twelve from the same date to that of Æthelbald's death, give twenty-five years, although three individuals, at least, in this descent were younger sons; and the average of the whole series of seventeen generations to Eadweard the Confessor, is but thirty years, although, (besides the younger sons just noticed),—

Ælfræd was the sixth son of Æthelwulf;

Eadmund the son of Eadweard, by his third wife, three sons and seven daughters having been the issue of the first and second marriages;

Eadgar, the second son of Eadmund;

Æthelræd the son of Eadgar by his second wife;

as well as in the possibilities it suggests, affords a criterion whereby to measure the rest; all of which we shall find to be as nearly coincident with it, as we have any right to expect. In researches of this kind, where our authorities are discordant, the safest course is to follow the earliest, because it is most probable that they have preserved for us ancient traditions in their purest form, (unless, in any particular instance, there be good grounds for preferring one more recent). For the ancestry of Woden, therefore, I refer to the History of the Britons, and on its authority, supported as it is by the genealogies in the Textus Roffensis, (which uniformly call Woden the son of Frealaf), and by the Norse genealogy, (in which his father is called Fiarlef, Frialafr, or Fridleifr), I reject the name of Frithuwald, which Asser interposes between those of Woden and Frealaf, (although, by retaining it in the accompanying scheme, a more striking correspondence could have been shown between the Gothic and Anglo-Saxon genealogies, than even now will appear). Still, in making Folcwald the father of Fin, the author of this History has fallen into an error, for which it is easy to account; the memory of Fin, the son of Folcwalda, was fresh in men's minds when he wrote, and it was easy to confound him with Fin, the son of Godwulf; for, (those only excepted who have copied from him), all other authorities, Norse and Anglo-Saxon, tell us that Godwulf was the son of Geat, and the ancestor of Woden. To Geat he gives precisely the character which Jordanis gives him, saying that he was reputed to have

---

Eadweard the second son of Æthelræd's second marriage, six sons and four daughters having been the issue of the first.

It is obvious that the average would have been less than twenty-five years if the descent had been continued in the line of elder sons. The longer the series the more will be the chances of the succession passing into younger branches, and, of course, the greater the average; but under the most unfavourable circumstances, (and they can scarcely be more unfavourable than in the genealogy we have just examined), it will seldom exceed thirty years.

been the son of a god; whilst Asser goes farther, and says that he was actually worshipped as a god, (an instance of the corruption of tradition). Woden, then, the fifth descendant of Geat, stands in the same degree as Ostrogotha, and as we may presume that his was the younger line, he would be somewhat Ostrogotha's junior. The date, at which his descendants in the fourth degree, Horsa and Hencgest, appear in our annals, and the circumstances of their history, suggest that he lived during the latter half of the third century and the earlier of the fourth, and thus was cotemporary with Hunnuil, Athal, Achiulf, and his sons; and this inference, whilst on the one hand it is quite consistent with the facts of the Gothic genealogy, is abundantly confirmed by the other genealogies of Woden's descendants, and by the circumstances of his life as detailed in Scandinavian tradition.

For, whatever was the period in which he flourished, Woden is in truth a historical personage. As such he was regarded by all our early chroniclers; the author of the History of the Britons, without a hint as to his divinity, gives him a line of ancestors; in the eighth century, Bæda says of him, "from whose stock the royal races of many provinces "derived their origin;" in the tenth, Asser simply mentions him as one of the line of his patron's ancestors, and Æthelweard calls him "King of a multitude of Barbarians," and "King of many nations, whom now some Pagans worship as "a god;" the rest speak of him in similar terms, in exact accordance with what is related of him in the Ynglinga Saga; and in the Exeter Book we have a distinct allusion to the new worship which he introduced into the North.[5] If he became the object of divine honours after his death, it was because he was eventually confounded with the original

[5] Woden worhte weos,	Woden made idols,
wuldor alwalda	the glorious Almighty (made)
rúme roderas.	the spacious heavens. (Page 341.)

Woden, whose name it is said he assumed. The outlines of his history are by no means improbable.

At a time when many chieftains fled from their dominions, because the Roman generals were going about, subjecting all nations to the authority of the Empire, he is said to have left his home at the head of a powerful force of warriors, whose bravery and noble appearance, superior wisdom and civilization, caused them to be regarded, by the ruder peoples through whose territories they passed, as more like gods than men, and contributed materially to ensure the success which everywhere attended them. Woden invaded and conquered in succession Russia, Germany, and Denmark, and placed each conquered or submissive nation under the government of one of his sons; thus Suarlami was established in Russia, and Wægdæg, Bældæg, Sigge, and Skiöld, became founders of royal dynasties in East Saxony, Westphalia, Franconia, and Denmark. Passing over into Sweden, he was allowed to form a settlement there, by Gylf, the king of the country, who, knowing that he had no force to oppose him, adopted the wiser policy of receiving him amicably. A desirable site was chosen, the city of Sigtun founded, a temple built therein, and sacrifices established according to the rites of Asaland. Lastly, Norway was invaded, subdued, and given by Woden to Sæming, who appears to have been born, as well as other sons, after his father's arrival in the North. Returning into Sweden, and perceiving that death was near, he put an end to his own existence, and left the kingdom to his son Yngve.

In all this there is nothing improbable. It is a simple narrative of an expedition, by a comparatively civilized race, through regions inhabited by peoples less advanced than they; by a race who had the address to consolidate, by the arts of peace, the conquests of the sword. No wonder that success everywhere attended them, that plenty and prosperity followed them, that the dynasties they established remained secure. They were, in fact, Goths, far the most civilized of those whom Greeks and Romans called Barbarians;[6] Woden and the rest of their chiefs, the Asar, were those whom Jordanis calls Anses, (for *As* is the Norse equivalent of the Gothic *Ans*, Anglo-Saxon *Os*); and, through Woden, Swedes, Danes, Jutes, Angles, Saxons, and many other tribes of Germany, each received a royal dynasty, of the same blood as those who ruled the Goths.

It is implied that this expedition was consequent on reverses suffered in conflict with the forces of the Roman Empire. Of all the successes which the Romans gained over the Goths, during the period at which we have ascertained that Woden must have lived, Constantine's victories in Dacia, A. D. 323, seem the most likely to have occasioned it. Woden must have been far advanced in years at the time, for he had many sons who had themselves attained to maturity. If, therefore, we suppose that it commenced immediately after this defeat, we shall find this supposition confirmed by history, and consistent with the genealogies of Woden's children.

For Sarmatia was Woden's first conquest. War had commenced between the Goths and Sarmatians in the interval between A. D. 323 and 331, and the Goths during this interval had conquered Sarmatia; for it was in that country that they were eventually subdued, when Constantine responded to the appeal of the Sarmatians, and espoused their cause. I believe that Woden's career of conquest commenced about A. D. 325; and it seems not improbable that Hermanaric, who afterwards became king, was associated with him for some time, until circumstances prepared the way for his accession to the throne of the Ostrogoths, for the stories of their conquests remarkably coincide.

This conjecture receives a striking confirmation from the

---

6 "Pæne omnibus barbaris Gothi sapientiores semper extiterunt, Græ-"cisque pæne consimiles." JORDANIS, *De Reb. Get.* III.

history of the Longobards, and, in turn, invests with a character of truth their ancient tradition: that the Vandals, making encroachments on the territories of their neighbours, sent a message to them demanding tribute; that they replied, they would rather fight than submit to this demand, and that both nations prepared for war; that the Vandals besought Woden to grant them victory, whilst the Longobards, more wisely, made interest with his wife Freya; and that she so arranged matters, that her husband gave the victory to them. Paul Warnefrid calls this story ridiculous, because "victory "is not attributed to the power of men, but rather is dis-"pensed from heaven;" evidently intimating, that the tradition ascribed to human agency the victory which the Longobards obtained; but, if we consider attentively the nature of the case, it does not appear so very ridiculous. Woden claimed magical power. Northern tradition tells us that his people believed that victory was always his, and that not only was he always successful when he commanded in person, but that, whenever he sent them on any expedition, he laid his hands upon their heads, and invoked a blessing on them, and that then they went forth, confident of victory. This mighty chief was in the neighbourhood of the place, where the Longobards and Vandals had arrayed their forces in preparation for battle; both parties sought that blessing from him, the utterance of that charm, which would ensure them victory; and we can easily understand what effect in raising the spirits of one, and depressing those of the other party, the knowledge that he had espoused the interests of the former would have.

Let us, then, compare this tradition with the history. The Vandals were actually in motion at the time we have conjecturally fixed for Woden's expedition. About A.D. 334 they had migrated in the course of one year from the shores of the German Ocean into the territory in which they suffered defeat at the hands of Geberic. They had, therefore, as Paul says, been pressing on the settlements of their neighbours, and that of the Longobards on the Elbe was in the line of their migration. The supposition that their hasty eastward movement was consequent on their defeat, is not unreasonable.

The chronology of the Longobards is perfectly consistent with the supposition that Ibor and Ayo, their first historic chiefs, were living at this time, and were cotemporary with Woden. Although their genealogical succession does not commence before their third king Lethu, yet, as his reign was of forty years' duration, and Agelmund's was thirty-three, we may fairly take the succession of their kings as equivalent to a genealogy; and, if we place Ibor and Ayo in the same line as Ostrogotha and Woden, we observe that Ildigisl, who was eighth in succession from Ayo, and was slain in A.D. 548, is but one degree above Theodoric the Ostrogoth, who died in A.D. 526. Further, if we suppose Ildigisl to have been born about A.D. 500, and allow thirty years' average for the generations, the birth of Lethu would be about A.D. 350. Then, taking A.D. 333 as the date of the victory, ten years of Ibor and Ayo's chieftainship bring us to A.D. 343, Agelmund's thirty-three years' reign to A.D. 376, and Lamissio's reign of three years to A.D. 379, for the time of Lethu's accession, at the age of twenty-nine, (according to the former computation), and his forty years' reign would close at the age of sixty-nine.[7] Thus the succession of their

[7] Paul gives no dates for the succession of these first kings. Some uncritical hand has interpolated the following series in Prosper's Chronicle.

A.D.
379. Ibor and Ayo conquered the Vandals.
389. Agelmund reigned thirty-three years.
423. Lamissio reigned three years.

Lethu's reign, therefore, would be from A.D. 426 to 466; but as this would scarcely allow an average of twenty years for the five succeeding generations, we can have little hesitation in rejecting these dates as erroneous.

kings, for the most part genealogical, corresponds with the genealogy of the Goths, their history coincides with that of the Goths, and their chronology is consistent with the theory, that Woden, after his Russian and German conquests, had reached the borders of Denmark in A. D. 333.

The genealogies of the Anglo-Saxon Kings are very variously stated in the Notes by some anonymous Cambrian authority, appended to some MSS. of the History of the Britons, in the Textus Roffensis, in the Saxon Chronicle, and in the Tables of Florence of Worcester; but, as I have already said, throughout this inquiry, I adhere to the principle of following the earliest authority;[8] and the Cambrian genealogist must have been living a century earlier than the time of the compilation of the Saxon Chronicle, (for the latest name he gives is that of Ecgfrith, the son of Offa); was evidently well acquainted with the history of the times of which he has left us these brief notes; and supplies, in several instances, information which we have not elsewhere. In the East Anglian genealogy, for example, he gives a descent, which enables us to understand the relationship of Aldwulf to his predecessors; and in that of the Mercian Kings, we have an opportunity of testing his accuracy, for the poem of Beowulf tells us that Offa was cotemporary with Hygelac, who was slain A. D. 511; and he gives three generations between him and Penda, who was born A. D. 576, which will

[8] In several of the lines of descent we observe that the later chronicles give more names than the earlier. The Ynglinga Saga illustrates the process by which this has been brought about; for the succession of kings there given cannot possibly be genealogical in its full extent, although it is probably historical. So I apprehend that the additional names which appear in these later genealogies, are those of chieftains who ruled the tribes during minorities, or represent elder lines which failed, and made way for younger branches of the same family. If we take the historical succession of the kings of any one of the Anglo-Saxon kingdoms, and suppose the records of their relationship to have been lost, and the series represented as genealogical by a writer who knew only of their names and their succession, we can readily understand this process of augmentation.

answer exactly; whilst the Saxon Chronicle and Florence give the manifestly excessive number seven. His authority, therefore, I do not hesitate to prefer, and shall follow, except in one instance, in which I think he may possibly have been mistaken. Next in value to these Notes, I consider the genealogies in the Textus Roffensis, originally compiled, I believe, not later than the beginning of the ninth century, since Coenwulf of Mercia is the latest whose descent is traced, and Beornwulf, his second successor, the latest who is named.

I. All authorities are agreed with respect to the ancestors of Horsa and Hencgest. They arrived in Britain in A.D. 428; Horsa fell at Episford, A.D. 435; Hencgest reigned after him until A.D. 443, when he was defeated at Conisbrough, fell into the hands of Ambrosius, and was put to death. A Frisian tradition, quoted by Suffridus,[9] tells us that two nephews and namesakes of theirs, sons of Udolph Duke of Frisia, and of their sister Svana, completed the conquest of Britain, which they had begun. In accepting this tradition, we need have no difficulty. It is by no means unlikely that there were in the same family more persons than one of each name, and we can easily account for the circumstance that the second Hencgest is not distinguished, in our history, from the first.[10] In the original records, or sagas,

---

9 "De Frisionum Antiquitate et Origine." It is uncertain what was the authority he followed, for he seems to have been mistaken in quoting Ocka Scharlensis, who mentions indeed a second Horsa and Hencgest, but represents them to have been the sons of Odilbalt King of Frisia. (See Thorpe's Lappenberg, I. 79). Suffridus' story appears the more probable, inasmuch as he connects the second Hencgest with the first, and so accounts for his succeeding him.

10 We shall have occasion to notice the presence of Chrocus, an Alamannic chief, in Britain, in the beginning of the fourth century; he might easily have been confounded with his namesake who figures in the history of Gaul, A.D. 258, were not the death of the latter distinctly recorded. In the West Saxon genealogy, which is more detailed than that of the other Anglo-Saxon royal dynasties, we have two Cuthas and three Ceols in two parallel generations, (abbreviated names, which, however, we can write at full by the aid of their history); so also in the Danish

from which the Saxon Chronicle was compiled, the name of Hencgest simply was given in the narratives of his exploits, in much the same way as we find it in one of the episodes in Beowulf; the chronicler set down an epitome of what he found recorded, and later writers, who knew nothing of a second Hencgest, have completely identified the two; just as the author of the History of the Britons, in assigning sixteen years as the duration of the reign of Constantine of Armorica, has added to his twelve years the four of Constantine the tyrant, who was slain about the time of his accession, and so confounded them together.

We shall be the more ready to admit the possibility of such confusion as this, arising out of the unsystematic records of the fifth century, if we consider the exactly parallel circumstances of the tenth, a period in which the Saxon Chronicle was being regularly kept, and the events of successive years entered as they occurred. The history of this later period is involved in perplexity almost as great as that of the earlier, owing to the frequent recurrence of the same names. There were certainly two Anlafs at least, a son of Sitric, and his nephew a son of Guthfrith, connected with the history of Northumbria in the tenth century; but in the Saxon Chronicle they are undistinguished, except that once Anlaf the son of Sitric is mentioned, and once Anlaf Quiran. So also there were two Erics, sons respectively of Harald Blaatand, and Harald Haarfagr, of the first of whom we have coins,

---

genealogies we have frequent repetitions of Frode, Halfdan, Ingiald, &c.; in later times Æthelfrith, King of Northumbria, had a brother, as well as a son, named Eanfrith; and the names of two ancestors of Eadwine, Wuscfrea and Iffi, were given to his two grandchildren. There is, therefore, no reason why Swane might not have named her children after her brothers. The feeling which usually dictates the choice of names in a family is nothing new. S. John the Baptist's name was objected to by his relatives on this very account, that it had been borne by none of his kindred; and doubtless it has been the practice in all ages, and amongst all peoples, as it certainly was amongst the Teutonic tribes, to give to children the names of their kindred, or illustrious ancestors.

whilst the second only is named in the Chronicle. If, then, in the tenth century, the Saxon Chronicle affords us no means of discriminating between princes of the same name, it is no wonder that the history of two Hencgests, in the fifth, should have been confounded.

This Frisian tradition affords a satisfactory solution, of what would otherwise have been an insuperable difficulty, the notices of a Hencgest in our history, after the time to which the fall of the first, (recorded in the Brut, Boece, and Ocka), must be referred; and enable us in part to reconcile the conflicting statements in our Chronicles, relative to the genealogy of the Kings of Kent. It is the second Hencgest, (as I shall endeavour to show), who figures in Beowulf; whose death is recorded in the fortieth year of the coming of the Angles, A. D. 467; and who stands at the head of the Kentish genealogy, in the Cambrian's Notes. For it is remarkable that this alone is not traced to Woden,[11] (as it could not have been, without including the name of a female, and so departing from the universal rule of these genealogies).

Again, Boece says, that after the death of Octa, in the last year of the reign of Uther, the Saxons made another Octa, the son of his brother, King of England, and shortly afterwards he notices his giving Northumbria to Colgrim, and going to the South. Buchanan also speaks of a second Octa, a son of the former. In the History of the Britons, the passage which immediately precedes the notice of Arthur's twelve victories, informs us that on the death of Hencgest, (A. D. 467), his son Octa passed from North Britain to Kent, and that he was the progenitor of all the Kings of Kent. Henry of Huntingdon says that Æsc was Hencgest's successor, and we learn from the Saxon Chronicle that the Kings

[11] To the objection which might be raised, that the genealogy of Hencgest is already given in the body of the History, the fact that the History and these Notes are distinct and independent documents, is a sufficient answer.

of Kent were called Æscings. Æthelweard enables us to reconcile these statements, by saying that Octa, whose forename was Ese (Æsc), was the son of Hencgest, and grandfather of Eormenric, and that from him the Kings of Kent were called Esings (Æscings).

The evidence of these Scottish historians as to the existence of a second Octa, is equally important with that of the Frisian tradition of a second Hencgest; it shows how the recurrence of the same names in this family has given rise to the confusion which exists with regard to the ancestry of Eormenric; and enables us to complete the restoration of this genealogy. The conflicting statements of our different authorities will be seen in the following table:—

Cambr.	Text. Roff.	Æthelweard.	Flor. Worc.	Bæda.
Hengest.	Hengest.	Hengest.	Hengest.	Hengest.
Octha.	Ocga.	Ese-Octa.	Ocga vel Oric.	Oeric-Oisc.
Ossa.	Eosa.		Oesa vel Oisc.	Octa.
Eormoric.	Eormiric.	Eormenric.	Eormenring.	Irminric.

Æthelweard, it will be seen, agrees with the Cambrian, adding that Octa had also the name of Æsc; and in this he is supported by the Scalæ Chronicon, which informs us that Arthur's antagonist, (whom Boece calls Octa, and who is certainly the person whom the Saxon Chronicle and Henry of Huntingdon call Æsc), was named Octa and Osca. He omits the name of his son; but there can be no doubt it was Ossa, for Henry of Huntingdon says that he reigned between Æsc and Eormenric, and his name occurs in this succession in the Textus Roffensis, and in the double pedigree which Florence of Worcester gives.

Florence appears to have had the two distinct descents before him; one the same as that recorded by the Cambrian, *Hengest, Ocga, Oesa, Eormenring;* the other, *Hengest, Oric, Oisc;* and not knowing how to reconcile them, has adopted the expedient of writing *Ocga vel Oric, Oesa vel Oisc.* Oeric and Oisc belong to the first Hencgest; their names certainly followed his in the genealogy, and although Bæda has represented them as borne by the same person, I suspect that they were, as Florence represents them, names of a son and grandson.[12]

Hencgest I. had a son Octa, who came to Britain soon after him, and, with occasional interruptions, reigned in Northumbria until A.D. 466, when he fell in battle near Verulam; but Octa and Ossa of the genealogy belong to Hencgest II. This Octa, generally called Æsc, succeeded the first Octa in Northumbria, and on the death of Hencgest II. in the following year, relinquished it in favour of Colgrim, and reigned in Kent thenceforward until A.D. 491.

In the accompanying table the conflicting statements are attempted to be reconciled as follows; the descent from Woden to Hencgest I. is that upon which all authorities are agreed; that from Hencgest II. to Eormenric is given by the Cambrian genealogist; and the connecting link, Swane, is supplied by the Frisian tradition. Æthelberht, Eormenric's son, is in the ninth degree from Woden; but it is evident that in his person this genealogy has fallen one generation into arrear, for he was born in A.D. 552, and must have been the son of Eormenric's old age.

II. Our authorities are accordant with regard to the East Anglian dynasty, as far as the name of Eni the son of Tytla.[13] Bæda notices particularly only the family of Anna the son of Eni. The Cambrian genealogist, and the Textus Roffensis, evidently independent authorities, take up the line of another son of Eni, the former concluding it with the name of Elric, otherwise unknown, the latter with that of Ælfwald.

---

12 Oisc is not Æsc, but Wisc, as Mr. Kemble has shown. Latin writers frequently used O before A or I to express the Teutonic W.

13

Cambrian.	Casser,	Titinon,	Trigil,	Rodmunt,	Rippa,	Guillem,	Guecha,
Florence.	Casere,	Tytmon,	Trygils,	Hrothmund,	Hryp,	Wilhelm,	Wewa, or Wehha,
Text. Roff.	Caser,	Tytiman,	Trygil,	Hrodmund,	Hryp,	Wilhelm,	Wehh,

Camb.	Guffa,	Tidil,	Ecni	Edric,	Aldul,	Elric.
Flor.	Wuffa,	Tytla,	Eni,	Anna.		
Text. Roff.	Wuffa,	Tytla,	Erri,	Ætherric,	Aldulf,	Ælfwold.

III. Later chroniclers differ from the Cambrian in inserting four generations between Eomær and Pybba in the Mercian line.[14] I follow him for the reason stated above, and as Creoda was certainly King of the Mercians before Pybba, I think it probable that these four names represent a collateral descent. This arrangement is supported by a statement in the Life of S. Guthlac, viz. that "he was of the oldest "and noblest family in Mercia, who were called Iclings;" for if Æthelbald, who was King of Mercia when this Life was written, had been an Icling, the author would not have passed over the fact of S. Guthlac's having been of his family. The Iclings, therefore, were not then in possession of the throne of Mercia, and Pybba was not of their line. In this instance, and in others, later chroniclers have interpolated in the genealogies, names of persons, who actually reigned perhaps, but who belonged to collateral descents.

IV. Florence's third and fourth names in the Bernician genealogy, Beorn and Beornd, as well as Beonoc which is given in the Saxon Chronicle, seem to be false spellings of Beornec; this last I adopt as the true orthography, on the authority of the Cambrian genealogist and the Textus Roffensis, since it suggests the derivation of the name of the Beornicas.[15] Angengeat and Ingengeat in Florence's list, Angenwit and Ingwi in the Saxon Chronicle, appear to be variations of one name, Ingwi or Ingwingeat; the Textus Roffensis agreeing with the Cambrian genealogist, in placing

---

14

Cambrian.	Guedolgeat,	Gueagon,	Guithleg,	Guerdmund,	Offa,	Ongen,
Sax. Chronicle.			Wibtlæg,	Wærmund,	Offa,	Angeltheow,
Florence.	Weothelgeat,	Waga,	Wibtlæg,	Wærmund,	Offa,	Angengeat,
Text. Roff.	Weodegeot,		Withlæg,	Weremund,	Offa,	Angelgeot,

Camb.	Eamer,					Pubba.
Sax. Chr.	Eomær,	Icel,	Cnebba,	Cynewald,	Creoda,	Pybba.
Flor.	Eomær,	Icil,	Cnebba,	Cynewald,	Creoda,	Pybba.
Text. Roff.	Eomer,	Icel,	Cnebba,	Cynewald,	Creoda,	Pybba.

15

Cambrian.	Beldeg,		Beornec,		Gechbrond,	
Saxon Chronicle.	Beldæg,	Brand,	Beonoc,			
Florence.	Bældeag,	Brand,	Beorn,	Beornd,	Wægbrand,	Ingebrand,
Textus Roffensis.	Bældæg,		Beornic,		Wægbrand,	Ingebrand,

Camb.	Aluson,		Inguec,	Ædibrith,	Ossa,	Eobba,	Ida.
Sax. Chr.	Aloc,	Angenwit,	Ingwi,		Esa,	Eoppa,	Ida.
Flor.	Alusa,	Angengeat,	Ingengeat,	Æthelbryht,	Oesa,	Eoppa,	Ida.
Text. Roff.	Alusa,	Angelgeot,		Æthelberht,	Eosa,	Eoppa,	Ida.

one name only between Aloc and Æthelberht. Ingebrand, the only name which the Textus Roffensis gives in addition to those of the Cambrian genealogist, may be collateral.

V. In the Deiran genealogy I suspect the Cambrian has fallen into an error, in placing at the head of the line, the ancestors of the Bernicians and West Saxons, instead of their own, Wægdæg.[16] It is easy to understand how Florence, who is the only authority for Swærta, finding the name Swerting after that of Seomel, took it for a patronymic, indicating that his father was Swærta. But Swerting is not a patronymic here; it is mentioned in Beowulf as a proper name, and was probably common enough; for, in the eleventh century, we find it borne by two of the Law-men of the city of Lincoln, the sons respectively of Harthacnut and Grimbald.

VI. In the West-Saxon genealogy I follow the Textus Roffensis and Asser,[17] for the Cambrian genealogist affords us no assistance here. Asser was certainly living at the time, when the Saxon Chronicle was first arranged in its present form; and, as chaplain to the King whose pedigree he gives,

---

[16]

Cambrian.	Beldeyg,	Brond,	Siggar,			Sebald,	Zegulf,
Saxon Chronicle.	Wægdæg,		Sigegar,	Swæbdæg,	Sigegeat,	Sæbald,	Sæfugel,
Florence.	Wægdeag,		Siggar,	Swæbdæg,	Siggæt,	Sæbald,	Sæfugol,
Textus Roffensis.	Wægdæg,		Siggar,	Swæbdæg,	Siggeot,	Sæbald,	Sæfugal,
Henry Hunting.				Wepdeg,	Sigegeat,	Seabald,	Sefugil,

Cambr.		Soemil,	Sguerthing,	Guilglis,	Usfrean,	Iffi,	Ulle.
Sax. Chr.			Westrefalcna,	Wilgils,	Uscfrea,	Yffe,	Ælle.
Flor.	Swærta,	Seomel,	Westorwalcna,	Wilgels,	Wyscfrea,	Yffi,	Ealle.
Text. Roff.		Seomel,	Westerwalcna,	Wilgilsing,	Wuscfrea,	Yffe,	Ælle.
H. H.			Westrefalcna,	Wilgils,	Uscfrea,	Iffa,	Ella.

[17]

Asser.	Belde,	Brond,			
Textus Roffensis.	Bældæg,	Brand,			
S. C. Tiberius, B. IV.	Beldæg,	Brand,	Frithogar,	Freawine,	
Tiberius, B. I. and A. VI.	Bældæg,	Brand,	Frithogar,	Freawine,	Wig,
C. C. Cambr. CLXXIII.	Bældæg,	Brand,	Frithogar,	Freawine,	Wig,

Asser.	Gewis,		Elesa,	Cerdic,	Creoda,	Cyneric.
Text. Roff.	Giwis,		Aluca,	Cerdic,	Creoda,	Cyneric.
S. C. Tib., B. IV.	Gewis,		Elesa,	Cerdic,	Creoda,	Cyneric.
Tib., B. I. & A. VI.	Gewis,	Esla,	Elesa,	Cerdic,	Creoda,	Cyneric.
C. C. Camb. CLXXIII.	Gewis,	Esla,	Elesa,	Cerdic,		Cyneric.

After the other genealogies in the Textns Roffensis, a second is given of the West-Saxon dynasty, extended to the sons of Eadgar. This appears to be a distinct document, derived from a sonrce different from that which has supplied the rest, none of which come down to a later period than the first half of the ninth century; and whilst the former which ends with Ine, agrees with that given by Asser, in every respect except that Cuthwnlf takes the place of Cutha, this agrees with the genealogy as stated in the MSS. Tiberins, B. I. & A. VI.

may be supposed to have enjoyed particular opportunities of acquiring the most accurate information. In his list, the (probably collateral) names of Freothegar, Freawine, Wig, and Esla, do not appear, but another name, Creoda, is inserted between those of Cerdic and Cyneric, and this, as we shall see, is very important. The genealogy of Ine in the Textus Roffensis is exactly the same as his; three MSS. of the Saxon Chronicle support him with regard to this name, and one in omitting Wig and Esla. Gewis, we may observe, is the eponymus of this race, as Beornec of the Beornicas.

VII. Florence of Worcester and Henry of Huntingdon give the genealogy of the East-Saxons, agreeing as to the number of descents, but differing as to their order.[18]

VIII. Florence and the Textus Roffensis agree in their statements of the genealogy of the Lindisfaras; but as the individuals, whose names appear in this series, are quite unknown in history, we have no means of comparing it with the rest, or of testing its accuracy.[19]

Let us now place these genealogies side by side for the sake of comparison. We find the result to be a remarkable vindication of their genuineness, and of the justice of our preference of the earliest authorities. The inequalities in the number of generations as stated by later authorities disappear, and Æthelbert, Tytla, Penda, Cuthwine, Ida, and Sleda, all of whom were living in the latter half of the sixth century, all appear in the ninth degree of descent from Woden; Ælle, their cotemporary, is in the tenth; and there are, in fact, no greater disparities in this earlier division of the genealogies, than in the later, which is undoubtedly historical. Referring to the Longobardic and Gothic lines, we find Hildigisl, who

[18]

Florence.	Seaxnete,	Gesecg,		Antsecg,	Swæppa,
Henry Huntingdon.	Saxnat,	Andesc,		Gesac,	Spoewe,
Flor.	Sigefugel,	Bedca,	Offa,	Æscwine,	Sledda.
H. H.	Sigewlf,	Biedean,	Offa,	Erchenwin,	Slede.

[19]

Florence.	Winta,	Cretta,	Queldgils,	Cædbæd,	Bubba,
Textus Roffensis.	Winta,	Cretta,	Cwædgils,	Cædbæd,	Bubba,
Flor.	Beda,	Biscop,	Eanferth,	Eatta,	Ealdfrith
Text. Roff.	Beda,	Bisceop,	Eanferd,	Eata,	Alfrid.

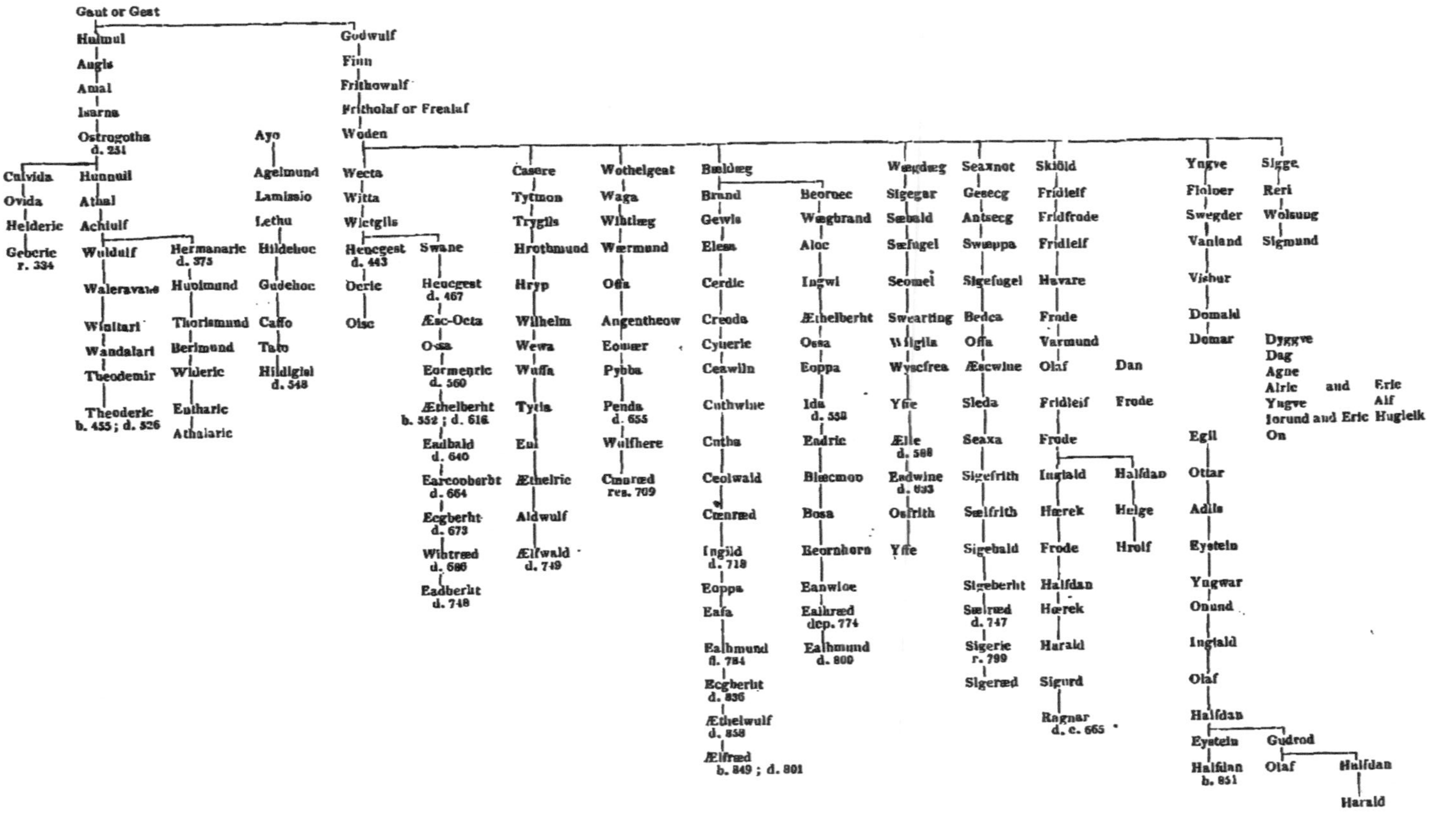

Gaut or Geat
Hulmul
Augis
Amal
Isarna
Ostrogotha
d. 251
Culvida
Ovida
Helderic
Geberic
r. 334
Hunnuil
Athal
Achiulf
Wulduif
Waleravans
Winitari
Wandalari
Theodemir
Theoderic
b. 455 ; d. 526
Hermanaric
d. 375
Huniumund
Thorismund
Berimund
Wideric
Eutharic
Athalaric
Ayo
Agelmund
Lamissio
Lethu
Hildehoc
Gudehoc
Caffo
Tato
Hildigisl
d. 548
Godwulf
Finn
Frithowulf
Fritholaf or Frealaf
Woden
Wecta
Witta
Wictgils
Heucgest
d. 443
Oeric
Oisc
Swane
Heucgest
d. 467
Æsc-Octa
Ossa
Eormenric
d. 560
Æthelberht
b. 552 ; d. 616
Eadbald
d. 640
Earconberht
d. 664
Ecgberht
d. 673
Wihtræd
d. 686
Eadberht
d. 748
Casere
Tytmon
Trygils
Hrothmund
Hryp
Wilhelm
Wewa
Wuffa
Tytla
Eni
Æthelric
Aldwulf
Ælfwald
d. 749
Wothelgeat
Waga
Wihtlæg
Wærmund
Offa
Angentheow
Eomær
Pybba
Penda
d. 655
Wulfhere
Cœnræd
res. 709
Bældæg
Brand
Gewis
Elesa
Cerdic
Creoda
Cynric
Ceawlin
Cuthwine
Cutha
Ceolwald
Cœnræd
Ingild
d. 718
Eoppa
Eafa
Ealhmund
fl. 784
Ecgberht
d. 836
Æthelwulf
d. 858
Ælfræd
b. 849 ; d. 901
Beornec
Wægbrand
Aloc
Ingwi
Æthelberht
Ossa
Eoppa
Ida
d. 559
Eadric
Blæcmon
Bosa
Beornhorn
Eanwine
Ealhræd
dep. 774
Ealhmund
d. 800
Wægdæg
Sigegar
Sæbald
Sæfugel
Seomel
Swearting
Wilgils
Wyscfrea
Yffe
Ælle
d. 588
Eadwine
d. 633
Osfrith
Yffe
Seaxnot
Gesecg
Antsecg
Swæppa
Sigefugel
Bedca
Offa
Æscwine
Sleda
Seaxa
Sigefrith
Sælfrith
Sigebald
Sigeberht
Sælræd
d. 747
Sigeric
r. 799
Sigeræd
Skiöld
Fridleif
Fridfrode
Fridleif
Havare
Frode
Varmund
Olaf
Fridleif
Frode
Ingiald
Hærek
Frode
Halfdan
Hærek
Harald
Sigurd
Ragnar
d. c. 665
Dan
Frode
Halfdan
Helge
Hrolf
Yngve
Fiolner
Swegder
Vanland
Vishur
Domald
Domar
Egil
Ottar
Adils
Eystein
Yngwar
Onund
Ingiald
Olaf
Halfdan
Eystein
Halfdan
b. 851
Gudrod
Olaf
Halfdan
Harald
Sigge
Reri
Wolsung
Sigmund
Dyggve
Dag
Agne
Alric and Eric
Yngve Alf
Jorund and Eric Hugleik
On

was slain in A.D. 548, in the same degree as Eormenric who died in A.D. 560, Ceawlin who died in A.D. 592, Pybba the father of Penda, Eoppa the father of Ida, and Æscwine the father of Sleda; and Hermanaric and Theodoric are each removed one degree farther from their common ancestor Geat, than their respective cotemporaries Wihtgils and Eormenric; so that the whole series of the genealogies of the children of Woden, appear to be a little in advance of the Gothic genealogy, in the fourteenth degree from Geat.

Again, Hencgest came to Britain in A.D. 428, at which time he was the father of a warrior of full age, and of the maiden who became the wife of Vortigern, so that we may safely set down his age at about forty-five; and reckoning the generations upwards at thirty years each, (though a less average would suffice), the birth of Wecta might be about A.D. 291. In the case of Penda, born A.D. 576, a larger average would be required, to get a date for the birth of Weothelgeat within reasonable limits of the same period; but we are expressly informed that Wærmund was far advanced in years when Offa was born; that Offa did not marry until a late period of his life; that Penda had eleven brothers, of whom nine probably were older than himself; and, in the collateral descent, we seem to have an indication that the elder line had been superseded by a younger.[20] If we compute thirty years to a generation, from A.D. 849, the date of Ælfræd's birth, that of Bældæg's might fall about A.D. 309; and the same average from A.D. 586, when Eadwine was born, would place the birth of Wægdæg about A.D. 296. In fact every one of these genealogies is perfectly consistent with the supposition, that the close of the third century and the beginning of the fourth was the period of the births of Woden's sons, (who are said to have been thirty in number), and that consequently they were of full age to un-

[20] The Iclings, or descendants of Icæl, were "the oldest and noblest family in Mercia."

dertake the government of kingdoms, at the time we have assigned for his expedition.

The Danish genealogy in the Langfedgatal[21] gives us twenty generations down to Ragnar Lodbrok, who was the cotemporary of the West Saxon Æthelwulf; but it is to be remarked that Dan is not called the son of Olaf, nor Fridleif the son of Frode Fridsami, nor Sigurd Hring the son of Haralld Hilditavnn. Dan and his son, therefore, are probably collaterally related to this line, and one or two generations may be deducted from this number. In the former case, the average of the generations would be about twenty-eight years, in the latter thirty;, supposing Ragnar to have been about sixty years old at the time of his death, and Skiold to have been born during the last decade of the third century.

It is evident that a correct genealogy cannot be deduced from the Ynglinga Saga; for the notices it contains of the cotemporary Danish kings show, that kings have been erroneously fathered upon their predecessors, in many instances. Fiölner, the second of this line, was cotemporary with Fridfrode, the third of the Danish; and it is said that Domar, the seventh, married the sister of Dan, the ninth of the Danish, a confirmation of our suspicion that his name is collateral, and must be placed in the eighth degree of descent. In the fourth degree after Domar, we have Alric and Eric, the latter of whom is said to have married Dag's daughter Dagrid; it is, therefore, probable that Agne, his father, was not the son, but (if related) the brother of Dag. Again, under the reign of On, the seventh from Domar, we are told, that during these

[21] Odenn, Skioldr h. s., Fridleifr h. s., Fridfrode h. s., Fridleifr h. s., Havare Handrami h. s., Frode h. s., Varmundr Vitri h. s., Olafr Litillate h. s.; Danr Mikillate, Frode Fridsami h. s., Fridleifr, Frode Fækni h. s., Ingialdr (Starkadar fostri) h. s.; Halfdan brodir hans, Helgi oc Roar, hans synir, Hrolfr Kraki Helga son, Hærekr Hnavggvanbaugi, Ingiald's son, Frode h. s.; Halfdan h. s., Hærekr Slavngvanbaugi h. s., Haralldr Hilditavnn h. s., Sigurdr Hringr, Ragnar Lodbrok h. s.

seven generations, and the two intermediate reigns of Alf and Hugleik, Dan, Frode, his son, and Fridleif and Halfdan, his grandsons, reigned in Denmark; eight generations in the Swedish line corresponding to three in the Danish; so that, besides the errors already indicated, it is probable there are several others. Egil, the son of On, made an alliance with Frode Fækni; Ottar, Egil's son, broke the treaty, and fell in conflict with Frode; Adils, Ottar's son, was at war with Helge, Frode's grandson; and Hrolf Krake, Helge's son, perished during the reign of Eystein, Adils' son. Thus, for four generations these lines coincide again; and for the rest, the Swedish succession appears to be one in excess of the Danish, which is not inconsistent with probability. Ingiald by this genealogy appears to be the fifth, and his conqueror, Ivar Vidfadme,[22] was the sixth ancestor of Harald Haarfagr.

---

[22] Ivar Vidfadme is said to have conquered the fifth part of England. The statement that he was the sixth ancestor of Harald Haarfagr, who was born in A.D. 851, would make it appear that he flourished during the latter part of the seventh century. He was, therefore, cotemporary with Ine, King of the West-Saxons, whose brother Ingild was the sixth ancestor of Ælfræd, who was born in A.D. 849. It is not stated in our chronicles how Ine obtained the kingdom; but this notice shows, that there may be some truth in the story which we find in the Brut, and most fully in Layamon's version—that Cædwealha, on the eve of his departure for Rome, A.D. 688, invited Inyr and his cousin Ivor to take possession of his kingdom, and that they came with a large fleet.

Ivar may really have been Ine's cousin, for the occurrence of the name Ingild, (so common in Swedish and Danish histories), but once in our genealogies, and then as that of Ine's brother, suggests the probability that Cœnræd, their father, contracted an alliance with a Danish princess. Under all these circumstances we may regard it as almost certain, that Ivar assisted Ine in defeating the pretensions of rival claimants to the throne, and in establishing his authority, and then returned to his own dominions.

Lappenberg observes, that "the Welsh historians adopted the policy of "purloining from a successful enemy, and skilfully transferring to his "British cotemporaries, if not to imaginary personages, the object and "reward of his battles, the glory and lastingness of his individuality in "history." Thus, Cædwealha, Ine, and Ivar are claimed by them as Cadwaladyr, Inyr, and Ivor.

It has seemed requisite to enter into these particulars, in order to show that this genealogy cannot be fairly collated with the rest. But, indeed, it cannot claim to be considered of equal authority, for it is presented to us for the first time in a work of the thirteenth century, whilst those we have had under consideration, come to us on the authority of writers of the sixth, eighth, ninth, and tenth; nor can the evidence of one document have much weight when opposed to that of ten others. The succession of kings is probably historical, and appears to be genealogical in the beginning and at the end; but there are certainly interruptions in the direct descent, in the middle, at the very time, too, when a similar interruption is indicated in the Danish succession. It is, however, of great value, inasmuch as it coincides with and confirms the Danish genealogy, in that part which may be regarded as most open to suspicion, which comprises the names of the immediate descendants of Woden.

Thus, an examination of the various lines of descent of the posterity of Geat, has shown us that the Gothic, Longobardic, Anglo-Saxon, and Danish genealogies, are perfectly consistent each with the others. Presenting, as they do, so many remarkable parallels, they are surely entitled to be received in good faith, regarded as real genealogies, not mere arbitrary successions of fictitious names. They are, in fact, witnesses, and, (seeing that they are entirely distinct and unconnected), unimpeachable witnesses, each to the truth and genuineness of the others. It can hardly be believed that the Goths in Eastern, the Longobards in Central, and the Danes in Northern Europe, could have constructed at hap-hazard so many genealogical series, as nearly coincident as we could have expected to find them, even if we had been able to verify them historically in each successive degree. They are, therefore, substantially genuine; errors there may, indeed, be in them, but not many.

There is nothing inconsistent with the theory, that Geat

flourished about the end of the first century, and that Woden was born in the latter half of the third; that he commenced his migration about A.D. 325, and conquered Russia and Germany in the years immediately following. On the contrary, it is confirmed by many facts connected with the history of the Goths and Longobards, and with the genealogies; and Geat's and Woden's places in history may be considered as probably determined.

It is admitted, of course, that these were names of gods, but that did not prevent them from being assumed by men. Thor was also the name of a god; it was that of one of Woden's twelve chiefs, according to Norse tradition; and, sixty years earlier than the date we have assigned for his migration, it was borne by Thuro, one of the four Gothic chieftains who ravaged Asia Minor in the reign of Gallienus. So the original Geat and Woden may have had many namesakes, though probably only in the line of the Anses, Asar, or Osas, who claimed descent from them.

The son of Vortigern by Hencgest's daughter is called Gotta in the triads; the Scald Deor celebrates the love of another Geat and Mæthhild; the great-grandfather of Ingiald I, King of Hleidre, and a Viking, who is named in several Runic inscriptions in Scandinavia and Man, were called Gaut.

The name of Woden would certainly not be given to any one after the conversion of our forefathers to Christianity, yet it occurs so frequently in neighbourhoods connected with the memory of Horsa and Hencgest, that I am convinced one of their associates was so named.

Thurscross in Yorkshire, Thursby in Cumberland, Thursford in Norfolk, Thurston in Suffolk, Thurstable in Essex, Thursfield in Staffordshire; Geatescumb[23] in Berkshire, Gatesden and Gatesbury in Hertfordshire, and Gateshead[24] in

[23] Codex Diplomaticus, 1171. Ibid. 410.

[24] Bæda explains this name "ad capræ caput," but, strange as it may

Durham; Wansford in Northamptonshire, Wansford in Yorkshire, Wansbeck in Northumberland, Wednesbury and Wednesfield in Staffordshire, Wodnesborough in Kent, Woodnesborough and the Wansdyke in Wiltshire; all I believe bear the names of men, early settlers in this country, not of gods.

Bald (the Norse Baldr) was the name of a god, yet it was borne by men. Jordanis tells us that the Balthas were next in nobility to the Amalas, and as the Amalas were descendants of Amal, so must the Balthas have been descendants of Balth. Bald was also a personal name amongst the Franks, and must have been amongst our forefathers also, as Baldslow in Essex shows.

In the last chapter we had occasion to notice an epitaph, written for one of his *gesithas* by the first King of the East Angles, before his coming to Britain; an inscription containing the names of two of the forefathers of Ida; and bracteates impressed with names which occur in the Mercian and Kentish genealogies; and as an additional, and very important illustration of the subject of the present chapter, we may fitly conclude it with a notice, of what may be regarded as the epitaph of the grandfather of Horsa and Hencgest, written in Roman capitals on a stone pillar at Kirkliston in Lothian.

IN (H)OC TVMVLO IACIT VETTA F VICTI'
"In this tomb lies Vetta son of Victus."

---

seem, his explanations of local names are not to be depended upon. For instance he translates *Strenæshalch*, "sinus phari," but we have a Strensall in Yorkshire, a Strenshall in Warwickshire, and a Strensham in Worcestershire, all inland; showing that these places bear the name of an individual *Stren*. *Heruteu* he translates "insula cervi," and *Selæscu*, "insula vituli marini," yet *eu*, in his dialect is "water," not "island," and neither of these places is an island, but each has a considerable mere adjoining. Both are on the coast; but we have an instance of the same termination in *Læstingaeu*, which is far inland. So *Geátes heáfod* is really the hill of Geat, *heáfod* being commonly applied to rising grounds.

The name of Wecta, (Wehta or Wihta), the son of Woden, might well be written Wict or Wiht by a Teutonic, or Victus by a Latin hand, (as we have the forms Hors and Horsus, for Horsa); and, indeed, it appears to be the primary element in that of his grandson Wictgils or Wihtgils; so that in "Vetta son of Victus" we have actually the "Witta son of "Wecta" of the Kentish genealogy. This coincidence has been remarked by Dr. Simpson of Edinburgh, as well as by myself; and as the history of the province in which this monument stands, (the ancient Valentia), speaks of the presence of Saxons there, at a time when Wecta and Witta may have been living, it is probable that we have more than a mere coincidence here, that this is really the sepulchral memorial of the grandson of Woden.

For Ammianus Marcellinus[25] tells us, that the Picts, *Saxons*, Scots, and Attacots, were continually ravaging the Roman provinces in Britain, from A. D. 364 to 368, and at length reduced them to the last extremity; that Severus was despatched to Britain, but immediately recalled, and Jovinus sent in his stead; and that the intelligence of the state of Britain, which he sent home, was so alarming, that Theodosius was entrusted with the charge of restoring the fortunes of the Empire there, because it was felt that none but a commander of the highest character, such as his, was equal to the emergency. He landed at Rutupiæ in A. D. 368, marched towards London, which was in the greatest danger, defeated on the way several parties of marauding Barbarians, by judiciously dividing his forces, and entered the city triumphantly. So strong, however, was the Barbarian confederacy, that he was convinced it was to be overcome rather by craft[26]

[25] xxvi. 4; xxvii. 8, 9.

[26] "Ubi ad audenda majora prospero successu elatus, tutaque scrutando "consilia, futuri morabatur ambiguus, diffusam variarum gentium plebem "et ferocientem immaniter, non nisi per dolos occultiores et improvisos "excursus superari posse, captivorum confessionibus et transfugarum

than by force of arms; and his first step was to detach from it those who had deserted from the Roman cause, many of whom, by promises of impunity, he induced to return to their allegiance. In A.D. 369 he marched from London, defeated the Barbarians, restored the cities and fortresses, and gave to the province which he thus recovered for the Empire, the name of Valentia, in honour of his master. If Claudian's[27] and Pacatus'[28] flattering panegyrics may be accepted as evidence, he was victorious by sea as well as by land, and pursued the Picts, Scots, and Saxons, as far as the Orkneys.

We have fuller details of these transactions in the pages of Fordun, Boece, and the Brut, for it is evident that they are the same as those of which these historians make Maximus the hero. To Maximus the Britons would naturally give all the credit possible, as being a descendant of their native kings; and Zosimus[29] tells us that he actually served with Theodosius in Britain at this time. These historians must have been indebted, for their narratives of the events of this war, to independent sources; for whilst they differ in many details, and in the dates[30] they assign to them, they are accordant as to the leading facts; and these, which strikingly illustrate Ammianus' story, we may accept. It will be necessary, in order to establish their credibility, to go back to an earlier period of the history.

"indiciis doctus. Denique edictis propositis impunitateque promissâ, de-"sertores ad procinctum vocabat, et multos alios per diversa libero com-"meatu dispersos. Quo monitu ut rediere plerique, incentivo percitus, "retentusque anxiis curis," &c.

27 "Maduerunt Saxone fuso
"Orcades; incaluit Pictorum sanguine Thule;
"Scotorum cumulos flevit glacialis Ierne."
CLAUDIAN. *In iiii. Cons. Honorii*, 31.

28 "Saxo consumptus bellis navalibus offeretur? Redactum ad paludes "suas Scotum loquar?" PACATUS, *Panegyr.* c. 5.

29 c. 35.

30 Fordun represents the war as enduring five years, from A.D. 355 to 360, Boece dates its conclusion A.D. 379, and the Brut five years previous to Maximus' abandonment of Britain.

The Emperor Constantine was assisted in his struggle with Maxentius, by three British princes,[31] Trahern, Leolin, and Mauricius. After his departure, one Octavius, with a few adherents, rose against aud slew the Roman governors, was elected King of the Britons, and then expelled the Imperial forces. Trahern was sent against him, and was defeated; but sailed to Scotland, and, after ravaging the country, encountered him again, and put him to flight. Octavius went to Norway,[32] and thence sent messages to his partisans in Britain, instigating them against Trahern. One of them, a magistrate of a municipal town,[33] at length found an opportunity of assassinating him.[34] Octavius then returned, dispersed the Imperial troops, recovered the kingdom, and by uniting the Picts and Scots in firm alliance with the Britons, was enabled to maintain his independence until the reign of Gratian and Valentinian. This brings us to A. D. 364, the year of Valentinian's accession, as the earliest, (and I believe that it is the true), basis for the dates of the events which follow.

In his struggle with Maxentius, British auxiliaries certainly formed part of Constantine's forces; and after he found himself firmly seated on the throne, Eusebius says he passed over to Britain, and subjugated it. There had, therefore, been a rebellion in the interval, and, (as it is not necessary to suppose that the Emperor went in person), the British story merely supplies the names of the rebel, and of the general who was sent to oppose him. It is consistent with the information which Eusebius supplies, with regard to the circumstances of

---

[31] The Brut calls them uncles of Constantine; neither Fordun nor Boece mention this relationship.

[32] Boece and the Brut say he went to Norway; Fordun says, to Scotland.

[33] Layamon calls him Aldolf.

[34] Boece, in accordance with the Brut, says that Traherius was slain in Octavius' absence; Fordun, that Octavius killed him in battle.

the commencement of Octavius' reign; and as we shall see that it is also consistent with regard to those which occurred at its close and afterwards, we may assume that it is true in substance with regard to the events of the interval. The statement, that a British prince was enabled to maintain his independence during half a century, is by no means inconsistent with the few notices which we find in classical authors, relative to Roman affairs in Britain during the interval. Octavius, though unable to expel the Romans from the country, may yet have been strong enough to hold his own, and to give them occasional annoyance, such as that which provoked the visits of Constans and Lupicinus;[36] and, indeed, the confederacy which he organized, of Britons, Picts, and Scots, was so strong, that even Theodosius despaired of being able to cope with it, by force of arms alone.

In his old age, as he had no son, Octavius desired to settle the succession to his throne. Caradoc, one of his chief princes, advised him to name Maximus[37] as his successor, and thereby incurred the displeasure of Octavius' nephew Conan, and of others who advocated his claims. Caradoc, however, sent his son Mauricius to Rome to invite Maximus; and, it is said, found him disaffected towards Gratian and Valentinian, on account of their refusal to give him a third part of

---

[36] Julius Firmicus says, that Constans went to Britain during the winter, and awed the Britons by his presence:—"Insperatam imperatoris "faciem Britannus expavit;" about A.D. 340. Ammianus alludes to his narrative of this event, but the narrative itself, unfortunately, is lost.

In A.D. 353, after the fall of Magnentius, Paulus was sent to Britain, to punish those who had favoured his cause.

In A.D. 360 the Picts and Scots ravaged the border provinces, and Julian, afraid to leave the Gauls exposed to the hostility of the Alamanni, sent Lupicinus to oppose them, but it does not appear that he achieved anything of importance.

[37] The Brut calls him the son of Leolin, Constantine's uncle; Fordun, "consanguineus" of Constantine. Leolin, who accompanied Constantine to Rome, might be his uncle, but the father of Maximus could not.

the Empire. This is not impossible; for the Empire was divided in this year, and the East given to Valens,—Valentinian, (at whose court their father Gratian, though not yet Augustus, doubtless enjoyed the highest consideration), retaining the West; and, as Boece says that Maximus was sent by Etius (Æquitius) with the sanction of the Emperor, the invitation from Britain might seem to them a favourable opportunity, of satisfying the ambition of a dangerous rival. Maximus gladly responded to it, and came to Britain with an army which he had collected on his way. Octavius, fearing that this was a hostile invasion, commanded Conan to oppose him with all the forces of his kingdom. Maximus, however, was received with welcome [38] by those who had invited him, and civil war was the result, in which, after several conflicts, he overcame his opponents. Conan retired to Scotland, raised an army of Britons, Picts, Scots, *and others collected from all quarters*, passed the Humber, encountered Maximus, and was again defeated. Octavius now submitted,[39] acknowledged Maximus his successor, and bestowed on him the hand of his daughter in marriage. These events, I suppose, occurred in A.D. 364. A year, probably, must be allowed between them and the renewal of the war.

Conan fled to Scandinavia,[40] collected a fresh army, invaded the provinces south of the Humber, and the war was continued for three years,[41] (*i. e.* from A.D. 365 to 368), with alternate success. Probably Maximus found himself in the end unequal to the struggle, and his demands for assistance from Rome procured the appointment of Theodosius; the

---

[38] I follow Fordun here, as his narrative seems more probable than that in the Brut, which says that Conan allowed himself to be persuaded by Caradoc to refrain from hostilities.

[39] According to the Brut, his determination to bestow his kingdom and the hand of his daughter on Maximus was the occasion of Conan's first flight.

[40] Fordun says, to Scotland again.

[41] Fordun.

working of whose plans to break the Barbarian confederacy by craft, we now discern in this story.

The Scots, it is said, had suffered much in this war, and desired peace, but without prejudice to their allies. The Britons, who favoured Conan's pretensions, afraid of being abandoned, made peace also, and Conan agreed to make common cause with Maximus. Here we observe the result of Theodosius' promises of immunity; Conan and his party were the deserters, whom Ammianus represents as returning to their allegiance.

For a year Maximus maintained peace outwardly with the Scots, but secretly stirred up the Picts to make war upon them, and made a treaty with the Picts at York, intending to subdue each nation in its turn. The Picts, supported by all the Britons save Conan and his party, attacked the Scots fiercely, and a destructive war ensued, the scenes of which Boece places in Westmoreland, Annandale, and Galloway.

In the following year Maximus took the field in person with his Pictish allies, and defeated the Scots in a bloody battle, in which their King Eugenius was slain. Ethodh, his brother, fled with his son Erth to Ireland,[42] others to Norway. Maximus buried the bodies of the slain, and performed the funeral obsequies for Eugenius.[43] The reduction of the Picts, who had been much weakened by their conflict with the Scots, was now an easy task, and all their fortresses fell into the hands of Maximus. He is said, however, to have maintained friendly relations with them, and, five years later, we shall find Vortigern, who married his daughter, "holding "under the Romans the sovereignty of the Picts."

Throughout this struggle with the forces of the Empire it

---

[42] Boece says that they fled to Norway, that Erth married a Danish princess, and had by her a son, Fergus, who was afterwards associated with Alaric in the capture of Rome. Norway, in these accounts, is not the country now known by the name, but Holland.

[43] Boece.

is clear that the Teutonic race were actively engaged. It was by their aid that Octavius established his independence. Ammianus enables us to add the name of the *Saxons*, to the Picts and Scots, as the *other allies* of the revolted Britons, whom Fordun mentions but does not name. It was to Scandinavia, (according to the Welsh Brut), that Conan's second flight was directed; the panegyrists say that the Saxons were vanquished by Theodosius; and Fordun and Boece that Norway was the refuge of some of the fugitives from this contest. It is far from improbable that Wecta and Witta were the leaders of these Saxons, and that Witta fell in the conflict[44] which restored Valentia to the Empire; and Boece's statement, relative to Maximus' care for the obsequies of the slain, will happily account for the fact, that this epitaph is written in the Latin language and characters; had the monument been erected for Witta by his own people it would have been written, we may believe, in the same dialect as Woodurid's, and in runes. With these probabilities,—or even with the alternative which presents itself, that Witta might be the leader of the Saxons who were received by Vortigern, in A. D. 375,—our chronology, in which we have fixed the date of Wecta's birth in the last decade of the third century, is perfectly consistent.

---

[44] The name of this monument, the Cat (*i.e.* "battle") stane, suggests the inference that Witta fell in a battle, of which the neighbourhood seems to present other traces. Sixty yards to the west stood a large tumulus which was opened in 1824, and found to contain several skeletons; near Edinburgh, about four miles to the east, there were formerly two very large conical cairns, called also Cat-stanes, beneath which were found cists containing skeletons, and weapons of iron and bronze; a few yards to the north-west of these still stands a monument, eleven feet high, called the Caiy-stane, in the neighbourhood of which a quantity of human bones have been found irregularly interred without cists; not far from it are still visible the rude earthworks of an ancient camp, and much more extensive intrenchments, of an oval form, once existed in the vicinity; and about half a mile distant from the site of the Cat-stanes, there is another standing stone, and two larger ones lying together.—(See Wilson's Prehistoric Annals of Scotland).

CHAPTER IV.

Local Nomenclature, as Illustrative of the Conquest of Britain.

THE verification of these genealogies has an important relation to the history of the conquest of Britain. The kindred of Hencgest are frequently mentioned, and it is probable that the descendants of their common ancestor, Woden, would be the leaders of the various tribes who followed his fortunes. As these were cotemporary in the ninth and tenth degrees, Hrothmund and Hryp, Wærmund and Offa, Icæl and Cnebba, Aloc and Ingui, Sæfugel and Seomel, Elesa and Cerdic, Swæppa and Sigefugel, Cædbæd and Bubba, would be cotemporary with Hencgest and Octa. Accordingly, wherever these historic chieftains have left the traces of their victorious career, in the names of places derived from theirs, we find similar traces of their kindred, most of whom are known to us only by their being named in these genealogies.

The instances which the Saxon Chronicle supplies, of Wippedes-fleot, so called after Wipped who fell in the battle there fought; of Cymenesore, named after Cymen who landed there with his father and brothers; and of Cerdicesore, Cerdicesford, and Cerdices-leah, marking the scenes of Cerdic's landing and conflicts; show that it was customary to bestow the names of the invaders of Britain on their battle-fields, or settlements. So the many traces of Horsa and Hencgest, which remain on the face of England from north to south, may fairly be presumed to indicate their gradual career of conquest, from their first battle near Stamford, and their subsequent settlement in Northumbria, to their final establishment in Kent; and as we always find such traces in the districts, in which the history tells us these brothers were actually engaged, so they will serve in some measure to fill up what is wanting, when the history is silent.

It is possible, of course, that others might have borne these names besides the first Hencgest and Horsa and their nephews, although we know of none who did; but the occurrence of these and a certain class of other names, grouped together in different districts, from Northumberland to Hampshire, and from Norfolk to Somersetshire, requires some cause to account for it, antecedent to the division of this country into kingdoms; and, therefore, necessarily refers us to the fifth century, the epoch of the Horsas and Hencgests.

Following, therefore, the career of these chieftains, we have first, in the district around Stamford, Horsey hill, near Peterborough, and Horsegate, near Market Deeping; then, in Yorkshire, Horsefield and Hinchcliff, near Holmfirth, Horseforth, near Leeds, Horsall, near Halifax, and Horsehouse, near Middleham; in Northumberland, three Horseleys; in Norfolk, Horsey, Horsford, Horsham, Horstead, and Hensthead; in Suffolk, Hensthead; in Essex, Horsey isle, and Hinckford; in Kent, Hinxhill; in Surrey, Horsall and Horsley; in Sussex, Horsebridge, two Horsteads, Horsell, and Horsham; in Derbyshire, Horsley; in Leicestershire, Horsepool and Hinckley; in Staffordshire, Horseley and Hincksford; in Worcestershire, Hengestesheale,[1] (not far

[1] Codex Diplomaticus, 570, 1251.

from Hincksford), Horseley and Horsecliff in the same district, Horsham, Hengestesbróc,[2] and Hengestesheafod;[3] on the borders of Oxfordshire and Berkshire, Horsepath in the former, near Hincksey (Hengestesige) in the latter, Hengestes-geat,[4] and Hengesthescumb; in Gloucestershire, Horsley; in Somersetshire, Henstridge (Hengesteshricg)[5] and Horscumb;[6] in Hampshire, Horsdon, Hursley (Horsanleah),[7] Horsford, Hensting, Hengistbury head, Hincstes gréf,[8] and Hengestes path;[9] in Cornwall, Hengeston (Hengestesdún) and Horsebridge; in Hertfordshire, Hinxworth (Haingesteuuorde);[10] and on its borders in Cambridgeshire, Horseheath and Hinxton.

The events of their history enable us to account for the presence of Horsa and Hencgest in nearly every one of these districts, as well as for the more frequent occurrence of the name of Horsa. It is impossible, of course, to determine in every case which of the two pairs of brothers are commemorated in these local names; but it seems very probable that those in Oxfordshire and Berkshire indicate a settlement of the second, and that those in Huntingdonshire, Lincolnshire, Yorkshire, Northumberland, and the Eastern coast counties, mark the career of the first.

Associated with their names we find those of their kindred and cotemporaries, and of others who may be believed to have followed their fortunes, from the frequent occurrence of their names in this connection, although it does not appear that they were of the same race.

Thus we meet with the name of Ossa, the brother of Horsa and Hencgest, at Ossett in Yorkshire, Oslow and Oscott in Staffordshire, Oseney near Oxford, Osanstoc[11] in Dorsetshire, and Osanlea;[12] that of Octa, the son of Hencgest, at Otley in

---

[2] Codex Diplomaticus, 536. [3] Ib. 150. [4] Ib. 648. [5] Ib. 714.
[6] Ib. 566. [7] Ib. 1065. [8] Ib. 597. [9] Ib. 1235.
[10] Domesday. [11] C. D. 701. [12] Ib. 1280.

Yorkshire; Otford (Ohtanford), Otham, and Otanhyrst[13] in Kent; and Otley in Sussex; that of Oeric, a younger son, at Orricesdén,[14] near Sandhurst, in Kent; and at the two Orchestons, near Stonehenge, in Wiltshire, (in which district Hencgest was, soon after the only mention of this name in the history); that of Oisc or Wisc at Wishley in Surrey, and Wishford in Wiltshire; that of Ebissa, whom the Irish version of the History of the Britons calls the son of Hencgest's sister, at Ebbsfleet in Kent, Ebbesborne in Wiltshire, and perhaps also at Happisburgh in Norfolk, Hapsford in Cheshire, and Apspond near St. Albans; and that of Æsc very frequently in all the districts above-named, as, for instance, at Ashbury (Æscesbyrig) in Berkshire; Ashbury, Ashcomb, and Ashford in Devonshire; Ashby in Leicestershire; and Ashford near Hinxhill in Kent.

All these were immediately related to Horsa and Hencgest. Frisian tradition tells us of a sister of theirs named Swane; her name we find at Swanwick in Derbyshire, not far from Horsley; three Swantons (Swanetún)[15] in Norfolk, a few miles to the west of the group of parishes which bear the name of Horsa; Swanborough near Horstead in Sussex; Swanthorpe, about a mile from Horsdon in Hampshire; Swanage on the coast of Dorsetshire, opposite to Hengistbury head; and Swanborough in Wiltshire.

Another female name occurs so frequently in this connection, that I am convinced she must have been of this family, if not the wife of Hencgest, whose coming is expressly noticed. We find it at Wilber clough, near Holmfirth, and at Wilberfoss in Yorkshire; Wilburge-wella[16] in Kent;

---

[13] Codex Diplomaticus, 198, 409. [14] Ib. 281.

[15] The ancient forms of the names of these places determine the sex of their original possessor. The masculine name *Swan* formed the genitive *Swanes;* the feminine genitive was *Swane.* Thus Swanscombe bears the name of a man, Swanetun, and the rest in the text, that of a woman.

[16] Codex Diplomaticus, 282.

Wilburge weg,[17] near Ashbourne, in Derbyshire; Wilbraham (Wilburgeham), about eight miles from Horseheath and Hinxton, and Wilburton, in Cambridgeshire; and at Wilburge gemæro,[18] and Wilburge mere[19] in Wiltshire, not far from Ashcombe and Ebbesbourne.

The name of Hrothmund, the ancestor of the East Anglian kings, appears at Romanby (Romundebi)[20] in Yorkshire; Rodmundesdæn,[21] near Endford, in Wiltshire; Romansleigh in Devonshire; and in that of the river Roman in Essex. As, however, these compound names have generally become contracted in pronunciation, in the course of time, it is not unlikely that Hrothmund's name may be concealed in those of the Rothleys, Rothburys, &c., of which we have many in this connection. That of his son Hryp occurs at Ripton in Huntingdonshire, Ripley in Yorkshire, and many other places of the same or similar names, in Derbyshire, Worcestershire, Kent, and Sussex.

With regard to Wærmund, the ancestor of the Mercian kings, we have a positive statement that he reigned over the West Angles, that is, in the districts which were afterwards known as the kingdom of Mercia; and whatever may be the truth with regard to Warwick, we certainly find his name at Warmley in Warwickshire; Warmlow (Wærmundeshlǽw),[22] Wærmundes-erne,[23] and Wærmundingc-ford[24] in Worcestershire. We find it also in other districts connected with the memory of Horsa and Hencgest; at Warmfield and Warmsworth in Yorkshire; Wærmundesham[25] (now Mundham) in Sussex; Warmscomb in Oxfordshire; Warmwell in Dorsetshire; and Wærmundestrew[26] in Wiltshire. His father's name Wihtlæg occurs at Wihtlachesford[27] in Worcestershire, and possibly also at Whittlesford and Whittlesea in Cambridgeshire, and Whittlebury in Northamptonshire.

[17] Codex Diplomaticus, 588. [18] Ib. 641. [19] Ib. 387.
[20] Domesday. [21] Codex Diplomaticus, 1110. [22] Ib. 1368.
[23] Ib. 262. [24] Ib. 649. [25] Ib. 18.
[26] Ib. 641. It is named next after Wilburge gemæro. [27] Ib. 493.

Of Icæl, whom, for reasons before stated, I regard as a co-temporary and relative of Wærmund, we have traces at Icklesham in Sussex, Icæles æwylmas[28] in Hampshire, Ickleton, near Hinxton, in Cambridgeshire, and Ickleford, about six miles to the south-west of Hinxworth, in Hertfordshire; and at about the same distance to the south of this last, one of Cnebba at Knebworth.

The Beornecas, or family of Beornec, appear to have left their name to Barnack, near Stamford, in Northamptonshire, where we begin to trace the career of these chieftains, and to Barnacle in Warwickshire. That of Wægbrand may perhaps be traced at Weybread in Suffolk, and at Wyburnbury in Cheshire. That of Aloc appears more distinctly at Aukley (Alcheslie)[29] in Nottinghamshire; Alkborough in Lincolnshire; Aukland in Durham; and Alkham in Kent; and that of Ingui at Ingthorpe near Stamford; Ingham, not far from Aukley and Alkborough, in Lincolnshire; Ingoe in Northumberland; Ingham and Ingworth in Norfolk; Ingham in Suffolk; and Ingestrie in Staffordshire.

Of Elesa we have several traces; at Elsdon and Elswick in Northumberland; Elston and Elswick in Lancashire; Elston in Nottinghamshire; Elsworth in Cambridgeshire; Ellesborough in Buckinghamshire; Elston in Wiltshire; and Ellisfield in Hampshire.

The name of Scylf, which, (for reasons which will be given in the sequel), I regard as belonging to the Deiran genealogy, appears at Shelf in Yorkshire; Shelfanger in Norfolk; Shilton (Scylftún)[30] and Scylfrycg[31] in Oxfordshire; Shilton in Warwickshire; and Shelve in Shropshire. Of Seomel the Cambrian genealogist, (intending no doubt to inform us how the ancestors of Ælle first became connected with Northumbria), says, "He first conquered Deira and Bernicia."[32] Samlesbury, in

---

[28] Codex Diplomaticus, 595.

[29] Domesday.

[30] C. D. 775.

[31] Ib. 311.

[32] "Ipse primus superavit Deur o Berneich." "Superavit" is the

Lancashire, bears his name; as, perhaps, does Semley in Wiltshire, near Wilburge gemæro and Wærmundestrew.

The name of Swæppa occurs at Swepstone in Leicestershire; that of Sigefugel, perhaps, at Segglethorpe and Sigglesthorne in Yorkshire; and that of Bedca at Bakewell (Badecanwyl) in Derbyshire, near Ashborne; Badecanlea and Badecandene[33] in Hampshire; and Bedford (Bedcanford).

That of Cædbæd may perhaps be traced at Cadeby in Yorkshire; Cadeby in Leicestershire; two Cadburys in Somersetshire; another Cadbury and Cadleigh in Devonshire; and that of Bubba at Bubwith in Yorkshire; and Bubbenhall in Warwickshire.

Havar and Frode of the Danish line may also have been associated in Horsa's and Hencgest's enterprise. We have the name of the former at Haverholme and Haverstoc in Lincolnshire; Havercroft in Yorkshire; Haverthwaite in Lancashire; Heversham, near it, in Westmoreland; Haverhill in Essex; Haversham (Hæfæresham)[34] in Buckinghamshire; and Haverford in Pembrokeshire, the district in which Uther defeated the Irish and Saxon allies of Pascent. The name of Frode we have at Froggatt (Frodesgeat) in Derbyshire; Frodesham in Cheshire; Frocester in Gloucestershire; and Frodesley in Shropshire. The last is not in any of the districts connected with the memory of Hencgest, but in one referred to at a later period of our history, as containing the names of the Hrethlings, Geats, and Wihstan.

In Beowulf, (and there only), we have a notice of Wæls, the father of the Wælsings, and that in a way which suggests the probability, that he was a cotemporary of Horsa and Hencgest. There can be no doubt that a person of this name accompanied them; for we have Walsden, near Horsall,

---

reading of the Cottonian MS. which Gale used, and is certainly better than "separavit" of the others.

[33] Codex Diplomaticus, 595. [34] Ib. 721.

in Lancashire; Walsley, near Ashby, in Leicestershire; Walsall in Staffordshire; Walsgrove hill in Worcestershire; two Walshams in Norfolk; another in Suffolk; and Wælsleáh[35] in Somersetshire. Walsingham in Norfolk, and perhaps also Wolsingham in Durham, and Wolsington in Northumberland, bear the name of his family, the Völsungr of the Norse Sagas. Now in the Edda, Völsung is said to have been the grandson of Sigge, one of the sons of Woden; it seems, therefore, that he and Wæls are one; if so, (or if Wæls be his father), Wæls will be one degree higher than Horsa and Hencgest, and his probably a younger line of the family of Woden.

His son was Sigemund, and Sigemund's nephew was Fitela. Both these names are found in the same connection at Simondsley in Derbyshire; Simondstone in Lancashire; Simondside in Durham; Simondside hill in Northumberland; Simondsbury in Dorsetshire; Fittleworth in Sussex; and Fittleton in Wiltshire.

Besides these, who were all kinsmen and cotemporaries of Horsa and Hencgest, we have traces of other persons who appear to have lived at the same period, and who may be believed to have been associated with them.

Childeric, who accompanied or followed Octa and Ebissa, has given name to Hilderthorpe in Yorkshire, Ilderton in Northumberland, Hildersham (Hildricesham)[36] and Childerley in Cambridgeshire; Hilderston in Norfolk; Hildercle[37] in Suffolk; Childerditch in Essex; and Hilderstone in Staffordshire. I am satisfied of his identity with the historic Childeric, King of the Franks; and their name also occurs at Frankby in Cheshire, Frankley in Worcestershire, and Frankton in Warwickshire.

Wada is noticed in the Traveller's Tale, as having ruled the Hælsings. Hæls, the father of this family, would seem to have taken part in the conquest of Britain, for he has given

---

[35] Codex Diplomaticus, 816. [36] Domesday. [37] C. D. 1349.

name to Halsham in Yorkshire; Halsall in Lancashire; Halstead in Leicestershire; Halston in Shropshire; Halstead in Essex; Halstead and two Halstows in Kent; and Halse in Somersetshire; and at Helsington in Westmoreland we have the name of his family. In the districts in which Horsa and Hencgest landed, when advancing against the Picts, Wada has given his name to Wadenhoe; and his sons Ægel and Weland to Ailsworth, and the river which separates Lincolnshire from Northamptonshire; in Lincolnshire we have Aylesby; in Yorkshire, Wadsworth, Wadworth, Wadsley, and Aylesthorpe, the scene of one of the battles between Vortimer and the Angles; in Norfolk, Aylsham and Wayland hundred; in Kent, Aylesford near the Halstows; in Sussex, Wadhurst and Aylsham; in Leicestershire, Aylestone; in Worcestershire, Wadborough, Ægelslona,[38] and Welland; and in Buckinghamshire, Waddesdon and Aylesbury.

Procopius speaks of the Frisians as having settled in this country along with the Angles. Friesthorpe and Frieston in Lincolnshire, two Frystones in Yorkshire, two Friestons in Suffolk, another in Sussex, two Frisbys in Leicestershire, Friesden in Buckinghamshire and Frisdon in Wiltshire, seem to bear their name; whilst that of Fin, who is named as their king in Beowulf and the Traveller's Tale, occurs at Fineston in Lincolnshire, Finsthwaite in Lancashire, Finsham in Norfolk, Finsbury in London, and Finstock in Oxfordshire; that of Hildeburh, his queen, at Hillborough (Hildeburh wella)[39] near Finsham, and Hildeburhuurth[40] in Warwickshire; and that of Hoce, her father, at Hockham and Hockwold in Norfolk, Hockley in Essex, Hockcliffe in Bedfordshire, Hockley in Staffordshire, Hockworthy in Devonshire. Perhaps Hoces byrigels,[41] near Bedwin in Wiltshire, marks his resting-place.

A party of Longobards, or Winilas, (their original name

---

[38] Codex Diplomaticus, 549, 1361.
[39] Domesday.
[40] C. D. 62.
[41] Ib. 1266.

according to Paul Warnefrid), seem to have taken part in this enterprise, for we have indications of their presence at Windleden in Yorkshire; Winlaton and Windlestone in Durham; and Winnall in Hampshire. Not far from the first of these, Sheffield bears the name of Sceafa, whom the Traveller names as one of their princes; so also do Shafton near Barnsley, and the Sheffords in Bedfordshire and Berkshire.

Traces of the Wenlas or Vandals occur twice. An extensive earthwork in the parish of Barwick in Elmet, Yorkshire, is called Wendel-hill; and we have Wendlebury in Oxfordshire.

The Wærnas, another well-known race, have left their name to Warnford in Northumberland; Warnham in Sussex; Warnford and Warnborough in Hampshire: and Billing, their chief, to Billing in Northamptonshire; Billingborough and Billinghay in Lincolnshire; Billingley in Yorkshire; Billinge and Billington in Lancashire; Billingham and Billingside in Durham; two Billingfords in Norfolk; Billingsgate in London; Billingshurst in Sussex; and Billingsley in Shropshire.

Hrethel, the king of the Geats, the brother or brother-in-law of Swerting, has left his name to Raddleside dale in Yorkshire, Hredlestede[42] in Kent, and Rattlesden in Suffolk. The occurrence of a very similar name, Netel, near Hredlestede and Rattlesden, suggests the probability that it may have been that of a brother of his. Nettleham and Nettleton in Lincolnshire; Nettlestead in Suffolk; Nettleswell in Essex; Nettlestead in Kent; Nettlesden in Buckinghamshire; Nettlebed in Oxfordshire; Nettleton in Wiltshire; Nettlecombe in Somersetshire, and another in Dorsetshire, indicate the active part he took in the transactions of his time.

---

[42] Codex Diplomaticus, 377.

It seems probable that Healfdene and his sons, Heremod, Heorogar, Hrothgar, and Halga, already settled in Northumbria when Horsa and Hencgest came,[43] assisted them in their wars; for we find their names in Lincolnshire at Harmston (Hermodestone),[44] Harmthorpe (Hermodestorp),[44] and Harrowby (Herigerbi);[44] in Yorkshire at Haldenby, Harmby, Rogerthorpe, Hellaby (Helgebi),[44] Helwick (Helguuic),[44] and Hellifield (Helgefelt);[44] in Middlesex at Harmondsworth (Hermodesworde)[44] and Halliford (Helgeford);[45] in Dorsetshire at Halstock (Halganstoc);[46] and in Wiltshire at Hermodesthorne.[47] Throughout the whole range of these districts we have traces of their subjects the Danes, in such names as Denbury, Denby, Denton, &c.

Hnæf is mentioned in Beowulf as associated with Hencgest in the assault on Finnesham, and another Hnæf, prince of the Hocings, is noticed in the Traveller's Tale. Navisford and Navesby in Northamptonshire; Navistock in Essex; Hnæfes scylf[48] and Hnæfleáh[49] in Somersetshire; bear this name. Wod of the Thyringas, and Hringweald of the Here-faras, commemorated by the Traveller, probably also belong to the list of Hencgest's allies.

Thus do we find, in the districts which are connected with the memory of these great chieftains, the names not only of their kinsmen, but of all the heroes, who, (from the notices of them which occur in the few existing remains of the Anglo-Saxon Sagas), may be believed to have been associated with them. Doubtless, if we had more of these Sagas to assist us, this identification might have been extended. Such personal names as Alr, Beonæt, Beowa, Brada, Cynfar, Eormen, Fear, Hlyd, Hræfn, Hungar, Nægel, Pendere, Sumær, (an Alamannic name), and Thurstan, with others; and names of

---

[43] See the chapter on the history of this family. [44] Domesday.
[45] Codex Diplomaticus, 483. [46] Ib. 701.
[47] Ib. 174. [48] Ib. 595. [49] Ib. 430, 463.

tribes or families as the Herulas or Herelingas, Leonas, Seaxas, Sweordas, Hundingas, Wætlingas, Eormeningas, Stæningas, Hedingas, Beormingas, and Eardingas constantly occur in this connection.

Lappenberg's conjecture that the kindred tribes of Germany, and, in particular, the Frisians, Franks, and Longobards, took part with the Angles, Jutes, and Saxons in the subjugation and colonization of Britain, is abundantly confirmed, and the truth of the narratives of authors hitherto neglected, which tell us of Hencgest's conflicts in the North, is vindicated by our local nomenclature. The history of the conquest of Britain is written upon the face of the country.[50]

---

[50] I have seen a notice in the Athenæum, of a work on the subject of "Local Nomenclature;" but I have not seen the work itself, nor do I know whether the author takes the same view as I do. The present work was compiled long before the notice in question appeared.

CHAPTER V.

Early Settlements of the Teutonic Race in Britain.

IT is extremely probable that the Teutonic tribes had effected settlements in this country even during the time of its occupation by the Romans; the "Notitia Imperii" reveals to us the fact, that towards the close of the fourth century, a considerable extent of the eastern and southern coasts of Britain was so numerously colonized by Saxons, (emigrants no doubt from the opposite shores of Gaul), that it obtained the name of "Littus Saxonicum per "Britannias;" and the etymology of several local names, which occur for the first time in this document, is most readily deduced from Teutonic sources.

Thus Regulbium is but a Latinized form, of the name by which it was known in Anglo-Saxon times, and which, with a very slight orthographical variation, it retains to this day, commemorating its first possessor Raculf;[1] Anderida, as well as Andredes-ceaster and Andredes-leage, (noticed in the Saxon Chronicle), bore the name of a Teuton Anderid; Segedunum is evidently *Secga-dún*, the "fort of the Secgas," of whom we shall hear more in the sequel; Magnis probably derived

[1] Raculf, Raculfes-ceaster, Reculvers.

its name from that of a Teutonic chieftain, Mægen,[2] for we have a Mainsforth in Durham, a Mainsborough in Hampshire, and a Mainstone in Shropshire, which certainly were so called after some person of this name; and the same may probably be said of Dubris,[3] first mentioned in Antonine's Itinerary, of Æsica and others. So also Hunnum, on the wall, may bear the name of the Huns, who are repeatedly mentioned in the history of Britain, during the fourth and fifth centuries, (engaged, it is said, by the Emperor Gratian to oppose the usurper Maximus);[4] and it is interesting to notice this, because we shall have to speak of settlements of this race in Britain during the course of the present inquiry.

Again, the decidedly Teutonic names of the usurper Tetricus in the third century, of the ninth and tenth bishops of London, Dedwin and Thedred, and probably also of the thirteenth, Vodin,[5] who was killed by Hencgest, are evidence not only of the presence of Teutons in this country previous to the great immigration, but of their rank and importance also.

These indications are certainly of great value, but we have evidence to the same fact of a more precise character. From Dion Cassius we learn that Marcus Antoninus transplanted multitudes of the Marcomanni to Britain; and from Zosimus,

---

[2] As Magn, this name is found amongst the ancestry of Woden, and it is of common occurrence in Scandinavian history.

[3] We have Dovercourt, Doverdale, and Doverburne, in other parts of England, and Dovrefjeld in Norway.

[4] The Huns first entered Europe A.D. 374. The story of Gratian's engaging them to oppose Maximus, about ten years later, acquires some probability from the fact, that they were employed by Theodosius to keep the Goths in check, and that they decided for Honorius the battle of Florence, A.D. 405.

[5] These names appear in the list given by Joannes Phurnius, a Greek author of the eleventh century; and I see no reason to doubt its authenticity, though the (rather titular than proper) name of Restitutus, the representative of the See of London at the council of Arles, does not occur in it. I quote from the Rev. Beale Poste, as I have not access to the work in question.

that Probus established colonies of Vandals and Burgundians in this island. Aurelius Victor tells us that Constantine was accompanied by Crocus, a king of the Alamanni, when he fled from Rome to Britain; and that he relied chiefly on the support of this prince, when he declared himself Emperor, on the death of his father, A.D. 306. And Ammianus Marcellinus says that Valentinian appointed Fraomarius king of the Butinobantes, an Alamannic tribe settled near Mayence, in opposition to Macrianus, A.D. 371; and shortly afterwards, when his territory had been devastated by war, and he was unable to maintain his ground, invested him with tribunitial power, and sent him with his people to Britain. Their settlement was probably in Norfolk, where Bramerton seems to bear the name of the chief, and four Buckenhams that of the tribe.

Two passages in the History of the Britons refer to an arrival of Saxons in this country a little later. In the Vatican and Paris MSS. we read—

"When Gratian Æquantius reigned at Rome, the Saxons "were received by Gurthergirn, in the year CCCXLVII after "the Passion of Christ."

And—

"When Gratian Æquantius was consul in Rome, because "then the whole world was governed by the consuls of the "Romans, the Saxons were received by Guorthegirn, in the "year CCCXLVII after the Passion of the Lord."[6]

The Harleian MS. 3859, gives the former passage with this variation, "Gratiano Secundo Æquantio" for "Gratiano "Æquantio Romæ."

The Irish edition reads—

---

[6] "Regnante Gratiano Æquantio Romæ, Saxones autem a Gurther-"girno suscepti sunt anno CCCXLVII post Passionem Christi.

"Quando Gratianus Æquantius consul fuit in Româ, quia tunc a "consulibus Romanorum totus orbis regebatur, Saxones a Guorthe-"girno anno post Domini Passionem CCCXLVII, suscepti sunt."

"Gortigern held in peace under the Romans the government of the Cruithneans, Gratian and Æquit in the sovereignty of the Romans at that time. But it was from the birth of Christ CCCXLVII years."

A MS. of the tenth century, in the library of Corpus Christi College, Cambridge, contains the following variation after the genealogies of the kings:—

"When Gratian was consul the second time, and Æquitius the fourth, the Saxons were received by Wyrtgeorn, in the year CCCXLVIIII from the Passion of Christ."[7]

This last, and the reading of the Irish version are important, inasmuch as they clearly explain in one particular that of the MSS. first quoted, and show, that by Æquantius is meant, not a surname of Gratian, but a distinct person, Æquitius, his colleague in the consulate, A.D. 374.

The author of this history followed the authority of those who dated the Passion of Our Lord in the year of the consulate of the two Gemini A.D. 29; therefore the computation from the Passion must be reduced to that of the Incarnation by the addition of twenty-eight years; and thus we have A.D. 375 indicated as the date of an arrival of Saxons.[8] In A.D. 374 Gratian was consul for the third time, and Æquitius for the first; in A.D. 375 it is said there was no fresh election of consuls, because, in the preceding year, the Sarmatians had ravaged Pannonia, and this year is generally designated "Post consulatum Gratiani et Æquitii." It may, however, have been considered as a prolongation of their consulate,[9] in fact as the fourth of Gratian and the second of

---

[7] "Quando Gratianus fuit consul secundo, et Æquitius quarto, Saxones "a Wyrtgeorno suscepti sunt anno CCCXLVIIII a Passione Christi."

[8] It cannot of course be doubted that the scribe who interpolated this notice in the History of the Britons, has confounded this early arrival of Saxons, with their later coming under Horsa and Hencgest.

[9] The Fasti for A.D. 413 present a case exactly parallel to this. Idatius gives the year "Post consulatum Honorii IX et Theodosii V," then adds "Lucio cons." and mentions the execution of Heraclianus. Prosper

Æquitius, for the transposition of the numerals in the C. C. C. MS., and the reading, "when Gratian was consul for the "fourth time and Æquitius for the second," seems the easiest way of correcting the passage, and preferable to that which Mr. Hardy has suggested.[10] The year given in this MS., A.D.P. 349, answers to A.D. 377, the year of the actual fourth consulate of Gratian, not, however, with Æquitius, but with Merobaudes; and probably was designed as a correction of A.D.P. 347, which may have occurred in the original MS. from which this was copied, as it does in the Paris and Vatican MSS. A.D. 375, then, "Post consulatum "Gratiani et Æquitii," or, as it may have been reckoned in Britain, "Gratiano IIII et Æquitio II coss." is marked as the date of an arrival of Saxons; and the Irish version tells us that Vortigern then held, under the Romans, the government of the Picts. This statement deserves attention, because the author of this version has incorporated with it much other matter relative to the Picts, and may be well believed to have had the authority of tradition for it. It will appear in the sequel, that Vortigern's death must have occurred about A.D. 443; and as he certainly lived to a very advanced age, it is not impossible that he might have received a force of Saxons in A.D. 375. What is said of his governing the Picts, seems to be corroborated by the facts subsequently related, that the Picts had friendly relations with Constantine, and were admitted to offices of state during his reign, when Vortigern first appears in our history as his chief counsellor; and that, after the assassination of Constantine, he

---

naming Lucianus alone, says that Heraclianus had been his colleague, but, having rebelled against the Emperor, lost his dignity and life. So that this year was known as "Post consulatum, &c.," and also "Luciano "cons.;" as A.D. 375 may have been "Post consulatum, &c.," and also "Gratiano IV et Æquitio II coss."

[10] Monumenta Historica Britanniæ. Introductory remarks, p. 110, note 1.

placed a guard of Picts about the person of Constantius. The intimation that he was in alliance with the Romans, is substantiated by the fact, revealed to us by the Valle Crucis inscription, that he was married to a daughter of Maximus. This settlement of the Saxons must have been in the North, and its date was more than half a century prior to the great advent, with which Anglo-Saxon history properly commences.

CHAPTER VI.

Dates of the Accession of Vortigern, and of the Coming of the Angles.

THE date of the coming of the Angles is the basis of the subsequent chronology for seventy years; and fortunately we are enabled to establish it in the most satisfactory way.

The following Chronological Notes, which may have been written as early as the sixth century, are appended to four MSS.[1] of the History of the Britons.[2]

"From the two Gemini, Rufus and Rubelius, to the con-" sul Stilichio, are CCCLXXIII (read 'CCCLXVIII') years."

"Also, from Stilichio to Valentinian, the son of Placida, "and the reign of Guorthegirn, XXVIII years.

"And from the reign of Guorthegirn to the quarrel of "Guitolin and Ambrosius, which is Guoloppum, that is Cat

---

[1] Harl. 3859; Cotton. Vespasian, D. XXI. 1, B. XXV. 7, and Vitellius, A. XIII. 11.

[2] "A duobus Geminis, Rufo et Rubelio, usque in Stilichionem consulem "CCCLXXIII anni sunt. Item, a Stilichione usque ad Valentinianum filium "Placidæ, et regnum Guorthegirni, XXVIII anni. Et a regno Guorthe-"girni usque ad discordiam Guitolini et Ambrosii, anni sunt XII, quod est "Guoloppum, id est Cat Guoloph. Guorthegirnus autem tenuit imperium "in Brittanniâ, Theodosio et Valentiniano consulibus, et in quarto anno "regni sui Saxones ad Brittanniam venerunt, Felice et Tauro consulibus, "quadringentesimo anno ab Incarnatione Domini nostri Jesu Christi. Ab "anno quo Saxones venerunt in Brittanniam et a Guorthegirno suscepti "sunt, usque ad Decium et Valerianum anni sunt LXIX."

"Guoloph, are XII years. But Guorthegirn held rule in "Britain when Theodosius and Valentinian were consuls, "and in the fourth year of his reign, when Felix and Taurus "were consuls, in the four hundredth year from the Incar- "nation, (read 'from the Passion'), of our Lord Jesus "Christ, the Saxons came to Britain.

"From the year, in which the Saxons came to Britain, "and were received by Guorthegirn, to Decius and Valerian, "(read 'Joannes'), are LXIX (read 'LXX') years."

In this precious document, we have a series of dates, all connected with the history of Britain, except the first; and that is the basis of the computation from the Passion of Christ, the consulate of Rufus Geminus and Rubelius Geminus, A.D. 29. An excess of five years, (owing to the carelessness of a scribe who substituted X for V), must be deducted from the second in order to bring it into harmony with that which follows; it cannot refer to the consulate of Stilicho, A.D. 400, an event of no particular interest to Britain,[3] but to an event which was of the greatest interest, his coming to the assistance of the Britons; and the necessary correction of the numerals enables us to fix its date, A.D. 397. Twenty-eight years from this date bring us to the third consulate of Theodosins and first of Valentinian, A.D. 425, the year of Vortigern's accession; three years more to the consulate of Felix and Taurus, A.D. 428, the year of the coming of the Angles, A.D.P. 400; and seventy years again to the consulate of Decius Paulinus and Joannes Scytha, A.D. 498.[4] The reason why this date is given is, doubtless, this: that the seventy-first year from the coming of the Angles was,

---

[3] It would of course be quite natural to speak of one who had attained to consular rank, as the "consul," even in a relation of events which occurred before his elevation.

[4] In the last date, the scribe appears to have written LXIX for LXX, and given Valerian as the colleague of Decius, doubtless from his having been accustomed to associate their names together, as persecutors of the church in the third century.

(according to Henry of Huntingdon), the date of the establishment of the West-Saxon kingdom, with which his computation from the coming of the Angles ceases.[5]

The History of the Britons itself confirms the date, which these notes supply, for the accession of Vortigern. After the first notice of the colonization of Armorica by Maximus, it is said,—

"We have learned from the tradition of our elders, that "there were of the Romans seven emperors in Britain;"[6]— and shortly afterwards, evidently referring to the time of Maximus, and to the aforesaid tradition:[7]—

"So, as we have read, the Romans reigned among the "Britons during four hundred and nine years."

A comparison of these with other passages in this work, clearly shows that this period of four hundred and nine years must be computed from the time, when Augustus received the submission and tribute of the kings of Britain. This fact is recorded in the Ancyran inscription with the names of the kings, Dumno, Bellaunus, and Timantius; and this history records it in the following words:[8]—

"Octavianus Augustus holding the monarchy of the whole "world, for he alone received tribute from Britain."

Augustus was on the point of invading Britain B.C. 26, but was prevented by a revolt of the Salassii. During that and the following year, he was occupied in Spain, and when

---

[5] This coincidence seems to show that Henry of Huntingdon derived his materials from some source related to these notes; probably from the complete work, of the rough draft of which they formed a part.

[6] "Traditione vero seniorum didicimus fuisse a Romanis VII impera- "tores in Brittannia." C. 27.

[7] "Ita, ut legimus, apud Brittones regnaverunt Romani per CCCC^{os} "VIIII^{em} annos." C. 28. Between these a passage, (which is evidently a parenthesis, and may have been a marginal note, introduced later into the text), intervenes, noticing the assertion of the Romans,—that is, the Roman clan in Britain, to which Constantine, Ambrosius, and Uther belonged, (and this is an indication of the early date at which it was written),—as follows, "Romani autem IX affirmant," &c.

[8] "Tenente Octaviano Augusto monarchiam totius mundi; nam et "censum a Brittanniâ ipse solus accepit." C. 20.

his wars in that country were concluded, and peace established throughout the world, the temple of Janus was closed for the second time, A.U.C. 729, B.C. 24. Now Gildas dates the submission of Britain, "not to arms but to menaces," after the first peace,[9] that is, after A.U.C. 725, when Augustus closed the temple for the first time; and this is clearly the occasion to which the Ancyran inscription, Dio Cassius, (who says that the Britons sent a submissive embassy to Augustus), and the History of the Britons refer. It was subsequent to the first peace, and it must have been subsequent to B.C. 26, and the war in Spain which followed. It was, therefore, immediately antecedent to the second peace, which was in B.C. 24; and, commencing with this date, we find that the period of four hundred and nine years terminates with the revolt of Maximus, A.D. 385.

Again, in the History of the Britons we read,[10]—

"It came to pass, after the aforesaid war which was be-
"tween the Britons and the Romans, when their leaders
"were slain, and the victory of Maximus who slew Gratian,
"and the transfer of the Roman Empire from Britain, that
"they were forty years in fear. But Gurthegirn reigned in
"Britain."

---

[9] "Etenim Romanorum reges, cum orbis imperium obtinuissent, subju-"gatisque finitimis quibusque regionibus vel insulis orientem versus, "*prima* Parthorum, Indorum confinium, *pace partâ, quâ peractâ in omni* "*terrâ cessavere bella*, potioris famæ viribus firmassent, non acies flammæ "quodammodo rigidi tenoris ad occidentem cæruleo oceani torrente vel "cohiberi potuit vel extingui; sed transfretans, insulæ parendi leges, nullo "obsistente advexit, imbellemque populum sed infidelem, non tam ferro "et igni machinisque ut alias gentes, quam solis minis vel judiciorum con-"cussionibus, in superficie tamen vultus, impresso in altum cordis dolore, "sui obedientiam proferentem edictis subjugavit." C. 5.

[10] "Factum est autem post supradictum bellum quod fuit inter Brit-"tones et Romanos, quando duces eorum occisi sunt, et victoriam Maximi, "qui Gratianum occidit, transactoque Romanorum imperio a Brittanniâ "per XL annos fuerunt sub metu. Gurthegirnus autem regnavit in "Brittanniâ." C. 31.

This author's mention of the removal of the Empire from Britain, as coincident with Maximus' usurpation, shows that, although he has noticed the assertion of the Romans, he is still following the traditions of his fathers.

These forty years from the victory of Maximus, and the removal of the seat of his empire from Britain, bring us, as before, to A.D. 425, for the accession of Vortigern.

In the Irish version we have the following important variation of the passages just quoted:—

"Four hundred and nine years were the Britons under "Roman tribute;"—

and

"It came to pass, after the aforesaid battle, and after the "slaughter of the Roman chieftains three times by the Bri-"tons, after they had been four hundred and forty-nine years "under the Roman tribute, that Gortigern, son of Gudail, "took the chief sovereignty of Britain."

These variations from the Latin copies clearly show, that the two periods of four hundred and nine, and four hundred and forty-nine years, commenced with the payment of the tribute, which the latter testify, (although this does not), was paid to Augustus; that the shorter period terminated with the victory of Maximus, the longer with the accession of Vortigern;[11] and as the date of Maximus' victory is certainly A.D. 385, that of Vortigern's accession is as certainly A.D. 425.

Again, the section which has been already referred to, as indicating an edition of A.D. 857, corroborates the date, which these notes furnish, for the coming of Angles. For the forty-five cycles and two years of another, which it numbers, leave no doubt as to the year in which it was written, A.D. 857; and this is also stated to have been four hundred and twenty-nine years after the arrival of the Saxons, the date of which must therefore have been A.D. 428.

---

[11] This period of four hundred and forty-nine years is made to include the reigns of Constantine and his son; for although Honorius' letter in A.D. 410 finally closed the connection between Rome and Britain, the succession of Roman Emperors was considered by their party to include them, as they were of Roman lineage; and it is also mentioned at the end of the passage, which speaks of the repeated insurrections of the Britons, and their embassies to Rome.

An additional corroboration is furnished by the notice which immediately follows the account of the reception of Horsa and Hencgest;[12]—

"In that time came S. Germanus to Britain to preach;"—for S. Germanus certainly came to Britain for the first time in A.D. 429.

Again, Osbern, in his Life of S. Dunstan, furnishes us with a date nearly coincident with these, saying that the saint was born in the first year of the reign of Æthelstan, and in the four hundred and ninety-seventh from the coming of the Angles. According to this statement, as Æthelstan began to reign in A.D. 925, the coming of the Angles should be dated A.D. 429; but it is possible that Osbern, in his computation from that æra, did not include the year in which it commenced.

Thus we have abundant confirmation of the dates given in these chronological notes, for the accession of Vortigern, and the coming of the Angles; dates which, independently, might be received with perfect confidence, since they are accompanied by the names of the cotemporary consuls.

The genealogies of the descendants of Vortimer, Catigern, and Pascent, are perfectly consistent with this date for their father's accession, as well as with the statements that he married the daughter of Maximus, and that he was reigning over the Picts as early as A. D. 375. According to the usual chronology, (although it is certain that much less than the usual average of years for generations, is sufficient for the verification of genealogies of these early times), they must be rejected altogether.[13]

Vortimer's daughter, Anna, was married to Gynyr of Caer Gawch; they had a son Giustilianus, who became Bishop of Menevia, and two daughters, Non and Gwen; Non gave

---

[12] "In tempore illo venit sanctus Germanus ad prædicandum in Brit-" tanniam." C. 32.

[13] See note to the chapter on the genealogies.

birth to S. David in A.D. 462; his great grandfather, therefore, was most probably born in the fourth century.

Cadell, who reigned about A.D. 500, was son of Pasgen, son of Rheiddwy, son of Rhudvedel, son of Cyndeyrn (or Catigern). If Catigern was born about A.D. 380, the computation of twenty-five or twenty-six years to a generation, would allow of his fourth descendant reigning about the beginning of the sixth century.

A genealogy is given in the History of the Britons, which, as it occurs in every MS., probably first appeared in the edition of A.D. 675. Fernmail, who was then reigning, was son of Teudubir, son of Pascent, son of Gaidcant, son of Moriud, son of Eldat, son of Eldoc, son of Paul, son of Meuprit, son of Briacat, son of Pascent, the third son of Vortigern, by his first wife. If Pascent was born between A.D. 380 and 390, an average of about twenty-seven years would allow of his tenth descendant reigning in A.D. 675.

Thus the date, which we have ascertained for the accession of Vortigern, assists us in verifying these genealogies, (all of which indicate that his sons must have been born before the close of the fourth century), and receives in its turn important confirmation from them.[14] We may, therefore, accept with perfect confidence the following series of dates, as the basis of our chronology, deduced from the notes above-cited.

A.D. 29. Rufus Geminus and Rubelius Geminus, consuls. Beginning of the computation "from the Passion of Christ."

A.D. 397. Expedition of Stilicho to Britain.

A.D. 425. Theodosius III. and Valentinian consuls. Accession of Vortigern.

A.D. 428. Felix and Taurus consuls. Arrival of Horsa

---

[14] In his "Essay on the Welsh Saints," (p. 134), Mr. Rees has remarked, without suspecting where the error lies, that the chroniclers have placed the æra of Vortigern several years too late. It is indeed the source of most of the difficulties which have hitherto perplexed the students of the history of the fifth century.

and Hencgest, in the fourth year of Vortigern, and the four hundredth from the Passion of Christ.

A. D. 498. Decius Paulinus and Joannes Scytha consuls. Foundation of the West-Saxon kingdom, in the seventy-first year of the coming of the Angles.

Adopting A. D. 428 as the epoch of the coming of the Angles, (so frequently referred to by Henry of Huntingdon), we shall find the result to be, that the British and Saxon narratives of the events of the fifth century, during this period of seventy years, are brought for the first time into striking harmony; that we can construct a perfectly clear and consistent history, out of materials which hitherto have seemed to present nothing but error and confusion.

The Venerable Father of our history is the father of all this.[15] To him must be traced the false dates A. D. 409 for the cessation of the Roman rule in Britain, and A. D. 449 for the arrival of Horsa and Hencgest; the result of his misconception of the time, from which the computation of these two terms begins. They are certainly not reckoned from the Incarnation, but from the period of the submission of Britain to the Romans, and the first payment of tribute; events which the author of the History of the Britons understood to have occurred during the reign of Augustus, and Gildas says were subsequent to his first peace. By this probably Bæda understood what was really his third peace, and so has made

---

[15] Mr. Hardy has conjectured that this error arose from some corrupt MS. of the History of the Britons, in which the name of Martian, and the year 449, were substituted for that of Gratian, and the year 347, from the Passion of Christ, in the passage cited above. These corrupt MSS. however are of very late date, and these errors must rather be imputed to scribes, who undertook to correct the text on the authority of Venerable Bæda, but who were not learned enough to change at the same time the word "Passion" into "Incarnation," and left it to condemn their work. On the other hand, Bæda's adoption of these dates of four hundred and nine, and four hundred and forty-nine years, convinces me, that he was acquainted with and made use of, either this History of the Britons, or the larger work, which I have supposed was founded upon it.

this æra coincident with that of the Incarnation. He does not, however, always compute from this date. Three passages in his Ecclesiastical History show that, for some reason or other, he regarded A.D. 446 or 447 as the year of the coming of the Angles.[16]

---

[16] I. 23.	A.D. 597	is about the one hundred and fiftieth year	from the coming of the Angles.
II. 14.	" 627	" one hundred and eightieth ..	
V. 23.	" 731	is the two hundred and eighty-fifth ..	

CHAPTER VII.

The Forty Years' Interval.

THE date of Vortigern's accession being computed from the revolt of Maximus, an examination of the history of the interval between these events becomes necessary, as an introduction to that of the fifth century. It must be shown, that all the events which are recorded previous to the coming of the Angles, really occurred during this interval.

Zosimus says that Maximus excited the Britons to revolt, because Theodosius, in A.D. 379, was associated in the Empire by Gratian, and that they saluted him Emperor, and invested him with the purple. The fact of his assuming the Imperial dignity at this time is not inconsistent with the British tradition, which represents him as having been King in Britain, (and this I have supposed was sanctioned by Valentinian by way of compromising his claims), some years before.

The date of Maximus' victory over Gratian, Gratian's death and Theodosius' accession, is fixed by Orosius in A.U.C. 1138, A.D. 385. In that year, through fear of Theodosius, Maximus made a treaty with Valentinian. This he violated two years later, by invading Italy at the head of a large force collected from Britain and Gaul, and compelled Valentinian to flee for protection to Theodosius. In the following year, A.D. 388, Theodosius and Valentinian led an army into Italy, defeated Maximus, and put him to death near Aquileia.

Gildas speaks of Maximus passing over into Gaul, extending his empire from Spain to Italy, and making Treves his capital, of the slaughter of one emperor and the flight of the other, and of the fall of Maximus. Then he adds,[1]—

"Thenceforth Britain, deprived of all her armed soldiery, "and military forces, an immense band of youths who, ac-"companying the career of the above-mentioned tyrant, "never returned home, is abandoned to cruel governors; "and, utterly ignorant of the practice of all warfare, trodden "down for the first time by two very cruel nations—of the "Scots from the north-west, and of the Picts from the north—"is amazed and will groan for many years."

In the History of the Britons, Maximus is noticed as the sixth Emperor, with a record of his conference with S. Martin of Tours; and again, as Maximian, the seventh Emperor, with the circumstances of his leaving Britain, defeating Gratian, and extending his empire over all Europe. His history is afterwards resumed, with fuller details; and a second notice of S. Martin in nearly the same terms as the first, and the story of the fall of Maximus and his son Victor. The colonization of Armorica, obscurely alluded to in the above-cited passage of Gildas, is more circumstantially related.[2]

---

[1] "Exin Britannia, omni armato milite, militaribusque copiis, rectoribus "linquitur immanibus, ingenti juvene spoliata, quæ comitata vestigiis su-"pradicti tyranni domum nunquam ultra rediit, et omnis belli usu ignara "penitus, duabus primum gentibus transmarinis vehementer sævis, Scoto-"rum a circione, Pictorum ab aquilone, calcabilis, multos stupet, gemetque "per annos." C. 14.

[2] "Noluitque dimittere belligeros suos comites Brittones, ad uxores "et filios et possessiones suas. Sed multas illis largitus regiones, a stagno "quod est super verticem Montis Jovis, usque ad civitatem quæ vocatur "Cantguic, et usque ad cumulum occidentalem, id est Cruc Occident. "Hi sunt Brittones Armorici, et illic permanserunt usque in hodiernum "diem. Propter illorum absentiam, Brittannia superata est ab alienis "gentibus, et heredes ejecti, usquequo a Deo auxilium largiatur." C. 27.

"He would not send away the Britons, his comrades in "war, to their wives and children and possessions; but "granted to them many regions from the pool which is at the "summit of Mons Jovis, to the city which is called Cantguic, "and to the western mound, that is Cruc Occident. These "are the Armoric Britons, and they have remained there "even to the present day. By reason of their absence, Bri-"tain was vanquished by foreign nations, and the heirs cast "out, until help be granted by God."

These circumstances are related in the Brut; very briefly in the Welsh version; but in Geoffrey's the slaughter of Gratian and the flight of Valentinian, are mentioned as if they were the result of one engagement, and Maximus is said to have fallen at Rome; for Geoffrey did not always follow very closely, and has sometimes misunderstood, the original work. The history of the colonization of Armorica is fully detailed; and if, as I believe, the author of this work was himself an Armoric Briton, it may be received without hesitation; but we are concerned with it, only so far as to notice the fact, that the withdrawal from Britain of the whole of her warlike population, left her defenceless, and was the cause of all the miseries which afflicted her for so many years.

Boece has fallen into the mistake of making two Emperors,[3] Maximus and Maximian; relating the events of his reign, first in their proper place, and then again after the deaths of Marcus and Gratian Municeps. He seems to have had two distinct narratives before him, and, not knowing that Maximus and Maximian were one, has incorporated both into his history; overlooking, (what ought at least to have raised a suspicion in his mind), the necessary recurrence of the same

[3] Thus his wars with the Picts and Scots are related in VI. 16, 17, and in VII. 10, 11; his usurpation in VII. 1, and again in VII. 12; his death in VII. 1, and his colonization of Armorica in VII. 12.

names and the same circumstances in these two accounts. He had in fact authentic materials before him, but wanted the judgment to use them aright; and thus, whilst his particular statements may be entitled to credit, (and some of them are certainly very valuable), his chronology is altogether wrong, and the succession of events in his history must be received with very great caution.

The cruel governors, of whom Gildas speaks, were those who were sent from Rome to Britain, and their rule was so oppressive that the Britons three times rose against and slew them.[4] The first of these insurrections seems to have been at the time of Maximus' revolt, the second previous to the coming of Stilicho, and the third about A. D. 407.

The Brut informs us that Guanis and Melga, kings of the Picts and Huns,[5] whom Gratian had sent into Germany to harass the friends of Maximus, invaded Britain when they heard that it was left defenceless, and that Maximus sent against them two legions, under the command of Gratian Municeps,[6] who, after several bloody engagements, compelled them to flee to Ireland. Coming from Germany, as it is stated, of course the Scots were not with them; the invasions, of which Gildas speaks, were subsequent to their flight to Ireland.

Boece says[7] that the Britons sent an embassy to Valentinian

---

[4] Hist. Brit. 30.

[5] It is said that Guanis was king of the Huns, and Melga of the Picts, but there can be no doubt of the identity of Guanis with a celebrated leader of the Picts, of whom more in the sequel; and Melga or Melias is a Hunnish name, given in the Sagas to another of their kings. Shortly afterwards Geoffrey speaks of the leaders of the Picts and Huns, Guanis and Melga, and this I believe is the right order.

[6] It is, of course, possible that Gratian Municeps was sent to Britain by Maximus in A. D. 387; and the author of the Brut, not having any information relative to the events of the following twenty years, may have supposed that his reign occupied the whole of that period.

[7] VII. 13. This expedition appears to be mentioned earlier, VII. 2; but the name of the general is not there given.

requesting aid, and that he sent Gallio Ravennas who defeated the Picts and Scots, and then returned. We cannot fix the date of this expedition precisely, but it must have been soon after the events noticed in the Brut; at any rate previous to A. D. 392.

A. D. 393 Chrysanthus was appointed Vicar of the British isles.[8]

Gildas and the History of the Britons speak of two embassies from Britain to Rome, and of aid sent to Britain in consequence; it is evident that they are relating the same circumstances, but in the latter the order of these embassies is transposed.[9]

"The nation of the Britons, unable to endure the attacks of "the Scots and Picts, in consequence of their ravages, and "most cruel oppression, sends ambassadors with letters to "Rome, asking with pitiful entreaties for a military force to "avenge them, and promising constant hearty submission to "the Roman Empire, if the enemy should be repelled. Forgetting the past evil, a legion sufficiently provided with "arms is immediately sent; which, transported over sea to "our country, and engaging with the cruel enemies, and "destroying a great multitude of them, drove them all beyond "the frontier, and delivered the oppressed citizens from so "cruel a scourge, and from impending captivity; and com-

---

[8] Socrates.

[9] "Gens igitur Britonum, Scotorum Pictorumque impetum non ferens, "ob horum infestationem ac durissimam depressionem, legatos Romam "cum epistolis mittit, militarem manum ad se vindicandam lacrimosis "postulationibus poscens, et subjectionem sui Romano imperio continue "tota animi virtute, si hostis longius arceretur vovens. Cui mox destinatur "legio præteriti mali immemor, sufficienter armis instructa, quæ ratibus "trans Oceanum in patriam advecta, et cominus cum gravibus hostibus "congressa, magnamque ex eis multitudinem sternens; et omnes a finibus "depulit, et subjectos cives tam atroci dilaceratione et imminenti captivitate liberavit. Quos jussit inter duo maria constituere trans insulam "murum, ut esset arcendis hostibus a turba instructus terrori, civibusque "tutamini; qui vulgo irrationabili absque rectore, factus non tam lapidibus quam cespitibus, non profuit. Illa legione cum triumpho magno "et gaudio domum repetente," &c. C. 15.

" manded them to make a wall across the island between the " seas, that, properly guarded, it might be a terror to the " enemy to keep them at a distance, and a defence to the " citizens. This, however, being made of turf, instead of " stones, was of no use to the silly people, who had no leader. " That legion returning home with triumph and great " joy, &c."

The " past evil " is the slaughter of the Roman governors, mentioned in the History of the Britons:[10]

" But the Britons slew the governors of the Romans, on " account of the severity of their rule, and afterwards asked " help from them. But the Romans came to command, and " help, and avenge their kindred; and having spoiled Britain " of gold, silver, and brass, and all manner of precious cloth- " ing, honey, and gifts, returned with great triumph."

The mention of the wall, in the former of these passages, shows that they refer to an expedition conducted by Stilicho, which is alluded to by Claudian in his first and second books " to Eutropius." In the first of these[11] Rome is personified, complimenting Stilicho on the pacification of the sea by the conquest of the Saxons, and security restored to Britain by the overthrow of the Picts. In the second,[12] which celebrates his first consulate, A. D. 400, Britannia is introduced, acknow-

---

[10] Bryttones autem, propter gravitatem imperii, occidebant duces Ro- " manorum, et auxilium postea petebant ab eis. Romani autem ad im- " perium, auxiliumque, et vindictam proximorum veniebant, et spoliata " Brittannia auro, argento, atque ære, omnique pretiosa veste, melle, et " muneribus, cum magno triumpho revertebantur." C. 30.

[11] " Quantum te principe possum
" Non longinqua docent; domito quod Saxone Tethys
" Mitior, et fracto secura Britannia Picto." I. 391. 3.

[12] " Me quoque vicinis pereuntem gentibus, inquit,
" Munivit Stilichon, totam quum Scotus Iernen
" Movit, et infesto spumavit remige Tethys.
" Illius effectum curis, ne tela timerem
" Scotica, ne Pictum tremerem, ne litore toto
" Prospicerem dubiis venturum Saxona ventis." II. 249. 255.

ledging the services he had rendered her when on the point of perishing, his fortification of her frontier against the Scots and Picts, and her shore against the Saxons.

From the Chronological Notes it appears that the time of his coming was A. D. 397. The particular services he rendered to Britain, seem to have been the restoration of the rampart of Antonine,[13] and the completion of the fortification of the Saxon shore.[14]

Boece, after the expedition above-mentioned, speaks of another under Marcus and Victorinus, the former of whom he says was stationed at London, the latter at York. This is very important, inasmuch as it accounts for the first coming to Britain of two persons, both of whom, on the authority of classical authors, we know to have been engaged in this country, both of whom are mentioned later in our history. Victorinus, indeed, is not noticed by the historians of his time, but his friend Rutilius Numatianus speaks of him, in terms[15] which are perfectly consistent with Boece's narrative, and indicate that he had governed the Britons, in such a way as to

---

[13] Bæda says the work executed on this occasion extended from Penneltun to Dunbarton.

[14] Six out of the nine stations on this shore, Othona, Branadunum, Gariannonum, Regulbium, Anderida, and Portus Adurni, are only mentioned in the Notitia Imperii, which was compiled shortly after this time.

[15] " Victorinus enim, nostræ pars maxima mentis,
" Congressu explevit mutua vota suo.
" Nec tantum duris nituit sapientia rebus,
" Pectore non alio prosperiora tulit.
" Conscius oceanus virtutum, conscia Thule,
" Et quicumque ferox arva Britannus arat.
" Quâ præfectorum vicibus frænata potestas,
" Perpetuum magni fœnus amoris habet.
" Extremum pars illa quidem discessit in orbem,
" Sed tanquam mediâ rector in urbe fuit.
" Plus palmæ est illos inter voluisse placere,
" Inter quos minor est displicuisse pudor.
" Illustris sacræ nuper comes additus aulæ,
" Contempsit sacros ruris amore gradus."

CL. RUTILII *Itiner*. 493–507.

win their affection; his conduct in this respect presenting a marked contrast to that of other governors, who, in that distant region, had presumed on their misdemeanours escaping the notice of their masters at home, and shamelessly tyrannized over the unhappy people.

The circumstances of his sojourn in Britain, as related by Boece, seem to warrant the supposition, that he and Marcus accompanied Stilicho, and were left by him in Britain. He says,[16] that he subjected the Picts to his authority, that they afterwards rebelled against him, that he led an army into Pentland, besieged and took Camelon, seized on the person of their king, and sent him captive to Rome, drove them beyond the Forth, exacted tribute from them, and compelled them to build the wall of Abercorn, (*i. e.* the rampart of Antonine). Again he says,[17] that he assembled an army, invaded Pentland, and besieged Camelon, fought a battle of which the result was doubtful, still occupied Pentland with his forces, whilst the Picts and Scots withdrew beyond the Clyde and Forth, and then that he commanded the Britons to build the wall of Abercorn, as a defence against them. Here again we have evidently two distinct narratives of the same events; one, in the Roman interest, claiming a victory; the other, in that of the Picts, denying it; but both agreeing as to the facts of a war in Pentland, of the withdrawal of the Picts and Scots beyond the Forth, of a cessation of hostilities, and of the building of the wall from the Forth to the Clyde. These I regard as detailed narratives of the events recorded in Gildas' fifteenth chapter; and I understand him, the author of the History of the Britons, and Boece, as relating the story of an expedition, of which Stilicho was the commander-in-chief, and Marcus and Victorinus his lieutenants. As then, Victorinus had the command in the North, and rebuilt the wall, so Marcus, whom Boece places in the South, and of whom, (as

---

[16] VII. 2.

[17] VII. 6

having nothing to do with Pictish affairs), he says nothing more at this time, may have occupied himself with the fortification of the Saxon shore; both the one and the other, as a matter of course, being placed to Stilicho's credit, by his panegyrist Claudian.

This Victorinus, the only one of the name who is connected with the history of North Britain, must be the person who, with Cælianus, dedicated the altar which was found at Kirksteads in Cumberland.[18] It is inscribed:—

L IVNIVS VICTORINVS ET L CAELIANVS LEG AVG LEG VI VIC P F OB RES TRANS VALLVM PROSPERE GESTAS,—

and may be a record of his victory over the Picts. The friend of so determined a foe to Christianity as Rutilius, could hardly be otherwise than a Pagan; and it is worthy of remark, that the first part of this inscription, which contained the dedication, has been designedly effaced.

The Britons revolted again, A. D. 407,[19] and raised Marcus to the throne, but soon afterwards put him to death. They then invested Gratian Municeps with the purple, allowed him to enjoy his dignity about four months, and murdered him in his turn. The Brut says that the common people rose against him in a tumultuous manner, and slew him on account of his tyranny; and Layamon, in perfect accordance with the fact, already noticed, of the arrival in Britain of a colony of Alamanni more than thirty years before, and the probability that they settled in Norfolk, supplies us with a detailed

---

[18] Now preserved at Kirk Andrews. Neither of the other Victorini, who are mentioned in the history of Roman Britain, can claim this monument. The usurper, who is commemorated in an inscription found near Neath in Glamorganshire, and of whom we have so many coins, was *M. C. Piavonius Victorinus;* and the other, who came to Britain in the reign of Probus, was a Moor, and remained no longer in Britain than the business, for which he came, required. It is therefore most probable that this inscription belongs to the Victorinus of whom Rutilius and Boece make mention.

[19] Before, (according to Olympiodorus), during, (according to Zosimus), the seventh consulate of Honorius.

account of a conspiracy by two twin-brothers in East Anglia, Æthelbald and Ælfwald, who collected a mob of seven hundred ceorls, and cut him to pieces whilst he was hunting.

Constantine succeeded Gratian. Not content with his insular dominions, he collected all the forces he could command, abandoned Britain, invaded Gaul and Spain, for four years struggled with Honorius for the Empire, and at length was slain in Gaul, along with his son Constans, whom he had associated with himself in his usurped dignity, A.D. 411.

Immediately after his departure, a fresh inroad of the Picts and Scots forced the Britons again to seek aid from Rome. Gildas says,[20]

"Those former foes, brought by the blades of oars and

---

[20] "Illi priores inimici, alis remorum remigumque brachiis, ac velis "vento sinuatis vecti, terminos rumpunt, cæduntque omnia, et quæque "obvia, maturam ceu segetem metunt, calcant, transeunt.

"Iterumque mittuntur queruli legati, scissis, ut dicitur vestibus, "opertisque sablone capitibus, impetrantes a Romanis auxilia. At illi, "quantum humanæ naturæ possibile est, commoti tantæ historiâ tragœdiæ, "volatus ceu aquilarum, equitum in terra, nautarum in mari, cursus "accelerantes inopinatos primum, tandem terribiles inimicorum ungues "cervicibus infigunt mucronum,—æmulorum agmina auxiliatores egregii, "si qua tamen evadere potuerant, propere trans maria fugaverunt, quia "anniversarias avide prædas, nullo obsistente trans maria exaggerabant.

"Igitur Romani patria reversi, denuntiantes nequaquam se tam "laboriosis expeditionibus posse frequentius vexari, et, ob imbelles erra"ticosque latrunculos, Romana stigmata, tantum talemque exercitum, "terra ac mari fatigari; sed ut insula potius, consuescendo armis ac "viriliter dimicando, terram, substantiolam, conjuges, liberos, et, quod his "majus est, libertatem vitamque totis viribus vendicaret, et gentibus "nequaquam se fortioribus, nisi segnitia et torpore dissolverentur, ut "inermes vinculis vinciendas nullo modo, sed instructas peltis, ensibus, "hastis, et ad cædem promtas protenderet manus, suadentes; quia et hoc "putabant aliquid derelinquendo populo commodi accrescere, murum, "non ut alterum, sumtu publico privatoque, adjunctis secum miserabilibus "indigenis, solito structuræ more, tramite a mari usque ad mare inter "urbes, quæ ibidem forte ob metum hostium collocatæ fuerant, directo "librant: fortia formidoloso populo monita tradunt, exemplaria instituen"dorum armorum relinquunt. In litore quoque oceani ad meridianam "plagam, qua naves eorum habebantur, quia et inde Barbariæ feræ bestiæ "timebantur, turres per intervalla ad prospectum maris collocant, et "valedicunt tanquam ultra non reversuri." C. 16. 18.

" arms of rowers, and sails filled with wind, burst the barriers, " and cut down everything; mow, trample on, pass over " all things in their way, as it were a ripe harvest. And " again querulous ambassadors, with garments rent, as it is " said, and heads covered with dust, are sent entreating help " of the Romans. But they, moved as much as is possible to " human nature, by the story of so great a tragedy, hasten- " ing like the flight of eagles, the course of cavalry by land, " of sailors by sea, unexpected at first, fix the terrible claws " of their swords in the necks of their foes. The noble " auxiliaries quickly drove the troops of the enemy across the " seas, (if any could so escape); for beyond the seas they " greedily accumulated their plunder year by year, when no " one opposed them.

" Then the Romans leave the country, declaring that they " could not be so often harassed by such laborious expeditions, " nor could the Roman soldiery, so great and brave an army, " be fatigued by sea and land, on account of cowardly vaga- " bond robbers; but advising that the nation should rather " defend with all their might their land, substance, wives, " children, and, what is of more value than these, liberty and " life, by inuring themselves to arms and fighting bravely; " and stretch forth hands,—not as unarmed to be bound with " bonds by nations in no wise stronger than they, were they not " enervated by idleness and torpor,—but armed with shields, " swords, and spears, and ready for slaughter. And because " they thought that this would be some advantage to the " people about to be left, they erect, in conjunction with the " miserable nation, at public and private cost, a wall, not like " the former, but in the usual mode of building, between the " cities which had been placed there, perhaps for fear of " enemies, in a direct line from sea to sea. They give brave " counsels to the timid people, and leave patterns of arms to " be made. On the shore also of the ocean, towards the " south, because from that quarter the wild beasts of Bar-

"baria were dreaded, they place towers at intervals to com-"mand the sea, and bid farewell, as it were never to return."

The corresponding passage in the History of the Britons is:[21]

"Three times were the governors of the Romans slain by "the Britons, and when they were harassed by the nations "of the Barbarians, that is, the Scots and Picts, the Britons "entreated help of the Romans; and when the ambassadors "were sent with great grief, and entered with dust upon their "heads, and carried great gifts, for the acknowledged crime "of the murder of the governors, and the consuls received "from them their acceptable gifts, they promised with an "oath to receive the yoke of the Roman Empire, although "it were severe. And the Romans came with a great army "to the aid of the Britons, and they appointed governors and "an Emperor in Britain, and an Emperor and governors "being appointed, the army returned to Rome, and thus they "did by turns for CCCCXLVIIII years."

The last sentence shows that this is really the conclusion of this account of Roman transactions in Britain, and ought to come next before the passage which speaks of the forty years' interval.

The narrative in the Brut is in exact accordance with Gildas' statements, supplying the names of the persons concerned, but omitting the mention of the towers along the

---

21 "Tribus vicibus occisi sunt duces Romanorum a Brittonibus, et "Brittones dum anxiarentur a Barbarorum gentibus, id est Scottorum "atque Pictorum, auxilium Romanorum flagitabant. Et cum legati "mittebantur cum magno luctu, et cum sablonibus super capita sua, in-"trabant et portabant magna munera pro admissâ occisionis culpâ ducum, "et accipientes grata dona consules ab illis, promittebant jurando accipere "jugum Romanici imperii licet durum esset. Et Romani cum magno "exercitu ad auxilium venerunt Bryttonum, constituebantque duces et "imperatorem in Bryttanniâ, et composito imperatore cum ducibus "revertebatur exercitus ad Romam. Et sic alternatim per CCCCXLVIII "annos agebant." C. 30.

For CCCCXLVIII we must read CCCCXLVIIII as we find it in four MSS.

shore. After the death of Gratian Municeps, we are informed, Guanis and Melga collected a fresh army of Norwegians, Danes, Scots, and Picts, invaded Britain, and ravaged it from sea to sea. The Britons, unable to oppose them, solicited and obtained a legion under the command of Severus; the enemy were speedily driven beyond the borders; and then the Britons and Romans together built up the stone wall, which separates Deira from the north country, to impede the incursions of foreigners for the future. Returning to London, the Romans desired Guitolin the Archbishop, to inform the Britons that they would now give up the tribute, as it cost more in men and money to defend the island, than they ever gained from it. This declaration called forth a piteous cry from the multitude, but the Romans were inexorable, betook themselves to their ships, and returned home.

Questions of great importance now suggest themselves, the discussion of which will delay for some time our resuming the series of the history. With respect to the leader of the Picts in these several invasions of Britain, Fordun and Boece supply an interesting corroboration of the statements in the Brut. We have learned that Guanis was expelled from Britain by Gratian Municeps, who had been sent against him by Maximus; that he returned, when he heard of Gratian's death, with a force of Norwegians and Danes, in addition to those of the Picts and Scots; and one of the results of this invasion was the abandonment of the northern wall, by the Britons and their Roman auxiliaries; for that which was subsequently built was across the southern isthmus. Fordun speaks of a noble Briton named Gryme, who claimed the provinces north of the Humber, in right of his descent from Fulgentius,[22] as expelled from Britain by Maximus, seeking refuge in Denmark, returning thence after the departure of the Roman legions, and destroying the rampart of Antonine,

[22] The leader of the Britons in their wars with the Emperor Severus.

in the ninth year of Honorius, A.D. 403. Boece[23] calls him Grahame, and says that some authors represented him as the son of one of the Scots who were exiled to Denmark, and of a Danish mother; others as a Briton, who had shared the banishment of the Scots; that he married a virgin of the blood-royal of Denmark; that he attacked the Britons as they were building the dyke, (Antonine's rampart), slew a great number of them, and afterwards carried his arms southward. In the second narrative,[24] (which we have had occasion to notice before), he says that Grahame destroyed the wall, and proceeds to speak of the Britons repairing the wall of Hadrian, and of their mission to Etius. It is evident that Guanis, Gryme, and Grahame are one and the same person,[25] and thus we find the Scottish historians substantiating the story in the Brut. The date which Fordun gives for the destruction of the northern rampart is probably near the truth.

Severus, the builder of the stone wall, is mentioned only in one Welsh MS. of the Brut; but the mention of this name is important, as identifying an Emperor of whom the History of the Britons makes mention.[26]

"The eighth was another Severus; he sometimes sojourned "in Britain, and sometimes abode at Rome, where he died."

The Irish version presents a remarkable variation from this:—

"Who died as he was going to Rome from the island of "Britain."

Probably his death occurred immediately on his arrival at Rome; but either this supposition, or that of his death on the journey, will account for the omission of all notice of him in

---

[23] VII. 6. [24] VII. 14.

[25] The difference in these names is no greater than what the negligence of copyists has introduced in other instances.

[26] "Octavus fuit alius Severus. Aliquando in Britannia commorabatur aliquando Romæ manebat, ubi defunctus est." C. 27.

the classical historians. In the prefatory notes of the Vatican MS. he is called Severus Æquantius,[27] and in the Capitula which are placed at the beginning of the Cambridge MS., F. f. i. 27, (but which are believed to have belonged to some other, since they do not correspond with the matters contained in this), we have additional evidence to the fact of his having built the wall.[28]

"The second Severus, who commanded that another wall, "of the usual construction, should be built to restrain the incursions of the Picts and Scots, from Tynemouth to Boulness."

Bæda says the wall built on this occasion was not far from that which the first Severus had built, and which was merely a rampart of earth. By this he means, of course, the rampart of Hadrian; for the statement, first made by Spartian, (about seventy years after the time of Severus), and repeated by Eusebius, Aurelius Victor and others, that Severus built a wall in Britain, has been very justly called in question;[29] since his cotemporary Herodian, an eye-witness of his campaigns in Britain, is altogether silent on the subject, and so also was Dion Cassius, if we may judge from Xiphilinus' abridgment of his history. If, however, there be any truth in it, the length of the wall, as stated by Eusebius, as well as the fact that he carried his arms far beyond the wall of Hadrian, would make it more probable that he repaired or completed that of Antonine; but no inscriptions have been found to attest that he had any part in it, on either of these works.

A careful consideration of the arguments, adduced by Dr. Bruce, in support of his theory, that Hadrian built the wall as well as the rampart, has failed to convince me that he did

---

[27] "Octavus alius Severus Æquantius."

[28] "De secundo etiam Severo, qui solitâ structurâ murum alterum "ad arcendos Pictos et Scottos, fieri a Tinemuthe usque Boggenes præ-"cepit."

[29] See the Rev. J. C. Bruce's excellent work on the Roman Wall.

anything more than complete two ramparts of earth, intended as defences, one against the Britons on the South, the other against the Caledonians on the North; the former still existing, the latter the foundation of a grander work, the stone wall, along its line. Had he built a stone wall, Antonine's legate, Lollius Urbicus, would scarcely have been satisfied with doing less when engaged in the fortification of the northern isthmus; and as he contented himself with a rampart of earth, it is probable, and indeed appears to be implied by Julius Capitolinus,[30] that Hadrian's work was of similar construction. The analogy of the Devil's Wall in Germany seems to agree with the supposition, that the stone wall was an addition to Hadrian's rampart, for there also the earthen mound is ascribed to him, and the stone wall to some of his successors.

In the absence, then, of any evidence to the contrary, and with what appear to be strong probabilities in its favour, I must declare my adhesion to the authority of Gildas, (who wrote at no very great distance of time from the event, and was born within eighteen years after it), supported as it is by the Brut and Boece; and express my conviction that the Romans, on the eve of their final departure from Britain, provided for the Britons, whom they were leaving to themselves, a stronger defence than they had deemed necessary whilst they occupied the country, by building the wall on the northern rampart of Hadrian. It is observable that Gildas speaks of the wall as built to connect the towers, that is, the stations, which had been constructed previously. This is quite consistent with the fact, that they are of very different masonry from the wall, and are admitted to be older. The stations may well be a part of Hadrian's work, but the wall I claim for Severus Æquantius.

---

[30] "Antoninus Britannos per Lollium Urbicum legatum vicit, *alio* " *muro cespiticio*, submotis Barbaris, ducto."

Gildas further speaks of the building of towers along the coast, to the South, where the Roman fleet was stationed, clearly indicating the Saxon shore. Here also there may have been some improvement on what Stilicho had done, an erection of stone walls, where there had previously been works of less strength.

Boece, perhaps, supplies the names of the governors, who are said to have been left to direct the energies of the Britons. He says[31] that, after Constantine's departure, Victorinus took the command of the army in Britain; that Honorius began to suspect him of intending to usurp the dominion of Britain, and that it was thought he would be recalled; that Victorinus, abetted by the army and a part of the nation, though opposed by Dioneth and the rest, took upon himself the sovereignty; and that Honorius then sent against him Heraclius, who made him prisoner and sent him to Rome, where he was put to death. These notices of Victorinus, like the former, are valuable; Rutilius intimates that his prosperous career had been followed by adversity, but as he testifies that he was still living when he wrote his Itinerary, (in A.D. 417), and had recovered the good graces of the Emperor, Boece is certainly in error in saying that he was put to death. He proceeds to say,[32] that Heraclius left in Britain, as governor, one Placidus; that, the Picts and Scots, having renewed the war, (as stated in Gildas and the Brut), he was unsuccessful, and made a treaty with them; that he died soon after, and was succeeded by Castius; that the Picts and Scots again invaded Britain, and were joined by Dioneth and his party; that Castius with the rest of the Britons opposed them; that he fell in battle;[33] and that his army was discomfited and fled into Wales, leaving all the fortresses of the country defenceless.

Besides that these statements seem to supply the names

[31] VII. 5. [32] VII. 8. [33] VII. 9.

which are wanting in the History of the Britons, they are supported in part by the traditions which still remain, in the memories of the primitive population who inhabit the districts traversed by the wall.[34] One of these relates that the Britons, (*i. e.* Dioneth and his party), tired of Roman oppression, rose and drove the garrison of the wall from all the stations with great slaughter, and that they fled into Wales, because a seer told them that they would be drowned if they attempted to quit the island, and slain if they returned to the stations.

The usurpation of Victorinus was immediately subsequent to the departure of Constantine, A. D. 407; the expedition of Severus, and the short præfectures of Placidus and Castius probably occupied the years 408 to 410.

Cunedda Wledig[35] and Brychan, with their sons, who were driven from the North by the Picts, expelled the Gwyddyl Ffichti who had seized on Wales after the departure of Maximus, and gave their names to the regions in which they settled, Gwynedd and Brycheiniog, were probably those who are said to have retreated into Wales from the stations of the wall.

The renewal of the war after the departure of Severus is the subject of Gildas' nineteenth chapter.[36] The Ro-

---

[34] Bruce's Roman Wall, p. 204.

[35] "Cunedag, cum filiis suis, quorum numerus octo erat, venerat prius "de parte sinistrali, id est de regione quæ vocatur Manau Guotodin, "centum quadraginta sex annis antequam Mailcun regnaret, et Scottos "cum ingentissima clade expulerunt ab istis regionibus, et nusquam "reversi sunt iterum ad habitandum." Cambrian Genealogist's Notes appended to the History of the Britons.

[36] "Itaque illis ad sua revertentibus, emergunt certatim de curicis, "quibus sunt trans Cichicam vallem vecti, tetri Scotorum Pictorumque "greges, cognitaque condebitorum reversione, et reditus denegatione, "solito confidentiores omnem aquilonalem extremamque terræ partem, "pro indigenis muro tenus capessunt. Statuitur ad hæc in edito arcis "acies, segnis ad pugnam, inhabilis ad fugam, trementibus præcordiis "inepta, quæ diebus ac noctibus stupido sedili marcebat. Interea non "cessant uncinata nudorum tela, quibus miserrimi cives de muris tracti, "solo allidebantur." C. 19.

mans, he says, "returning home, the hateful hordes of "the Picts and Scots hastily disembark from their vessels, "in which they were conveyed across the sea; and, having "heard of the departure of our friends and their refusal to "return, more bold even than they were wont to be, they "seized upon all the north and extreme part of the land, as "far as the wall, for their own. A garrison, slow to fight, "and unfit for flight, useless by reason of their timid hearts, "who dozed away days and nights in stupid sitting, is arrayed "against them on the height of the wall. Meanwhile the "hooked weapons of their naked foes are not idle, whereby "the wretched citizens, dragged from the walls, are dashed "to the ground."

Another of the traditions collected by Dr. Bruce[37] has preserved to this day a remembrance of these circumstances; relating how the Romans lay basking in a state of torpor on the south side, (*i. e.* behind the parapet), of the wall, and how the Scots threw lines with hooks attached to them over the wall, caught them by their clothes or flesh, dragged them over, and made them prisoners.

In the remainder of the chapter, Gildas speaks of the flight of the Britons from the wall and stations, of the cruelty of their enemies who pursued them, and of civil war amongst themselves,[38] which is explained by Boece's story of a party of the Britons under Dioneth being in league with the Picts and Scots. In the next chapter he says:[39]—

"Meanwhile a terrible and most famous famine attacked "the wandering and unsettled people, and compels many of

---

[37] P. 203.

[38] "Laniant et seipsos mutuo—augebantur extraneæ clades domesticis "motibus." C. 19.

[39] "Interea fames dira ac famosissima vagis ac mutabundis hæret, quæ "multos eorum cruentis compellit prædonibus sine dilatione victas dare "manus, ut pauxillum ad refocillandam animam cibi caperent, alios vero "nusquam; quin potius de ipsis montibus, speluncis ac saltibus, dumis "consertis, continue rebellabant." C. 20.

" them to surrender without delay to the bloody robbers, so " that they might have a little food to refresh their souls; " but not so others, who rather made sallies continually from " the mountains, caves, forests, and thickets."

Idatius, cotemporary with Gildas, says this famine was attended with pestilence, and prevailed all over the world, A.D. 409, 410. The " meanwhile" indicates that it had preceded what Gildas had just recorded,[40] viz. that the Britons sent letters to Agitius, a powerful Roman citizen :—

" To Agitius, thrice consul, the groans of the Britons. " The Barbarians drive us into the sea, the sea drives us " back to the Barbarians; between them two kinds of death " are offered to us, we are either killed or drowned ; "—but, he says, they obtained no help.

The Brut informs us, that Guanis and Melga landed in Scotland, as soon as they heard of the departure of the Romans, and ravaged the country as far as the Humber; that the Britons sent an embassy to implore the help of Agitius; but that the Roman senate refused to comply with their petition, and renounced the tribute.

Boece[41] gives the letter in full, with the passage quoted by Gildas about the middle of it, and then a more circumstantial account of the reply, viz. that he was very sorry that the Roman empire was so beset on every side, that he could scarcely defend France from the Barbarians, and therefore could send no assistance to Britain; that, nevertheless, he exhorted them to make the best defence they could, in hope of better fortune.

Now, when Zosimus tells us, that the Emperor Honorius,

---

[40] "Igitur rursum miseræ reliquiæ mittentes epistolas ad Agitium " Romanæ potestatis virum hoc modo loquentes, inquiunt; 'Agitio ter " 'consuli gemitus Britannorum,' et post pauca loquentes, 'Repellunt " 'nos Barbari ad mare, repellit nos mare ad Barbaros; inter hæc " 'oriuntur duo genera funerum, aut jugulamur aut mergimur;' nec pro " eis quisquam adjutorii habent." C. 20.

[41] VII. 16.

A.D. 410, wrote in answer to the cities of Britain, exhorting them to defend themselves, I am satisfied that he is speaking of this very embassy and its result. In both accounts the terms of the reply are the same, but Boece adds details which truly describe the condition of the Empire at the time; consistent with the fact that Honorius was in Gaul in this very year, opposing Constantine; and corresponding with Procopius' statement, that after Constantine's fall, A.D. 411, it was no longer in the power of the Romans to make any effort for the recovery of Britain.

Bæda has substituted the name of Aetius, who was consul for the third time A.D. 446, for that of Agitius, and so also has Polidore Vergil in his edition of Gildas; yet I cannot believe that this event has been so strangely misplaced, as the identification of Agitius with Aetius would imply. For not only the Brut and Boece, but Bæda and Gildas also, speak of a great victory gained by the Britons after it, and then of a considerable period of prosperity intervening between it and the invitation of the Saxons by Vortigern; which of course is irreconcileable even with the supposition that the letter was written A.D. 446, and that Vortigern invited the Saxons A.D. 449. As, however, we have ascertained A.D. 449 is twenty-one years too late, even for the arrival of Horsa and Hencgest, either the letter must have been written about A.D. 410, or Gildas and the rest must have erred, in representing these circumstances as having occurred, previous to the victory, and the reign of Constantine. But it is scarcely possible that Gildas could have fallen into this error, for in A.D. 446 he was in his native land and twenty-one years of age. Instead, therefore, of Aetius, I would read Æquitius for Agitius; and as the Vatican MS., which reads Æquantius for Æquitius, calls Severus also Æquantius, believe that he is the person here intended. His successes in Britain would distinguish him as worthy of the consulate, and it would be natural for the Britons to apply to him, as having recently aided them.

Now it is very remarkable that this precise year, A.D. 410, presents circumstances connected with the consulate, perfectly consistent with the supposition that Æquitius discharged the office in the commencement of the year, or at least was elected consul. Prosper, giving only the name of Fl. Varro, says:—

"Rome, once the conqueror of the world, in this year was "taken by the Goths under Alaric, and on this account there "was only a consul of the East, which was the case in the "following year also."

Varro was created February 1, and Tertullus six months afterwards, at Rome, by Attalus; but his name was erased from the Fasti, because Attalus, deposed in the year preceding, had joined the Goths. Æquitius, then, might have been created by Honorius, January 1, and on his death, Varro might be appointed his successor; or he might have been Varro's colleague, and on his death, either by sickness or in opposing the Goths, Tertullus might be nominated in his place by Attalus, their ally; and thus, if the Britons reckoned A.D. 375 as the year of his second consulate, they would regard A.D. 410 as his third. For the omission of his name from the Fasti, as well as for the fact that the letter addressed to him was answered by Honorius, his death either on the journey or immediately after his arrival in Rome, and the confusion consequent on the sacking of Rome by Alaric, will readily account; so that, although actually created consul, he might have no opportunity of performing any public act in which his consulate would be recorded, or if he did, the record might have perished.

Boece's successive notices of the person to whom the letter was addressed, and whom he calls Etius, fully bear out the identity here supposed of Agitius and Æquitius. He says[42] that Maximian was sent by him, with the authority of the Emperor, to the assistance of the Britons. Now Æquitius was himself nominated to the Imperial dignity, and assisted

---

[42] VII. 10.

by his influence in securing the election of Valentinian, who was preferred to him, in A.D. 364, the very year in which, as we have seen, Maximus first came to Britain; and he was consul in A.D. 374. Boece's statement,[43] therefore, may very well be true with regard to Æquitius; it is perfectly consistent with the rank he held, and with the influence which he possessed, on account, not only of his merits in time past, but also of the service he had recently rendered to the Emperor; it cannot be true with regard to Aetius.

Again he says, that Etius stirred up the Armoricans to resist Maximian's authority, that he sent into Britain for the legion which Maximian had left there, to oppose him in Gaul, and that Britain was then left wholly unprotected. This statement again may apply to Æquitius, but it certainly cannot to Aetius.[44]

After the return of Gallio Ravennas,[45] he notices an unsuccessful embassy of the Britons to Etius, and lastly[46] he mentions this letter and the reply to it. Doubtless one of his authorities supplied these successive notices of Æquitius, all of which, except the last, must be referred to years preceding A.D. 410. This letter, therefore, was addressed to their deliverer Severus Æquitius, by the Britons, who supposed him to be discharging the functions of the consulate, and as he was dead, it was answered by Honorius.

Zosimus' mention of this letter is the last of the notices of Roman transactions in connection with Britain, which classical authors supply; and he also informs us, that during the usurpation of Constantine, therefore not later than A.D. 411, the Britons took up arms, braved every danger, and freed their cities from the invading barbarians. It will not be questioned that this was subsequent to the letter of Honorius,

---

[43] VII. 12.

[44] There was another Æquitius, who is thought to have been his son, a relation of the Emperor Valens. He fell in battle at Hadrianople A.D. 378.

[45] VII. 14.

[46] VII. 16.

and in the exact agreement between Zosimus and Gildas, in the passage which immediately follows the notice of the letter, we have one more confirmation of what has been already advanced. After speaking of the famine, contemporaneous with the ravages of the Picts and Scots, he says:[47]—

"Then, for the first time, trusting, not in man but in God, "they gave slaughter to their enemies, who for many years had "infested the land. The boldness of the enemy ceased for a "time, but not so the wickedness of our people; foes withdrew "from the citizens, but not the citizens from their crimes."

For the details, as usual, we must refer to the Brut and Boece. The Brut says, that after the Britons' hope of aid from Rome had failed, Guitolin, Archbishop of London, was sent to Aldroen, King of Armorica, to ask the assistance of their kindred in that country, and that he sent an army, two thousand strong, under the command of his brother Constantine, to their assistance; that Constantine fought many battles with Guanis and Melga, and in the end was completely victorious; that he assumed the sovereignty, and reigned prosperously and peacefully for twelve years; and that at last he was assassinated by a Pict, who had obtained an audience on pretence of business.

Boece's story is consistent with this in the main, but furnishes additional particulars, and some variations. A British prince, he says,[48] named Conan, stirred up the Britons to resistance, and was associated with Guitolin in the embassy, but died at sea.[49] In the battle he says that the Britons were

---

47 "Et tum primum inimicis per multos annos in terra agentibus "strages dabant, non confidentes in homine, sed in Deo.

"Quievit parumper inimicorum audacia, nec tamen nostrorum malitia, "recesserunt hostes a civibus, nec cives a suis sceleribus." C. 20.

48 VII. 15.

49 It is important to remark the difference in these two accounts; the Scottish narrative of Boece naming the two ambassadors who were sent, the Armorican of S. Albinus only the one who arrived at the court of Aldroen; the latter claims a victory for the Britons, whilst the former denies it, but in such a way as to convince us that they did really prevail.

defeated with the loss of sixteen thousand, whilst the Picts and Scots lost fourteen thousand, but that a cessation of hostilities was the result, and admits that the Picts ceded many fortresses to Constantine. He bears witness to the general prosperity and peace of Constantine's reign, says that many of the Picts, (of whom probably Vortigern was one), settled in Britain, and obtained situations of trust about his court, and that at last he was murdered by some of them, who had gained admission to his presence, under pretence of a conference on state affairs.

John Ross, who says he had gained his information from MSS. in Wales and Anglesey, is an additional witness to these circumstances. He gives a few details which are neither in the Brut nor Boece, but these are of small consequence, except that Constantine's founding and rebuilding cities may be taken as a confirmation of the peaceful character of his reign.

Earlier, however, than any of these, we have a notice of Constantine and of the treason to which he fell a victim, in the History of the Britons.[50]

" The ninth was Constantine; he reigned sixteen years in
" Britain, and in the seventeenth year of his reign he died;
" slain, as they say, by treachery in Britain."

Thus Gildas and the History of the Britons support the Brut and Boece, except with regard to the duration of his reign; and in this particular I prefer the Brut, for we have seen that the term of forty years from Maximus' revolt fixes A.D. 425 as the date of Vortigern's accession, and as some time, about a year, must be allowed for the reign of Constantius, that of Constantine commencing A.D. 411 cannot much have exceeded twelve years. I suspect that the error in the History of the Britons has arisen from a confusion of

---

[50] " Nonus fuit Constantinus ('Constantius,' V). Ipse regnavit XVI
" annis in Britanniâ, et in XVI ('XVII,' V.) imperii sui anno obiit, quasi
" dolo voraciter occisus in Britanniâ, ut aiunt." C. 27.

the two Constantines, and that the sixteen years assigned to Constantine of Armorica, include the four years of Constantine the usurper.

It is said that he married a Roman lady, and had by her three sons, Constantius, Ambrosius, and Uther; but Constantius must certainly have been born before his coming to Britain, for he was not only old enough to succeed to the throne, (which Ambrosius and Uther were not), at the time of his father's death, but was also a professed monk and subdeacon.

His monastic profession and holy order excluded him from the throne, and disputes arose relative to the succession; but his right, notwithstanding these disqualifications, was insisted on by Vortigern, who was highest in authority in the council. Vortigern induced him to leave his monastery, and take the kingdom, having previously obtained from him a promise that the chief direction of affairs should be entrusted to himself; and consecrated him king, because no prelate dared to perform the ceremony. Constantius was neither fitted nor inclined to take upon himself the cares of government, and everything was left to Vortigern; who was carefully laying his plans for the usurpation of the throne, took care to place partizans of his own in all the fortresses of the kingdom, surrounded the person of his sovereign with a guard of Picts, attached to his own interests, and eventually procured his assassination by their hands.

This is the account given in the Brut, and Boece substantially agrees with it. Gildas alludes to the sacrilegious consecration of Constantius, and his being murdered by his consecrator, in the following terms:[51]—

"Kings were anointed, yet not by God, but by those who

---

[51] "Ungebantur reges et non per Deum, sed qui cæteris crudeliores "exstarent; et paulò post ab unctoribus, non pro veri examinatione, "trucidabantur, aliis electis trucioribus." C. 21.

"were more cruel than the rest; and shortly afterwards, not "for the vindication of the truth, were murdered by those "who anointed them, others more cruel being elected."

The Brut and Boece agree in saying, that Vortigern feigned great indignation at the murder of Constantius, and caused the Pictish guard to be put to death. The former tells us that he crowned himself king; the latter, more probably, that after he had persuaded the people to set aside the brothers of Constantius, on account of their tender age, he was elected king by acclamation; that he massacred all the Picts and Scots who were in London, and immediately after his coronation put to death or banished all the kindred and friends of Constantius; Ambrosius and Uther alone escaping with their tutors to Armorica. To these last circumstances Gildas alludes when speaking of Ambrosius:[52]—

"Who had survived in the crash of so great a storm, in "which his relatives, clothed with the purple, were slain."

Thus every event that is recorded as having occurred previous to the coming of the Angles, really occurred within the limits we have ascertained, and there is positively no notice whatever of any connection between Rome and Britain, subsequent to A. D. 410.

---

[52] "Qui tantæ tempestatis collisione, occisis in eadem parentibus, pur- "pura nimirum indutis, superfuerat." C. 25.

CHAPTER VIII.

The Reign of Vortigern, A. D. 425 *to* 433.

IN the History of the Britons, in continuation of the passage cited above, p. 170, we read:[1]—

"Gurthegirn reigned in Britain; but in "his time the Britons were harassed by fear "of the Scots and Picts, and by the hostility of the Romans, "and also by dread of Ambrosius."

Gildas speaks of the invasion of the Scots and Picts:[2]—

"God wishing to purify His people, the winged flight of a "rumour, not for the first time heard, penetrates the quick- "ened ears of all, of the approach of their ancient foes, bent "on destroying the land, and occupying it as they had been "wont, from end to end."

In the Life of Merlin[3] we are informed, that after the

---

[1] "Gurthegirnus autem regnabat in Brittanniâ; sed in tempore illius "Brittones urgebantur a metu Scottorum Pictorumque, et a Romanorum "impetu, nec non et a timore Ambrosii." C. 31.

[2] "Interea, volente Deo purgare familiam suam,—non ignoti rumoris "penniger ceu volatus arrectas omnium penetrat aures, jamjamque ad- "ventus veterum hostium volentium penitus delere, et inhabitare solito "more a fine usque ad terminum, regionem." C. 22.

[3] "Crimen quod memini, cum Constans proditus esset
"Et defugissent parvi trans æquora fratres
"Uter et Ambrosius, cœperunt illico bella

death of Constantius, Vortigern traversed the whole country at the head of his troops, terrified the people into submission, usurped the crown, and put many of the nobility to death; and that the kindred of Ambrosius and Uther raised an insurrection against him, destroyed his fortresses and disturbed his reign.

The Book of Basingwerk says, that Vortigern's assumption of the royal dignity was by no means pleasing to the nation in general; that they would not assist him against the Picts, who had declared war against him on account of the murder of their kindred; that he invited foreigners to his assistance, but was disappointed for some time; and that he was defeated in several battles with his adversaries. Thus the History of the Britons is confirmed, with regard to the invasion of the Picts, and the hostility of the Roman nobility, as sources of annoyance to Vortigern; and we are told, that it was on account of these that he had recourse to the Saxons, in exact agreement with the words of Gildas:[4]—

"They begin to deliberate what was best and most expe-
"dient to be determined, to repel so frequent and cruel

"Per regnum fieri, quod tunc rectore carebat.
"Vortigernus enim consul Gewissus in omnes
"Agmina ducebat patrias, ut duceret illas,
"Lædens innocuos miserandâ clade colonos.
"Deniqne vi subitâ rapuit diadema, peremptis
"Nobilibus multis, et regni cuncta subegit.
"Ast hii qui fuerant cognato sanguine juncti
"Fratribus, id graviter tolerantes, igne cremare
"Cœperunt cunctas infausti principis urbes,
"Et turbare suum crudeli milite regnum,
"Nec permiserunt illum cum pace potiri." L. 982. 995.

[4] "Initur namque consilium, quid optimum quidve saluberrimum ad "repellendas tam crebras et tam ferales supradictarum gentium irrup- "tiones prædasque, decerni potius deberet.

"Tunc omnes consiliarii una cum superbo tyranno Gurthrigerno, Bri- "tannorum duce, cæcantur, et adinvenientes tale præsidium, imo ex- "cidium patriæ, ut ferocissimi illi nefandi nominis Saxones, Deo homini- "busque invisi, quasi in caulas lupi, in insulam ad retrudendas aquilo- "nales gentes intromitterentur." C. 22, 23.

"irruptions and plunderings of the aforesaid nations. Then "all the councillors, together with the proud tyrant Gurth-"rigern, the leader of the Britons, are blinded, devising for "their country such a protection, (or rather destruction), as "this, that the most fierce Saxons, of abhorred name, hated "by God and men, should be introduced into the island, like "wolves into the fold, to repel the northern nations."

That the Saxons were invited by Vortigern, appears certain. If he had friendly relations with them in his youth, as we have authority for believing that he had, he would naturally have recourse to them in his perplexity; and perhaps to the family, whose fathers had been associated with the Britons and Picts, in their wars with Maximus, sixty years before, if Wecta and Witta were really the same as Victus and Vetta of the Kirkliston monument. But I believe that the Book of Basingwerk states the truth with regard to this embassy, viz. that it was unsuccessful, and that the later coming of two princes of this family was, as it is uniformly represented, casual; for it is very improbable that a request for military aid would be responded to, by the sending of so small a force, as Horsa and Hencgest are said to have brought with them.

Disappointed in his expectations of assistance from this quarter, Vortigern was compelled to carry on the war with his northern enemies unaided, and its issue was most disastrous. A great part of his army, says Geoffrey of Monmouth, perished in this campaign, and Boece confirms this in a circumstantially detailed narrative. The Picts and Scots, he says, when they heard of the massacre of their kindred, invaded and ravaged Britain. Vortigern, knowing how unpopular he was with the British nobility, and not choosing to expose his own person to danger, sent Gwitell, prince of Wales, at the head of an army to oppose the invaders. Proceeding at once into the North, Gwitell came upon them, whilst free from apprehension of resistance on the part of the

Britons, they were all in disorder, laying the country waste, took five hundred prisoners, whom he executed on the spot, and put the rest to flight. They soon rallied, however, and surprised the Britons in their turn. Frequent skirmishes followed, and eventually a general engagement, in which the Britons were defeated, and Gwitell, with twenty thousand of his army slain, the loss on the other side being scarcely four thousand. All the fortresses of the borders now fell into their hands.

To add to Vortigern's perplexity, (according to the Brut), he now received intelligence that the sons of Constantine were assembling a force in Armorica, for the recovery of their father's kingdom; and this completes the agreement between these authorities, and the History of the Britons.

It was at this juncture that Horsa and Hencgest arrived. The History of the Britons continues:[5]—

"Meanwhile three ceols come to Britain, driven into exile "from Germany, in which Hors and Hencgest, who also "were brothers, were commanders.—Gurthegirn received "them kindly, and delivered to them the island which in their "tongue is called Tanet, in British Roihin."

"But it came to pass after the Saxons pitched their "tents in the aforesaid island Tanet, the aforesaid king pro-"mised to give them food and clothing without fail, because "that they had engaged to fight manfully against his enemies."

Gildas, after some comments on the folly of which Vortigern was guilty in inviting the Saxons, proceeds to say:[6]—

---

5 "Interea tres ceolæ, a Germaniâ in exilium expulsæ, Britanniam ad-"veniunt, in quibus dominabantur Hors et Hencgest, qui et ipsi fratres "erant. Gurthegirnus autem suscepit eos benigne, et tradidit eis insulam "quæ linguâ eorum vocatur Tanet, Brittannice Roihin." C. 31.

"Factum est autem postquam metati sunt Saxones in supradictâ in-"sulâ Tenet, promisit rex supradictus Gurthegirnus dare illis victum et "vestimentum absque defectione, pro eo quod sese promiserant viriliter "contra inimicos ejus pugnaturos." C. 36.

6 "Tum erumpens grex catulorum de cubili leænæ Barbariæ, tribus

"Then a litter of cubs issuing forth from the lair of the "lioness of Barbaria, in three cyuls, as it is expressed in her "tongue, in ours long ships,—on their arrival, by command "of the unlucky tyrant, fixed their terrible claws in the "eastern part of the island, as it were with the intention of "fighting for, but more truly of invading, our country."

The story in the Brut, of the coming and reception of the Saxons, is perfectly consistent with these. Tidings, it is said, were brought to Vortigern, who was then at Canterbury, of the arrival of three ships in the Thames, manned by three hundred strangers, of tall stature and noble bearing. On his sending to inquire if their intentions were peaceable, they replied that they were, and that they were willing to enter into his service. He then invited them to his court, and, when they were come, in answer to his questions, they said that their leader was named Hencgest, and his brother Horsa; and that the occasion of their coming was this, that the customs of their nation obliged them to leave their homes, and seek their fortunes in foreign countries. Vortigern at once enlisted them in his service, and promised to give them lands, if they would assist him in his wars with the Picts. They accepted his proposal, and remained at his court.

The result of these statements appears to be as follows; that on account of the disaffection of the British nobility, Vortigern had invited the Saxons to aid him in his war with the Picts, but without success; that he engaged in the war with such forces as he could command; that after its disastrous issue, and when fresh danger was threatening from Armorica, on the part of the sons of Constantine, a small force

"ut lingua ejus exprimitur cyulis, nostrâ linguâ longis navibus, secundis "velis, secundo omine auguriisque, quibus vaticinabatur, certo apud eum "præsagio, quod ter centum annis terram cui proras librabat insideret; "centum vero quinquaginta, hoc est dimidio temporis, sæpius quoque "vastaret. Evectus primum in orientali parte insulæ, jubente infausto "tyranno terribiles infixit ungues, quasi pro patria pugnaturus, sed eam "certius impugnaturus." C. 23.

of Saxons under Horsa and Hencgest opportunely arrived on the coast of Kent, whom he engaged as stipendiaries in his service; and that they were located in Thanet for a time, receiving supplies from him. This occupation of Thanet was merely a temporary encampment, and this was in A.D. 428; their settlement in Kent belongs to a later period of their history.

It was not long before intelligence reached Vortigern that the Picts had crossed the Humber, and were committing fresh ravages.[7] Hereupon he reassembled his forces, and advanced to meet them, in conjunction with his new allies. An obstinate and bloody engagement ensued which lasted until noon, when Vortigern obtained the victory, mainly through the bravery of the Saxons, and pursued the enemy until evening.

Henry of Huntingdon, quoting, I believe, from the lost work of Gildas, not only confirms this statement of Layamon, but determines the scene of battle:[8]—

" The Saxons, therefore, by command of the same king, " received a place of abode in the eastern part of the island, " ostensibly as defenders of our country, but really as its in- " vaders. They engaged in battle with the Picts and Scots, " who had now advanced as far as Stamford, which is situate " in the southern part of Lincoln, distant therefrom forty

---

[7] Brut. The details are Layamon's.

[8] " Saxones igitur in orientali parte insulæ, jubente eodem rege, locum " manendi, quasi pro patria pugnaturi, re autem verâ hanc expugnaturi, " susceperunt. Inierunt autem certamen contra Pictos et Scottos qui " jam venerunt usque ad Stanfordiam, quæ sita est in australi parte " Lincolniæ, distans ab eâ quadraginta miliariis. Cum igitur illi pilis et " lanceis pugnarent, isti vero securibus gladiisque longis rigidissime de- " certarent, nequiverunt Picti pondus tantum perferre, sed fugâ saluti " suæ consuluerunt; Saxones vero triumpho et prædâ potiti sunt. Quod " ubi Saxoniæ nuntiatum est, simul et insulæ fertilitas ac segnities Bri- " tonum, mittitur confestim illo classis prolixior armatorum ferens ma- " num fortiorem; quæ præmissæ adjuncta cohorti invincibilem fecit " exercitum."

"miles. When, therefore, the latter fought with javelins "and lances, whilst the former contended most fiercely with "axes and long swords, the Picts were unable to resist so "great a pressure, but consulted for their safety by flight, "and the Saxons obtained triumph and booty. And when "the intelligence hereof, as well as of the fertility of the "island, and the sluggishness of the Britons, is conveyed to "Saxony, a larger fleet than the former, carrying a stronger "force of warriors, is immediately dispatched; which, united "to the band which had been previously sent, constituted an "invincible army."

The first part of this passage corresponds to that which has been already cited from Gildas; and the last, to the sentence which immediately follows it.[9] The rest explains the nature of the "success," which is said to have attended the first comers, and encouraged their kindred at home to send them reinforcements.

The tradition of the district in which this battle was fought, tells how the Saxons came from Kent by sea, entered the Nen, and landed near Peterborough; in perfect accordance with what we know of the habits of this people, who always preferred a sea-voyage to a land-journey; and the local nomenclature of the district remarkably illustrates the history and the tradition. For besides several places in the neighbourhood of Stamford, which bear the names of those whom I regard as probably the associates of Horsa and Hencgest, some of which have been already noticed, an ancient entrenchment, Horsey hill, about two miles from Peterborough, bears the name of Horsa. In this district, then, I believe the Saxons sojourned for a while, until succours from Germany enabled them to act on the offensive, and follow the Picts into the North.

---

[9] "Cui supradicta genitrix, primo comperiens agmini fuisse prosperatum, item mittit satellitum canumque prolixiorem catastam, quæ "ratibus advecta adunatur cum manipularibus spuriis." C. 23.

Boece says nothing of the arrival in three ships, nor of the battle of Stamford, but represents Horsa and Hencgest as having a force of ten thousand at their command; which may perhaps represent the number they were able to bring to the standard of Vortigern, after they received this reinforcement.

The next battle appears to have been fought in the district which is now called Yorkshire, and which the Pictish leader, Gryme, is said to have claimed as his hereditary right. Geoffrey says that the Saxons attacked the Picts beyond the Humber; Boece, that they had passed it before their enemies knew of their arrival, (*i. e.* of the arrival of this reinforcement), in Britain; both are agreed that the victory was easily gained, and that the enemy were completely discomfited. Thus we have distinct accounts of two battles, fought in different localities, and with different circumstances; the first an obstinate conflict near Stamford, when the Saxons were few in number; the second in Yorkshire, after the Saxons had been largely reinforced, resulting in an easy victory.

After this Vortigern is said to have given large possessions to Hencgest and his followers. These, Geoffrey says, were in Lindsey, a mistake I suspect for Luidis, for I am satisfied that Boece is correct in saying, that the first settlement of the Saxons was in Yorkshire, and that it was in the neighbourhood of Leeds. The whole history of these incursions of the Picts shows, that their object was to gain possession of the territory north of the Humber; in that district this battle was fought, and the usual result of a battle is to give to the conquerors possession of the battle-field. Moreover, Vortigern's object in giving lands to the Saxons was, that they might be a defence to his kingdom against his northern foes, and this, Layamon and Boece say, that they actually were. It is therefore far more probable, that the lands which were given to them were centrally situated in Yorkshire, than that Vortigern would leave a wide frontier undefended, by locating the Saxons in Lincolnshire. Accordingly, whilst in Lindsey itself, we find no traces of Horsa and Hencgest, we have several in Yorkshire; and the analogy of Cerdicesford, (see p. 149), suggests that Horsforth, five miles from Leeds, may possibly have been the scene of this second victory of the Saxons.

The Saxon chiefs, however, did not content themselves with defending Vortigern's kingdom from the incursions of the Picts and Scots, but prosecuted the war with vigour, resolved on the entire conquest of North Britain. For the details of this war we are indebted to Boece, and the very character of his narrative is of itself an argument for its substantial truth; for it cannot be supposed, that a Scottish historian would have invented stories such as these, reflecting only discredit on his own nation. He is not wholly unsupported; Layamon, as we shall see, speaks of this war, in general terms indeed, but in such as suffice to corroborate his testimony.

Not content, he says, with the slaughter of the Scots and Picts between the Humber and the Tyne, the Saxons ravaged Merse and Pentland with fire and sword, hoping, after the extermination of the Picts, to effect an easy conquest of the Scots. The Picts sent a message to the Scots, entreating them to come to their assistance; but the messengers were scarcely gone, when tidings came that the combined forces of the Britons and Saxons were at hand, and the king of the Picts assembled his troops in haste, and went to meet them. Hencgest, who had the chief command of Vortigern's army, arrayed it in three divisions, and by a simultaneous assault overpowered the Picts, and put them to flight. He then followed up his success by expelling the Picts and Scots from all their settlements in Britain.

The Picts now sent a second message for help to the king of the Scots, and he accordingly summoned his forces to meet within twenty days in the southern part of the wood of Caledon. An army, forty thousand strong, was thus assembled, and soon after they had joined the Picts, they met the forces of Hencgest, whose numbers and martial bearing so terrified them, that many took to flight. The confederate kings, however, sending a detachment in pursuit of the fugitives, compelled them to return to the ranks, and caused several of them to be executed, for an example to the rest. Soon afterwards the battle began with showers of arrows and javelins, and then was continued most furiously with swords and spears and bills, without any apparent advantage on either side, until at length the Britons, who were opposed to the Scots on the right, began to give way. Then suddenly a storm of hail came on, accompanied with so dense a fog, that both armies were compelled to desist from fighting. Hencgest now gathered his people to his standard by sound of trumpet; and when the fog passed away, the Scots and Picts, believing the victory was theirs, intent only on slaughter and spoil, began to pursue the Britons without order, and so fell an easy prey to the Saxons, who turned upon their rear, and spared none whom they could overtake. The greater part of the British division fell, in the battle and in the flight.

Horsley, between Newcastle and Hexham, and another Horsley twenty miles to the northward, may possibly indicate the scenes of this war.

Hencgest did not think fit to pursue his success any further, but, in order that his assistance might still be necessary to the Britons, abandoned the district between the Tyne and Tweed, and returned with his victorious army into Yorkshire. Then, leaving them in their tents because winter was coming on, he repaired to London to Vortigern; to whom he represented the dangers he had undergone in the late war, advised him to send an army to the borders, to keep the enemy in check, and promised on his part to bring in a reinforcement of Saxons, against the next summer. Many of the Britons regarded this proposal with distrust, yet dared not express their suspicions openly, for fear of Hencgest; others on the contrary, and Vortigern, above all, approved his design.

Vortigern richly rewarded his services, and made him his lieutenant in Britain; and Hencgest, perceiving that he had enemies by whom his influence might be undermined, if he were to absent himself, determined to reside constantly at court.

This proposal is mentioned in the History of the Britons, although the events which had intervened, since Vortigern engaged the services of the Saxons, are passed over; for it is evident that some time had elapsed, and it is intimated that the Saxons had been reinforced; and the author of this history represents the jealousy, of which Boece speaks, as more openly expressed, the Britons saying that they had no farther occasion for the services of the Saxons.[10]

" But when the Barbarians were multiplied in number, " the Britons could not feed them, when, as they were wont, " they demanded that food and clothing should be given to " them, as had been previously promised to them. And the " Britons said, ' Your number is multiplied, we do not need " ' your help, depart from us, we will give you neither food " ' nor clothing;' and they deliberating amongst themselves, " seeking how they might have peace, went their way. But " Hencgest, as he was a clever and crafty man, and had found " out the king and nation to be silly and unwarlike, having

---

10 " Cum autem Barbari multiplicati essent numero, non potuerunt " Brittones cibare illos, cum solito more cibum vestemque sibi dari pos- " tularent, ut eis antea fuerat promissum. Dixeruntque Bryttones, " ' Numerus vester multiplicatus est, adjutorio vestro non indigemus, re- " ' cedite a nobis, victum vel vestitum dare nolumus;' et ipsi consilium " inter se facientes, quærentes qualiter pacem haberent, abierunt. Henc- " gistus autem, cum esset vir astutus et callidus, explorassetque regem " indoctum ac gentem [vagitantem], et sine armis commorantem, inito " consilio dixit ad regem Gurthegirnum, ' Pauci sumus, si vis mittemus " ' ad patriam nostram, et invitabimus milites de regione nostra, ut am- " ' plior sit numerus ad certandum pro te et gente tua.' Et impetrata a " rege licentia, miserunt legatos, qui transfretantes Scithiam venerunt ad " patriam suam, electisque inde militibus ac viris bellicosis, reversi sunt " cum XVI ceolis, adducentes secum filiam Hencgisti pulchram valde de- " coraque facie." C. 36, 37.

"devised a scheme, said to King Gurthegirn, 'We are few, "'if thou wilt, we will send to our country, and will invite "'soldiers from our land, that our number may be greater to "'contend for thee and for thy nation.' And having obtained "leave from the king, they sent messengers, who, passing "over Scithia, came to their own country, and soldiers and "warriors being chosen thence, they returned with sixteen "ceols, bringing with them the daughter of Hencgest, who "was very fair, and of beautiful countenance."

Gildas says:[11]—

"They complain that their monthly pay is not given libe-"rally to them, colouring occasions on purpose, and protest "that they will break the treaty and devastate the whole "island, if greater liberality be not extended to them, and "without delay they carry their threats into execution."

But it is evident that he passes over a considerable interval, for nothing had yet occurred on the part of the Saxons to break the peace. The Britons wished to get rid of them, now that they had rendered them the service for which they were engaged, and certainly gave them occasion for dissatisfaction by refusing their pay; but Hencgest was too prudent to lose the opportunity of a settlement in a fertile country like Britain, and was determined to remain, not as the enemy, but as the ally of Vortigern. This the subsequent story shows, and I gladly adopt the "quærentes qua-"liter pacem haberent" of the Paris MS., (which represents an earlier version of the History of the Britons than any other extant), in preference to the "quærentes qualiter pacem "rumperent" of the Vatican MS., and similar expressions in others. Throughout the whole history of Hencgest we must bear in mind, that it comes to us through inimical channels

---

[11] "Queruntur non affluenter sibi epimenia contribui, occasiones de "industria colorantes, et nisi profusior eis munificentia cumularetur, "testantur se cuncta insulæ, rupto fœdere, depopulaturos. Nec mora, "minas effectibus prosequuntur." C. 23.

only, and we must judge him by his actions, not by the motives which the author of the Brut and Boece impute to him.

Layamon speaks in general terms of the battles, of which Boece gives so detailed a narrative; saying, that whilst Hencgest occupied the lands which Vortigern had given him, the Picts dared not enter Britain, or if they did they were soon slain; and afterwards representing Hencgest as pleading with the king, on a festival day when he was rejoicing with his people, how faithfully he had served him, how he had been foremost in every fight, and as taking the opportunity to suggest the policy of inviting from Germany a fresh body of his countrymen, and to prefer a request, that some strong castle or city might be assigned to him for his security. Vortigern adopted the suggestion, but dared not accede to the request, for fear of exasperating his subjects, with whom he was already unpopular. Hencgest then begged that he might have as much land given to him for the site of a castle as he could encompass with a bull's hide. This was granted; and accordingly, after having sent to Germany for fresh forces, he encompassed with a thong made of a bull's hide a rocky place which he had chosen, and built thereon a castle, surrounded by a stone wall and a deep ditch, which was called Kaer-Carrei by the Britons, and by the Saxons, Thwong-caster or Thong-castle.[12]

[12] The circumstance of the thong of bull's hide is sufficient, in the opinion of many persons, to condemn the whole story, because it occurs also in that of the foundation of Carthage, in the Saga of Ragnar Lodbrok, and elsewhere; and if we had only the English name, the probability might have been admitted, that this had suggested the tradition of its origin. But the fact, that not only the English name, but its British equivalent, are given in a work which I regard as originally composed by S. Albinus, in the sixth century, not more than a hundred years, if so much, after the event; at a time when the British race still formed a considerable proportion of the population of the district in which this castle was situated, suggests the possibility that this tradition may have its foundation in truth, and that the encircling of the site of an intended stronghold with the hide of a bull, recorded as having happened here, as

Boece alludes to this story as accounting for the name of the castle, which he says was in Yorkshire; and he adds that, whatever might be thought of the alleged derivation of the name, it was certain that the Saxons had their first settlement in that district.

I have already stated my conviction, that their second victory and their first settlement were in the neighbourhood of Leeds; and considering the fact, that Hencgest, after his expulsion from Britain, laid the foundations of a city, the name of which is almost identical with that of Leeds, (Leide, or Leyden), I think it is very probable that the name Caer Carrei may still be traced in that of Quarry hill, in Leeds. The ancient fortress which crowned this hill is now scarcely traceable, but there were remains in the time of Thoresby, which clearly indicated a place of great strength. It is believed that a numerous British population continued to dwell about Leeds, even in the times of the Northumbrian kings, and the name Caer Carrei may have been retained on account of the tradition of its origin, along with that of Caer Loitcoit.

After the invitation had been sent to Germany for fresh forces, Boece says that Vortigern, by Hencgest's advice, sent an army of five thousand Britons to defend the northern frontier; that these were destroyed during the winter by the Picts and Scots; and that a second force, ten thousand strong, followed and met with the same fate. In due course, an army of five thousand Saxons arrived, with Hencgest's wife and daughter, and ten men of noble blood. Hencgest paid a hasty visit to his kindred, and then returned to London, to make preparations for a war with the Picts and Scots in the following summer.

---

elsewhere, may really have been a religious rite, intended to secure impregnability to the place. If the Hindoos, as is probable, were acquainted with such a rite, it would be easy for them to be persuaded, that the English merchants had practised it, when they obtained possession of Calcutta.

The daughter of Hencgest is called Rowena in the Brut, but in the Capitula prefixed to the Cambridge MS. of the History of the Britons, Romwenna. Rumwen is a true Teutonic female name, and as this form is preserved in these Capitula, and is one which was very likely to be changed to Rowena in the course of transcription, we may accept it without difficulty. The "ten men of noble blood" are probably the ancestors of the Anglo-Saxon royal dynasties, the kindred of Hencgest, whose names we have traced in districts connected with his memory. The number of auxiliaries, here stated by Boece, is probably not far from the truth, for that of the vessels is said in most MSS. of the History of the Britons to have been sixteen, seventeen in others, and eighteen in the Brut; and it appears from the Brut, and from Procopius also, that these vessels were capable of containing from two hundred and fifty to three hundred men each. Layamon says it was fifteen hundred, but the circumstances of the story seem to require a larger number; and possibly Layamon misunderstood the authority he followed.

These four first victories of the Saxons belong to A. D. 428; the two defeats of the Britons are said to have occurred in the winter, and the fresh arrival of Saxons would be in A. D. 429, followed by the events which we have now to consider.

In the summer, according to Boece, Hencgest proceeded leisurely into the North, and there awaited the coming of Vortimer, to whom the command of the British army was entrusted. On his arrival, the Britons and Saxons combined advanced beyond the Tyne to meet the Picts and Scots, who were moving southward, sixty thousand strong. Frequent skirmishes occurred between the two armies, but Hencgest would allow no provocation on the part of the enemy to bring on a general engagement, knowing that nothing was so effectual as delay to cool their ardour; and a valley and morass between his forces and theirs, favoured his purpose. To obviate this impediment, the allied kings commanded their people to cut turf and make a pathway through the moss; this done, they passed quietly over to a hill that overlooked the position of the Britons and Saxons, and from this elevation they contrived to annoy them, by hurling fragments of rock down upon them. Finding that they could neither provoke them to battle, nor drive them from their tents by this artifice, they had recourse to another; they collected an immense quantity of heather, made it into bundles, and after nightfall set them on fire, and cast them among the tents. This caused great confusion amongst the Britons and Saxons; some ran to guard the trenches, others occupied themselves in trying to quench the flames, but the burning faggots fell so fast, and the darkness of the night added so much to their perplexity, that their leaders had no alternative but to prepare for battle. Accordingly they led their troops forth into the plains in good order, where Hencgest gathered them to his standard by sound of trumpet, and waited for the dawn of day. The enemy came down from the hill, expecting an easy victory over an army thrown into disorder, but, finding it was quite otherwise, they too delayed the attack until day-break, and then the battle began. For some time the advantage seemed to be on their side; but eventually a reserve of three thousand, whom Hencgest had posted in a wood, assailed the Scots in the rear, and they were forced to give way, and their king was severely wounded and carried off by his friends to the neighbouring mountains. Meanwhile, the Picts had routed the Britons who were opposed to them, slain great numbers and driven the rest into a river; but the approach of night prevented an encounter between them and the Saxons; and, as they dared not wait for an opportunity of measuring their strength with them on the morrow, they collected all their carts and waggons, and everything that could impede their flight, under cover of the night, set them on fire, and then effected their escape with the remnant of the Scots. Hencgest did not pursue them, but returned with his army into Yorkshire, and after instructing them to be on their guard, in case of any fresh invasion, repaired to London, to consult with Vortigern as to the future conduct of the war. Four thousand Saxons are said to have fallen in this contest, which appears to have lasted from morning until night of a summer's day.

This battle is not noticed at all in the British Chronicles. It appears to have been fought in Northumberland, as well as the two last of the previous year's campaign; and the description of the country is so circumstantial, that I have no doubt it was in the neighbourhood of Long Horsley, between the rivers Coquet and Wansbeck; the former, probably, flows through the valley which separated in the first instance the hostile armies, and the latter is the river into which the Britons were driven by the Picts; Wingates the hill at the foot of which the Britons and Saxons were encamped, until compelled to abandon their position; and the hills to the west, the neighbouring mountains, to which the Scots fled with their wounded king. The relative situation of these places agress exactly with the indications in Boece's narrative.

The fortress of Thwong-caster being now completed, Hencgest invited Vortigern thither to visit his wife and daughter, and to encourage by his presence the Saxon troops. In the History of the Britons we read:[13]—

---

13 "Hencgistus convivium rege et militibus suis et interpreti suo "nomine Ceretic præparavit, ac filiam suam puellam jussit illis ministrare, "vinumque et siceram ubertim propinare, quatenus saturarentur nimis-"que inebriarentur. Sed illis bibentibus et valde inebriatis, diabolo in-"stigante, Guorthegirnus amore inardescens puellæ, per interpretem "suum illam postulavit a patre suo, promisitque ei dicens, 'Quicquid "'postulaveris pro ea a me voluntarie tibi præstabo.' Hencgistus autem "inito consilio cum senioribus comitibusque suis, qui secum venerant de "genere Ochgul, vel Ongle, petiit pro puella provinciam quæ vocatur "Anglice Centland, Brittonnice autem Ceint. Et data est illis ipsa pro-"vincia, ignorante Guorancguono qui tunc temporis regnabat in Cantia. "Quem quidem dolor nimius exagitabat, quia regnum suum clam dolose-"que et imprudenter alienigenis traditum est. Sic tamen puella regi "tradita est, dormivitque cum ea, et ultra modum amavit." C. 37.

"Hencgest prepared a banquet for the king, and his "knights, and his interpreter, Ceretic by name, and com-"manded the maiden, his daughter, to serve them abundantly "with wine and mead, so that they might be filled, and be "made very drunk. And whilst they were drinking, and "much inebriated, by the devil's instigation, Guorthegirn, "burning with love of the maiden, demanded her of her "father through his interpreter, and promised him, saying, "'I will willingly give thee whatever thou shalt ask of me "'for her.' But Hencgest having deliberated with his "elders, and his comrades, who had come with him of the "race of Ongle, demanded for the maiden the province which "is called in English Centland, but in British Ceint. And "the province was given to them without the knowledge of "Guorancgon who at that time reigned in Kent.—So the "maiden was delivered to the king, and he slept with her, "and loved her above measure."

The Brut and Boece relate this story in nearly the same terms. In the former the feeling of hostility to Hencgest which is displayed in this passage, does not appear. Instead of imputing to him the design of making Vortigern drunk, it is merely stated that Rumwen came into the hall during the feast, and presented to the king a cup of wine with the words, "Hláford cyning wes hǽl," and that Vortigern, instructed by his interpreter, replied, "Drinc hǽl." This was but the ordinary custom of Teutonic hospitality, as exemplified more than once in Beowulf; and this circumstance, related by a British author, with the preservation of the words, appears strongly to confirm the truth of the story.

Layamon says that Guorancgon was the hereditary prince of Kent; and that the mother of Vortigern's three sons, Vortimer, Catigern, and Pascent, was dead at the time of this second marriage. Boece says she was living, and that Vortigern repudiated her for the sake of Rumwen; and his statement appears the more probable, as he connects it with the following circumstances which are not noticed by the British authorities.

After Vortigern had returned to London with his bride, Vodin, Bishop of London, visited him at Vortimer's request, reproached him with having repudiated his lawful wife and married a Pagan, and represented to him the mischief which would inevitably follow. Vortigern with grief lamented his wickedness, and promised to make reparation; but at that moment Hencgest came in, rebuked him for giving way to grief at the time of his marriage, slew Vodin[14] and his attendant clergy, and would have slain Vortimer also, if he had not made his escape.

Thus for the first time, about a year after his arrival, was the peace broken between Hencgest and the Britons, and Boece supplies a sufficient and satisfactory cause for the breach. The friendship between him and Vortigern still continued, and with his aid, although a great part of the British nation had forsaken him, and espoused the cause of Ambrosius, he still maintained his power. He was now obliged to depend on his foreign auxiliaries; and the History of the Britons informs us that a larger force was sent for at this time, than had been deemed necessary before:[15]—

---

[14] This Vodin is named as the successor of Guidelin in the see of London, with a notice of his having been put to death by the Saxons, in the catalogue of bishops compiled by Joannes Phurmius in the beginning of the eleventh century, a circumstance which adds considerable weight to the statements in the Brut and Boece relative to these prelates; for Phurmius lived considerably earlier than the time of the first appearance of the Brut in England, and of Veremund, from whom probably Boece's information was derived.

[15] "Hencgistus autem pater puellæ Guorthegirno regi dixit, 'Ego ero " 'pater tuus et consiliator, cave ne transgrediaris consilium meum, quia " 'nunquam ab ullo homiue vel ulla gente superari timebis, quoniam gens " 'mea valida est, ad bellandumque robusta. Si vis mittam ad filium " 'meum cum fratruele suo qui sunt viri bellatores, invitans eos ut " 'dimicent contra Scottos, et da illis regiones quæ sunt in Aquilone " 'juxta murum qui vocatur Guaul.' Licentia autem improvidi regis in-" vitavit eos, Ochta videlicet et Ebisa cum XL ceolis. At vero ipsi cum

"Hencgest, the father of the maiden, said to King Guor-
"thigern, 'I will be thy father and counsellor, take care not
" 'to transgress my counsel, for thou shalt never be overcome
" 'by any man or nation, since my nation is strong, and
" 'mighty for war. If thou wilt, I will send to my son and
" 'his cousin, who are warriors, inviting them to fight against
" 'the Scots, and do thou give them the regions which are in
" 'the North near to the wall.' So, by the permission of the
" short-sighted king, he invited them, namely Ochtha and
" Ebisa with forty ceols. But they, whilst they sailed around
" the Picts, wasted the Orkney Isles, and occupied very
" many regions, as far as the frontiers of the Picts. So
" Hencgest invited, by little and little, the ceols of his
" country to himself, so that they left the islands whence they
" came without inhabitant. But when their nation had in-
" creased in might and multitude, they came to the aforesaid
" region of the Cantuarii."

Boece, (who, however, erroneously places these events before the banquet, and the marriage of Vortigern), says that on account of the arrival of fresh intelligence, of the preparations Ambrosius and Uther were making in Armorica, for the recovery of the kingdom, Hencgest suggested that the Saxons in Yorkshire, whom Horsa commanded, should be placed in all the fortresses along the coast opposite to Gaul; and that, when a messenger brought word from Pentland, that the Scots were preparing to invade Britain again, others who were in Hencgest's interest proposed to Vortigern, that Occa, Hencgest's son, should be invited; that he should have the charge of defending the northern frontier, whilst Horsa

" navigarent circa Pictos vastaverunt Orcades insulas, et occupaverunt
" regiones plurimas usque ad confinium Pictorum. Hencgistus autem in-
" vitabat paulatim ceolas suæ regionis ad se, ita ut insulas aliquas (a qui-
" bus) venerant absque habitatore relinquerent. At dum gens illorum
" crevisset in virtute et in multitudine venerunt ad supradictam regionem
" Cantuariorum." C. 38.

guarded the coasts, and that Hencgest should remain with Vortigern.

It is not a little remarkable, as confirmatory of this story, that we have many traces of the presence of Horsa in the counties in question, but scarcely any of Hencgest, who is represented as having remained at court. It was necessarily after the arrival of Octa, that Horsa left Yorkshire, for otherwise the northern frontier would have been left undefended. Boece says that Octa brought with him a force of ten thousand warriors, and this agrees with the statement in the History of the Britons, allowing two hundred and fifty to each vessel; but he adds that their wives and children also came and settled in Northumberland, and this,—taken in connection with the statement above quoted that so large an immigration of Saxons took place in consequence of Hencgest's invitations, that the islands whence they came were left without inhabitant, and with the name of another leader, who may be believed to have conducted them, in the Brut,—enables us to account for the larger number of three hundred ships, which are represented, in the Brut, as having come at this time. This leader is called Chledric, (*i. e.* Childeric), in the Welsh Brut; we have many traces of his presence in the districts which are connected with the memory of Horsa and Hencgest; and we shall meet with him again later in the history.

The district along the wall was to be given to these new comers. This, therefore, would be a real immigration, not a mere military adventure; and so ten thousand warriors in forty ceols may well have been followed by their wives and children, as well as by other bodies of their countrymen. The Welsh Brut mentions Ossa, the uncle of Octa, as having accompanied him, but not Ebissa, (who is said to have been the son of Horsa in Capitula, and the son of Hencgest's sister in the Irish version of the History of the Britons); Layamon mentions all the three in the subsequent story.

Fordun here supplies important information, which enables

us to understand the above-quoted passage, and Boece also; showing that there was a concerted movement on the part of the Scots and of Ambrosius, which rendered necessary the invitation of fresh forces, and the defence of the coasts as well as of the frontier. He says, (and Buchanan, although he omits some details, agrees with him), that Ambrosius sent messengers to Drostan, King of the Picts, (Drust Mac Erp, A.D. 409 to 454); desiring to form an alliance with him, but that Hencgest was beforehand, and had already engaged him to assist him against the Britons; that after Hencgest had established his kingdom in Kent, relying on the faith of the Picts, he sent Octa and Ebissa to occupy the northern parts of Britain, resist the Scots, and prevent them from co-operating with Ambrosius; that they were well received by the Picts, and made war upon the Scots, in conjunction with them. This is precisely in accordance with the motive assigned for their being invited, "that they may fight against the Scots," and for the limits stated of their occupation, "as far as the "frontiers of the Picts."

This is the earliest notice of any actual movement on the part of Ambrosius; there can be no doubt that Vortimer had made common cause with him; and that, although their names are not mentioned, they were Vortigern's opponents in many battles of which the Brut speaks; in all of which, through the assistance of the Saxons, he was victorious. Of this war we seem to have many traces in Leicestershire, Staffordshire, Worcestershire, Oxfordshire, Berkshire, Hampshire, and even as far west as the borders of Cornwall, in places named after Horsa and Hencgest, and their followers.

Hencgest was now bent in securing for himself and his family, including of course the issue of Vortigern's marriage with his daughter, the sovereignty of Britain. The Saxons everywhere, (according to the Brut), endeavoured to strengthen their interest by intermarriages with the Britons, and Boece tells us that Octa, in compliance with instructions received from Hencgest, put to death all the British nobles who dwelt in the North, alleging in excuse to Vortigern, when called to account for it, that they were in treasonable correspondence with his enemies. Vortigern, he says, was very much perplexed; on the one hand, the Britons who still remained faithful to him implored him to break with the Saxons; on the other, the suspicions which recent events had excited conflicted with his attachment to Hencgest; but whilst he hesitated what course to pursue, Hencgest solved the difficulty by retiring to Kent, and expelling therefrom, under pain of death, all the Britons who dwelt therein.

This estrangement, however, did not last long; for in the subsequent wars with Vortimer, it is said that Vortigern was always with Hencgest; indeed his deposition, and the election of Vortimer to the sovereignty, which occurred not long afterwards, would naturally lead to a reconciliation between them, if it had not taken place before.

The arrival of Octa, and of Ambrosius, and the commencement of the war between Ambrosius and the Saxons, must be referred to the latter part of A. D. 429.

This year was also marked by the first mission of S. Germanus to Britain, as the decisive authority of Prosper of Aquitaine,[16] his cotemporary, testifies. His family was connected by the marriage of his sister with that of Ambrosius;[17] and this connection seems to throw some light on the history

---

16 "Florentio et Dionysio Coss. Agricola Pelagianus, Severiani Pela-"giani episcopi filius, Ecclesias Britanniæ dogmatis sui insinuatione cor-"rupit. Sed ad actionem Palladii Diaconi, papa Cœlestinus Germanum "Autissiodorensem episcopum vice sua mittit, et deturbatis hæreticis "Britannos ad catholicam fidem dirigit."

17 Rhedyv — children: Germanus; N. (a daughter) = Aldor
Cynvawr — children: Aldor; Constantine
N. (a daughter) = Aldor — child: Emyr
Constantine — children: Ambrosius; Uther
Emyr = N. (a daughter of Uther) — child: Hoel
Uther — child: Arthur

of both his missions. His first was in A.D. 429, the year in which Ambrosius returned to Britain, and the second, (as the sequel will show), was about A.D. 443, the time of Ambrosius' second return. This cannot have been a mere coincidence; and when it is considered that the murder of Vodin, and the flight of Vortimer, must be referred to A.D. 429, the conjecture may be admitted, that the representations of Vortimer to Ambrosius suggested this mission, and that S. Germanus was chosen for it, as connected with the family of Ambrosius, no less than on account of his character for learning and holiness. The statements in the Capitula[18] that he came for the first time during the reign of Vortigern, and for the second just before its close; the accounts of his intercourse with Vortigern, in the History of the Britons; Roger of Wendover's notices of his influence with Vortimer; and Constantius' description of the Alleluia victory; which have presented difficulties so great, under the supposition that the Saxons arrived in Britain in A.D. 449, are all perfectly consistent with the true dates of the accession of Vortigern, A.D. 425, and of the arrival of the Saxons, A.D. 428. These events will all be noticed in their chronological order; here I will only remark that there is nothing, in the Life of S. Germanus written by Constantius forty years after his death, (and transcribed almost word for word by Bæda, as far as it relates to events in Britain), to warrant the notion that his visit was of short duration. So far from its being a simple mission, resulting in a synod, and the condemnation of the heresy, it appears to have been a true apostolate, in the benefits of which the whole country shared. It is evident, from

---

[18] "XXIX. Quando Sanctus Germanus fidem prædicaturus Brittanniam "venerit et Pelagianam hæresim exstirpavit, damnavit, et omnino destruxit. "XLVIII. De secundo adventu Sancti Germani in Brittanniam, et qualiter "fugientem Vortigernum, ut ei fidem prædicaret, Sanctus Germanus "sollicite subsecutus sit; et nocte, igne de cœlo cadente, rex in arce cum "suis exustus fuit."

the terms in which it is described, that S. Germanus remained in this island for a considerable time, until, by preaching through the length and breadth of the land, he had thoroughly accomplished his work of bringing back the churches of Britain to the orthodox faith,—a work which must necessarily have been very tedious and laborious, compared with what it would be now. When, in addition to this, we consider that the story of the last twenty years of S. Germanus' life is almost wholly devoted to his proceedings during his two sojourns in Britain, the probability is confirmed, that a considerable part of those twenty years was spent in this country. I have therefore the more confidence in accepting the British traditions relative to S. Germanus; and, (in substance at least), that story in particular, of which the probability may be thought most open to question, on account of some of its circumstances. It is found in the most ancient MSS. of the History of the Britons;[19] it is related, (with some difference), in the Life of S. Germanus by Heric of Auxerre, on the authority of Marcus; and, as Mr. Gunn informs us, is still current in Wales.

Benlli Gawr, of whom it is related, appears from other sources to have been a chieftain resident at the time, in the district which is the scene of the story. That he refused hospitality to S. Germanus, that he came to a miserable end which was regarded as a Divine judgment upon him for so doing, and that Cadell Deyrnllwg, the herdsman who received S. Germanus, was raised to the principality of Powys, and was the ancestor of a long line of princes, are circumstances by no means improbable. It is said that Benlli perished in the destruction of his castle by fire from heaven; but Boece, who erroneously substitutes the name of Kenrik, (Cyneric the son of Cerdic), for that of Benlli, says that he was slain by the people, because he made S. Germanus lie out doors in

[19] C. 32. 35.

an evil night; and this may be the true version of the story, that the people rose against him and destroyed his castle by fire, because he refused shelter to S. Germanus and his company, in a severe winter's night, as Marcus related it to Heric.

S. Germanus' labours for the conversion of the Pelagians were closed by a synod[20] in which their clergy were confuted; and it is not improbable that the deposition of Vortigern, related in the following passage of the History of the Britons, may have been one of the acts of the same synod:[21]—

"In addition to all his other crimes, Guorthegirn took his "daughter to wife, and she bare him a son. When this became known to S. Germanus, he came to rebuke him with "all the British clergy. And whilst a great assembly of

---

[20] Camden says the synod was at S. Albans, misunderstanding the statement, that S. Germanus and his companion S. Lupus, after it was concluded, "petierunt Sanctum Albanum," that is, repaired to S. Albans, to give thanks for their success.

[21] "Ac super omnia mala adjiciens, Guorthegirnus accepit filiam suam "sibi (in) uxorem, quæ peperit ei filium. Hoc autem cum compertum "esset Sancto Germano, venit eum corripere cum omni clero Brittonum. "Dumque congregatio magna sinodi clericorum laicorumque esset una in "consilio, rex stolidissimus præmonuit filiam suam ut exiret ad sinodum, "diceretque coram omnibus quod ipse pater esset infantis. Mulier vero "impudica fecit sicut prius erat edocta, suscepitque infantulum Sanctus "Germanus et dixit, 'Pater tibi ero nate, nec te dimittam donec mihi "'novacula cum forcipe pectineque detur, et tibi liceat hæc patri tuo "'carnali dare.' Sicque factum est, et infans Sancto obedivit Germano, "perrexitque ad avum suum, patrem scilicet carnalem, Guorthegirnum, "et dixit illi puer, 'Pater meus es, caput meum tonde et comam capitis "'mei.' Et ille erubescens siluit, et infantulo respondere noluit, sed "surgens iratus est valde, a facieque Scĩ Germani fugiens maledictus ac "dampnatus est a sancto, et ab omni sinodali conventu." C. 39.

The child, who is the subject of the story, is mentioned afterwards:—

"Quartus (sc. filius Guorthegirni) fuit Faustus, qui a filia sua illi genitus est, quem Sanctus Germanus baptizavit, enutrivit, et docuit, et ædificato monasterio non parvo super ripam fluminis nomine Renis, sibi "consecravit, ibique perseverat usque in hodiernum diem." C. 48.

This notice appears, from the concluding words, to have been written whilst he was living. There can be no doubt of his identity with Edeyrn, a son of Vortigern, who founded a community of monks, at a place which is still named from him Llanedeyrn, on the river Rumney in Glamorganshire.

" clerics and laics was deliberating in synod, the most foolish " king suggested to his daughter, that she should go to the " synod and say before all, that he (S. Germanus) was the " father of the child. The shameless woman did as she had " before been instructed, and S. Germanus took the infant, " and said, 'I will be a father to thee, my son, and I will not " 'let thee go until a razor, scissors, and a comb be given me, " 'and thou be allowed to give them to thy carnal father.' " And so it was done, and the infant obeyed S. Germanus, " and went to his grandfather, his carnal father, Guorthegirn; " and the boy said to him, 'Thou art my father, shave my " 'head, and the hair of my head.' And he blushed and was " silent, and would not answer the child, but rose and was " very angry, and, fleeing from the face of S. Germanus, was " cursed and condemned by the saint, and by all the synodal " assembly."

Two MSS., of no great authority, but useful inasmuch as they have perpetuated in this instance what was doubtless an old tradition, contain a passage to the effect, that Vortimer was present at the synod, fell at the feet of S. Germanus, begged him to pardon the outrage that had been offered to him, and gave him the land upon which the synod had been held, as a reparation for it; and that it was thenceforth called Guartheuniaun, which signifies "the calumny justly retorted." It is probably Worthen, a parish partly in Shropshire, and partly in Montgomeryshire; and one of the churches which are believed to have been founded by S. Germanus, is in the neighbouring parish of Castell Caereinion.

This story is in exact accordance with chronology, for as S. Germanus came in A. D. 429, and Vortimer's first victory over the Saxons is dated five years after their arrival, *i. e.* in A. D. 433, we have an interval of four years, for a child to be born at least a year after his arrival, (so as to give some colour to the calumny), and to have attained to an age when he could walk and speak. Moreover, we seem to have an incidental confirmation of part of the story at least, in the conclusion of the inscription on the pillar of Eliseg at Valle Crucis; the more valuable, because it speaks of a circumstance which is not related here, the blessing of Vortimer by S. Germanus, and that, not in the way of narrative, but alluding to it as something well known. The name of Pascent, the brother of Vortimer, occurs distinctly in the line which precedes this passage, and I have no hesitation in supplying the blanks as follows:—

GUA[R]T[IMER] FILIUS GUARTHI
[GERNI] QUE BENED GERMANUS QUĒ
PEPERIT EI SEEIRA FILIA MAXIMI
[RE]GIS QUI OCCIDIT REGEM ROMANO
RUM.

The last line of course alludes to the slaughter of Gratian by Maximus; and, whether the name of Vortigern has been correctly connected with the coming of the Saxons in A. D. 375, or not, the mother of his three sons, Vortimer, Catigirn, and Pascent, (who must themselves have been fathers at the time when Horsa and Hencgest came), may very well have been a daughter of Maximus. Here, then, we have a valuable notice of "Guarthimer whom Germanus blessed, the "son of Guarthigern whom Severa bare to him, the daughter "of King Maximus, who killed the King of the Romans."

Boece speaks of an assembly of the British nobility at London, in which Vortigern was formally deposed, and Vortimer raised to the throne. This may be supposed to have immediately followed the synod; after which S. Germanus is said to have repaired to S. Albans to give thanks for his success, probably on his way to London.

CHAPTER IX.

The Reign of Vortimer, A. D. 433 *to* 436.

THE accession of Vortimer must be dated A. D. 433. Ambrosius' title to the throne was doubtless better than his, but Vortimer had the advantage of maturer years. It is evident that the party in Britain, who were attached to the family of Vortigern, was very strong, and the safety of Britain demanded that both parties should coalesce, and make common cause against the Saxons. The influence of S. Germanus may have influenced Ambrosius to acquiesce in the choice of the British nobles, to recognize Vortimer as sovereign, and to accept of a share in the government or a subordinate principality; for the supposition, that Ambrosius also began to reign in this year, will enable us to account for the different statements as to the length of his reign, in the Life of Merlin and in other authorities. Accordingly we find him associated with Vortimer in the struggle which ensued, and S. Germanus still appears, assisting Vortimer with his counsels during the intervals of rest.

The accounts of the war, which Vortimer renewed with the Saxons, immediately on his accession, vary considerably, but may be reconciled without much difficulty. That in the History of the Britons must be cited first, as being the earliest:[1]—

"Guorthemer, the son of Guorthegern fought bravely "against Hencgest and Hors and their nation, and drove "them to the aforesaid Isle of Tenet, and there three times "shut them up, besieged with slaughter, reduced by his "assaults; and they sent messengers over sea to Germany, "to increase their fleet, and invite ceols with a great number "of warriors; and with these so collected they fought against "the kings and princes of the British nation, and sometimes "by conquest extended their boundaries, but sometimes were "conquered and expelled. But Guorthemer waged war with "them manfully four times; first as has been said above; the "second battle he fought upon the river Derguint; the third "upon the ford which in their tongue is called Episford, but "in our tongue Secthergabail, and there fell Hors and a son "of Guorthegirn, named Catigirn, fighting in battle; but "the fourth battle he fought against the Saxons near the "stone which is on the shore of the Gallic sea, and obtained "the victory, but the Saxons fled to their ships."

The text of this passage is evidently corrupt in all the MSS. of this history, Latin as well as Irish. The Latin, (with the exception of the Paris and Vatican MSS.), give the

---

[1] "Guorthemer filius Guorthegirni contra Hencgestum et Horsum et "gentem illorum petulanter pugnabat, et usque ad supra dictam insulam "Tenet expulit; eosque tribus vicibus ibi conclusit, obsedit occidens, "comminuit atterens. Et ipsi legatos ultra mare ad Germaniam trans- "mittebant, ad classem augendam, ceolasque provocandas cum ingenti "numero virorum bellatorum; atque his ita congregatis pugnabant contra "reges et principes Brittannicæ gentis, et aliquando dilatabant terminos "suos, aliquando autem vincebantur et expellebantur. Guorthemer "autem quater contra illos bellum viriliter egit; primum ut supra dictum "est; secundum super flumen Derguint bellum fecit; tertium super "vadum quod lingua eorum Episford vocatur, in nostra autem lingua "Secthergabail, et ibi cecidit Horsus, et filius Guorthegirni, nomine "Catigirn, in pugna bellantes; quartum vero bellum juxta lapidem qui "super ripam maris Gallici est contra Saxones egit, et victoriam optinuit, "Saxones vero fugerunt usque ad naves suas." C. 43, 44.

number of battles as four, but enumerate only three; the first on the Derwent, the second at Episford, the third on the sea-shore, and in this order the Brut agrees with them. The Irish MSS., (with one exception which omits Episford), enumerate four; the first on the Derwent, the second Rethenegabail, the third on the shore of the Iccian sea, the fourth at Episford; thus making two battles out of the second or third of the Latin copies. I suspect that the words "ut" to "secundum" had been omitted by a scribe, supplied in the margin of one MS., and then restored, but in the wrong place, to the text of that from which the Paris and Vatican editions were derived; that they were wanting in the original of the other MSS. and that such alterations were made in the numerals, as the defect of the text seemed to require. I regard this as the only way of accounting for the variations which the MSS. now present, and I venture to restore the passage thus:—

"Primum super flumen Derguint bellum fecit, secundum "ut supra dictum est, tertium super vadum quod lingua "eorum Episford vocatur," &c.

According to Boece, Vortimer made an alliance with the Picts and Scots, promising to give up to them all the lands beyond the Humber. Their united forces at once invaded the territories of the Saxons between the Humber and the Tyne; but whilst they were ravaging the country the troops of Octa appeared, and although he perceived that their numbers were greater than his own, he gave them battle at once. The issue was doubtful for a time, but at length, overpowered by the superior force of their enemies, the Saxons were forced to give way. Octa used his utmost endeavours, by promises and threats, to restore the battle, but in vain. His army was completely discomfited; greater numbers fell in the flight than had fallen in the battle; and he escaped with but few followers, reached the Humber, and thence sailed to Kent. Vortimer now raised the standard of the cross, called upon all Christians to follow it, and thus gathered together an army of eighty thousand men, as well of priests and monks, as of the laity. With these he gained so great a victory, ten thousand Saxons falling in the battle, that Kent and the neighbouring provinces were recovered by the Britons, and the country between the Humber and the Tyne restored to the Picts and Scots. Hencgest and Octa fled with their vanquished forces into Northumberland, hoping to maintain themselves there, until succour should arrive from Germany; but they were attacked by the Picts and Scots, and driven to the mouth of the Humber, whence they took to their ships and returned home.

Roger of Wendover, an authority of very little weight in general, furnishes an account of this war which enables us to understand the statements in the History of the Britons, and to connect them with those of Boece. He says:[2]—

"In the year of grace 454, the nobles of Britain, abandon-"ing altogether King Vortigern, unanimously raised to the "throne his son Vortimer; and he, acquiescing entirely in "their counsels, began to expel the Barbarians, and pursuing "them as far as the river Derwent, there gained a victory. "Vortigern, who assisted them as much as he could, on "account of his wife, fled with the rest. Then Vortimer, "having gained the victory, began to restore to his country-"men their lost possessions, and commanded that the destroyed "churches should be rebuilt, and ecclesiastics honoured in all "things."

There are several Derwents in England, but the position

---

[2] "Anno gratiæ CCCCLIV magnates Britanniæ, regem Vortigernum "penitus deserentes, unanimiter Vortimerum filium ejus in regem subli-"maverunt. Qui consiliis eorum in omnibus acquiescens, cœpit expellere "Barbaros, et insequens eos usque ad flumen Derewent, ibi victoriâ "potitus est. Fugit autem cum aliis Vortigernus, qui, propter uxorem "suam, quod potuit illis auxilium impendebat. Tunc Vortimerus, victoriam "adeptus, cœpit possessiones amissas civibus reddere, ipsosque diligere, "ecclesias destructas renovare, atque viros ecclesiasticos in omnibus "honorare præcepit."

of the Derbyshire Derwent, and the occurrence of Horsley on its banks, induce me to give it the preference as the scene of this first battle.

Having defeated the Saxons, and driven them into Yorkshire, where their position was too strong to be assailed by the Britons alone, Vortimer appears to have employed the interval of rest, thereby secured for South Britain, in the organization of his kingdom, assisted by the counsels of S. Germanus, (as we are told in the Brut), and also in securing the alliance of the Scots; for the next battle, recorded by Roger of Wendover,[3] is the first of Boece's, fought between the Humber and the Tyne:—

"In the year of grace 455, which is the seventh year of "the coming of the Angles into Britain, the nation of the "Angles, with Vortigern, having recruited their strength, "began to challenge Vortimer King of the Britons to battle. "Their battalions coming together from different parts at "Ailestorp, fought fiercely and long; at length the fortune "of the battle turned against the Saxons, who declined the "combat and fled. The Britons, boldly pursuing them, slew "an immense multitude, and the rest being dispersed, Vor-"timer returned victorious to his quarters."

This description of the battle agrees exactly with Boece's, and I have no doubt that it was fought between the Humber and the Tyne, at the only place that will answer to the name, Aylesthorpe near Middleham in Yorkshire. Not far from this is a place called Horsehouse, and another, Warthermask, which seems to bear the name of Vortigern, where many

---

[3] "Anno gratiæ CCCCLV, qui est annus adventus Anglorum in Bri-"tanniam septimus, gens Anglorum cum Vortigerno viribus resumptis, "cœperunt iterum Vortimerum, regem Britonum, in bellum provocare. "Convenientes autem hinc et inde apud Ailestorp cunei, acriter et diu "pugnaverunt; tandem pondus prælii in Saxones est conversum, (qui) "pugnam deseruerunt et campum. Britones vero, viriliter insequentes "eos, innumeram multitudinem peremerunt; cæteris autem dispersis, "Vortimerus cum victoriâ ad propria remeavit."

objects of antiquity have been found, and amongst others the head of an axe and part of a golden shield, possibly relics of this battle.

Regarding this as the battle which is particularly described in the History of the Britons, and afterwards referred to, "secundum ut supra dictum est," (according to the restoration of the text which I have proposed), I suppose that Vortimer pursued Octa into Kent, and that this was the first of the three occasions, on which he blockaded Thanet, as therein related.

Wendover clearly distinguishes this battle of Aylesthorpe from the following, which, (although he does not mention the name of the battle-field), is certainly that of Episford, in which Horsa and Catigern fell; and he prefaces his account of it with words which correspond to Boece's:[4]—

"Not long after, Vortimer with his brothers Catigern and "Pascent, and all the people of the island, declared war "against the Saxons; and they, being assembled together, "disposed their ranks for battle. But Hors, the brother of "Hencgest, to whom Vortigern had given the province of "Kent, and who was called king by his countrymen, charged "the troops of Catigern with such impetuosity, that they were "scattered like dust, and unhorsed and slew Catigern. King "Vortimer his brother, seeing this, rushed upon and killed

---

[4] "Nec multo post Vortimerus, cum fratribus suis Katigerno et Pas- "centio et universo insulæ populo, Saxonibus bellum indixit; quibus con- "gregatis, acies disposuerunt ad bellum. Horsus vero frater Hengisti, "cui Vortigernus Cantiæ provinciam contulerat, et rex a suis concivibus "dicebatur, percussit aciem Katigerni fratris Vortimeri regis tanto im- "petu, ut ad modum pulveris dispersa dissiparetur; deinde Katigernum "ab equo prostratum interfecit. Quod videns rex Vortimerus frater "ejus, irruit in eum, et illo interfecto reliquias cohortis suæ ad Hengis- "tum (qui cum Ambrosii cuneo invicte confligebat)* fugavit, totumque "prælii pondus in Hengistum conversum; cum probitati Vortimeri re- "sistere nequivisset, tandem non sine magno Britonum detrimento, qui "nunquam fugerat aufugit."

---

* Henr. Hunt.

"him, and drove the rest of his cohort back upon Hencgest," (who was contending with Ambrosius, according to Henry of Huntingdon), "on whom the whole weight of the battle now "fell; and as he could not resist the valour of Vortimer, at "last, but not without having made great slaughter of the "Britons, he fled who had never fled before."

It seems to be the battle of which Boece speaks, in which ten thousand Saxons fell, and I believe it was fought at Hapsford in Cheshire, the only place in England which bears a name at all resembling Episford; for Boece, whilst he agrees with Wendover, in saying that Vortimer raised the whole force of the island to combine in one vigorous effort for the expulsion of the Saxons, adds the important circumstance, that this war was regarded as a sort of crusade, and that priests and monks formed a considerable part of his army; and the proximity of Hapsford to Mold in Flintshire suggests the probability, that the victory of Hapsford was the sequel to the Alleluia victory, gained in that neighbourhood by S. Germanus, of which the History of the Britons speaks in the following terms:[5]—

"That most blessed man, being constituted on one occasion "commander against the Saxons, not by the clang of trumpets, "but by praying to the Lord with chaunting of psalms and "Alleluia, and the whole army by shouting to God, turned "the enemies to flight even to the sea."

Here Saxons only are mentioned as adversaries of the Britons, and so also at the conclusion of Constantius' narrative of this event in the Life of S. Germanus, but at its commencement he names the Picts also. The Picts had been allied with the Saxons, against the Scots and Britons, in the war with Ambrosius, and the mention of them would seem to in-

[5] "Iste beatissimus vir dux belli contra Saxones una vice factus, non "tubarum clangore, sed ad Dominum orando cum cantu psalmorum et "Alleluia, totusque exercitus ad Dominum vociferando, hostes in fugam "usque ad mare convertit." C. 47.

dicate that they were so still. If so, Boece must be mistaken in including them in the league which the Scots made with Vortimer, (a mistake which the constant association of the two nations might easily occasion); and Buchanan represents the confederacy of the Picts and Saxons, as continuing until that alliance of the Picts and Britons was formed, which the union of Loth with the sister of Ambrosius cemented; and from Boece's own account of the Alleluia victory it appears, that the Picts and Saxons were really leagued together at the time. He says that Loth, King of the Picts, made a league with Octa against the Britons, and endeavoured to induce Conran, King of the Scots, to do the same, but without success; that the Britons, by the advice of S. Germanus, assembled their forces, and were engaged in the solemnities of Easter, when they received tidings that the Saxons and Picts were at hand; that Uther arrayed the forces of the Britons; and that S. Germanus and the priests marched in the van, and put the enemy to flight, by the simultaneous Alleluia of the whole army.[6]

This victory was certainly gained in the neighbourhood of Mold, where Maes y Garmon preserves the remembrance of it, and the British tradition, embodied in the above passage, that S. Germanus drove the enemy to the sea, is perfectly consistent with the supposition, that Vortimer pursued and engaged with them at Hapsford, which is but two miles from the shore. Under a general such as Hencgest appears to have been, the Saxons would not be long before they recovered from their panic.

As Catigern fell in this battle, and the head-quarters of the

---

[6] Boece is in error in placing this event under the reign of Uther, and in naming Severus as S. Germanus' companion. Severus was the companion of his second mission, and Constantius tells us that this victory was one of the events of his first. Uther might hold an important command at this time, but S. Germanus certainly died before he came to the throne. Bæda has also fallen into the mistake of connecting the Alleluia victory with S. Germanus' second mission.

Britons were at Mold, he seems to have a very fair claim to the gold corslet which was found in a tomb at Mold, and is now in the British Museum.

The Saxons fled into Kent, (according to Layamon), and thither they conveyed the body of Horsa, whose tomb was to be seen in the eastern part of that province in Bæda's days. Very little has been said of him in the course of this history; but there can be no doubt, (notwithstanding a statement in the Brut to the contrary), that he was the elder brother; for not only is his name mentioned first in the oldest authorities, but we are told expressly, that it was not until after his death that Hencgest became king. Doubtless the reason why his name is so seldom mentioned is this, that he was always with his people, whilst Hencgest, continually present at the court of Vortigern, came more particularly under the notice of the Britons. Yet, if history says little about him, he has left many more traces of his name on the face of the country, than his more famous brother.

The second blockade of Thanet must have followed this battle, and as Hencgest is said to have fought three battles in this year, and only suffered one defeat, Vortimer must have been repulsed. The dates of these events, A. D. 454 and 455, as they are computed from the false date of the coming of the Saxons, must be reduced to A. D. 433 and 434.

Wendover proceeds to say:[7]—

"In the year of grace 456 (*i. e.* A. D. 435), Horsa being
" dead, the Saxons raised Hencgest to the throne of Kent;
" in which year we read that he fought three times with the
" Britons, but not being able to withstand the valour of Vor-

---

7 " Anno gratiæ CCCCLVI Horso defuncto, Saxones Hengestum fratrem " ejus, in regnum Cantiæ sublimaverunt. Quo etiam anno ter contra " Britones pugnasse legitur; sed probitati Vortimeri resistere non valens " ad insulam Thanet confugit, ubi prælio navali quotidie vexabatur. " Tandem Saxones ciulas suas vix ingressi, relictis mulieribus et filiis, " Germaniam redierunt."

"timer, he fled to the Isle of Thanet where he was daily "harassed by naval attacks. At length the Saxons having "with difficulty entered their ships, return to Germany, "leaving their wives and children."

Layamon says that the Saxons, pursued by Vortimer, halted on the sea-shore, and fought a desperate battle, in which they were defeated with the loss of four thousand; and that they took shipping which lay in the adjacent haven and crossed over into Thanet, which lay close by, on the right hand. Thus he clearly indicates Stonar as the scene of the battle on the sea-shore, the "Lapis Tituli" of the History of the Britons. It is now included in, but anciently appears to have been separated by a wide channel from, the Isle, which would be on the right hand of the Saxons as they confronted the forces of Vortimer. Its name *Stán áre*, the "stone of "honour," may very well be equivalent to "lapis tituli."[8]

Henry of Huntingdon says, that Hencgest fled, once to Thanet and once to his ships, and sent to Germany for others who had departed. This agrees with Boece's statement, that the object of his withdrawing to Northumbria, was to wait there until succours should arrive from Germany.

The following summary of the events of the last year of this war, is offered as a harmony of all the above-cited statements. After his election to the throne in A.D. 435, Hencgest continued the war, fought three battles with Vortimer, was defeated in the last at Stonar, retired into Thanet, was blockaded by Vortimer for some days, sent Vortigern to ask for leave to depart, made his escape whilst his request was under consideration, sent to Germany for some of his people who had fled and for succours, repaired to Northumbria to await their coming, but was attacked by the Scots, and compelled to return to the Continent.

Boece says that Vortimer reigned for some years, that he

[8] All the MSS. except the Paris and Vatican give this name.

was very merciful to the Saxons, of whom he allowed some to remain in Kent in subjection to the Britons, and others to return home; that he suffered Rumwen, who was pregnant, to remain in the Tower of London with guards to wait upon her; and that he governed his subjects well, applying himself to the restoration of churches, and purging the land of false doctrine with the aid of S. Germanus and S. Lupus. This probably applies to the whole duration of his reign; for the History of the Britons and the Brut agree in saying that he did not live long; and Henry of Huntingdon says that he reigned scarcely a year, after the expulsion of the Saxons. All authorities are agreed, that S. Germanus was in Britain during his reign, assisting him by his counsels.

The History of the Britons thus records his death:[9]—

"But he died after a little interval, and before his death, "considering what would happen, he said to his family, "'Bury my body in the port of the haven of the entrance of "'the Saxons, that is, on the shore of the sea whence they "'first came; for although they may dwell in other parts of "'Britain, yet in that they will never remain if you do this.' "But they, imprudently contemning his command, did not "bury him in the place which he had requested."

Henry of Huntingdon simply says,[10] "Vortimer, the flower "of youth, died of disease in the year following" (the expulsion of the Saxons); yet the Brut tells us, that he died by

---

[9] "Ipse autem post modicum intervallum mortuus est; et ante obitum "suum futuræ rei casum animadvertens, dixit ad familiam suam, 'Sepelite "'in portâ ostii introitus Saxonum corpus meum, id est super ripam "'maris a quo primum venerunt, quia quamvis in aliis partibus Bryt- "'tanniæ habitaverint, tamen in istâ si sic facitis nunquam in æternum "'manebunt.' Illi autem imprudenter mandatum ejus contempnentes, "eum in loco quem postulaverat, non sepelierunt." C. 44.

All the MSS. agree in this, but one (Cambridge, F. f. i. 27) introduces a passage, to the effect that he reigned five years after the expulsion of the Saxons.

[10] "Anno vero sequenti morbo periit flos juvenum Gortimerus, cum quo "simul spes et victoria Brittonum extincta est."

poison administered to him at the instigation of Rumwen; and Boece says the same, with the addition of a circumstance, which a British historian might well suppress, that the British nobles were accessory to her guilt. These statements are strengthened in some degree, by the passage in S. Gildas which follows the allusion to Vortigern's treason, and which can only refer to Vortimer; implying that he incurred the hatred of the Britons, on account of his zeal for the reformation of public morals, and that his services to his country were forgotten:[11]—

"But if any of them appeared more gentle, and somewhat "more attached to the truth, the hatred of all and their darts "(of calumny) were hurled against him, without regard, as "though he were a subverter of Britain."

Their disregard to his dying request, and the restoration of Vortigern after his death, warrant the suspicion that there was disaffection towards him on the part of the British nobility, even if they were clear of the treason. The Brut says he was buried at London; an interpolated passage of little value, in a late MS. of the History of the Britons, at Lincoln.

---

[11] "Si quis mitior eorum, et veritati aliquatenus propior videretur, in "hunc, Brittaniæ quasi in subversorem, omnium odia, telaque, sine re- "spectu, torquebantur." - C. 21.

CHAPTER X.

The Restoration of Vortigern, A.D. 436 *to* 443.

AFTER the death of Vortimer, the nobles of Britain restored Vortigern to the throne, ignoring the claims of Ambrosius. The treason, to which Vortimer fell a victim, may partly account for this injustice, and the brief notice of the battle of Guoloph, in the Chronological Notes, is sufficient to show, that there was a strong party in Britain opposed to his pretensions. As soon as Vortigern was confirmed in the sovereignty, Rumwen sent to Germany to recal Hencgest, desiring him to bring with him a sufficient number of followers; but Vortigern, who concurred in the invitation, (according to Geoffrey), advised him to bring but a small retinue, lest the jealousy of the Britons should be roused. Hencgest, who, (according to the Chronicles of Holland), was occupied at the time with the foundation of Leyden, immediately returned to Britain, and made his appearance in the Thames near London, accompanied by his sons Oeric-Oisc[1] and Octa, with a fleet of sixty sail. The Britons were alarmed, and called on Vortigern to expel them from the country.

---

[1] Here Bæda incidentally confirms the accounts of his expulsion and the invitation to return, when he says that he and Oeric came in consequence of an invitation. (Book II. 5).

The History of the Britons is silent with regard to the invitation, but notices the return of the Saxons.[2]

"Taking advantage of this," (the death of Vortimer), "the "Barbarians," (apparently those who had been allowed to remain), "assembled in great force, and were aided by the "Pagans from over the sea, especially because Guorthegirn "was their friend, on account of the daughter of Hencgest "whom he had taken to wife, and loved them so much that "no one dared to oppose them."

"After the death of Guorthemer, the son of Guorthegirn, "Hencgest being reinforced, and having again collected together many ships," &c.

Geoffrey says he brought an army of no less than three hundred thousand, and Layamon that his fleet consisted of seven hundred ships each containing three hundred men. Excessive as these numbers appear to be, it is not unlikely that much greater numbers would immediately follow, those whom Hencgest had at his disposal when he received the invitation, and whom he conducted in person; and Henry of Huntingdon, in a passage to be cited immediately, says that the forces of the Saxons were extraordinarily numerous.

Boece says that he landed peaceably, and did nothing to provoke the people, for his object was evidently not a hostile invasion, but a peaceable resumption of territories, which Vortigern had conceded to him and Octa, in Kent and Northumbria. Obviously, he could not be expected to be content to fill the station of a noble at the court of Vortigern, a station so inferior to that to which he was now raised by the

---

[2] "Barbari vero per hoc magnopere congregati sunt, et transmarinis "paganis auxiliabantur, maxime quod Guorthegirnus illis esset amicus "propter filiam Hencgesti quam acceperat in uxorem, atque adeo diligebat ut nullus auderet contra illos pugnare." C. 45.

"Factum est autem post mortem Guorthemeri filii regis Guorthegirni "Hencgestus confortatus, et ad se multis iterum navibus congregatis," &c. C. 46.

voice of his people. However, it is said, that the Britons were very much incensed when they heard of his coming with so great a multitude, and resolved on driving him out of the country; and that Vortigern commanded all the nobles of Britain to assemble their forces, and march into Kent with this object. A battle was fought, which doubtless was the result of this gathering, but which neither Boece nor the Brut record. Henry of Huntingdon speaks of it in the following terms:[3]—

"Hengest and Esc his son, having received help from their "own country, and encouraged by the death of the youth "(Vortimer), prepare themselves for war at Creganford. "The Britons, on the other hand, array against them four "very large phalanxes, commanded by four most brave "leaders. But when the Britons had begun the game of "war, they could not withstand the number of the Saxons, "which was greater than usual, and these new comers were "chosen men, and cut the bodies of the Britons terribly with "their axes and swords, and did not desist until they beheld "the four leaders fallen and slain. Then, terrified beyond "what can be believed, they fled from Kent to London, and "never again dared to enter Kent with warlike intentions. "From that time Hengest and Esc his son reigned at Can-"terbury."

Mr. Thorpe considers the introduction of the name of Æsc

---

[3] "Hengist igitur, et Esc filius suus, receptis auxiliis a patriâ suâ "bello se præparant apud Creganford. Brittanni vero quatuor pha-"langes maximas, quatuor ducibus munitas fortissimis, bello prosti-"tuunt. Sed cum ludum belli Brittones inissent, numerum Saxonum, "majorem solito, male ferebant: recentes quippe qui supervenerant, et "viri electi erant, securibus et gladiis horribiliter corpora Brittonum "findebant, nec tamen cesserunt donec quatuor duces eorum prostratos "et cæsos viderunt. Tunc vero, ultra quam credi potest perterriti, a "Cantiâ usque in Londoniam fugerunt, et nunquam in Cantiam postea "gratia pugnandi venire ausi sunt. Exinde regnavit Hengist et Esc "filius suus in Cantuariâ: regnum igitur Cantiæ incepit VIII. anno "adventus Anglorum."

a later addition to the text, the verb "regnavit" being left in the singular.

The scene of this battle is rightly placed at Crayford in Kent. The date in the earliest edition of the Saxon Chronicle is A.D. 457, *i. e.* (according to the true reckoning), A. D. 436. Henry of Huntingdon places it immediately after the death of Vortimer. His narrative, taken in connection with Boece's, of Vortigern's preparations for war, and advance towards Kent, leaves no doubt that the battle was the sequel thereto.

In A. D. 437 an event occurred which is mentioned only in the Chronological Notes, the quarrel between Guitolin and Ambrosius, and the battle of Guoloppum, twelve years after the accession of Vortigern. This was doubtless an attempt, on the part of Ambrosius, to obtain the sovereignty, resulting in his discomfiture; and this may account for his not appearing again in the history for some years. Guoloph may be Wallop in Hampshire, not many miles distant from Ambresbury, (the city of Ambrosius), in the neighbourhood of which the tragedy was enacted, which claims our next attention.

In the History of the Britons we read:[4]—

[4] "Hencgestus—cum senioribus suis dolum Guorthegirno regi et suo "exercitui præparavit; mittensque ad regem legatos, dolose pacem inter "se firmari deprecatur, ut perpetua amicitia inter se uterentur. Rex "autem, inscius doli, cum senioribus suis consiliatus est pacem cum "Hencgesto habere, et discordia bellorum renuere. Legati vero rever-"tentes id ipsum renuntiaverunt Hencgesto. Hencgestus postmodum, "grande præparans convivium regi Guorthegirno et senioribus militibus "ejus ccc, convocavit regem omnemque familiam ejus ad firmandam "pacem. Latente autem sub specie pacis dolosa machinatione, Henc-"gestus ex suis totidem elegit milites, initoque cum eis consilio, prædixit "eis, ut unusquisque artavum suum in ficone sub pede suo poneret, et "milites regis ad convivium venientes inter se commiscerent, illosque "sollerti cura inebriarent; 'Et cum clamavero,' inquit, 'ad vos, et dixero, "'"Nimiad is sexa," cultellos vestros ex ficonibus educite, et in illos "'irruite, et unusquisque propiorem sibi jugulet. Veruntamen regem "'custodite, et nolite eum interficere, sed pro connubio filiæ meæ "'quam amat eum servate, melius enim est ut a nobis redimatur, "'quam ut occidatur.' Rex autem ad convivium cum suis venit, ut "pacem, quam sibi invicem servare promiserant, certius firmarent. Ad-"venientibus vero cum rege suo Brittonibus, Saxones pacifice loquentes,

"Hencgest with his elders prepared a snare for King "Guorthegirn and his army; and, sending messengers to the "king, he treacherously entreats that peace may be estab- "lished between them, that they might mutually enjoy per- "petual friendship. But the king, unconscious of the deceit, "determined with his elders to have peace with Hencgest, "and to have done with the discord of wars. The messengers "returning told this to Hencgest. Hencgest afterwards, "preparing a great banquet for King Guorthegirn and three "hundred of his elder knights, invited the king and all his "family to establish the peace. But a crafty design being "concealed under the guise of peace, Hencgest chose as "many knights from amongst his own people, and having "arranged his plan with them, he premonished them that "each one should place his knife in his shoe, and that they "should mingle themselves amongst the king's knights who "were coming to the banquet, and carefully make them "drunk; 'And when,' said he, 'I shall say to you "Nimiad is "' "sexa," draw your knives from your shoes, and fall upon "' them, and let each one kill the nearest to himself. But "' guard the king, and do not kill him, but, on account of "' his marriage with my daughter whom he loves, preserve "' him, for it is better that he should be ransomed from us "' than slain.' But the king came with his people to the "banquet, that they might establish more securely the peace "which they had mutually promised to observe. But when

---

"dolumque in corde vertentes, convivis suis Judaico more parabant "mortem. At, inscii malorum, Brittones mixti Saxonibus discubuerunt. "Quibus nimis epulantibus et bibentibus, et ultra modum inebriatis, "Hencgestus ut prius suis prædixerat comitibus, elevata voce subito "vociferatus est, 'Nimiad is sexa.' Ad cujus vocem Saxones, protinus "exurgentes suosque extrahentes cultellos, irruerunt super Brittones, "unusquisque super consessorem suum, et de senioribus Guorthegirni "regis ccc sunt jugulati. Rex autem captivitati subditus est. Pro sua "siquidem liberatione tradidit illis III regiones, East Sexā, Suth Sexā, "Middel Sexā, cum reliquis regionibus quas ipsi eligentes nomina- "verunt." C. 37.

"the Britons came with the king, the Saxons, speaking "peaceably and meditating treachery in their hearts, pre-"pared death for their messmates, after the example of "Judas. But the Britons unconscious of mischief sat down "promiscuously with the Saxons; and as they feasted and "drank freely, and were exceedingly drunk, Hencgest, as he "had before premonished his comrades, raising his voice "shouted suddenly, 'Nimiad is sexa.' At his voice the "Saxons, rising at once and drawing their knives, fell upon "the Britons, each upon his neighbour, and three hundred of "King Guorthegirn's elders were slain, but the king was "made captive. For his liberation he surrendered to them "three regions, Essex, Sussex, and Middlesex, with other "regions which they had chosen and named."

Our other authorities are agreed, that Hencgest sent a messenger to Vortigern protesting that he had come with no hostile intention, but rather to be a protector to him, placing himself and his people at his disposal, and desiring that a conference might be held between them. The Brut says, that Vortigern and his council agreed to the proposal, and appointed the first day of May for a meeting at Ambresbury; but Boece tells us, (and this statement throws great light on the subsequent tragedy), that there was a party amongst the Britons, who, distrusting Hencgest, and determined to get rid of him, were prepared to take any measures, fair or foul, to effect their object, and banded themselves together in a conspiracy to watch the course of events, and seize any opportunity that might present itself to them. The meeting took place, and after it, at the banquet (which is mentioned only in the History of the Britons), the British nobles fell beneath the daggers of the Saxons. According to the Brut, however, they defended themselves bravely, and slew many of their foes; and Eldol in particular, the consul of Gloucester, took up a stake, (or, as Boece has it, snatched a dagger from a Saxon), slew seventy of them, and then made his escape.

There can be no reasonable doubt, that the conference and massacre really occurred at Ambresbury, and that the bodies of the slain were interred where Stonehenge now stands. The History of the Britons, the Brut, and Boece, present us with distinct accounts of it, the two last evidently so, and neither of them derived from the first.

This unhappy affair has shrouded with disgrace the memory of Hencgest; but we must not forget that we have only one side of the story, the Saxon accounts of the actions of this great chieftain being almost entirely lost, and very little indeed being known of him, but what his enemies, the Britons and the Scots, have recorded. Yet even what they admit, taken in connection with what is preserved to us elsewhere, although they have left it unnoticed, extenuates in no slight degree even the vileness of this transaction. For they admit that Hencgest's coming was the result of invitation, and his coming with so great a multitude, to reoccupy districts which had been granted to him and his son by Vortigern, was a matter of course; they allow that Vortigern and the Britons prepared to expel him by force, and it appears that they actually invaded Kent, and attacked him. If Hencgest's party, then, went to the conference armed, and provided with a signal to be given in case of emergency, what were these but precautions, necessary to be taken, in intercourse with a people whom they might regard as having already broken faith with them, and at whose hands they had reason to apprehend treachery?

Boece tells us, that there were those amongst the British nobility, who were prepared to rid the country of him by foul means, if they could not succeed by fair; and, if we but knew the whole truth with regard to this massacre, we should probably discover, that Hencgest detected their designs, and that it was not altogether unprovoked.

Two circumstances seem to warrant the view here taken, that Hencgest's object in returning was a peaceable resumption of his own territories, not conquest; the first, that he did not follow up the decisive victory of Crayford by any aggressive movement, when, with the forces at his command, the empire of Britain was, humanly speaking, at his feet; the second, that when Vortigern was in his hands, and he might have demanded the sovereignty of Britain, he contented himself with asking for the provinces which bordered on his own kingdom, Essex, Middlesex, Sussex, and perhaps Surrey. Moderation such as this is hardly consistent with the character which is generally imputed to him.

For some time afterwards, Hencgest refrained from aggression. We are not told, (nor is it likely that we should be), whether he received provocation or not; but eventually he determined to seize upon the whole kingdom, overran the island, and everywhere destroyed the churches, and slaughtered the clergy. S. Gildas devotes his twenty-fourth and part of his twenty-fifth chapter[5] to a notice of this war, and the Brut and Boece speak of it in nearly the same terms.

Vortigern, not knowing what to do, fled into the district of

---

[5] "Confovebatur—de mari usque ad mare ignis orientalis sacrilegorum "manu exaggeratus, et finitimas quasque civitates agrosque populans, "qui non quievit accensus, donec cunctam pene exurens insulæ super-"ficiem, rubra occidentalem trucique oceanum lingua delamberet.—Ita "ut cunctæ columnæ crebris arietibus, omnesque coloni cum præpositis "ecclesiæ, cum sacerdotibus et populo, mucronibus undique micantibus, "ac flammis crepitantibus, simul solo sternerentur, et miserabili visu, in "medio platearum, ima turrium edito cardine evulsarum, murorumque "celsorum saxa, sacra altaria, cadaverum frusta, crustis ac semigelantibus "purpurei cruoris tecta, velut in quodam horrendo torculari mixta vide-"rentur, et nulla esset omnimodis, præter horribiles domorum ruinas, "bestiarum volucrumque ventres, in medio sepultura, salva sanctarum "animarum reverentia, si tamen multæ inventæ sint, quæ arduis cœli per "id temporis a sanctis angelis vehebantur.—Itaque nonnulli miserarum "reliquiarum, in montibus deprehensi, acervatim jugulabantur; alii fame "confecti accedentes, manus hostibus dabant in ævum servituri, si tamen "non continuo trucidarentur, quod altissimæ gratiæ stabat in loco; alii "transmarinas petebant regiones:—alii a montanis collibus, minacibus "præruptis vallati, et densissimis saltibus, marinisque rupibus vitam, "suspecta semper mente, credentes, in patria licet trepidi perstabant."

Snowdon, where he attempted to build a fortress, but is said to have been dissuaded by Merlin. Thence he retired to Genoreu (now Ganerew) in Herefordshire, and there built a castle, which was named after him Caer Guorthegirn, on Mount Doward.[6]

The date of this conquest is established by the cotemporary testimony of Prosper Tyro, who says, that in the eighteenth year of Theodosius, A. D. 441,[7] "the Britons, up to this time "torn by various slaughters and disasters, are subjugated by "the Saxons." Vincent of Beauvais adopts this date for the flight of Vortigern, and we obtain the same result after deducting the usual twenty-one years from A. D. 462, the date given by Roger of Wendover.

It was probably in this war, that Brychan, (who settled in and gave name to Brecknock about the time that Cunedda settled in North Wales), and his children perished. He was murdered, with his sons Rhawin and Rhun, and his daughter Tydfyl, at the place which is now called Merthyr Tydfyl, by a party of Saxons and Picts, who were afterwards defeated by his grandson Nefydd. Cynawg, Cyflefyr, Cynbryd, and Dogfan, also his sons, and probably ecclesiastics, are said to have been murdered by the Saxons in other localities.

At length, (according to Roger of Wendover, in A. D. 464, *i. e.* 443), the Britons sent a message to Ambrosius and Uther, begging them to come to their assistance. They responded to the call, and began immediately to make preparations for their expedition, and Wendover says that Ambrosius was the commander of the British forces in the next battle, which he erroneously places under the year 473, (evidently owing to

---

[6] Sir F. Madden has pointed out the identity of the mountain, which Geoffrey calls Cloarius, Layamon Cloard, and Wace Clouart, with Doward, (some early scribe having read **d** as **cl**), and thus has established the identity of Genoreu also.

[7] "Britanniæ, usque ad hoc tempus variis cladibus eventibusque "laceratæ, in ditionem Saxonum rediguntur."

his having misunderstood the second for the first coming of Hencgest, from which it was the seventeenth year).

S. Gildas notices the coming and victory of Ambrosius as follows:[8]—

"Some time, then, intervening, when the most cruel "robbers had returned home, the remnant,—to whom the "wretched citizens resort from every quarter, that they might "not be utterly exterminated,—strengthened by the Lord, "recruit their forces, challenging their conquerors to battle, "and by God's favour they gained the victory according to "their vow; under the conduct of Ambrosius Aurelianus, a "modest man, who alone was gentle, faithful, brave, and true, "perchance of Roman lineage; who had survived the crash "of so great a tempest, in which his relatives, clothed with "the purple, were slain; whose offspring now in our times "has greatly degenerated from the goodness of their an-"cestors."

This passage, which immediately follows that last referred to, speaks of Ambrosius' eventual success, previous to which he had suffered some reverses. For although neither the Brut nor Boece notice his having sustained defeat, the Life of Merlin[9] implies that he did more than once, and as it

---

[8] "Tempore igitur interveniente aliquanto, cum recessissent domum "crudelissimi prædones, roboratæ a Domino reliquiæ, quibus confugiunt "undique diversis in locis miserrimi cives,—ne ad internecionem ita "usquequaque delerentur, duce Ambrosio Aureliano, viro modesto, qui "solus fuit comis, fidelis, fortis, veraxque, forte Romanæ gentis, qui "tantæ tempestatis collisione, occisis in eadem parentibus, purpurâ "nimirum indutis, superfuerat, cujus nunc temporibus nostris soboles "magnopere avitâ bonitate degeneravit, vires capescunt, victores pro-"vocantes ad prælium, quibus victoria, Deo annuente cessit." C. 25.

[9] "Hæc ita dum fierent, in finibus Armoricanis
"Uter et Ambrosius fuerant cum rege Biduco;
"Jam gladio fiunt cincti belloque probati,
"Et sibi diversas sociabant undique turmas,
"Ut peterent natale solum gentesque fugarent
"Quæ tunc instabant patriam vastare paternam.
"Ergo dedere suas ventoque marique carinas,

is a British authority its testimony is important. The brief notice of the reign of Ambrosius there given, is most useful as a guide, in the arrangement of the events it comprised.

Ambrosius landed at Totness with his brother Uther, and an army ten thousand strong, in A.D. 443, and about the same time, and we may believe in his company, came S. Germanus for the second time. Immediately on his arrival the clergy and people in council elected him their king, and urged him at once to lead them against the Saxons. He was determined, however, on the destruction of Vortigern first, as the murderer of his father and brother, and the cause of all the misfortunes which had befallen Britain. Accordingly they proceeded at once to attack the fortress in which he dwelt.

Boece says, that Vortigern, aware of the approach of Ambrosius, assembled his troops and advanced to give him battle; that he was deserted by the greater part of his army before the battle began; that seeing all hope was gone, he stripped off his armour, and fought desperately, seeking death in battle, rather than by fire; which Merlin had predicted to him; but that he was rescued by his friends, and conveyed to

---

"Præsidioque suis concivibus applicuerunt:
"Nam Vortigernum per Cambrica regna fugatum,
"Inclusumque, sua pariter cum turre cremarunt.
"Enses inde suos vertere recenter in Anglos;
"Congressique simul vincebant sæpius illos,
"Et vice transversâ devincebantur ab illis.
"Denique consertis magno conamine dextris,
"Instant nostrates, et lædunt acriter hostès,
"Hengistumque necant, Christoque volente triumphant.
"Hiis igitur gestis, cleri populique favore,
"Ambrosio regnumque datur, regnique corona.
"Postmodo quam gessit tractando singula juste,
"Emensis autem per lustra quaterna diebus,
"Proditur a medico, moriturque bibendo venenum."

L. 1043–1063.

the castle where he had left his son. For the rest, Boece and the Brut are agreed in saying, that Ambrosius followed and besieged him in the fortress of Genoreu, and finding his engines ineffectual to destroy it, set it on fire, and consumed him with all who were therein.

The History of the Britons[10] gives three distinct traditions relative to the end of Vortigern; the first, taken from the book of S. Germanus, that the saint laboured for his conversion, following him first to Guorthegirniaun, and then to Caer Guorthegirn, but without success, and that whilst he was praying for him in the neighbourhood of the latter, fire fell from heaven, and destroyed the citadel with all who were therein; the second, that hated by all the people for his crimes, he wandered from place to place, until he died in obscurity of a broken heart; the third that the earth opened, and swallowed him up alive on the night when his castle was burned, because no remains of him were ever found.

These traditions are important, because they show that the Britons believed, that the time of the destruction of Vortigern was coincident with that of S. Germanus' second coming, and that the saint laboured earnestly for his conversion. Indeed the Capitula, as has been observed already, expressly mention the second coming of S. Germanus as immediately antecedent to the destruction of Vortigern; and there appears to be sufficient ground for the surmise, that Ambrosius did not resort to extremities, until every endeavour, on the part of S. Germanus, to bring Vortigern to a better mind, and detach him from the interests of Hencgest, had failed. It is clear that great uncertainty prevailed as to his actual fate, that search was made for his remains in the ruins of his castle, but that none were found. We prefer, of course, (as in the case of Benlli), the story which represents the fire as having been kindled by his enemies; but the tradition that he escaped

---

[10] C. 47, 48.

from the conflagration, and died in obscurity, is confirmed by another, which has constantly designated a tomb at Llanhaiarn in Caernarvonshire, in which the bones of a man of tall stature were found, as Bedd Gwrtheyrn or the "Tomb of "Vortigern."

CHAPTER XI.

The Reign of Ambrosius Aurelianus, A.D. 443 *to* 449.

ACCORDING to the Brut, Hencgest fled into the North, on hearing of the destruction of Vortigern; but Hencgest was not the man to take flight, before he had measured strength with his enemy; and Boece enables us to account for his presence in the North more satisfactorily, by telling us, that after he had completely subjugated Britain, he engaged in a contest with the Picts and Scots who dwelt between the Humber and the Tyne. With them, he says, Ambrosius formed a league as soon as he had destroyed Vortigern, and Layamon supports him by mentioning Scots amongst his forces in the battle which ensued. Loth, a king of the Picts, and Conran a commander under the King of the Scots, brought a large army to his aid.

Thus strengthened, Ambrosius lost no time in renewing his contest with Hencgest, "challenging his conquerors to "battle;" and on his northward march, we are told, he was very much grieved at witnessing the devastation which the Saxons had made, and vowed that he would rebuild the churches, if he should gain the victory,—a circumstance which explains the "ex voto" of S. Gildas' brief narrative. Hencgest advanced to meet him to a place called Maes Beli, through which he knew the line of his march lay. A fierce battle was fought, Hencgest was defeated, and fled to the fortress of Caer Conan. Then, observing that he was pursued closely by Ambrosius, and perhaps apprehending a fate such as had befallen Vortigern, he abandoned the fortress, and prepared for a renewal of the conflict. He was again defeated, and fell into the hands of Eldol, who escaped from him at Ambresbury; and, after some deliberation what was to be done with him, it was decided that he should suffer death. Accordingly he was beheaded by Eldol, but honourably buried, and a mound raised over his remains by order of Ambrosius.

There is a great appearance of truth in the circumstantial detail with which this part of the history is related,—the deliberation, Bishop Eldad's reasons why mercy should be withheld from him, his decapitation, and the honourable sepulture accorded to his remains,—and we may consider it as a fact that Hencgest perished at this time, since Boece, and a Frisian tradition given by Ocka Scharlensis, attest it; though the former says that he perished in the flight from Maes Beli, and the latter that he was hanged by Eldol, a very slight variation from the statement in the Brut.

Maes Beli is doubtless Belgh in Nottinghamshire; and here we have one of the many proofs that Layamon had ancient and authentic sources of information before him; for he does not mention the name, but represents Ambrosius as saying after the battle, "Hencgest is gone North;" and Belgh is about twenty miles to the southward of Conisbrough in Yorkshire, which is unquestionably the Caer Conan of our story. Polidore Vergil, who says that the battle took place on the river Don near Doncaster, testifies that the fame of it was still current amongst the inhabitants of the place, in his time, the sixteenth century; and, early in the following century, Camden mentions the mound near to the castle wall of Conisbrough, as Hencgest's tomb. The tradition still continues; the mound, now almost levelled, still bears his name.

Octa has not been once mentioned since Hencgest's return to Britain, when Boece says that he and his two brothers accompanied their father. The chroniclers keep in view the principal characters in the story only, and take little or no notice of the rest. Henceforth Octa is the chief hero; Boece speaks of him alone; the Brut associates with him his uncle Ossa; and Layamon mentions his cousin Ebissa, who accompanied him at his first coming to Britain, also.

When Hencgest had fallen into the hands of Ambrosius, Octa and (according to Layamon) Ebissa fled with the greater part of the army to York, and Ossa with the rest to Alclud. Ambrosius followed, and laid siege to York; Octa and Ebissa resolved on submission, and were received to mercy, at the instance of Bishop Eldad. Ossa and the rest, on hearing of this, followed their example, and with them were permitted to occupy certain districts bordering on Scotland, doubtless the principality granted originally to Octa by Vortigern.

Peace being thus established, Ambrosius assembled a council of his nobles at York, and fulfilled his vow by giving orders for the restoration of the churches. Thence he proceeded to London, and (according to Boece) received the submission of the garrison which Hencgest had left there, and commanded all the warriors to quit the country, except such as were content to embrace Christianity. At a feast held to celebrate his triumph, he ceded to Loth and Conran the districts north of the Humber, which had so long been the object of contention, and gave to them in marriage his sisters Anna and Ada, the more firmly to cement his alliance with them. Anna, the wife of Loth, became the mother of three children, Modred, Walgan, and Thamete; Ada died in childbirth.

It is impossible entirely to reconcile the statements in the Brut and Boece relative to Loth; but on the one hand there is an evident mistake which runs through the narrative in the Brut, which represents Anna as the sister of Arthur, who was not born until after Ambrosius' death, whilst it says that Loth was married to her, during Ambrosius' reign; and on the other, Boece's story is more consistent, and affords a satisfactory explanation of many subsequent events, and of the conduct of Modred in particular. Fordun says that Loth was a descendant of the celebrated Fulgentius; he was, therefore, in some way related to the Pictish leader Guanis, Gryme, or Græme, who has figured in the earlier part of this history, and was probably his son, as he appears to have inherited his rights. This probability the sequel will show to amount almost to certainty. Boece calls him king; but we need not understand thereby that he was sovereign; like Græme, probably, he held a subordinate principality.

The peace, which Ambrosius established, was broken in the following year, A. D. 444. The Brut says nothing of this affair; it rarely records the defeats of the Britons; but Henry of Huntingdon says:[1]—

"Reinforcements arriving after some time, King Hencgest, "and Æsc his son, gathered together a most invincible army "in the seventeenth year of their coming into England; "against whom all Britain, having collected her forces, "opposed twelve phalanxes nobly arrayed at Wippedesflede. "They fought long and fiercely, until Hencgest slew the

[1] "Supervenientibus vero auxiliariis post aliquantum temporis, Hengist "rex, et Esc filius suus, invictissimun congregaverunt exercitum anno "XVII adventus eorum in Angliam; contra quos omnis Britannia, viribus "congregatis, duodecim phalanges nobilitèr ordinatas opposuit apud "Wippedesflede. Pugnatum est diu et acriter, donec Hengistus duo"decim principes cuneorum prostravit, et vexillis eorum dejectis, et "manipulis eorum proturbatis, in fugam coegit. Ipse autem multos "principum suorum et gentis amisit, et quendam magnum principem qui "vocabatur Wipped, ex cujus nomine locum belli illius prædicto nomine "vocavit. Victoria igitur illis lacrymabilis fuit et odiosa, ita ut postea "non parvo tempore, nec ipse inter Britannorum fines, nec Britanni in "Cantiam venire præsumerent."

"twelve leaders of their battalions, overthrew their standards, "scattered their bands and put them to flight. He, however, "lost many of his chiefs and nation, and one great chief "named Wipped, after whom he called that place by the "name aforesaid. That victory was lamented, and the "memory of it odious, so that for some time neither did he "venture beyond the frontiers of Britain, nor did the Britons "presume to enter Kent."

This is the first notice in our history of the second Hencgest, of whom we should have known nothing, but for the Frisian tradition, which tells us, that he completed the conquest of Britain which his uncles had begun. He may have been the captain of the garrison which the first Hencgest left in London, when he departed on his expedition against the Picts and Scots, (the submission of which to Ambrosius in the previous year Boece records). The battle of Wippedesfleet must be dated A. D. 444, as it was the seventeenth year from the coming of the Angles; and it would appear that Hencgest II, having returned with reinforcements from abroad, was enabled to assert a claim to the province of Kent, succeeded in establishing it, and was allowed by Ambrosius to hold it undisturbed; in the same way as Octa was permitted to retain his principality in the North. Policy would dictate to Ambrosius, as to Arthur at a later time, (and to Ælfræd still later), the expediency of ceding certain districts, as the best security against aggressions, which defeat only served to kindle with fresh ardour.

The name Wippedesfleet is lost, and the scene of this battle cannot be determined.

Ambrosius had now leisure to devote himself to the re-establishment of law and order in the kingdom. The ancient laws were revived, all those who had been deprived of their estates during the late troubles were reinstated in their rights, whilst the lands for which no claimants could be found were distributed amongst his soldiers. The History of the Britons incidentally records an instance of this restitution,[2] when it has occasion to notice Pascent, the third son of Vortigern, "who reigned in two provinces, Buelt and Guorthegirnaim, "by the gift of Embresius, who was a great king amongst "the kings of Britain."

The restoration of Winchester and other cities also occupied Ambrosius. When this was done he proceeded to Ambresbury, to visit the tombs of those who were slain by Hencgest, resolved on the erection of a monument to their memory; and through the aid of the mechanical skill of Merlin, at whose disposal a force of fifteen thousand under the command of Uther was placed, transported from Kildare to Salisbury Plain, the grand circles of Stonehenge, after a victory over one of the kings of Ireland, who attempted to impede the execution of their design.

I see no improbability in this story. There the monument stands, erected at some period or other by the hands of men; a force such as that which is said to have been sent to Ireland was more than sufficient for the work; and its energies were directed by the master-mind of Merlin, whom we have no occasion to suppose anything more than a philosopher, though he may have had the credit of being a magician, like others who have been in advance of their age. The constant tradition of Wales assigns the erection of it to Ambrosius, and calls it Cor Emrys; and the Rev. W. D. Coneybeare has satisfactorily proved that its geological character is decidedly in favour of this tradition. It consists of four concentric circles; of which the innermost and the third are composed of single tapering stones of greenstone rock, which is not found nearer to the spot than Dartmoor in Devonshire on the one hand, and Charnwood in Leicestershire on the other, each fully one hundred miles distant; but the mountains

[2] "Tertius Pascent, qui regnavit in duabus provinciis Buelt et Guor-"thegirnaim, post mortem patris sui, illi largiente Embresio qui fuit "rex magnus inter reges Britanniæ." C. 48.

which rise from the Bog of Allen in Kildare are composed of it; and as the carriage of such stones would be more easily accomplished by water than by land, it is far more probable that they were brought down the Liffey, across the Channel, and up the Avon to within a few miles of the site of Stonehenge, than that they should have been transported one hundred miles over land. These stones are much inferior in dimensions to those of the second and fourth circles which enclose them, and which consist of gigantic trilithons of the coarse sand-stone which abounds on the neighbouring downs; and there seems to be no more probable way of accounting for the circumstance of two such noble circles, of indigenous material, enclosing two others of meaner character, which have certainly been brought from an immense distance, than that which the story supplies and suggests; viz. that the latter, on account of their supposed virtue, were transported by Ambrosius from a mountain in Kildare, (or from Killair in the adjoining county of Meath, in which circles of the same kind still exist), to their present home, and that he there surrounded them with the two circles of trilithons, which differ from all other works of the kind.

The stones being brought over, and the circles erected, Ambrosius celebrated the feast of his coronation at Pentecost, and nominated Dubricius and Sanxo to the metropolitan sees of Caerleon and York. S. Dubricius had already been Bishop of Llandaff, and as we are informed in his Life, that S. Germanus performed the ceremony of his consecration to that see, and that of his translation to Caerleon, we have additional evidence that S. Germanus' second sojourn in this country was during Ambrosius' reign.[3] The History of the

[3] S. Germanus is further said to have appointed S. Cadoc, the cotemporary and friend of S. Gildas, abbot of a monastery which he founded at Llancarvan, where we shall find him some years later in this history. S. Iltut, also, is said, by Vincent and in the Register of Llandaff, to have been one of his disciples; a fact which Usher has noticed as

Britons[4] says, that he returned to his own country after the death of Vortigern. This cannot have been later than A. D. 447, and may have been earlier; he died at Ravenna, July 25, A. D. 448.

Buchanan says, that Ambrosius attempted to take Westmoreland from the Scots, and that the matter was on the point of being settled by the sword, when fears of the common enemy put an end to the dispute. This probably occurred towards the conclusion of his reign, when Pascent, the son of Vortigern, began to aspire to the crown of Britain, formed a league with Octa, accompanied him to Germany, raised an army there, and returned with him to Northumbria. Ambrosius marched against them promptly and defeated them, yet (says Boece) with so great loss, that he refrained from further hostilities, and granted them a four months' truce. Octa availed himself of this respite to send Pascent to Germany for reinforcements; and he, being driven by contrary winds to Ireland, found Gillomaur inflamed with desires of revenge on account of the removal of the stone circles, and glad to embrace the opportunity of an alliance with him and Octa. Accordingly they fitted out a large fleet, and landed near Menevia. Ambrosius lay sick at Winchester, and was consequently unable to lead his forces in person, but placed

---

incompatible with his chronology, but which is perfectly consistent with ours. Some accounts say, that S. Iltut was appointed by S. Germanus abbot of Caer Worgorn, now Llaniltyd; others that he was a soldier at the court of Arthur, was persuaded by S. Cadoc to renounce the world, and appointed by S. Dubricius, (who is said to have had the monastery committed to his charge by S. Germanus), his successor. These statements again are quite in accordance with our chronology, as well as with that which may be deduced from the pedigree of S. Iltut. For he was the grandson of Aldor, S. Germanus' brother-in-law, and as S. Germanus was born in A. D. 378, S. Iltut may well have been a pupil of his, and, (as being of Arthur's kindred), may have been present at his court at the beginning of his reign.

4 "Sanctus vero Germanus post mortem Guorthegirni reversus est ad "patriam suam." C. 50.

them under the command of Uther, and sent him against the enemy. Meanwhile Octa, who despaired of success so long as Ambrosius was alive, sent one of his people, named Eoppa, to visit him under the guise of a physician, and administer poison to him.

The story of these events is differently related in the Brut and by Boece, but their accounts are perfectly reconcileable in every respect but one; and that is, where Boece says that Ambrosius was carried in a litter against the Saxons, a circumstance which seems rather to belong to Uther's history. This confusion, doubtless, has arisen from the fact that both died by poison, and under very similar circumstances. It must be observed, that the Brut says nothing of Octa's part in these affairs, and consequently the guilt of the murder of Ambrosius is therein ascribed to Pascent, but the agent is said to have been a Saxon, and his name is evidently the same as that given by Boece. The Life of Merlin merely says, that Ambrosius was betrayed by a physician, and died by drinking poison.

The body of Ambrosius, in obedience to his dying request, was conveyed to Ambresbury, and interred within the circles of Stonehenge. The events of his reign, though important, are few, and must have been comprised within a very few years. Boece says that he died in the seventh year of his reign, and a Scottish Chronicle, cited in the notes to "Excerpta e Chronicis Scocie," that he reigned seven years. If, then, he arrived in Britain in A.D. 443, his death must have occurred towards the close of A.D. 449, or at the beginning of A.D. 450; and the former is the more probable, on account of the notice of the appearance of a remarkable comet at the time; one being mentioned in the Chinese records as having been first observed on December 11, A.D. 449.[5] In

[5] There was another comet in June, A.D. 451, but I believe this of December, A.D. 449, marked the close of Ambrosius' reign and the be-

the Life of Merlin sixteen years are assigned as the duration of his reign. These must be computed from the deposition of Vortigern, A. D. 433.

---

ginning of Uther's. Others were observed in A. D. 467 (Chron. Pasch.), 499 (Zonaras), 501 and 507, (Chinese Records), but none in 504, the year generally marked as the first of Uther.

CHAPTER XII.

The Reign of Uther, A.D. 449 *to* 467.

UTHER received the tidings of his brother's death whilst on his march against the Saxons and the Irish, but would not suffer it to hinder the prosecution of his enterprise. He soon fell in with the enemy; after an obstinate and bloody conflict, the scale began to turn in his favour towards evening; and at length Gillomaur and Pascent were driven with great slaughter to their ships. He then returned to Winchester, where the unanimous vote of the clergy and people awarded to him the sovereignty of Britain.

Octa, Ossa, Ebissa, (now for the first time associated together by Layamon), and the rest of the kindred of Hencgest in the North, now renewed the war, made themselves masters of Northumbria, and were besieging York, which was bravely defended by its British garrison, when Uther came to the rescue. They retreated, were pursued by him to Mount Damian, now Windgates in Northumberland, and besieged in their turn. At the suggestion of Gorlois, prince of Cornwall, Uther made an assault upon their camp by night, captured their leaders, put several thousands to the sword, and the rest to flight. He then proceeded to Alclud, and when he had completely pacified the North, returned with his prisoners to London.[1]

The following events I regard as belonging to the first year of Uther's reign, following Boece's arrangement in preference to that in the Brut.

Uther being afflicted with sickness, the Saxon chiefs found means to persuade the soldiers who guarded them, to escape with them to Germany, whence they speedily returned with a very large fleet, and landed in Scotland.

According to the Brut, Uther deputed the command of his army to Loth, who frequently engaged the Saxons with various success, but was unable to gain any decided advantage over them, on account of the disaffection of his forces, and the contempt with which he was regarded. Boece says that the commander so appointed, Nathaliod, was a man of low birth, that his appointment gave great offence to the nobility, and that he was defeated by Octa, because Gorlois, who disdained to serve under him, withdrew his division from the field. Octa forbore from pursuing the defeated army because he suspected that this withdrawal was only a stratagem; and Gorlois, fearing lest his division should be attacked, fled to his own principality under cover of the night. In the morning, Octa found the camp of the Britons deserted, and sent a message to Uther, commanding him to retire into Wales, and leave the rest of the island to him. Seeing resistance hopeless, Uther proposed terms of peace, which were gladly accepted by the Saxons, viz. that they should have the eastern parts of the island, and he the western, and on these terms peace was maintained for a long time.

This battle is noticed in the Saxon Chronicle:—

"A.D. 473, (*i.e.* 452), Hengest and Æsc fought with the

[1] From the manner in which the events of Uther's reign are related by Geoffrey, it would appear that the captivity of the Saxon chiefs endured for several years. This would be in itself improbable, and is negatived by the story in Boece, which is more circumstantial and consistent than that in the Brut.

"Wealas, and took spoils innumerable, and the Wealas fled "from the Angles like fire."

The contempt of the Britons for their general, and his being unsuccessful in consequence, circumstances as to which the Brut and Boece are agreed, show that it is the same event they are relating; and the date in the Saxon Chronicle, corresponding to A. D. 452, marks a victory such as that which Boece speaks of, early in the reign of Uther; which may well be identified with it, by the circumstances of the precipitate flight of the Britons, and their leaving immense spoil in the hands of their enemies. The Saxon Chronicle, giving the traditions of Kent, speaks only of Hencgest II. and Æsc, as the commanders of the Saxons; whilst Boece, following those of Northumbria, speaks only of Octa; and he alone enables us to account for the long peace of Uther's reign,—a fact which is recorded in the Brut also, and alluded to, as we shall see, by S. Gildas.

The story of Uther's intrigue with Igerna, the murder of Gorlois, and the birth of Arthur, almost immediately follows the narrative of this event, in Boece's history. He discards, however, the marvellous circumstances related in the Brut, and says that Gorlois' defection, which occasioned the loss of the battle above-mentioned, was made by Uther the pretext for putting him to death. Arthur must have been born before the close of A. D. 452, or early in the following year, since he was in his fifteenth year at the time of his accession.

After this, we have nothing more recorded of the events of Uther's reign until we approach its termination; save that Boece mentions the arrival of two Saxon chieftains, Terdix and Kenrik, (*i. e.* Cerdic and Cyneric). An arrival of Saxons did take place about the middle of his reign, but Boece has confounded it with one later, and mistaken the names.

Henry of Huntingdon mentions it in a very remarkable passage:[2]—

[2] "Britanniæ igitur dum cessarent externa bella, non cessabant ci-

"But although Britain's wars with foreigners ceased, civil "wars did not; but amidst the ruins of cities destroyed by "the enemy, the citizens who had escaped fought with one "another. Whilst, however, the memory of the calamity "which had befallen them was fresh, kings, priests, private "men, and nobles, kept their relative places; but when the "younger generation, who had only experience of the peace "of their own time, was grown up, all the rules of truth and "justice were so shaken and subverted, that of them, I will "not say a vestige, but not even the remembrance appeared, "save in a few, a very few. Therefore God sent from the "parts of Germany many very fierce leaders in succession, "to destroy the nation hateful to God; and first came Ælle, "and his three sons, Cymen, Wlencing, and Cissa. So "the chief Ælle with his sons, and a fleet furnished with "the munitions of war, landed in Britain at Cymenesore. "But as the Saxons disembarked, the Britons gave the

---

"vilia; sed inter exterminia civitatum, ab hoste dirutarum, pugnabant "invicem, qui hostem evaserant, cives. Dum tamen recens esset me-"moria calamitatis inflictæ, servabant utcumque reges, sacerdotes, privati, "et optimates, suum quique ordinem; cum autem junior ætas crevisset, "præsentis solum serenitatis statum experta, ita cuncta veritatis et jus-"titiæ moderamina concussa sunt ac subversa, ut eorum non dicam ves-"tigium, sed nec memoria quidem, præter in paucis et valde paucis, "appareret. Immisit ergo Deus, ex partibus Germaniæ, duces plures "ferocissimos, per successiones temporum, qui gentem Deo invisam de-"lerent, et in primis dux Ælle venit, et tres filii sui, Cymen, et Plen-"ting, et Cissa. Igitur dux Ælle cum filiis suis, et classe militaribus "copiis instructissima, in Britannia ad Cymenesore appulerunt. Egre-"dientibus autem Saxonibus de mare, Britanni clamorem excitarunt, et "a circumadjacentibus innumeri convolarunt, et statim bellum initum "est. Saxones vero statura et vigore maximi, impudenter illos recipie-"bant: illi vero imprudenter veniebant: nam sparsim et per intervalla "venientes a conglomeratis interficiebantur, et ut quique attoniti venie-"bant, rumores sinistros ex improviso sentiebant. Fugati sunt igitur "Brittanni usque ad proximum nemus, quod vocatur Andredesleage. "Saxones autem occuparunt littora maris Sudsexe, magis magisque sibi "regionis spatia capessentes, usque ad nonum annum adventus eorum. "Annus autem quo Ælle venit in Angliam fere xxx fuit ab adventu "Anglorum."

"alarm, and great numbers came together from the neighbouring districts, and a battle immediately began. The Saxons, however, who were of great stature and strength, received them boldly, and they came on without any prudence, in detachments and at intervals, and were slain by the compact phalanx of the Saxons; so that as each new body answered to the alarm and came, it was only to hear of the defeat of those who had come before them. The Britons, therefore, were put to flight, as far as the neighbouring wood of Andredes-leage, and the Saxons occupied the coast of Sussex, more and more extending their territory, until the ninth year of their coming.—The year in which Ælle came to England was about the thirtieth from the coming of the Angles."

This passage, though not a transcript from the concluding chapter of the History of S. Gildas, has so much in common with it, that, (as it is evidently a quotation), I suspect it is a fragment of his lost history; but be this as it may, the subject is certainly the peace of Uther's reign, undisturbed by any but civil wars, and the relapse of the British nation into those habits of profligacy, from which their misfortunes, their deliverance, and the preaching of S. Germanus had roused them, when the generation which was then in its infancy had attained to years of maturity. Such being the case, this passage is of very great importance, inasmuch as its author represents the peace as having been first interrupted by the coming of Ælle, and this was in the thirtieth year from the coming of the Angles, *i. e.* A.D. 457.

Ælle and his people do not appear to have met with any opposition except the tumultuary resistance of the inhabitants of the district in which they landed, and they gradually made themselves masters of Sussex and Surrey. In the former county we find traces of Ælle at Elstead, of Cymen at Keynor (Cymenesore) in Selsey, of Wlencing at Lancing, and of Cissa at Chichester (Cissan-ceaster), and Cisbury, an ancient fortress in the parish of Findon; in the latter we have another Elstead, and Cissestede[3] near Merstham.

Henry of Huntingdon continues:[4]—

"Then when they had more boldly advanced into a dis-
"tant region, the kings and princes of the Britons came
"together at Mearcredesburne, and fought against Ælle and
"his sons, and the victory was very doubtful; for each army
"having suffered great loss, declined the conflict, and retired
"to their own territories. Ælle, therefore, sent to his coun-
"trymen requesting aid."

This was in the ninth year of their coming, A.D. 465. The name Mearcredes-burn is lost; it is obvious that it must be sought at a considerable distance from Ælle's settlement in Sussex, and to the west, for the eastern parts of the island were occupied by Saxons at this time; and it is not improbable that it may be represented by Margaret-marsh in the north of Dorsetshire; for we observe the following traces of the names of Ælle's sons, indicating their advance from Sussex in this direction: at Cissanbeorh[5] near Streetley, and Cumnor (Cumenesora)[6] in Berkshire, at Cymenesdene[7] near Bedwin, at Chisbury, a grand fortress on the Wansdyke in Wiltshire, and at Cissan-anstigo,[8] and Cissanham[9] in Hampshire.

Ælle's message to his compatriots resulted in a league with Octa, whom Boece represents as having favoured the recently arrived Saxons, and excited the suspicions of Uther that he intended to break the peace by so doing. Uther accordingly sent a remonstrance to him, and desired him to drive them from the country. To this Octa returned an insolent

---

[3] Cod. Diplom. 413.

[4] "Tunc vero cum audacius regionem in longinquum capesserent, con-
"venerunt reges et tyranni Brittonum apud Mercredesburne, et pugna-
"verunt contra Ælle et filios suos, et fere dubia erat victoria, uterque
"enim exercitus valde læsus et minoratus, alterius congressum devovens,
"ad propria remearunt. Misit Ælle igitur ad compatriotas suas auxilium
"flagitans."

[5] C. D. 1094. [6] Ib. 992. [7] Ib. 133. [8] Ib. 1235. [9] Ib. 658.

answer, and to a second message of a more conciliatory character, none whatever; so the Britons prepared for war. Shortly afterwards Octa invaded Uther's dominions, and slew fifteen thousand Britons, but followed the retreating army so closely, that he was slain with many of his companions.[10]

The Brut says that Octa and his forces had advanced to Verulam, and occupied it, when Uther, though afflicted with sickness, resolved to take the field in person, and prepared to besiege them, carried in a litter at the head of his army. The Saxons, preferring the chances of a battle to the tediousness of a siege, sallied forth and engaged with him, but were defeated with the loss of seventeen thousand, and their leaders Octa, Ebissa, and Ossa.

Ælle's advance into Dorsetshire was an invasion of Uther's territories, and Octa's abetting him was certainly a breach of the treaty. The result of Ælle's demand for assistance was Octa's advance to Verulam, and a renewal of hostilities after a peace of fourteen years. The battle was certainly fought not long before the death of Uther, and the date, which is assigned to it in the Orcamp additions to the Chronicle of Sigebert of Gemblours, is probably correct, A.D. 466.

Boece says, that after the death of Octa, the Saxons made another Octa, the son of his brother, king of England;[11] that he made preparations for a war with the Picts, because Loth had supported the Britons in the last battle, and invited Colgrim with reinforcements from Germany; that they fought with and defeated them; and that Octa then committed Northumbria into the hands of Colgrim, and led his own forces against the Britons.

In the History of the Britons, in a passage quite unconnected with what goes before, it is said:[12]—

---

[10] I suspect that Boece, who represents Nathaliod as having fallen in this battle, has confounded it with one fought in A.D. 487.

[11] Buchanan also speaks of a second Octa, a son of the former.

[12] "In illo tempore, Saxones invalescebant in multitudine magna, et

"At that time the Saxons were strengthened in great "multitude and increased in Britain. But Hencgest being "dead, Octha his son came from the northern part of Britain "to the kingdom of the Kentishmen, and from him all the "kings of the Kentishmen (are sprung) even to this day."

Henry of Huntingdon says,[13]—

"Hencgest, King of Kent, died in the fortieth year after "his coming to Britain, and Esc his son reigned in his stead "thirty-four years. But Esc, with hereditary valour, held "his country vigorously against the Britons, and extended "his kingdom at the expense of theirs."

Hencgest II, therefore, died in A. D. 467, and his son, whom the History of the Britons calls Ottha or Octha, the Saxon Chronicle Æsc, Æthelweard Esc-Octa, and the Scalæ Chronicon Osca Octa, succeeded him, having previously reigned for a year in Northumbria. His departure from the North to take possession of the kingdom of Kent, is the circumstance of which Boece speaks, when he says that he made Colgrim Prince of Northumbria, and proceeded against the Britons in the South. The notice of this Octa in the History of the Britons is introductory to that of Arthur's twelve battles, and Boece repeatedly mentions him as the opponent of Arthur.

Boece proceeds to say, that Octa defeated the Britons, and that Uther was poisoned by a Saxon, and died in the eighteenth year of his reign.

Layamon does not notice the second Octa, but, for the rest, his narrative is quite consistent with Boece's. He says, that the Saxons who survived the battle of Verulam returned to

---

"crescebant in Brittannia. Mortuo autem Hencgesto Ottha filius ejus "advenit de sinistrali parte Brittanniæ ad regnum Cantuariorum, et de "ipso omnes reges Cantuariorum usque in hodiernum diem." C. 56.

[13] "Mortuus est Hengist rex Cantiæ anno XL post adventum suum in "Brittanniam, et regnavit Esc filius ejus pro eo XXXIV annis. Esc autem "patria virtute patriam contra Brittannos potenter tenuit, regnumque "suum regnis eorum ampliavit."

the North, chose for their king Colgrim "the fair," and recommenced their ravages under his command. Uther's illness increased, and prevented him from pursuing them; and whilst he lay sick at Winchester, Saxons in disguise came to his court, and poisoned the water of a well from which he used to drink. His body was conveyed to Stonehenge, and buried with that of Ambrosius. His death and the accession of his son Arthur, are thus recorded in the Ulster Annals:—

"A. D. 467. Death of Uiter Pendragon, King of England, "to whom succeeded his son, namely, Cingh Airtur."

Vincent of Beauvais gives the same date, saying that Arthur's reign commenced in the eleventh year of the Emperor Leo; and Capgrave is an additional witness to the existence of histories, which placed the reign of Arthur thus early; for, (whatever was the authority he followed), he represents him as cotemporary with the Emperor Leo, A. D. 457 to 474, and with Pope Simplicius, A. D. 468 to 483. The same date is deducible from Boece also; for he says that Constantine was made king of the Scots in A. D. 465, and that Vortigern obtained the crown of Britain in the fifteenth year of his reign, *i.e.* A. D. 479. Here, of course, there is an error of fifty-four years, and this error pervades the whole of his history, until the accession of Arthur. He says that Ambrosius was elected king of the Britons in A. D. 498; he assigns to him a reign of rather more than six years, and to Uther one of seventeen years, and places the death of the latter in A. D. 521. From these data we obtain the following table of his chronology for comparison with our own:—

Accession of	Vortigern,	according to Boece,	A.D. 479,	true date	A.D. 425.
"	Ambrosius	"	498,	"	443.
"	Uther	"	504,	"	449.
"	Arthur	"	521,	"	467.

He therefore dates the accession of Arthur forty-two years after that of Vortigern, and as that was in A. D. 425, so must this be in A. D. 467.

This date I accept with perfect confidence; it is vindicated by the record of Arthur's battles in the History of the Britons, in immediate connection with the accession of Æsc-Octa to the throne of Kent, (which took place in the same year); and by Boece's notices of Æsc-Octa as his antagonist; and a chronology of his reign, based upon this date, will be found to be perfectly in harmony with the succession of events in the Saxon Chronicles, to acquire confirmation from other sources entirely distinct, and to obviate the many inconsistencies, anachronisms, and impossibilities, which are involved in the system which is based upon the dates in the Annals of Cambria, and that which Geoffrey of Monmouth assigns for his death.[14]

---

[14] This date, although not hitherto received, has certainly the preponderance of authority in its favour; but its importance is so great, that the following facts are here presented as illustrating and confirming it.

A story in Ludwig Van Velthem (Spiegel Historiael, Book III.) shows that this early date was recognized as the æra of Arthur in his days. He says that Edward I. during his invasion of Wales, found some gigantic armour, and amongst the rest a sword, on which was an inscription purporting that it had been made in the year of our Lord 466, and that it was at once concluded that these were the arms of Arthur. I say nothing of the fabulous details of the story, nor do I attach any importance to the question whether in its substance it be true or not. If there be any truth in it, and if such a sword was really found, why should they who were present at the discovery have concluded from the date, that it had belonged to Arthur? or if the poet invented it, why should he have fixed on this precise date, unless they or he had some reason for believing that it was the æra of Arthur?

S. Carantoc is said to have been the son of a British prince named Ceredic, and because his father was old and infirm, his people determined to raise him to the throne, on account of an invasion of his dominions by the Scots. To escape from the greatness thus attempted to be thrust upon him, he retired to a solitude, where he built an oratory and dwelt for some time. At length, affection for S. Patrick induced him to accompany him to Ireland, thirty years before the birth of S. David. After many years' residence in that country, he returned to his old hermitage in Cardiganshire, and thence after some time he crossed the Severn, and obtained from Arthur a grant of land for the site of a church. Not long after this he returned to Ireland, and there ended his days. His death is recorded in the Feilire of Aenghus, on the 16th of May, "the illustrious "death of Charnig the truly powerful," with the gloss "Cairnech of Du- "lane, in the neighbourhood of Kells, and he is of the Britons of Cornwall."

Now as his first journey to Ireland was thirty years before the birth of S. David, therefore in A.D. 432, the story of his return in the days of Arthur and Cador, after many years' residence in that country, is quite consistent with the statement, that Arthur began his reign in A.D. 467, but scarcely with that which places his accession in A.D. 512 or 516.

S. Kyned was born of the daughter of a prince of Bretagne, at a time when Arthur was entertaining, at a Christmas feast, the princes who were subject to his authority. This cannot have been earlier than the tenth year of his reign. After having spent eighteen years in solitude in one place, and many years in another, he was visited by S. David, S. Theliau, and S. Paternus, and shortly afterwards was invited by S. David to be present at a synod, evidently the synod of Victory. His story again is perfectly consistent with the earlier, but not with the later, dates of the accession of Arthur, which would only allow an interval of nineteen years between the birth of S. Kyned, and the death of S. David.

S. Cadoc was the cotemporary of S. German and S. Gildas, and must have been of mature age when he was made Abbot of Llancarvan, before A.D. 447, by the former. He and S. Gildas retired at the same time to islands in the Severn, and after this he is said to have gone to Beneventum, that is, Weedon in Northamptonshire, (Bennaventum in Antonine's Itinerary), where he was consecrated bishop, and at length he was murdered by a certain king. His retirement, as we shall see in the sequel, must have been about A.D. 475, and before this time he came in contact with Arthur twice.

Arthur was meditating vengeance on a British nobleman who had killed three of his soldiers, but at the entreaty of S. Cadoc, he consented to accept cattle as the price of their lives. On another occasion, Arthur is said to have met with a prince of Glamorganshire who was pursued by his enemies, and by the advice of Cai and Bedwer to have assisted him to recover his possessions.

In all these instances Arthur is spoken of in terms which leave no doubt of his identity with the great Arthur, the subject of our history. There was another Arthur, a son of Mouric, King of Glamorgan, mentioned in the Register of Llandaff. He it is, I believe, who is noticed in the Life of S. Paternus after his return from Jerusalem, not with the epithets by which the great Arthur is distinguished in these Lives, but merely as "quidam tyrannus."

CHAPTER XIII.

The first Four Years of the Reign of Arthur, A.D. 467 *to* 471; *his Twelve Victories.*

ARTHUR was in Armorica at the time of his father's death, but returned immediately, and was solemnly crowned by S. Dubricius at Silchester, A.D. 467, he being then in the fifteenth year of his age. Others, we are told, had a better title to the throne;[1] and of this number were Modred and Walgan, the sons of Loth, on behalf of whom their father preferred a claim,[2] which the Britons rejected with contempt.[3] Loth, in consequence, formed an alliance with Æsc-Octa, (according to the Scalæ Chronicon[4]); and this confederacy, of the Picts and Saxons against Arthur,

---

[1] "Licet multi ipso nobiliores essent." Hist. Brit.

[2] Fordun.

[3] Boece.

Fordun says, on account of their age; but although Walgan may have been an infant at the time of Arthur's accession, Modred could not have been much his junior. Geoffrey confirms Boece by saying, that the union of Loth and Anna took place during the days of Ambrosius, but afterwards confounds this Anna with the sister of Arthur, who was not born until after Ambrosius' death.

[4] The Saxon prince is called *Osca alias Occa;* a confirmation of Æthelweard's statement respecting him. Boece, as we shall see, also speaks of this confederacy.

called forth all his energies, during the first years of his reign. The earliest and the most authentic notice of him, is contained in the History of the Britons, in a passage, which follows immediately the mention of the death of Hencgest II, and Æsc-Octa's accession to the throne of Kent:[5]—

"Then the warrior Arthur, with the soldiers and kings of "the Britons, fought against them, and although many were "more noble than he, yet he was twelve times the leader of "the war, and conqueror in his battles. He began the first "battle against them near the mouth of the river which is "called Glem. The second, and third, and fourth, and fifth "battles, on another river, which is called in the British "language Duglas, which is in the district Inniis. The sixth "battle upon a river which is called Bassas. The seventh "battle he fought against them in the wood of Celidon, which "is named in the British language Cat-coit-Celidan. He "fought the eighth battle against the Barbarians near the "castle Guinnion, in which the same Arthur bore the image

---

[5] "Tunc belliger Arthur cum militibus Brittanniæ atque regibus "contra illos pugnabat; et licet multi ipso nobiliores essent ipse tamen "duodecies dux belli fuit, victorque bellorum. Primum bellum contra "illos iniit juxta hostium fluminis quod dicitur Glemu'. Secundum ac "tertium quartumque ac quintum super aliam amnem, quæ nominatur "Brittannice Duglas, quæ est in regione Inniis. Sextum bellum super "flumen quod vocatur Bassas. Septimum vero contra illos iniit bellum "in silva Celidonis, quæ Brittannice Cat toit Celidan nominatur. Octavum contra Barbaros egit bellum juxta castellum Guinnion, in quo "idem Arthur imaginem Sanctæ Mariæ Dei Genitricis semperque Virginis "super humeros suos portavit, et tota illa die Saxones per virtutem Domini nostri Jhū Xti, et Sanctæ Mariæ matris Ejus, in fugam versi sunt, "et multi ex eis magnâ cæde perierunt. Nonum egit bellum in urbe "Leogis, quæ Brittannice Cair Lion dicitur. Decimum vero gessit bellum "in littore fluminis, quod nos vocamus Trac Theuroit. Undecimum in "monte qui vocatur Breuoin, ubi illos in fugam vertit, quod nos Cat "Bregion appellamus. Duodecimum contra Saxones durissime Arthur "bellum in monte Badonis perpetravit, in quo corruerunt impetu illius "una die CCCCXL viri, nullo sibi Brittonum in adjutorium adherente, "præter ipsum solum, Domino confortante. In omnibus autem supradictis bellis protestantur semper eum fuisse victorem, sicut fuerunt et "alii perplures Brittones." C. 56.

"of S. Mary, the Mother of God, and ever Virgin, on his "shoulder, and all that day, through the might of our Lord "Jesus Christ, and of S. Mary, His Mother, the Saxons "were put to flight, and many of them perished with great "slaughter. The ninth battle he fought in the city Leogis, "which is called in the British language Cair Lion. But "the tenth battle he fought on the banks of a river, which "we call Trat treuroit. The eleventh battle on the mountain "which is called Breguoin, where he put them to flight, which "we call Cat-Bregion. The twelfth battle Arthur accom-"plished most fiercely against the Saxons, on the hill of "Bath, in which CCCCXL men fell by his valour in one day, "no one of the Britons assisting him, but himself alone, the "Lord strengthening him. But in all the aforesaid battles "they protest that he was always victor, as also were very "many warlike Britons."

If the attempts, which have hitherto been made to identify the scenes of these twelve battles, have failed, it has been because the authorities, who relate the history of Arthur, have been despised or neglected. With their aid we shall be able to trace his career, and to determine the locality of each with something like certainty. The Brut and Boece give detailed accounts of the war to which these battles belong, each supplying matter which the other has not. Besides these, in the metrical Life of Merlin, we have a valuable notice of four of them, in the form of a prophecy, which the poet puts into the mouth of the sister of the Caledonian Merlin, Ganieda; but there can be no doubt that it belongs to the times of his earlier namesake, and relates to the events of this war,—the deliverance of Oxford by the defeat of the Saxons at the mouth of the Glym, the siege of Caer-Loit-coit, the battle of Guinnion castle, and the raising of the siege of Bath. The notices of Hueil, in the Life of S. Gildas, and the Welsh traditions respecting him, enable us to complete the series.

Immediately after his coronation, (according to Boece[6]), Arthur assembled an army, fought with the Saxons, and made them tributary. The Britons then came to London, and remained there some months, making preparations for a war with the confederate Picts and Saxons of Northumbria.

This is the battle on the Glem, and its circumstances forbid us to look for the river far north; the Glen, therefore, in Northumberland, and the Glen in Lincolnshire, are out of the question. I am satisfied that it was fought at the confluence of the Glym and Evenlode, in Oxfordshire, about seven miles from Oxford; for the passage referred to in the Life of Merlin,[7] speaks of Oxford, under its British name Rytychen, as occupied by an army; of its clergy and religious women destined to captivity; and of the shepherd, (*i. e.* Arthur), compelled by the urgent entreaties of his young men, to open the vessel of his own ruin, that is, to begin the series of battles which ended in his destruction, (an allusion to Epimetheus' opening the vessel of Pandora).

About three miles from the junction of the Glym and Evenlode, to the north-west, there are some entrenchments, and a fort called Callow hill, and at the distance of a mile to the south-east, another fort, called the Round Castle; which may indicate the positions of the Saxon and British forces. At the time of Arthur's accession, I believe that the Saxons occupied Oxford, that they withdrew on his approach, and entrenched themselves in the neighbourhood; and that his first victory was gained over Æsc-Octa, of whom we last heard as having defeated the Britons in the South, and as en-

---

[6] He says the battle was fought "not ten miles from London," one of his geographical blunders. For "London" we must read "Oxford."

[7] "Cerno Ridichenam galeatis gentibus urbem
"Impletam, sacrosque viros, sacrasque tyaras,
"Nexibus addictos. Sic consiliante juventâ,
"Pastor in excelsâ mirabitur edita turris,
"Et reserare sui cogetur fictile dampni." L. 1477-1481.

tering into alliance with Loth, and who is said[8] to have been expelled from Britain about this time.

Finding the resources at his command insufficient for the prosecution of the war, Arthur appears to have retired to London for a time, to recruit his army, and,[9] by the advice of the clergy and people, sent to Armorica to invite his kinsman Hoel, who had accompanied him to Britain and returned, to co-operate with him in expelling the Saxons from the country. Hoel brought a large army to his assistance, and accepted the second command. Thus reinforced, Arthur immediately proceeded northward to attack Colgrim, who held in subjection the whole of Northumbria, and was in alliance with the Scots and Picts. Apprised of his movements, Colgrim sent his brother Baldwulf southward to the coast, to wait there for fresh forces, which Childeric was expected to bring from Germany; and at the head of a large army of Saxons, Scots, and Picts, advanced to meet the Britons and Armoricans. They encountered on the river Douglas, and after an obstinate contest, continued probably during four successive days, victory declared for Arthur, and the Saxons fled.

The river Douglas, which falls into the estuary of the

---

[8] In the sequel of Boece's narrative.

[9] "Et puer Arturus fuerat, nec debilitate
"Ætatis poterat tantas compescere turmas.
"Ergo, consilio cleri populique recepto,
"Armorico regi mittens mandavit Hoelo,
"Ut sibi præsidio festinâ classe rediret.
"Sanguis enim communis eos sociabat, amorque,
"Alter ut alterius deberet dampna levare.
"Mox igitur collegit Hoel ad bella feroces
"Circumquaque viros, et multis millibus ad nos
"Venit, et Arturo sociatus, percutit hostes
"Sæpius aggrediens, et stragem fecit acerbam."
Vita Merlini, L. 1080-1090.

Hoel was doubly related to Arthur—his cousin by the father's side, his nephew by the mother's. Geoffrey, alone of the editors of the Brut, gives the name of his father Dubricius; an evident mistake, traceable, as Mr. Roberts has remarked, to the mention of S. Dubricius just before.

Ribble, is certainly that which is indicated here; for Colgrim is said to have gone from York to meet Arthur; and although it was one of Arthur's tactics to get round his adversaries, so as to be able to attack them when least expected, (which will account for the scene of this conflict being considerably to the west of the direct line from London to York), it is extremely improbable that he would have gone so far north as the Douglas in Lothian, when his object was to attack Colgrim at York. The reading which the Paris MS. and Henry of Huntingdon give,[10] is, I believe, correct, and represents Ince; a name which is retained to this day by a township near to this river, a little more than a mile to the south-west of Wigan, and by another, about fifteen miles to the west; and which may possibly have belonged to a considerable tract of country.

In this district, and on this river, Arthur's second, third, fourth, and fifth battles were fought, and of all these, according to Mr. Whitaker, local traditions still preserved the remembrance in the last century. He says that in his days, (1775), these traditions spoke of a battle in the marshes south of the river, of two others on opposite sides of the town of Wigan, and of a fourth about six miles from Wigan, near Blackrode; that with regard to one of those said to have been fought near Wigan, the traditions had been confirmed by the discovery of a large space strewn with the bones of men and horses, from which six hundred-weight of horseshoes were taken, in the course of the formation of a canal, forty years before he wrote; and that, about the middle of the eighteenth century, three or four old men connected the battle of Blackrode with the memory of Arthur.

Neither the Brut nor Boece mention more than one battle at this time; but the latter says that Arthur "pursued the "Saxons, continually slaughtering them, until they took re-

[10] "Duglas, qui est in regione Inniis."

"fuge in York;" and that, "having had so frequent victories, "he there besieged them;" and these expressions may well imply the four victories, gained in one prolonged contest on the Douglas, and another on the river Bassas, *i. e.* the Bashall brook, which falls into the Ribble near Clithero, in the direct line of Colgrim's flight to York.

As soon as Baldwulf heard that Arthur was besieging York, he left his station on the coast, and hastened to relieve his brother. Intending to take Arthur by surprise, he halted in a wood seven miles from the city; but Arthur, who had gained intelligence of his design from a Briton who was with Baldwulf's troop, sent a detachment under Cador, Prince of Cornwall, to intercept him. Cador surprised the Saxons in their encampment, slew great numbers of them, and put the rest to flight. Baldwulf hastened to York, contrived to pass the British lines in the guise of a harper, and entered the city. The scene of this affair was probably Cawood on the Ouse.

Arthur had made his arrangements for carrying York by assault, when intelligence reached him of Childeric's arrival with a large fleet, on the coast of Scotland; and, as he knew that the Saxons, with this accession of strength, were more than a match for him, he retired to London until the following year.

Boece gives an interesting variation of these circumstances. He says, that after Arthur had besieged York for three months, he heard that Octa, who had been driven out of Britain, (after the battle on the Glym), had returned with a fresh army to Northumbria; that not being able to compete with him, he abandoned the siege, and fled with his army into Wales, leaving a small force under Hoel in Northumbria, to keep the Saxons in check during the winter; and that he soon afterwards returned to London, to oppose the Saxons who had re-entered Kent, and the neighbouring provinces.

This account, of course, is quite consistent with the other;

for Æsc-Octa may have returned with Childeric, and, after Arthur's withdrawal of his forces, have passed over to his own kingdom of Kent. Boece mentions Childeric later, and that in his account of a battle in which Octa was also engaged. The king of Kent could hardly have been an indifferent witness of the struggle, and Boece's notices of Octa are particularly valuable—supplying, as they do, information relative to the part he took in it, which is wanting in the Brut; and they are supported by the statement in the Scalæ Chronicon, that it was he who, as the principal leader of the Saxons in Britain at this time, made the league with Loth.

Hoel appears to have remained in Yorkshire for a time, thence to have gone to London, and thence to Armorica for reinforcements. So at least we must infer from a comparison of the statements in Boece and the Brut; and this inference is supported by a passage in the Life of Merlin,[11] which speaks of the siege of Caer Loit-coit, and of one of the leaders, who commanded its garrison, making his escape, only to return with a fresh army and with the prince. The leader of course is Hoel, and the prince Arthur, who in the following summer returned to the North, with reinforcements which Hoel had brought from Armorica.

Boece, again representing Octa as confederate with Colgrim, relates a circumstance, which is not in the Brut, but is perfectly consistent with its statements, that Arthur took York on the third night after his arrival, through the treachery of a Briton, who passed for a Saxon,[12] and admitted a large

---

[11] "Cerno Kaerloyctoyc vallatam milite sævo,
"Inclusosque duos, quorum divellitur alter,
"Ut redeat cum gente ferâ, cum principe vallis,
"Et vincat rapto sævam rectore catervam." L. 1482-1485.

[12] In this circumstance, as compared with what Layamon relates of similar treachery practised in the preceding year, we seem to have an indication of the ancient sources from which both these writers derived their details; and, (as they are entirely distinct), an incidental confirma-

number of his troops into the city; and that he slew the garrison, but spared the people.

Colgrim, Baldwulf, and Childeric, were engaged at the time with the siege of Caer Loit-coit. By thus taking advantage of their absence, Arthur not only gained a firm footing in Northumbria, and established a centre for future operations, but deprived them, at the same time, of an important place of refuge, and separated them from their countrymen who occupied the more northerly districts. This accomplished, he proceeded to attack them, and after a bloody contest, in which the British garrison of the fortress took part, completely routed them, and pursued them to the wood of Celidon. There he surrounded them, and besieged them for three days, until they were compelled to surrender by want of provisions, gave hostages as security for their keeping peace for the future, and were permitted to leave the country. This defeat of the Saxons, and their surrender in the wood of Celidon, are comprised in what is called Cat coit Celidon, "the battle of the wood of Celidon," Arthur's seventh victory.[13]

---

tion of their truthfulness. Layamon says, that Baldwulf had a British knight in his host, a relative of Arthur, named Mawron, who communicated intelligence of his design to Arthur; and Boece speaks of a Briton, who passed for a Saxon, admitting Arthur's forces within the walls of York. It is not unlikely that the same person played the traitor on both occasions; but, however this might be, the statements of these writers appear to gain credibility, from the facts that they are quite independent, and that the events of which they speak, are said to have occurred at different periods of the same war, and under different circumstances.

[13] In the passage of the Life of Merlin, above referred to, it seems to be implied that a distinguished leader of the Saxons fell in this battle; and, if it be the same as that which is noticed in a poem in the Welsh Archæology (I. 160), we have his name there given.

"Pacing to combat, a great booty,
"Before Caer Lwydgoed, has not Morial taken
"Fifteen hundred cattle, and the head of Gwrial."

A Saxon chieftain of this name appears, from the traces he has left in the districts which are connected with the history of Horsa and Hencgest, to have followed their standard; it occurs at Whorlton in Yorkshire, Whorlton in Durham, Whorlton in Northumberland, Worlcstone in Cheshire, and Whorwelsdown in Wiltshire.

The identity of Caer Loit-coit with Leeds in Yorkshire, I consider certain. Five miles therefrom is the village of Gildersome, which seems to bear the name of Childeric, and about a mile and a-half nearer thereto, there are the remains of an ancient earthwork, called the Giant's or Castle hill, possibly that which Layamon tells us he constructed during the siege. The wood of Celidon is doubtless that which occasioned the addition of *coit* to the name of *Caer Loit; celyddon* having been a common appellation of the forests of Britain.

Arthur's eighth victory, that of Guinnion Castle, was probably gained in the following summer, which Boece tells us was spent in frequent skirmishes, between the Northumbrian Saxons, and the Britons who occupied York. Unnoticed in other authorities, it is described at some length in the Life of Merlin,[14] in a very interesting, but, (on account of our ignorance of all the circumstances), somewhat unintelligible passage. Arthur and Hoel, with their forces, appear to be typified as "two lions," and "two moons," and the latter, at the conclusion, as the "Armorican boar." Against them were arrayed four chieftains with their bands, two against each; one of these was defeated and pursued by Hoel; the other three, united, attacked Arthur, and were also discomfited; two found safety in flight, the third was admitted to a

---

[14] "Inspicio binas prope Kaer Wen in aere lunas,
"Gestarique duos nimia feritate leones.
"Inque duos homines unus miratur, et alter
"In totidem, pugnamque parant, et cominus astant;
"Insurgunt alii, quartumque ferocibus armis
"Acriter obpugnant; nec prævalet ullus eorum,
"Perstat enim clipeumque movet, telisque repugnat,
"Et victor ternos confestim proterit hostes;
"Impellitque duos trans frigida regna Boetes,
"Dans alii veniam qui postulat. Ergo per omnes
"Diffugiunt partes totius sidera campi
"Armoricanus aper, quercu protectus avitâ
"Abducit lunam, gladiis post terga rotatis." L. 1488-1500.

treaty of peace. Thus the hostile army would seem to have comprised four distinct races, of whom three were certainly Picts, Scots, and Saxons; and Britons, opposed to Arthur, were probably the fourth.

The chieftain who made peace with Arthur was undoubtedly Loth, who, (according to the Scalæ Chronicon), was defeated by him, and, (according to Boece), made peace with him, at this time, on the following conditions: that Arthur should enjoy the crown of Britain during his life, and that Modred and Walgan should succeed him; that Modred should marry the daughter of Gawolan, the greatest of Arthur's princes; that Walgan should be educated at Arthur's court; and that the Picts should have the territory north of the Humber. Hitherto Loth had been leagued with the Saxons against Arthur; henceforth, until his death, he appears as Arthur's ally; and it would seem that Arthur had detached him from the common cause, by conceding to him the province for which the Picts had fought so long, and recognizing the claim of his children to the crown of Britain; for the rest of his nation, as well as the Scots, still remained hostile to Arthur.

There is every reason to believe that Guinnion castle, or Caer Wen, is Ptolemy's Winnowion, Antonine's Vinovia, now Binchester in Durham.

Secure at length from all fear of enemies, the Britons, (according to Boece), spent the whole winter at York in feasting and debauchery. They were not, however, allowed to remain inactive long; hostilities in the West involved Arthur in a campaign, (noticed only in the Life of S. Gildas), in which he gained his ninth and tenth victories. S. Gildas, it is said, was the friend of Arthur,[15] "but his twenty-three "brethren resisted the aforesaid rebel king, impatient of his

[15] "Confratres tamen tres et viginti resistebant regi rebelli prædicto, "nolentes pati dominium, sed crebro fugabant et expellebant a saltu et "bello. Hueil, major natu, belliger assiduus et miles famosissimus, nulli

"dominion, and often defeated him, and put him to flight, "from skirmish and battle. Hueil, the eldest, an active "warrior, and most famous knight, obeyed no king, not even "Arthur; but harassed him, and stirred up the greatest ani-"mosity between them. He came very frequently from "Scotland, made conflagrations, carried off spoil, with victory "and renown. •Wherefore the king of all Britain, hearing "that the magnanimous youth had done such things, and "was doing the like, pursued the victorious and excellent "youth, the future king, as the natives said and hoped. In "the prosecution of the war, and in a hostile encounter, he "killed the young marauder, in the isle Minau. After that "slaughter, Arthur returned victor, very greatly rejoicing "that he had conquered his bravest enemy."

Here the title, "rebel," bestowed on Arthur, illustrates what we have found elsewhere, as to the invalidity of his right to the throne; and the mention of frequent encounters between him and the brothers of S. Gildas, in which they had the advantage, confirms what Boece says of the frequent skirmishes in which he was engaged, during the summer which followed the capture of York. The MSS. of the History of the Britons, which we follow, record only Arthur's victories, and it is observable that they do not claim for him a series of victories, untarnished by reverses, but only state that he was victor on every one of these occasions.

Some traditions, relative to this war of Arthur and Hueil, are recorded in the Welsh MS. Chronicle[16] of Mr. Jones of

---

"regi obedivit, nec etiam Arthuro. Affligebat eundem, commovebat "inter utrumque maximum furorem. A Scotia veniebat sæpissime, in-"cendia ponebat, prædas ducebat cum victoriâ et laude. Unde rex "universalis Britanniæ, audiens magnanimum juvenem talia fecisse, et "æqualia facere, persecutus est victoriosissimum juvenem et optimum, "ut aiebant et sperabant indigenæ, futurum regem. In prosecutione "belli et in conventu bellico, in insulâ Minau interfecit juvenem præda-"torem. Post illam interfectionem, Arthurus victor remeavit, gaudens "maxime quod superaverat suum fortissimum hostem."

[16] Quoted by Mr. Roberts.

Gelly Lyfdy. One of these states that Arthur fought many battles with the King of Anglesey; another, that he and his army performed many gallant actions between Ystrad Meric, in Cardiganshire, and Anglesey; and another, that Arthur fought with Hueil and was wounded by him, but afterwards put him to death. It is evident that these traditions, and the passage above cited, speak of the same events; the Life of S. Gildas is certainly the more trustworthy authority; but the traditions are useful, inasmuch as they serve to fix the locality of Arthur's war with Hueil, and so to connect with this war his ninth and tenth victories.

The ninth was at Caer Lion, and the proximity of Chester to the district in which these traditions prevailed, warrants us in preferring it to Caerleon on Usk, and regarding it as the place where Arthur encountered Hueil on his arrival from the North, and for the first time defeated him.

The tenth was at Trath Trevroit, on the banks of a river Trevroit or Tribruit; and as we have two places called Trefdraeth, (one in Pembrokeshire, the other in Anglesey), guided by the mention of the isle Minau in the Life of S. Gildas, as the scene of Hueil's overthrow, and the notices of Anglesey in the traditions, we can have no hesitation in preferring the latter. The name of Anglesey indicates that it was occupied by the Angles at an early period, and as all the victories of Arthur are said to have been gained in conflict with the Saxons, it is probable that the king of Anglesey, Arthur's adversary and Hueil's ally, was of their race. Hueil was the son of Nau, king of the Picts; he had been previously opposed to Arthur, and had obtained some successes over him. It would seem that he had taken advantage of the security in which the Britons were indulging themselves at York, to make an incursion into Wales, and that Arthur marched against him and defeated him, in two successive engagements, at Chester and Trefdraeth. After his death, Arthur returned to the North, carried the war into Scotland against the Picts and the remnant of the Saxons, and gained his eleventh victory, Cat Bregion, on the hill of Agned, that is, Edinburgh. *Cat Bregion,* as Dr. Todd has suggested, indicates the nation who were opposed to Arthur, that is, the Picts.[17]

The war in Scotland was still proceeding, when Arthur received intelligence, which obliged him to hasten to the South, leaving Hoel, who was prevented by sickness from accompanying him, in the strong city of Alclud.

Henry of Huntingdon says:[18]—

"Auxiliaries had come to Ælle in the third year after the "death of Hencgest, (*i.e.* A.D. 470), and relying on his great "resources, he besieged Andredes-ceaster, a most strongly "fortified city. The Britons swarmed like bees, and attacked "the besiegers with stratagems by day, and with assaults by "night; there was no day nor night in which adverse and "fresh intelligence did not exasperate the minds of the

---

[17] Geoffrey mentions this expedition only incidentally; Layamon says that Arthur overran at this time Scotland, Galloway, Moray, and Man, (the last perhaps a mistake for Anglesey).

[18] "Venerant enim ei (Ællæ) auxiliares a patria sua anno tertio post "mortem Hengisti. Fretus igitur copiis ingentibus, obsedit Andrede-"cestre urbem munitissimam. Congregati sunt igitur Britanni quasi "apes, et die expugnabant obsidentes insidiis, et nocte incursibus; nullus "dies erat, nulla nox erat, quibus sinistri et recentes nuntii Saxonum "animos non acerbarent; inde tamen ardentiores effecti, continuis in-"sultibus urbem infestabant. Semper vero dum assilirent, instabant "eis Brittones a tergo cum viris sagittariis, et amentatis telorum missili-"bus. Dimissis ergo mœnibus, gressus et arma dirigebant in eos Pagani. "Tunc Brittones, eis celeritate præstantiores, silvam cursu petebant; "tendentibusque ad mœnia rursum a tergo aderant. Hac arte Saxones "diu fatigati sunt, et innumera strages eorum fiebat, donec in duas partes "exercitum diviserunt; ut dum una pars urbem expugnaret, esset eis a "tergo, contra Brittonum excursus, bellatorum acies ordinata. Tunc "vero cives diuturnâ fame contriti, cum jam pondus infestantium ferre "nequirent, omnes ore gladii devorati sunt cum mulieribus et parvulis, "ita quod nec unus solus evasit; et quia tot ibi damna toleraverant ex-"tranei, ita urbem destruxerunt quod nunquam postea reædificata est; "locus tantum, quasi nobilissimæ urbis, transeuntibus ostenditur deso-"latus."

The Saxon Chronicle dates this event A.D. 491, *i.e.* 470.

"Saxons, who thereby were rendered more resolute, and "beset the city with continuous assaults. Always, how-"ever, when they assailed it, the Britons attacked their rear "with arrows and javelins; so, leaving the walls, they turned "against them. Then the Britons, who excelled them in "swiftness, ran to the woods, and when they returned to the "walls, were again at their rear. The Saxons were harassed "for a long time in this way, and many of them were slain, "until they divided their army into two parts, so that whilst "one invested the walls, the other might be arrayed against "the Britons in their rear. Then the citizens, compelled by "famine to surrender, when they could no longer resist their "adversaries, were all put to the sword with their women "and children, so that not one escaped; and the foreigners, "because they had suffered so much in the siege, destroyed "the city, so that it was never rebuilt; but the site, as of a "most noble city, is shown desolate to passers by."

Evidently this attempt to raise the siege was not that of a disciplined army, but a tumultuary rising of the people, such as that which Ælle encountered on his arrival in Britain. The auxiliaries were probably Colgrim, Baldwulf, and Childeric, who, having recruited their forces, returned at this time to Britain. They landed, we are told, at Totness, overran Devonshire, Wiltshire, and Somersetshire, and at length laid siege to Bath. It would be but natural for them to unite their forces with those of Ælle, whom they would find in Wiltshire; and the time of their coming, coincident with that of his auxiliaries, suggests the probability that they did so.

Andredes-ceaster has been identified with Pevensey, and Pevensey is almost certainly Anderida, one of the fortresses of the Saxon shore; but as Ælle had been resident for more than twelve years in Britain, and had made advances into the interior during the time, it does not seem likely that he would have left the fortresses of the coast of Sussex so long unoccupied. We must, therefore, look for it inland, and within, or on the borders of, the great forest of Andred. In the Parliamentary Gazetteer it is said, that Silchester was destroyed by Ælle on his way to Bath. I do not know on what authority this statement is made, but it is exactly in accordance with my own conclusions, that the siege of Andredes-ceaster immediately preceded that of Bath, and that Ælle was present at the latter. Silchester, in the times of the Romans, was one of the largest walled towns of Britain, and was called by them Vindomum, (or Vindonum), and by the Britons Caer Vyddau. After their departure it was still a place of great importance, and the Brut records the coronation of Constantine there in A. D. 411, and of Arthur A. D. 467; but after the latter date, three years before the fall of Andredes-ceaster, it is mentioned no more in history, (Geoffrey's notice of the consecration of a bishop of Silchester in A. D. 490, being one of his additions to the original Brut). The space within its walls is now cultivated by the plough, with the exception of a small portion occupied by a church and village at its eastern extremity; this, and the record of its complete destruction by the Saxons, suggests that *syl*, a "plough," is the first element in its modern name, as it were *syl-ceaster* or *seó sylode ceaster*, "the ploughed city." Its ancient importance, according with the description "urbs "munitissima" and "nobilissima;" its present state, answering to the record of its entire destruction, and to the probable etymology of its name; and the time of its disappearance from the pages of history; concur to convince me, that the statement above referred to is correct, that Silchester is Andredes-ceaster, and that Ælle was assisted by Colgrim, Baldwulf, and Childeric, in this enterprise, and was immediately afterwards associated with them in the siege of Bath.

As soon as the intelligence of the siege of Bath reached Arthur, he gave orders for the execution of the hostages whom the Saxons had given him in the wood of Celidon, and marched at once into Somersetshire. Encouraged by S. Dubricius, his army attacked the Saxons, and, after a severe conflict of two days, gained the victory; Colgrim and Baldwulf were slain; Childeric fled across the Avon, hoping to regain his fleet. Cador, whom Arthur despatched in pursuit of him, proceeded direct to Totness, seized the Saxon vessels and manned them with the people of the country, between whom and the army of Cador, Childeric found himself hemmed in, when he arrived. His band was speedily destroyed, and he fled with twenty-four companions to a hill called Teignwick, by the river Teign, whither they were pursued by Cador, and all put to the sword.[19]

Boece speaks of this battle, but in different terms. He names Octa, Colgrim, and Childeric, as opposed to Arthur, and represents Colgrim as reproaching the Picts for their breach of faith in entering into an alliance with him. Now this is a circumstance which very strongly confirms the truth of the story. Boece has not mentioned the expulsion of Colgrim, after which, at the time of the battle of Caer Wen, Arthur and Loth were reconciled; and the first meeting of Colgrim and Loth afterwards, would be before the walls of Bath; so that the circumstance of such a conversation having taken place, is extremely probable. The result of the battle, he continues, was that Childeric was slain and his division routed by the Scots; that Colgrim, after unhorsing Loth, was slain by the Picts; that some of the Saxons sued for peace, offering to embrace Christianity, and become the subjects of Arthur; and that Octa and the rest returned to Germany, where the news of their defeat only served to stimulate their countrymen to further attempts for the conquest of Britain.

The principal difference between this account and that in the Brut is, that Boece appears to give the name of Childeric instead of that of Baldwulf, (whom he never names), as

---

[19] Layamon.

having fallen in the battle. He gives us besides the name of Octa as commander-in-chief.

In the Life of Merlin we have another notice of this battle. Bath is called "Collis Urgenius," from Urbgen, who, (according to the Brut), was its governor in the time of Arthur; "two stars," *i.e.* Arthur and Cador, are represented as opposed to the "wild beasts;" the union of the forces of Colgrim with the Saxons of the South, is spoken of under the names of "Deyri" and "Gewissi;" and "Cohel," *i. e.* Colgrim, is their commander.[20] The conclusion of the passage, "a star dashed against a star retreats to a covert, and hides "its light with renewed light," is very important; for it is evident that the flight of Childeric is alluded to, and yet the words "hides its light with renewed light," can hardly be understood in any other sense, than that, wounded and left for dead, he recovered and escaped; a perfectly possible supposition, and one which will be found to receive confirmation from what will be advanced in the sequel. Childeric's is not the only instance of one whose death on the field of battle has become matter of history, and who yet survived many years.

This is the last of Arthur's twelve famous battles. They are now for the first time localized, not according to mere conjecture, but according to a collation of the narratives in the Brut, Boece, and the Life of Merlin. Although none of these authorities mentions all of them, each supplies matter which the others have not, and the indications they furnish of Arthur's movements are perfectly in accordance with the History of the Britons, as to the order in which these battles

[20] "Sidera bina feris video committere pugnam
"Colle sub Urgenio, quo convenere Deyri
"Gewissique simul, magno regnante Cohelo.
"O quanto sudore viri, tellusque cruore
"Manat, in externas dum dantur vulnera gentes!
"Considet in latebras, collisum sidere sidus,
"Absconditque suum renovato lumine lumen." L. 1501-1507.

were fought. The Life of S. Gildas, and the Welsh traditions, come in to supply what is wanting. With these aids we obtain a tolerably clear view of Arthur's movements during the first four years of his reign, and are enabled satisfactorily to identify the scenes of his twelve victories.

CHAPTER XIV.

Testimony of S. Gildas to the Date of the last Victory. Identity of Childeric.

THE date of Arthur's twelfth victory is clearly fixed by the positive statement of a cotemporary, the earlier S. Gildas.

He was born about A. D. 425, one of twenty-four brothers, sons of Nau, a king of the Picts. He pursued his studies in his native land, during seven years from his childhood, then went to Gaul to complete them, and spent there seven other years. Returning to Britain he opened a school, and had many scholars; after some time, he preached with great fruit throughout the kingdoms of Britain, and eventually seems to have fixed his abode in Pembrokeshire, whence he passed over into Ireland, about A.D. 461, just before the birth of S. David. In Ireland he continued his preaching, and opened a school at Armagh, where he was resident when he heard of the death of his brother Hueil, and where also, as I believe, he composed the tract, which has been so frequently cited in the foregoing pages.

In the preface to this tract, the author says, that after ten years' delay, he had resolved on giving to the world his little history or admonition, which his friends had requested him to write; he enumerates the matters of which he proposed to treat; and he concludes it with a reference to his promise, and a statement of the fulfilment thereof, in nearly the same words as in the prefatory enumeration, but with one remarkable difference. This is shown in the following table, in which the two are collated, with references to the chapters in which the several matters are discussed, an explanation of their subjects, and the dates of the successive events.

Preface.		Summary.		
" Igitur		" Sed ante promissum		
" Deo volente pauca		" Deo volente pauca		
" de situ Britanniæ,	3	" de situ		
" de contumaciâ,	4	" de contumaciâ,		B.C.
" de subjectione,	5		Submission of Britain to Augustus	24
" de rebellione,	6		Rebellion of Boadicea	A.D.
" de secunda subjectione,	7		Subjugation of Britain by Suetonius	61
" ac diro famulatu,		" ac diro famulatu,		
" de religione,	8	" de religione,	Christianity preached in Britain, before	37
" de persecutione,	9	" de persecutione,	Diocletian's persecution	303 to 313
" de sanctis martyribus,	10, 11	" de sanctis martyribus,	S. Alban and others	
" de diversis hæresibus,	12	" de diversis hæresibus,	Arian and other heresies, about	320
" de tyrannis,	13	" de tyrannis,	Revolt of Maximus	385
" de duabus gentibus vas- " tatricibus,	14	" de duabus gentibus vic- " tricibus,	Picts and Scots	
" de primâ vastatione,			Their invasion of Britain, about	396
" de defensione,	15	" de defensione,	Expedition of Stilicho	397
" de secundâ vastatione,	16	" itemque vastatione,	Second invasion	407
" de secundâ ultione,	17, 18	" de secundâ ultione,	Expedition of Severus	408
" de tertiâ vastatione,	19	" tertiâque vastatione,	Third invasion	410
" de fame,	20	" de fame,	A famine	410
" de epistolis,		" de epistolis ad Agitium,	Letters to Æquitius, answered by Honorius	410
" de victoriâ,		" de victoriâ,	Victory of Constantine	412
" de sceleribus,	21	" de sceleribus,	Wickedness of the Britons, during the reigns of Constantine and Vortigern	412 to 425
" de nuntiatis subito hos- " tibus,	22	" de nuntiatis hostibus " subito,	Fourth invasion, about	426
" de famosâ peste,		" de famosâ peste,		
" de consilio,		" de consilio,	Invitation of the Saxons	
" de sæviore multo prim- " is hoste,	23	" de sæviore multo prim- " is hoste,	Their arrival	428
			Their hostilities, about	429
" de urbium subversione,	24	" de urbium subversione,	Their conquest of Britain	441
" de reliquiis,	25	" de reliquiis,	Victory of Ambrosius	443
" de postremâ pace quæ " temporibus nostris " Dei nutu ei donata " est,			Peace of Uther's reign	452 to 466
	26	" de postremâ victoriâ pa- " triæ, quæ postrema " victoria temporibus " nostris Dei nutu do- " nata,	Victory of Bath-hill	471
" dicere conamur."		" dicere curabo."		

In the preface, then, the last subject proposed to be treated of is the "peace;" and as this should have followed the notice of Ambrosius' victory, it is evidently the long peace of Uther's reign which is intended; this is merely alluded to in the last chapter; but instead of this, in the summary, we have the "last victory," and this is the victory of Bath-hill. This difference clearly shows that the work was begun during the peace of Uther's reign, but interrupted; then resumed and completed immediately after the battle of Bath; and the end of the twenty-fifth chapter is the point at which the interruption occurred.

In the fourth chapter, S. Gildas tells us that he had not had the writings or chronicles of his own country to guide him, for these had been destroyed by the fires of the enemy, or had been carried abroad in the fleet which conveyed his countrymen into exile, a circumstance related in the twenty-fifth chapter. This is an important statement, for it shows that there had been records carried to Armorica, which might supply materials for the work of S. Albinus. In the absence of these he had to rely chiefly on the *vivâ voce* information of persons who came over sea, and as this was frequently interrupted, it was by no means clear. This excludes the supposition that this tract could have been written in Armorica, the country to which the records had been conveyed, or in Britain, where persons were certainly living who could inform him as to events which had happened before his days, or during his youth, and absence in Gaul; it seems, therefore, almost certain that it was written in Ireland; and this account of the sources of his information sufficiently explains the character of his work, which is singularly deficient in names and details, and could not have been understood without the help of the Brut. Its chief value is that it is the earliest history of the times of which it treats, (all the events which are alluded to, from the thirteenth chapter to the end, having occurred within a period of ninety years previous to its publication), and enables us to receive with greater confidence the statements of other historians, by whom the details in which it is deficient are supplied.

The concluding chapter is most important, not only because it fixes decisively the date of the siege of Bath, but on account of the many allusions it contains to earlier events, which are not particularly noticed, but which of course were fresh in the memory of those for whom his work was designed. It is a hasty review of the affairs of nearly a quarter of a century.

This chapter, with illustrations of the allusions it contains, is here subjoined:[1]—

Of Ambrosius' victory.

"And from that time,
"at one time our people, at another
"the enemy were victorious,
"that in that nation, the Lord, as He

Uther having sometimes conquered, and at others suffered defeat, and Arthur's career of victory having been chequered with reverses.

[1] "Et ex eo tempore nunc cives, nunc hostes, vincebant, ut in ista "gente experiretur Dominus solito more præsentem Israelem, utrum "diligat eum an non; usque ad annum obsessionis Badonici montis, qui "prope Sabrinum Ostium habetur, novissimæque ferme de furciferis non "minimæ stragis, quique quadragesimus quartus, ut novi, oritur annus, "mense jam primo emenso, qui jam et meæ nativitatis est. Sed ne nunc "quidem, ut antea, civitates inhabitantur patriæ, sed desertæ dirutæque "hactenus squalent, cessantibus licet externis bellis, sed non tamen "civilibus. Hæsit etenim tam desperati insulæ excidii insperatique "mentio auxilii memoriæ eorum, qui utriusque miraculi testes extitere; "et ob hoc reges, publici privatique, sacerdotes, ecclesiastici, suum "ordinem servarunt. At illis decedentibus, cum successisset ætas tem-"pestatis illius nescia, et præsentis tantum serenitatis ac justitiæ experta, "ita cuncta veritatis ac justitiæ moderamina concussa ac subversa sunt, "ut eorum, non dicam vestigium, sed ne monimentum quidem, in supra-"dictis propemodum ordinibus appareat, exceptis paucis et valde paucis, "qui, ob amissionem tantæ multitudinis, quæ quotidie prona ruit ad "Tartara, tam brevis numeri habentur, ut eos quodammodo venerabilis "mater ecclesia, ut in sinu suo recumbentes non videat, quos solos veros "habet. Quorum ne quis me egregiam vitam, hominibus admirabilem, "Deoque amabilem, carpere putet, (quibus nostra infirmitas sacris "orationibus, ut non penitus collabatur, quasi columnis quibusdam ac "fulcris saluberrimis sustentatur,) dixi, si qua liberius de his, imo lugu-"brius, cumulo malorum compulsus, qui serviunt non solum ventri, sed "et diabolo potius quam Christo, qui est benedictus super omnia Deus in "sæcula, non tam disceptavero, quam deflevero. Quippe quid celabunt "cives, quæ non solum norunt, sed exprobrant jam in circuitu nationes?" C. 26.

" is wont, might try the Israel of our day whether they would " love Him or not, until the year of the siege of Bath-hill, " (which is situated near the mouth of the Severn), and of " almost the last, and not least " slaughter of the scoundrels; and " which is as I know the forty-fourth " year commencing, the first month, which is also that of my " nativity being now past. But not " yet are the cities of our country " inhabited as formerly, but still, de- " serted and destroyed, lie desolate; " external wars ceasing, " but not civil.

Not the last, for it was followed by the destruction of Childeric's band.

This was evidently written before Arthur commenced the work of restoration.

Arthur's conflict with the Saxons, A.D. 471.

His war with the Picts.

By Hencgest, A.D. 441.

" For the tradition of the devastation of the island, beyond hope of recovery; " and of the unexpected aid, " remained in the memory of those " who were witnesses of either marvel; and on this account " kings, public and private men, priests and ecclesiastics kept " their respective places; but when they departed, and a " generation succeeded that knew " not of that tribulation, and had " only experience of the tranquillity " and justice of their own days, all " the laws of truth and justice were " so shaken and subverted, that " thereof, I will not say a trace, but " not even a remembrance appears in the orders above- " named; a few, yea a very few, only excepted, who, (by " reason of the loss of so great a multitude daily descending " to the shades), are of so small a number, that our venerable " mother, the Church, scarcely beholds, as resting in her " bosom, those whom alone she has true. Whose illustrious " life, admirable before men, and lovely before God, (by whom, " by their sacred prayers, as by columns and most salutary

The arrival of Ambrosius, A.D. 443.

Here is the allusion to the peace of Uther's reign, A.D. 452 to 466, and the foregoing sentence, as will be seen by comparing it with the parallel passage in Henry of Huntingdon, indicates the mutual forbearance of the Britons and Saxons, of which Boece speaks.

"stays, our infirmity is prevented from utterly falling), let "no one, I have said, suppose that I censure, if compelled "by the accumulation of evils, I have too freely, yea mourn-"fully, not so much chidden as lamented over, those who "serve, not only the belly, but the "devil, rather than Christ who is "blessed above all, God for ever. "For why shall our people dissemble, "what the nations around not only know, but even make the "subject of reproach?"

Here is an allusion to the sensuality of the Britons of which, particularly during Arthur's days, we have much said elsewhere.

The full value of this passage seems never to have been sufficiently appreciated. The allusions it contains to the events of the history, as we have them related elsewhere, are clear; and it is evident that it was written immediately after the siege of Bath, which is called "almost the last slaughter," and in the summary the "last victory;" whilst Arthur was still engaged in civil war, for he proceeded against the Picts and Scots immediately afterwards, and before he had begun to restore the cities of Britain. But its chief value consists in its decisively fixing the date of that victory, in the beginning of the forty-fourth year of the coming of the Saxons, A.D. 471.

So this passage was understood by Bæda; but in modern times it has been taken to signify that the year of the siege was that of S. Gildas' nativity, and that this tract was written forty-four years afterwards. Yet surely the rules of grammatical construction will not allow of such a sense; for in the words,—"usque ad annum obsessionis—quique quadragesi-"mus quartus oritur annus, mense jam primo emenso, qui jam "et meæ nativitatis est,"—"annus" is clearly the antecedent of the first "qui," and "mensis" of the second.

The date, then, is certainly the forty-fourth year of the coming of the Saxons, therefore A.D. 471; and this treatise of S. Gildas, previously commenced and laid aside, was resumed and completed, as soon as the news could reach him at

Armagh, within the month, and that the month of his nativity. So the date, already determined for the accession of Arthur, receives additional confirmation; for the events which formed the subject of the last chapter occupied four years; the battles on the Glym, Douglas, and Bassas, and the siege of York belonging to the first; the capture of York, the deliverance of Caer Loit-coit, and the battle of the wood of Celidon, to the second; the battle of Guinnion to the third; the war with Hueil and the battle of Agned to the fourth year of Arthur's reign. Thus four summers are numbered by Boecé, previous to the battle of Bath; and Roger of Wendover places it in the fifth year. The forty-fourth year of the coming of the Angles being the fifth of Arthur, the fortieth is his first, and that is A. D. 467; and as Roger of Wendover and the Annals of Cambria are agreed, in dating the battle of Camlann twenty-one years after the siege of Bath, I shall take its date as A. D. 492, and that of Arthur's death as A. D. 493.

Our obligations to S. Gildas for this fixed point in our history are very great; but they would have been greater still, had it not been for the unhappy feud between Arthur and Hueil. He had written, so a British tradition preserved by Giraldus Cambrensis[2] informs us, noble books about the acts of Arthur and his race, but threw them into the sea when he heard of his brother's death; and this tradition, he says, satisfactorily explains,—what has been made the ground of an argument against the genuineness of the works ascribed to him,—his studied silence with regard to Arthur.

---

[2] "De Gildâ vero, qui adeo in gentem suam acriter invehitur, dicunt "Britones, quod propter fratrem suum, Albaniæ principem, quem rex "Arthurus occiderat, offensus, hoc scripsit; unde et libros egregios, quos "de gestis Arthuri et gentis suæ laudibus multis scripserat, auditâ fratris "sui nece, omnes, ut asserunt, in mare projecit; cujus rei causâ nihil de "tanto principe in scriptis authenticis expressum invenies." *De Illaudabilibus Walliæ*, c. 27.

It seems very probable, that Childeric, who played so conspicuous a part in this struggle, was the chieftain who followed Octa and Ebissa to Britain in A. D. 429, and who has left so many traces of his name in the districts, in which the presence of Horsa and Heucgest, at different stages of their career, is indicated by local names derived from theirs. Layamon, alone of all the editors of the Brut, furnishes particulars respecting him, which enable us, almost with certainty, to identify him with Childeric King of the Franks.

He says that he was "a powerful kaiser," and that "all "the land in Allemaine was his own," and afterwards that "he had with him all the strength of Rome," and he scarcely ever mentions him without the title "kaiser." Had he given him this title once or twice only, the circumstance would have called for no remark, for occasionally he graces Arthur with it, as well as one or two others; but when he bestows it uniformly on Childeric, I conceive he must have had some authority for thus distinguishing him, as well as for the statement that he had Roman forces under his command.

Now there was one person only, as far as we know, living at this period, to whom these circumstances could apply,— Childeric the son of Merovech. He is mentioned for the first time in history in A. D. 451, as having been taken captive by Attila, and rescued; and soon afterwards he became king of the Franks. About A. D. 459 his subjects deposed him for his vices, and placed themselves under the command of Ægidius, the general of the Roman forces in Gaul. In his exile he found refuge amongst the Thuringians, and during some part of it, (according to Fredegarius), he resided at Constantinople. He was restored in A. D. 463, and associated with Ægidius, as general of the Roman militia; and as such he would doubtless be graced with Roman titles, as Chlodovech was afterwards. His signet ring, on which his bust and the legend CHILDRICI REGIS are engraved, found in his tomb at Tournai, is a proof that he affected regal state, in a greater degree than the Barbaric chieftains of his time, and that Roman civilization was exercising its influence on Frankish customs. Before the death of Ægidius, in A.D. 464, he fought a battle at Orleans, after which nothing is recorded of him for some years. At the time of his reappearance, and in the district in which he reappears, events occurred, which are noticed by Sidonius Apollinaris, and circumstantially related by Jordanis, in which I believe he was interested.

Sidonius tells us,[3] that Arvandus, the præfect of the Gauls, was accused of sending letters to Euric, king of the Visigoths, dissuading him from peace with the Emperor, and instigating him to attack the Britons who were settled on the Loire; and one of his letters is addressed to the king of these Britons, whom he calls his friend,[4] claiming on behalf of the bearer some slaves, whom the Britons had seduced from his service. Jordanis says:[5]—

"Euric, the king of the Visigoths, observing the frequent "changes of the Roman princes, attempted to seize the Gauls "for his own. Anthemius, the Emperor, receiving intelli-"gence of this, immediately invited the aid of the Britons,

---

[3] "Legati provinciæ Galliæ—prævium Arvandum publico nomine "accusaturi cum gestis decretalibus insequuntur. Qui—interceptas "literas deferebant, quas Arvandi scriba correptus dominum dictasse "profitebatur. Hæc ad regem Gothorum charta videbatur emitti, pacem "cum Græco imperatore dissuadens, Britannos super Ligerim sitos im-"pugnari opportere demonstrans, cum Burgundionibus jure gentium "Gallias dividi debere confirmans." I. 7.

[4] "Sidonius Riothamo suo." III. 9.

[5] "Euricus ergo, Vesegotbarum rex, crebram mutationem Romanorum "principum cernens, Gallias suo jure nisus est occupare. Quod com-"periens Anthemius imperator, protinus solatia Britonum postulavit. "Quorum rex Riothimus, cum XII millibus veniens, in Biturigas civi-"tatem, Oceano e navibus egressus, susceptus est. Ad quos rex Vese-"gotharum Euricus innumerum ductans exercitum advenit, diuque "pugnans, Riothimum, Britonum regem, antequam Romani in ejus "societate conjungerentur, superavit. Qui, amplâ parte exercitus amissâ, "cum quibus potuit fugiens, ad Burgundionum gentem vicinam, Romanis "in eo tempore fœderatam, advenit. Euricus vero, rex Vesegotharum, "Arvernam Galliæ civitatem, occupavit." *De Rebus Geticis*, XV.

" whose King Riothimus, coming with twelve thousand, and
" disembarking from his ships, was received into the city
" Bourges. Euric, king of the Visigoths, came against them
" leading an innumerable army, and fighting for a long time,
" overcame Riothimus, the king of the Britons, before the
" Romans had joined company with him. Having lost a
" great part of his army, he fled with all whom he could save,
" and came to the neighbouring nation of the Burgundians,
" then confederate with the Romans. But Euric, king of the
" Visigoths, seized Auvergne, a city of Gaul."

Now, who were these Britons?

These events occurred in A. D. 469, the year after Childeric was expelled from Britain, the year that Arthur gained the victory of Guinnion castle or Caer Wen. It is in the highest degree improbable, that Anthemius would send to Britain for aid; and the passage above-cited does not necessarily mean that these Britons had come in consequence of invitation; it may equally imply that he had engaged them to assist him, when he heard of their arrival. Sidonius' expression "super "Ligerim sitos" shows that they had really made a settlement; and his letter, taken in connection with Jordanis' statement, shows further, that their settlement embraced the city of Bourges, and extended southward into his diocese of Auvergne. It is inconceivable that the subjects of Arthur, who were engaged with him in the defence of their native land, should have voluntarily emigrated to Gaul, and formed a settlement there in A. D. 469; yet it was from Britain they came, not from Armorica, for they came by sea. The conclusion is inevitable, that they were fugitives from Britain; and I think it very probable, that Riothamus was one of the four chieftains, who were defeated by Arthur in this very year, at the battle of Guinnion castle.

Immediately after the defeat of Riothamus, the Goths took Auvergne, and they appear to have extended their conquests westward, for at this very time Childeric reappears, in alliance with the Romans, opposed to the Goths, besieging and taking the city of Angers on the Loire. After this, the only recorded events of Childeric's history are, a joint expedition of the Romans and Franks to the isles of the Saxons, and an alliance with Odoacer, both of uncertain date. He died in A.D. 481.

Now the facts of our history fully bear out the theory of the identity of this Childeric with ours. Our Childeric is not once mentioned in our history, at the times to which the notices of the king of the Franks belong; nor does Gregory of Tours say anything of the king of the Franks, during the years when, (according to the Brut and Boece), Childeric was in Britain. Our Childeric conducted a large force to Britain in A.D. 429, and seems to have accompanied Horsa and Hencgest during the greater part of their career, which came to a close in A.D. 443. Childeric the Frank appears for the first time in A.D. 451, and is mentioned occasionally until A.D. 464, when the battle of Orleans was fought. Our Childeric brought a powerful armament to the aid of Colgrim in A.D. 467, and was defeated and expelled from Britain in A.D. 468. In the following year the Frank king reappears, apparently in connection with the fugitives from Britain, certainly in the same interest, in alliance with the Romans, as they were, and prosecuting the war with the Goths, in which they were engaged. After this we have Childeric again in Britain in A.D. 470 and 471.

Layamon, then, has unconsciously, (for it is clear that he had no suspicion of this identity, and for that reason his statements are the more worthy of credit), supplied us with grounds for identifying our Childeric with the king of the Franks, the ally and stipendiary of the empire, by describing him as the "powerful kaiser," the "lord of all Germany," the "leader of the forces of Rome." In favour of this identity we have the facts, that our Childeric is never noticed in our history when we know that Childeric was in Gaul; that

French history is silent with regard to Childeric, at the times when our Childeric was in Britain; and that the time of Childeric's expulsion from Britain coincides to a year, with that of Childeric's reappearance in Gaul. Against it, we have nothing but a statement in the Brut, that he was killed in Britain; a statement apparently contradicted by another in the Life of Merlin, which enables us to correct the former, by supposing, that he was so severely wounded that he was believed to be dead, but that he recovered and escaped. The conjecture, also, that Riothamus and his people were fugitives from Britain, perfectly harmonizes with this theory, and with our history; and this theory satisfactorily accounts for their presence in Gaul, in the same district as Childeric, and engaged in the same cause.

CHAPTER XV.

The Reign of Arthur continued, A.D. 471 *to* 493.

HAVING defeated Childeric, Cador hastened to join Arthur, who had raised the siege of Alclud, and driven the Picts and Scots into Moray. In that district Arthur and Hoel fought three battles with them, forced them at last to seek refuge in the islands of Loch Lomond, and there besieged them. Gillomaur came to their relief with a powerful force from Ireland, but was repulsed with great loss; and the blockade would have been continued by Arthur, even to the extermination of his adversaries, had not the entreaties of the clergy prevailed on him to show them mercy. These events must be referred to A.D. 471 and 472.

Returning now to York, to celebrate Christmas, Arthur gave order for the restoration of the churches; appointed his chaplain, Piram, Archbishop of York, in the room of Sanxo,[1] who had fled; and restored the lately conquered districts, which had belonged to their ancestors, to Loth[2] and his

---

[1] There were two Sanxos, successively Archbishops of Dol, in Bretagne, and both came from Britain. One had been Archbishop of York, carried his pall with him to Dol, and thus was the occasion of its being raised to the dignity of a metropolitan see. The other was a Welsh ecclesiastic.

[2] Geoffrey's, Gervase's, Wace's, and Layamon's editions of the Brut,

brothers Augusel and Urien; giving to the first Lothian, to the second Albania, and to the third Moray. In A.D. 473, as it seems, he went to London, held a council there, and settled the affairs of the kingdom.

Of this expedition into the North,—to which S. Gildas appears to allude, when he says, that civil war continued after the defeat of the Saxons,—Boece says nothing; but he mentions Arthur's coming to York, and his departure for London in the following year; adding, that the reason of his going thither was to repress the ravages, which the Saxons of Wight and Kent were committing in the British territories, and that he marched against them assisted by a force of twenty thousand Picts and Scots. On this occasion, he says, Modred with Gawolan, his father-in-law, quitted the main body of the army, at the head of a detachment of five thousand horse, intending to distinguish himself by some valorous exploit. The Saxons sent messengers to Arthur, when his forces were within five miles of their camp, desiring leave to depart from the country. Their request was granted, but when they further asked for three days' delay, Arthur refused it, suspecting treachery. Meanwhile Modred had attacked the Saxons, but was defeated, and driven back upon the main body. Hereupon Arthur recalled the Saxon messengers, upbraided them with this skirmish, at a time when a treaty of peace was under consideration, and refused ever to entertain proposals of the kind for the future; and when, immediately afterwards, forty chiefs of the Saxons came to offer

give the names of these three brothers with great uniformity. Augusel, Augesilin, Angesil, Aguesel, or Angel, is king of the Scots, and this appears to be a Teutonic name, Eangisl or Eangils, (which it is not improbable he might have, if his mother was a Dane); Urien is king of Mureif; and Loth is king of Lothian. In the Welsh copies great liberties are taken with these names. Augusel is changed into Arawn; Loth into Llew; the three are represented as sons of Cynfarch; and Urien is made king of Rheged, in order to identify him with the illustrious prince of Cumbria, who flourished in the latter half of the next century.

an explanation of what had occurred, saying, that it had been the act of young men, unsanctioned by their leaders, he ordered them, as well as the first messengers, to be detained. That night he attacked the Saxons, who were wholly unprepared, with such fury, that very few survived the conflict. The chiefs were now permitted to depart, and Arthur's allies returned home, after a few days' rest in London.

In this story there is a manifest inconsistency; Modred is represented as the aggressor, yet Arthur summons the Saxon messengers, and accuses their countrymen of breach of faith, and other messengers come to apologize for what had happened. I have no hesitation, therefore, in preferring Buchanan's version of the story as a correction of Boece's. He says, that Arthur marched against the Saxons of Kent, assisted by ten thousand Scots and Picts, the latter commanded by Modred; that, as they were encamped separately, within five miles of the enemy, the Saxons made a sudden attack on the Picts by night, and compelled Modred and his father-in-law, after a brave resistance, to flee to Arthur's camp; and that Arthur calmly spent the day in reorganizing the Pictish division, attacked the Saxon camp with all his forces during the following night, and made immense slaughter.

The Brut is silent with regard to this affair, and it is not noticed in the Saxon Chronicle, which only records Saxon victories. It seems very probable that Æsc-Octa and Ælle, who fled from Britain after the siege of Bath, returned very soon,—for it is said that the intelligence of their defeat, which they carried to Germany, stirred up their countrymen to make preparations for a fresh invasion; that the ravages, of which Boece speaks, committed by the Saxons of Wight and Kent, were the result of these preparations; and that this fresh army of Saxons was all but exterminated by Arthur. Thus we are enabled to account for the fact, that he undertook a foreign expedition in the following year; for he could hardly have done so, if he had not been able to leave Britain in security. This battle seems to have been fought near London.

About this time, (A. D. 473), S. Gildas returned from Ireland, as related in his Life. Arthur visited him by the advice of the clergy, entreated his forgiveness for the slaughter of his brother, and received from him the kiss of peace and his blessing. Thus the wound was healed; and had not Arthur's subsequent conduct with regard to Modred opened it again, we might yet have had, from the pen of S. Gildas, a circumstantial history of his reign.

Arthur now went into Cornwall, where he married Guanhumara, (or Guennuuar), a relative of Cador, and spent the following winter. In the summer, A. D. 474, he fitted out a fleet at Exeter, and sailed to Ireland, defeated and captured Gillomaur, and received tribute from other princes of the island. He then proceeded to Isoland, (Iselland, the country watered by the Yssel), exacted tribute from Ælc its king, and the person of his son Æscil as security for its payment. Gunfas, king of the Orkneys, Doldav, king of Gothland, and Rumareth, king of Winetland, (the coast between the Schlie and Vistula), also sent their sons to him, in obedience to his summons, promising to pay him tribute. He remained abroad during the winter, and returned to Britain in the following year, A. D. 475.

His object in this expedition was, doubtless, to punish or overawe the foreign princes, who had abetted his enemies in the late wars, and to secure his own dominions from future aggression, by exacting hostages for their peaceable behaviour. In this, however, he was a little too late. There was a fresh arrival of Saxons, in the year of this expedition, and most probably during his absence, as we shall see.

Gillomaur and Æscil appear henceforth attached to Arthur's interests, and both fell on his side in his last battle. Ælc, the father of Æscil, is named no more, (and this time by Layamon only); and it is not unlikely that he was the person who is called Aloc in the Bernician genealogy. Another name in this line, that of his grandson Æthelberht, appears amongst those of Arthur's allies, at the battle of Camlann.

The arrival of the Saxons, above referred to, is noticed as follows by Henry of Huntingdon:[3]—

"In the forty-seventh year of the coming of the Angles," (*i. e.* A.D. 474), "Cerdic and Cyneric his son came with five "ships to Cerdicesore. The same day a multitude of the "country came together, and fought against them. The "Saxons, in close array, stood immoveably by their ships. "The islanders rushed upon them boldly, and though they "retreated were not pursued, for the strangers never quitted "their position; so the battle was carried on with alternate "advances and retreats, until the darkness of night brought "the conflict to a close. The Britons therefore withdrew, "having had experience of the bravery of the Saxons, and "neither party claimed the victory; yet Cerdic and his son, "having obtained a footing in a hostile land, began further "and further to occupy the districts along the coast, but not "without frequent battles."

They landed, (according to John of Wallingford), at the mouth of a river which bore Cerdic's name; therefore, probably, at Charmouth in Dorsetshire. Chardstock, about eight miles to the north of Charmouth, Chard in Somersetshire, about four miles further, and Charborough in Dorsetshire, considerably to the east of these, indicate the presence of

---

[3] "Anno XLVII adventus Anglorum, Certic et Cinric filius suus, cum V "puppibus venerunt ad Certicesore. Eodem die convenit multitudo re- "gionis, et pugnatum est contra eos. Saxones, acie consertâ, coram "navibus immobiliter stabant. Insulani audacter in eos irruebant, et "sine persecutione revertebantur, advenis quippe nunquam locum dese- "rentibus; sic irruendo et redeundo bellatum est, donec noctis tenebræ "litem dirimerunt. Inventis igitur Saxonibus asperis, Britanni se re- "traxerunt, et neutrâ ex parte habita est victoria. Hospitati tamen "Certic et filius suus in terrâ hostili, magis magisque circa littora maris "cœperunt occupare, non sine frequentibus bellis, regiones."

Cerdic in this district. The frequent battles were with Arthur, as we shall see, but we have no particular account of them. Æthelweard alone tells us of an attempt on the part of Cerdic to extend his territory:[4]—

"In the sixth year of their coming, they compassed the "western part of Britain which is called West-Sexe."

In the following year, A. D. 480, Henry of Huntingdon speaks of another arrival:[5]—

"In the seventh year after the coming of Cerdic, Port and "his two sons, Beda and Megla, with two very great ships, "came to Portsmouth, and immediately a great cry to arms "filled all the province. So the governor of the province, "and all the people, engaging in conflict without order, and "as each came, perished in the twinkling of an eye; for "boldness impelled the Britons against the enemy, but the "valour of the enemy turned their imprudence into confusion. "So the leader and his people being slain or put to flight, "Port, from whom Portsmouth is named, and his sons gained "the victory."

In the Saxon Chronicle we are told, that the Saxons slew a young British chief of high nobility.

In Hampshire, Dorsetshire, and Somersetshire, we find many traces of Port and his sons. In the first, besides Portsmouth, we have Portsea, Portchester, Portsdown, and Bedhampton, in its immediate neighbourhood, and at some distance to the north-west, Portesbricg,[6] Porteswudu,[6] and Portstræt;[6]

---

[4] "Sexto etiam anno adventus eorum, occidentalem circumierunt Bri-"tanniæ partem, quæ nunc Uuest-Sexe nuncupatur."

[5] "Septimo autem anno post adventum Certici, venit Port et duo filii "ejus Beda et Megla, cum duabus navibus maximis, apud Portesmud-"ham, statimque clamor maximus implevit omnem provinciam. Dux "igitur provinciæ et omnis multitudo pugnam aggressi, absque ordine ut "quisque adveniebat, in ictu oculi deperiere; audacia namque agebat "Brittones in hostem, fortitudo vero hostis agebat imprudentiam eorum "in confusionem. Duce igitur et populo perempto vel fugato, victoriâ "potiti sunt Port, de quo dicta est Portesmudam, et duo filii ejus."

[6] Near Stoneham. Cod. Diplom. 776 and 1230.

in the second, Portland and Melcombe together on the coast, Portisham about six miles to the north-west, a fortress called Badbury near Wimborne, Bedhurst and three Melburys near the borders of Somersetshire, and another Melbury near the borders of Wiltshire; in the third, Portbury, Portishead, Portlock and Mells, Portanbeorg[7] and Bædwyl.[7]

In the Life of S. Gildas we have a story, which remarkably illustrates and confirms the indications which these names afford, of the residence of this family in Somersetshire. After his reconciliation with Arthur, he made a pilgrimage to Rome, which must have occupied about a year; on his return, he spent another year with S. Cadoc at Llancarvan, and then lived in solitude on an island in the Severn for seven years. Thus about ten years, added to the date of his reconciliation with Arthur, will bring us to A. D. 483, when, because an invasion of pirates from the Orkneys rendered his position untenable,[8]—

" He left the island, and came to Glastonbury, king Meluas " then reigning in Somersetshire. Glastonbury was beset by " the tyrant Arthur with an innumerable multitude, on ac- " count of his wife Guennuuar, who had been violated and " carried off by the aforesaid wicked king, and led thither " for safety's sake, for the refuge which the place, impreg- " nable by reason of the inundations of the thicket, and the

---

[7] Near Ham. Cod. Diplom. 1220.

[8] " Reliquit insulam, ascendit naviculam et ingressus est Glastoniam " cum magno dolore, Meluas rege regnante in æstivâ regione.—Obsessa " est itaque ab Arturo tyranno cum innumerabili multitudine, propter " Guennuuar uxorem suam violatam et raptam a prædicto iniquo rege, " et ibi ductam propter refugium inviolati loci, propter inundationes " arundineti, ac fluminis, et paludis, causâ tutelæ. Quæsiverat rex re- " bellis reginam per unius anni circulum, audivit tandem illam rema- " nentem. Illico commovit exercitus totius Cornubiæ et Dibueniæ; " paratum est bellum inter inimicos. Hoc viso, abbas Glastoniæ, comi- " tante clero et Gildâ sapiente, intravit medios acies, consuluit Meluas " regi suo pacifice, ut redderet raptam; reddita ergo fuit, quæ reddenda " fuerat, per pacem et benevolentiam. Inde redierunt reges pacificati."

" river, and the swamp, afforded. The king in arms had " sought her for the space of a year; at length he heard that " she was abiding there. Thither he assembled the armies " of all Cornwall and Devon; war between the enemies was " impending. Seeing this, the Abbot of Glastonbury, ac- " companied by his clergy and Gildas the Wise, went be- " tween the armies, and advised his king Meluas peacefully " to restore the woman he had carried off; she, therefore, " who ought to have been restored, was restored, through " peace and goodwill. The kings returned thence pacified."

The chieftain, who was associated with Guanis, at the end of the last and the beginning of this century, is called Melga by Geoffrey, and Melwas in the Welsh Brut; and here I believe that Melwas is the individual who is called Mægla in the Saxon Chronicle, the son of Port. After this, S. Gildas resided some years at Glastonbury, and then retired to a hermitage in the neighbourhood, in which he continued until the year of his death, A.D. 512.

An interval of twelve years is placed between the first and second foreign expeditions of Arthur, in the Brut; during which he is said to have devoted himself to the improvement of his people, and to the maintainance of peace.[9] These

---

[9] The story of the Round Table is adduced by Layamon as an evidence of Arthur's care for the preservation of peace, and I cannot believe that the traditions relative to it had not some foundation in fact, so constantly is it associated with his memory.

The story, as Layamon tells it, has in itself little of improbability. After Arthur's return from his first foreign expedition, at his Christmas feast in London, a quarrel arose, between the princes of different nations who were there assembled, which ended in bloodshed. Arthur severely punished the authors of the strife, threatened with death any who should renew it, and made all swear to observe peace. Then a clever workman proposed to make for him a round table, at which all might sit on an equality, without any question of precedence. " This," he adds, " is the " board about which Britons tell so many lies; for all is not true, nor " all falsehood, that minstrels sing about Arthur; for Britons loved him " much, and say many things about him, that never were transacted in " this world; but whoever will say the truth about him, may find enough years, however, were continually disturbed by the aggressions of Cerdic. Leland, quoting from the Chronicle "cujusdam Divionensis," says:[10]—

"Cerdic, often contending with Arthur, if he were van-
"quished one month, the next month more boldly rose again
"to battle. Arthur, wearied out at length, after the twelfth
"year of Cerdic's arrival, fealty to himself having been sworn,
"gave him the territory on the southern Avon, and Somer-
"setshire, which Cerdic called Wessex."

Cerdic doubtless had received large reinforcements, besides those which Port conducted to Britain, to enable him to maintain the contest with Arthur, and to occupy the territories which were at length ceded to him by treaty, that is, Hampshire and Somersetshire, and of course the intervening districts of Wiltshire and Dorsetshire; and this treaty must have been forced upon Arthur, not by the tediousness of the war, as the author just cited asserts, but by the necessity which called him from Britain to interfere in the affairs of Norway. For it was made after the twelfth year of Cerdic's residence in Britain, therefore in A.D. 486 or 487; and the twelve years' interval between Arthur's return from his first foreign expedition, and his departure on his second, terminates in A.D. 487. Thus, as the expulsion of the Saxons left Arthur at liberty to undertake the first, so a treaty with Cerdic was necessary as a preliminary to the second.

Sichelin, (evidently Sigehelm), the king of Norway,[11] on

"in writings, of his acts from beginning to end." I quote this passage in evidence of Layamon's sincerity, and his confidence in the authorities he used for the compilation of his work.

[10] "Cerdicius cum Arturio confligens sæpius, si uno mense vinceretur,
"in alio mense acrior surrexit ad pugnam. Tandem Arturius, tædio
"fatigatus, post duodecimum annum adventus Cerdicii, fidelitate sibi
"juratâ, dedit ei Avoniam meridianam et Somariam, quam partem vocavit
"Cerdicius Visi-Saxoniam."

[11] By Norway, in the following story, as in others which have been already discussed, I understand Holland.

his death, had named Loth, his sister's son, successor to his throne.

This statement vindicates the conjecture, already advanced, that Loth was the son of Gryme; for Gryme, (according to Boece), had married a virgin of the blood-royal of Denmark, during his exile; and thus we find Fordun, Boece, and the Brut, mutually, and quite incidentally, confirming each the others. Fordun tells us, that Gryme claimed the territory north of the Humber, as a descendant of Fulgentius; and afterwards, that Loth, a Scot, prince of Lothian, was of the same race. From Boece we learn, that Grahame, during his exile, married a princess of Denmark. From the facts of the history, that Loth of the same race as Gryme, (Grahame, or Guanis), appears as his successor struggling for the same rights,—for these districts were the object of contention, throughout the wars of the Picts and Britons, and whenever peace was made between them, the cession of these districts was one of the articles,—we have concluded that he was his son; and now the Brut confirms all this, by telling us, that Loth's mother's brother was Sigehelm, a king of Norway.

Tidings reached Arthur, that the Norwegians had resolved on rejecting Loth, and had chosen in his place Riculf, one of their own countrymen; so he prepared a fleet at once to assist Loth in obtaining the kingdom. As soon as he arrived on the coast of Norway, Riculf met him with the whole force of the country, but was defeated and slain. Arthur passed through the country, reducing it to subjection, and then gave it to Loth, to be held as a fief of his own crown. He then entered Denmark, and received the homage of its king Æscil,[12]—apparently the person who had been delivered to him as a hostage by his father Ælc, thirteen years before.

I cannot but regard these foreign expeditions of Arthur

---

[12] We are indebted to Layamon for this, as well as the former notice of Æscil.

as indubitable facts; and of this, in particular, the story is confirmed, by three other narratives, wholly independent, yet perfectly consistent with it.

I. Gaimar mentions, as reigning in Denmark, some twenty years later than these events, (since Havelok had grown up in the interval, from unconscious infancy to manhood, and married), Odulf, whom he calls the brother of this Æscil, and whom he represents as having betrayed Gunter, then king, when Arthur invaded his territory.

II. The Lay of Havelok says, that Hodulf slew Gunter by treachery, and then received Denmark as a fief. Æscil and Odulf may have reigned in different districts, and the latter in that which had belonged to Gunter.

III. Johannes Magnus,[13] in the sixteenth century, tells us, that Tordo, king of the Swedes, (possibly Doldav, king of Gothland, who is named in the Brut), defeated Harold, a prince of Denmark; that the latter fled for refuge to Arthur; and that Arthur, with a fleet collected from Britain, Gaul, and Holland, gained a victory over the Swedes by sea, and then conquered Denmark.

Thus we have three distinct notices of this expedition, and the particulars they furnish may well have been successive events of the same campaign; Arthur's victory over Riculf, and conquest of Norway; his war in Harold's behalf, and victory over the Swedes; his receiving the homage of Æscil, and his war with Gunter; and the appointment of Æscil's brother, Odulf, in Gunter's stead. Gaimar's notice of Æscil is a connecting link, between his narrative, and those in the Lay of Havelok and the Brut.

Roger of Wendover says, that Arthur returned to Britain after this campaign, a circumstance unnoticed in the Brut.

In A.D. 487, and probably during his absence, the treaty

[13] I am only acquainted with this notice through the Rev. Beale Poste's "Britannia Antiqua."

he had made with Cerdic was broken by a British prince, named Natanleod. Henry of Huntingdon, as usual, gives a circumstantial account of this affair, which has very much the character of a quotation, and from the beginning of a chapter or book, of his original authority :[14]—

"I am going to write of the war which Nazaleod, a very "great king of the Britons, waged with Cerdic and Cyneric "his son in the sixtieth year of the coming of the Angles, "(*i. e.* A. D. 487). Now Nazaleod was a man of great name, "and of great pride, after whom that district was called "Nazaleoi, which is now called Cerdicesford. All the forces "of Britain being gathered together, Cerdic and his son had "asked aid of Esc the king of the Kentishmen, and of Ælle "the great king of the South-Saxons, and of Port and his "sons who had lately arrived; and they arrayed their forces "in two divisions; Cerdic commanded one, and Cyneric his "son the other; Cerdic led the right wing, Cyneric the left. "When the battle began, king Nazaleod, seeing that their

---

[14] "Bellum scripturus sum quod Nazaleod, rex maximus Brittanno-"rum, egit contra Certic et Cinric filium ejus, sexagesimo anno adventus "Anglorum. Nazaleod vero magni nominis erat, et magnæ superbiæ, "a quo regio illa dicta est Nazaleoi, quæ modo dicitur Certichesforde. "Congregatâ igitur omni multitudine Brittanniæ, auxilium petierat in "supremis negotiis Certic et filius ejus ab Esc rege Cantuariorum, et ab "Ælla magno rege Sudsexorum, et a Port et filiis ejus qui nuper ve-"nerant; et duas acies bello statuerunt; unam regebat Certic, aliam "vero Cinric filius ejus. Certic regebat cornu dextrum, Cinric vero "sinistrum. Inito ergo prælio, rex Nazaleod dextrum cornu videns "præstantius, irruit ipse et omnes vires ejus, ut illud quod fortissimum "erat prius prosterneretur; prostratis ergo vexillis et acie perforatâ, "Certic in fugam versus est, et facta est strages maxima aciei ejus in "momento. Videns autem sinistrum cornu, ductum a filio, quod dex-"trum cornu patris sui destructum esset, irruit in terga persequentium, "et aggravata est pugna vehementer, et cecidit rex Nazaleod, et versi "sunt sui in fugam, et interfecti sunt ex eis quinque millia; cæteris "vero celeritas fuit subsidium. Saxones igitur prærogativâ victoriæ "potiti sunt, et quies data est eis annis non multis; adveneruntque eis "adjutores fortes et multi."

Compare this passage with 1 Macc. IX. 14.

"right wing was the stronger, attacked it with all his forces, "in order that that which was the strongest might be first "overcome. So, his standards being overthrown, and his "line pierced, Cerdic was put to flight, and there was im-"mediately a very great slaughter of his division. But the "left wing, commanded by the son, seeing that the right "wing of his father was destroyed, rushed upon the rear of "the pursuers, and the battle became very furious, and king "Nazaleod fell, and his people were put to flight, and five "thousand of them were slain, but swiftness proved the "safety of the rest. The Saxons therefore obtained the pre-"rogative of victory, and rest was given to them for a few "years, and auxiliaries came to them, brave and many."

Natanleod probably claimed the sovereignty of Hampshire, which had been lately ceded to Cerdic, and availed himself of Arthur's absence to assert his claim; and as he was the aggressor, and the Saxons merely defended their ceded rights, no notice was taken of this quarrel by Arthur; but the Saxons were allowed to retain their possessions undisturbed, and the treaty was faithfully kept on either side, until the last year of Arthur's reign. I believe all the notices of Natanleod relate to one and the same person, the commander of Uther's forces in A. D. 452 and 466. The Saxon Chronicle says that all the country was named after him Natanleaga, as far as Cerdicesford, and this name is still retained by two villages in Hampshire, Netley and Nateley Scures. Cerdicesford is Charford on the Avon in Hampshire.

Before we enter upon the history of Arthur's two campaigns in Gaul, we may remark, that the circumstances of each, as well as of the interval between them, are related with greater minuteness, than those of any other event of his reign. The theory that the author was an Armorican Briton, who might have become acquainted personally with Arthur in his youth, at the time of the first of these campaigns, and have actually been present at the scenes he describes, fully explains this fact, and confirms the story in general. Boece reprobates the whole on chronological grounds, as well he might; for if Arthur had reigned in the sixth century, it is simply impossible that these events could have occurred; whereas the story is consistent, not only with the true chronology, but with the history of the Roman Empire, and of its Gallic provinces in particular; and it is singularly in harmony, as we shall see, with the history of the Burgundians.

In the Life of Merlin, which speaks of a treaty of alliance, offensive and defensive, between Arthur and Hoel,[15] the motive of Arthur's first Gallic expedition is suggested. It must have been undertaken on Hoel's behalf, for hitherto Hoel has only appeared in Britain, assisting Arthur in the establishment of his kingdom; and now Arthur goes to Gaul to assist Hoel in the extension of his territorial dominion. The date is A. D. 490, and this is remarkable. A year earlier, no such invasion of Gaul could have taken place, for Odoacer was ready at any time to cross the Alps, and repress the turbulence of the enemies of the Empire; but now he was fully occupied at home. In A. D. 489 Theodoric invaded Italy, defeated him August 28th and September 30th, and again, (after some months' reverse of fortune), with the aid of the Visigoths, August 11th, A. D. 490; he then pursued him to Ravenna, and besieged him for three years. Thus Arthur and Hoel appear to have availed themselves of the opportunity, which this war afforded them, of invading the Roman province of Gaul.

In A. D. 490, then, at the head of the united forces of his own, and the tributary kingdoms, Arthur passed over to Gaul, and occupied Boulogne. Frollo, a tribune, who then governed Gaul,[16] hearing of his coming, collected all the

15 "Sanguis enim communis eos sociabat, amorque
"Alter ut alterius deberet dampna levare."

16 "Gallorum populos, cæso Frollone subegit

forces that were at his disposal, and advanced to give him battle, but was defeated and compelled to retreat to Paris. Arthur pursued him and laid siege to the city, and when the siege had lasted for a month, it was arranged that he and Frollo should decide the quarrel by single combat, on an island in the Seine. Frollo fell in the combat, and Paris surrendered to Arthur. Hoel and Arthur now separated; Hoel extended his own dominions by the conquest of Anjou, Touraine, and Berri, received the submission of Guitard the Lord of Poitou, carried his arms into Auvergne, and even as far south as Gascogne; whilst Arthur conquered Lorraine and Burgundy; Hoel, (it may be remarked), including in his conquests the districts in which Riothamus and his people had settled more than twenty years before, and Arthur the nation which had abetted their cause. Returning to Paris, Arthur held his court there at Easter, and committed the government of the conquered provinces to the most faithful of his followers. This was in A. D. 491, for Gervase of Tilbury says that Arthur was in Gaul nine months;[17] *i. e.* from July or August, A. D. 490, to April or May of this year.

Gaul was still nominally a Roman province; the Goths possessed the south-eastern provinces; the kingdom of Chlodovech was confined to Arras and Tournai and the Isle of the Batavians; and it was not until A. D. 508 that he was enabled to establish his throne at Paris. Five years before the date of this expedition, Syagrius, the son of Ægidius,—who was probably allowed by Odoacer to reign with the title, by which Gregory of Tours designates him, of King of the Romans,—was defeated at Soissons by Chlodovech, fled to

---

"Cui curam patriæ dederat Romana potestas."
Vita Merlini, l. 1100, 1101.

Layamon calls him "King of the French, born in Rome, of Roman "kindred."

[17] Thus Gervase, writing months for years, happily corrects the error in the Brut.

Alaric, the King of the Goths, at Toulouse, was betrayed into the hands of his enemy, and put to death. This is the only notice we have for some years, of Chlodovech's presence in Gaul, and on this occasion it was in the district immediately bordering on his own territory.

Frollo may have been a successor of Syagrius, a tribune sent from Rome to watch over the Roman interests in Gaul, as Gervase says, and perhaps graced with the same title, King of the Romans. Fortunately Jordanis has preserved the memory of a person of this name, as connected with the history of the Empire at this time; saying, that when the Huns were defeated by the Gepidæ, A. D. 453, and compelled to retreat to the shores of the Euxine, some of their nation accepted a settlement in Illyricum, and that of this race were Blivilas, Duke of Pentapolis, and his kinsman Froilas, and the patrician Bessa, cotemporary with himself.[18] Now Bessa played an important part in the Gothic war; and we may fairly infer that Blivilas and Froilas, who flourished at an earlier time, were singled out by Jordanis for honourable mention, because their names were also well known, as connected with Roman affairs. Odoacer was himself connected with the Huns; his father Edecon having been the confidential minister of Attila; and it is not unlikely that he appointed this Hunnish noble, Froilas, after the death of Syagrius, to the charge of the province of Gaul.

The Brut says that his master was the Roman general Leo; and the Life of Merlin speaks of an Emperor Leo as the colleague of Lucius in the campaign of the following year. Both the Leos died in A. D. 474, so that the mention of this name involves an anachronism, but one for which it is easy to account. There were chronicles, (on the model of which

---

[18] "Ex quo genere fuit Blivilas, Dux Pentapolitanus, ejusque germanus Froilas, et nostri temporis Bessa Patricius." *De Rebus Geticis*, XVII.

Capgrave formed his), in which, under the reign of Leo, his cotemporaries were noticed, the Popes Hilarius and Simplicius, and Arthur King of Britain; and with such a chronicle before him, Geoffrey inserted the name of Leo as the Emperor, when he had occasion to speak of Arthur's invasion of a Roman province. So also, earlier in the history, he had supplied the name of Supplicius (Simplicius) as that of the Pope, to whose care Walgan was entrusted, for the sake of learning Romau manners. We have fair grounds for regarding both these names as interpolations; for neither Gervase, Wace, nor Layamon mention Leo; Walter omits the name of the Pope, and Roger of Wendover gives instead, that of a later Pope, Vigilius.

Arthur now returned to Britain, and determined to celebrate his triumph, on the approaching feast of Pentecost, by a solemn festival at Caerleon, to be graced by the presence of all the kings and princes, his allies and vassals. Great preparations were made for this festival, which seems to have been one of extraordinary magnificence; and I fully concur with Mr. Roberts' remark, that several minute circumstances in the narrative, which would not have occurred to an inventor, indicate that the original author of it was an eyewitness of what he describes. This S. Albinus may very well have been.

To the list of princes and nobles present at this festival, given in Walter's version, other Welsh versions, and Geoffrey, add about a dozen other names, derived probably from some other source. All the versions agree[19] in recording the pre-

[19] With some variation in the names as nsual. Generally, I have greater confidence in the forms of the names which Geoffrey gives, because, whenever we have an opportunity of comparison, they agree better with those given by other authorities, as in the instance of Loth. I suspect that Walter's familiarity with Bardic traditions, led him to alter some of the names, in order to identify their owners with the heroes of those traditions. A palpable instance of this disposition occurs in the Book of Basingwerk, where Warin of Chartres, whom Walter calls Geraint of Caerwys, is transformed into Geraint ap Erbyn.

sence of Gillomaur, Doldav, Gunfas, Æscil, Loth, Augusel, and Urien, already noticed in the history, and of Cadwallo king of Gwynedd, Sater king of Dwyfed, and Maluas king of Isoland; and all agree in saying, that S. Dubricius presided at the religious functions of this festival, in his character of metropolitan.

This is, of course, inconsistent with the usual chronology, (according to which this feast should be dated A. D. 540, when S. Dubricius was dead, and S. David had been Archbishop of Menevia for many years), but quite consistent with ours. Geoffrey and Walter, (in his Welsh version of the Brut), say that S. Dubricius resigned his see, and that S. David was elected in his stead, on the occasion of this festival; and the latter adds, as the motive for S. Dubricius' resignation, that "considering how long a preparation had been made for a "festival of three days only, and struck with the perishable "nature of worldly enjoyments, he resolved to prepare for the "æternal joys of heaven." This may either have been Walter's own conjecture, (and a probable one, it must be confessed), or he may have derived it from some other source. In the Life of S. Dubricius it is said, that he resigned his see on account of old age and infirmity, (he had been a bishop for about forty-eight years in A. D. 491), withdrew to the Isle of Bardsey, and there continued until the time of his death; whilst in that of S. David we are informed, that S. Dubricius and S. Daniel were deputed to summon him to the synod, at which he was elected Archbishop. The time of the synod is not clearly marked, and there is no reason why it may not have been as early as the date of which we are speaking; but it is unnecessary to discuss this question, since all that concerns our present purpose is this, that both Geoffrey and Walter agree in representing S. Dubricius as presiding at this festival; and he was actually Archbishop of Caerleon in A. D. 491, the date our chronology requires, but he was dead, and the see had been transferred to Menevia, long before

A. D. 540, the date to which the usual chronology would refer this event.

In the midst of these festivities, an embassy is said to have arrived from Lucius, a Roman general or consul, demanding tribute and satisfaction on account of the invasion of Gaul, and requiring, on the part of the Roman senate, Arthur's appearance at Rome. Arthur, having held a council to deliberate on this message, returned an answer of defiance, announcing his intention to appear at Rome, not to pay tribute, but to exact it. Preparations for a renewal of the war were immediately commenced, and the first day of August following was fixed for a general rendezvous of his allies at Barbefleur. By the advice of the senate, Lucius summoned the kings of the east to assist him, as soon as he received Arthur's defiance.

Arthur appears to have repaired to Barbefleur before the appointed day, and to have waited there for his allies. When they were all assembled, he marched direct to the river Aube, on the banks of which Lucius was encamped; and as soon as he reached it, sent him an insolent message, commanding him to evacuate Gaul. This provoked a series of skirmishes, and eventually a general engagement, in which the Britons were victorious, and took many prisoners, who were sent to Paris, under the charge of Cador, Borel, and Richer. Lucius retreated to Langres, and Arthur hastened forward to the valley of Secy on the Saone, through which he was informed that Lucius intended to pass, in order to intercept him. Equally apprised of Arthur's movements, and determined to try the fortune of a battle once more, Lucius marched to meet him. A battle was fought with alternate success, and great slaughter on either side, until a charge of Arthur's cavalry decided the victory in his favour, and in this final charge Lucius fell by an unknown hand.[20] Arthur gave

[20] In the midst of his account of the battle of Secy, Walter inserts the

orders for the burial of the Britons in the neighbouring monasteries; sent the bodies of his Gallic confederates to their respective principalities, and those of Lucius and the Romans to their friends.

This story, hitherto regarded as one of the most improbable in the Brut, must now be discussed in detail, and confronted with Roman history. When we consider how miserably the History of the Britons has been corrupted, in the several editions through which it has passed, we cannot expect otherwise, than that the Brut should have suffered through the blunders of scribes, and the occasional introduction of marginal notes, and even of extraneous matter into the text, in the course of six centuries. Such an interpolation, I believe, is the story of an adventure with a giant, with which Arthur is said to have occupied his leisure, whilst waiting for his allies at Barbefleur; and I think the reference to another giant-story, (not in the Brut), with which it concludes, marks it as such. But I am convinced that the story of this Gallic campaign is a part of the original Brut, and is substantially true; and so far from being improbable, its most improbable circumstance, Arthur's projected invasion of Italy, proves to be that which is most strikingly consistent with the history of the time. The concluding incident of the battle of Secy imparts a character of truthfulness to the whole; for a romancer

---

remark, "the full description of it was a laborious work," an intimation that he was abridging the story. On the other hand, Geoffrey admits in the beginning of his eleventh book that he was indebted not only to the British book, but to his friend Walter's knowledge of old histories. One, therefore, curtailed, the other amplified; and part of the matter, which Geoffrey's version has in excess of Walter's, may have been derived from the original Brut, though we cannot say how much. In the Life of Merlin this campaign is briefly noticed, as follows:—

> " Romanos etiam, bello sua regna petentes,
> " Obpugnans vicit, procuratore perempto
> " Hybero Lucio, qui tunc collegaque Legnis
> " Induperatoris fuerat, jussuque Senatus
> " Venerat ut fines Gallorum demeret illi." L. 1102-1106.

would have represented Lucius as having fallen by the hand of Arthur, or at least of some favourite hero; yet after a conflict with Walgan, the decision of which a charge of the Roman cavalry prevented, we are told that a Briton, whose name is unknown, slew him with a spear in the final charge; and this statement appears to me to convey this much, that a body was found upon the battle-field, which was believed to be that of Lucius; for if his fall had been witnessed, his slayer's name would have been ascertained, and the deed rewarded; or the slayer would have claimed the credit of his exploit for the sake of honour and reward.

A speech is attributed to Cador, as he and Arthur were going to the council-chamber to deliberate on Lucius' message, in which he alludes to five years' rest from war. Evidently this does not refer to those who had accompanied Arthur to Gaul, for they had not rested more than a month in Britain, after their return, when this message arrived. But Cador was not of their number, and as he appears as second to Arthur, throughout the history, I have no doubt he was left as regent in Britain when Arthur went abroad in A.D. 487 and 490. He speaks, then, of himself, and of those who had remained with him; and this speech, which is recorded as if it had been overheard by the narrator, affords an incidental confirmation of the truth of the story, for exactly five years of peace had intervened in Britain, between A.D. 486, when the treaty was concluded with Cerdic, and this year, A.D. 491.

Arthur must have invaded Gaul about the end of July or the beginning of August A.D. 490, and yet it was not until the week of Pentecost, *i. e.* the first week in June, that he received this message at Caerleon. Ten months, then, appear to have elapsed before the Roman Empire resented an invasion of one of its provinces. Of course, Arthur had nothing to fear from Italy, for we have already remarked, that he availed himself of the opportunity which Theodoric's invasion of Italy afforded him; the last battle between Theodoric and

Odoacer must have been fought about the time that he encountered Frollo; the siege of Ravenna commenced soon after; and during the first months of the siege, at least, Theodoric must have been fully occupied. Neither had he anything to apprehend on the part of the Empire of the East, for Zeno, who had sent Theodoric into Italy, in order to rid himself of one whom his own folly had made a dangerous enemy, was neither able nor disposed to vindicate the honour of the Empire. He died April 9; Anastasius, who was crowned April 14, was a man of a very different character, prompt and vigorous in the discharge of his duties; and this story really acquires no slight degree of confirmation from the fact, that this embassy to Arthur must have been the result of measures concerted between Rome and Constantinople, within a month of Anastasius' accession.

The history of this precise period is so imperfect, that the silence of historians with regard to Lucius could in no wise impair the credibility of a story, which so many other circumstances tend to confirm; but Gervase calls him consul, and although this word is loosely applied in the Brut, I think it is not improbable, that he was no other than Olybrius, the consul for this year in the East;[21] for it is not difficult to divine the process by which his name has been transformed into the "Lucius" of the Welsh version, the "Lucius Tiberius" of Geoffrey, and the "Hyberus Lucius" of the Life of Merlin. It is well known that the name of the celebrated Christian King Lucius is translated "Lever maur;[22] and

---

[21] Baronius confounds this Olybrius with another of the name, to whom three of S. Ennodius' letters are addressed, but Pagi corrects this error. There was another, Fl. Anicius Olybrius, consul in A.D. 526.

[22] "Lucius, agnomine Lever maur, id est 'magni splendoris,' propter "fidem quæ in ejus tempore venit." *Hist. Brit.* (MS. C. C. Camb. F. f. i. 27).

Those who have attempted to throw discredit on the story of Lucius, are not aware, that Bæda's notice of him is merely a transcript, doubtless made for him by his friend Nothhelm, from an ancient Papal Register.

here I believe that Geoffrey has Latinized "Lybr" or "Lyvr" which represented Olybrius in his Armorican MS. into "Lucius," and added "Tiberius" as an alternative, (as it were suspecting an error),—"Lucius vel Tiberius;" that the "vel" has been dropped or its corresponding sign been mistaken for a hyphen, leaving "Lucius Tiberius" as we now have it; and that Walter adopted "Lucius" only.

That Lucius should have summoned to his assistance the Kings of the East, *i. e.* the governors of the provinces of the Eastern Empire, and some Barbaric chieftains, allies of the Empire, is quite consistent with probability; for no forces at all adequate to such an emergency as this could have been spared from Italy at this time; and when, in the following year, Gundebald invaded the Transalpine provinces, he was enabled to do so with impunity; neither can we have any difficulty in believing, that Lucius' muster-roll was something like what is described, when we consider the material of which the Imperial armies were composed at this period. Yet we must remark, that the list of the commanders is Geoffrey's, and (like that of Arthur's guests at Caerleon) has been augmented from some foreign source. Six names of Romans occur in Walter's account of this campaign; Caius, nephew of the general, and Marcellus, both slain in the first skirmish; Petreius, taken prisoner, in the second; Vulteius, slain in the battle on the Aube; Milvius, slain at Secy; and Quintus. Five Barbaric chieftains also are named; Evander, King of Syria, slain in the battle on the Aube, Alifantinam or Alifatima, King of Spain, Bocchus or Bacchus, King of Media, Sertorius, King of Libya, and Polyctetes or Polycletes, King of Bithynia, all slain at Secy. These are not impossible names, though we may not be able to identify them all.

This Register is two centuries older than Bæda's time, for the last Pope, whose acts it records, is Felix IV, A.D. 526 to 529; and under the name of Eleutherus, A.D. 170 to 185, it gives the following notice:—"Hic "accepit epistolam a Lucio Britanniæ rege, ut Christianus efficeretur per "ejus mandatum."

Petreius may have been the person to whom Sidonius Apollinaris wrote a letter[23] on the death of his uncle Claudian, A.D. 474; for as Claudian was a priest at Vienne, and his brother, S. Mammertus, Archbishop of Vienne, it seems that this family resided in Eastern Gaul. Procopius, in his history of the Vandalic war, mentions Salomon the brother, and Cyrus, Sergius, and Salomon, the sons of Bacchus, as having been associated with Belisarius against Gelamir, and the place of their origin was Dara, a city on the confines of Media. Bacchus himself was probably dead, since his brother and his sons are mentioned without him, and he may have been a leader of Median auxiliaries, thirty-nine years previously at the battles on the Aube and at Secy; or our Bacchus may have been another of the same family, since the occurrence of the names Sergius and Bacchus in connection, seems to indicate a devotion on the part of this family to the celebrated martyrs of Rasaphe in Syria, and a probability that these were favourite names with them. At any rate, it is important to discover a Median Bacchus at this time. Even Alifantinam, or Alifatima, which Mr. Roberts has stigmatized as an interpolation of a later date than the eighth century, may have been the name of an Arab chief; it is not unlike that of Alamundar, who is noticed in the history of the early part of the sixth century; and Spain may have been misread for "Scenitæ," the designation of the Arab tribes, in the chronicles of the time.

We are not bound to account for the other names in Geoffrey's list, because we have no means of judging of the character of the authority from which he derived them; but with regard to Mustensar, King of Africa, *i. e.* of the Vandals, it may be remarked, that this name is written Aius Gensar in the Book of Basingwerk, and this is not unlike the Vandalic names Genseric and Genso; and, (although we cannot

---

[23] Book IV. 11.

account for his being called King of the Parthians or of Persia), Hirtacus seems to represent Herduic one of Theodoric's most illustrious chieftains. Some of Geoffrey's names, —Epistrophus for instance, and Pandrasus,—are very suspicious.

Amongst the names of Arthur's captains, there is one of peculiar interest, Richer. There was a prince of the Franks of this name, who not long afterwards was murdered by Chlodovech, with his father Ragnachar, the seat of whose kingdom was Cambrai. In his route from Boulogne to Paris, in the preceding year, and from Barbefleur to the Aube in this, Arthur must have passed the settlements of the Franks, and we naturally look for the presence of their chieftains amongst his allies. Richer appears to have been one of the twelve consuls of Gaul, whom Warin of Chartres brought to Arthur's standard, and possibly the others also, and Leodegar of Boulogne, were Franks. Boso of Oxford was probably a Saxon, and as his name is not mentioned after the battle of Secy, Mount Bozon, about twenty miles south-east of Secy, may have been named after him, and mark his burial-place.

Arthur began to make his preparations for this war in the beginning of June, and as some time must be allowed for the return of the ambassadors, it is obvious that Lucius' arrangements to meet him in August, must have been made very hastily. Arthur had the advantage in this respect, as well as in having his allies present with him at Caerleon, and accordingly his forces are represented as far outnumbering those of Lucius; one hundred and eighty thousand, in about equal proportions from Britain, Scandinavia, and Gaul, opposed to forty thousand[24] from the provinces of the East.

Arthur is said to have remained in the district in which he

---

[24] I take Geoffrey's number as the most reasonable. Walter has four hundred thousand thousand, the Book of Basingwerk four hundred thousand.

gained this victory, until the winter was passed, employing his time in reducing the cities of the Allobroges. In the beginning of the following summer, A. D. 492, he was preparing to cross the Alps and invade Italy, when domestic troubles compelled him to return to Britain, and leave the prosecution of the enterprise to Hoel.

Here the history of the Burgundians supplies a striking confirmation of the truthfulness of the original Brut, and of our system of chronology. At the close of A. D. 490, or at the beginning of A. D. 491, we have been told that Arthur subdued Burgundy, and now we are informed that he was in Burgundy again, in A. D. 492, preparing to invade Italy. A. D. 491 was marked by a revolution in Burgundy. Hitherto the Burgundians had been, as represented in the story of Riothamus, the firm allies of Rome, and Gundebald had been invested with the dignity of Patrician by Olybrius, in A. D. 472; but in this year he rebelled against his brother Chilperic, defeated and slew him, and usurped his throne. In A. D. 492 he invaded Italy, ravaged Æmilia and Liguria, and took Turin, and returned with immense spoils to his own kingdom in the following year. These coincidences convince me, that Arthur supported him in his rebellion, and placed him on the throne; and that he was the instigator of the invasion of Italy, an enterprise in which he would have borne part in person, had not the affairs of Britain obliged him to leave it in the hands of Hoel and Gundebald; and the fact, that Gundebald could ravage with impunity the provinces in question, is the more readily accounted for, if we accept the Brut as evidence, that Arthur destroyed a Roman army in Gaul in the preceding year.

Independently of these coincidences, it is no more improbable that Arthur should have invaded Gaul, than that Maximus and Constantine should have done so. At the beginning of his reign he had successfully repelled the incursions of the Saxons; he had carried his arms even into the countries whence they came, and made the rulers of those countries his tributaries or allies; like Ælfræd at a later time, he had attached to his interests, by cession of territory, the Saxons whom he could not altogether drive out of the country; and thus he had secured his dominions from foreign invasion, and consolidated his power during a prosperous reign of twenty-three years. In A.D. 490 Britain was safe, and the weakness of the Roman Empire offered an opportunity to his ambition. Such an invasion of Gaul, as the Brut describes, was therefore possible, and with these coincidences to support its narrative, must now be regarded as an unquestionably historic fact.

For the little that we know of the events of this period we are rather indebted to incidental sources of information, than to professed histories. The latter are altogether silent with regard to these affairs, but in the former I think I can detect one reference to them. Writing to the senate, in A.D. 510, Theodoric recommends for their approval Felix, whom he had nominated consul for the following year.[25] He says, that he belonged to a family, which had once been illustrious and of consular rank, but had been reduced and obliged to leave their country, by some great calamity which had befallen Gaul, and had come to Rome, and achieved distinction there. Juret supposes, that he alludes to the invasion of Gaul by Maximus, and to something of the kind he certainly does allude; but when he says, that this nomination was regarded as a revival of the former consulate of Felix, it is clear that the revolution or invasion in question must have been subsequent to A.D. 428, the year of the consulate of

[25] "Jacebat nobilis origo sub Gallicano justitio, et honoribus suis privata peregrinabatur in patriâ. Tandem pressos divina levaverunt. Romam recepere cum gloriâ, et avorum antiquas laureas ab ornatâ Curiæ silvâ legerunt. Nam quis possit negare generi munus, cujus habeatis velut in arcâ depositum. In ore quippe rumoris est, quondam Felicis adhuc vivere consulatum." CASSIODOR. *Variorum*, II. 3.

Felix and Taurus; and now that we are enabled to place Arthur's invasion of Gaul amongst the facts of history, we may not unreasonably suppose, that this is the event to which Theodoric refers.

Arthur's designs for the invasion of Italy were checked by intelligence which reached him from Britain, that Modred, whom he had left as regent, had usurped his kingdom, and taken his queen to wife.

Boece says that Loth died about this time, and in this he is supported by the Brut, which records Loth's presence at the festival of Caerleon, but never mentions him again. After his death, he says, that Modred sent a message to Arthur, reminding him of his sworn engagements, and begging him not to allow himself to be influenced by the persuasion of those who, as he had heard, were endeavouring to set aside his claim to the succession, and favouring the pretensions of Constantine the son of Cador. An answer was returned to this effect, that the treaty with Loth was dissolved by his death, and that the Britons had chosen Constantine for their prince, because he was of the blood royal of their nation.

Buchanan, (an independent witness, inasmuch as he has not noticed the treaty in question, and speaks of Arthur's expedition to Gaul, the story of which Boece repudiates), tells us, that this nomination of Constantine took place whilst Arthur was absent from Britain, and Modred regent. It appears, therefore, that Loth died about the end of A.D. 491, or the beginning of A.D. 492, and as he must have been very far advanced in years, it is probable that he took no part in this campaign personally, but remained at home, sending his forces to assist Arthur.

Thus these Scottish historians place the conduct of Modred in a better light than the Brut does. His right to the succession, which his father had asserted on his behalf at the time of Uther's death, and maintained during three following years, and which Arthur at length guaranteed by treaty, was now set aside; his remonstrance had failed; and the absence of his cousin afforded him an opportunity of taking possession of the kingdom. With regard to his intrigue with Guennuuar, Boece is silent; Buchanan merely says it was suspected.

The Brút and Boece are agreed in saying, that the Picts, Scots, and Saxons were leagued together to support the claims of Modred; the former names the Irish also, and says that Modred sent Selix (or Cheldric) to Germany, to raise all the forces he could, promising him more than even Vortigern had granted, the districts between Kent and the Humber. Cerdic is probably intended here, for the Chronicle "cujusdam Divionensis" cited by Leland, says:[26]—

"He (Modred) aiming at the sovereignty and fearing only "Cerdic, gave him seven other provinces, Sussex, Surrey, "Berkshire, Wiltshire, Dorsetshire, Devonshire, and Gloucestershire, to secure his support. Cerdic peopled his provinces with Angles, and was crowned after the Pagan "manner at Winchester, but Modred over the Britons at "London."

We must understand that these districts were ceded to Cerdic and his allies. This notice, derived from a West Saxon source, names him alone, but Ælle was really at this time paramount chief of the Saxons in Britain.

---

[26] "Ille vero regnum appetens, sed solum Cerdicium timens, dedit ei "ut sibi faveret, septem alias provincias, Sudo-Saxoniam, Sudorheiam, "Berrochiam, Vilugiam, Duriam, Devoniam et Coriniam; Cerdicius "autem suas provincias, accitis Anglis, instauravit, et coronatus est more "gentili apud Wintoniam, Mordredus vero super Brittones apud Londoniam."

This author, however, has fallen into a palpable blunder with regard to Arthur's sojourn in Gaul, and has falsified his statement, in his endeavour to harmonize it with the false date of the battle of Camlann, by saying, that Cerdic died whilst Arthur was in Gaul, and that Cyneric had reached the seventh year of his reign before Arthur returned. Arthur returned as soon as the intelligence reached him, and he had not been a year in Gaul.

Modred, having constant intelligence of Arthur's movements, proceeded to Southampton to await his arrival, and a fierce battle commenced as soon as his troops began to disembark, in which Walgan and Augesil, King of Albania, fell. Arthur, however, made good his landing, and compelled Modred to flee to Winchester; where he had time to rally his scattered forces, and strengthen his position, whilst Arthur remained on the battle-field to bury the dead. This done, Arthur marched to Winchester and besieged it, but Modred made his escape to Southampton, (according to Layamon), took shipping there, and went to Germany for fresh forces, (according to a statement in the Life of Merlin[27]). Returning with large reinforcements, he prepared to renew the contest on the river Camlann. The bishops and clergy of the Picts, Scots, and Britons, (according to Boece and Buchanan), endeavoured to bring about a reconciliation; Modred consented to lay down his arms, on condition that the treaty should be observed; and Arthur was disposed to accept this condition; but the friends of Constantine dissuaded him, insisting that an appeal to arms was necessary for the vindication of his honour. The battle began, and was prolonged throughout the day; towards its close, Arthur attacked Modred's division, and slew him with great numbers of his people, but was himself severely wounded; a rumour of his death inspired his enemies with fresh ardour, and the battle con-

---

27 " Cœperat interea nostrum sibi subdere regnum
" Infidus custos, Mordredus, desipiensque;
" Illicitam venerem cum conjuge regis agebat.
" Rex etenim transire volens, ut fertur, in hostes
" Reginam regnumque suum commiserat illi.
" Ast ubi fama mali tanti pervenit ad aures,
" Distulit hanc belli curam, patriamque revertens
" Applicuit multis cum millibus, atque nepotem
" Oppugnans pepulit trans æquora diffugientem.
" Illic collectis vir plenus proditione
" Undique Saxonibus, cœpit committere pugnam
" Cum duce, sed cecidit, deceptus gente propbanâ
" In quâ confisus tantos inceperat actus." L. 1107-1119.

tinued, and was one of the severest ever known. Most of the leaders on either side fell; on Arthur's are named Etbrict, (or Olbrict), King of Norway, probably Loth's successor, Æscil, King of Denmark, Cador, and Caswallon; on Modred's, three Saxon chiefs, Elaes, Egbrict, and Bruning, Gillomaur and three other Irish princes, and all the commanders of the Picts and Scots. The Britons abandoned the field; Arthur was conveyed to Glastonbury; and the spoils of his camp, and his queen, fell into the hands of his enemies.

As no claim to a victory is made on behalf of the Britons, and as it is evident from the Brut that they suffered severely, we may confidently accept Boece's and Buchanan's account of this battle, which states that they were signally defeated; and the more so, because we find a battle recorded in our chronicles, fought in this very year, A. D. 492, twenty-one years after the siege of Bath, with circumstances which indubitably identify it with this.

In continuation of his narrative of Natanleod's attack on Cerdic, in which we have been told that many brave auxiliaries came to him, Henry of Huntingdon proceeds to say:[28]—

" In the sixth year after the aforesaid battle, Stuf and " Wihtgar, nephews of Cerdic, came with three ships to Cer" dicesore."

Obviously they are not the whole of the auxiliary force, of which he speaks, but they alone are specified, on account of

---

[28] " Sexto namque anno post bellum prædictum, venerunt nepotes " Certic, Stuf et Wihtgar, cum tribus navibus apud Certicesore.

" Primo autem mane, duces Brittannorum acies in eos secundum belli " leges pulcherrime construxerunt; cumque pars eorum in montibus, " pars eorum in valle progrederetur caute et excogitate, apparuit sol " oriens, offenderuntque radii clipeis deauratis, et resplenduerunt colles ab " eis, aerque finitimus clarius effulsit, timueruntque Saxones timore " magno, et appropinquaverunt ad prælium. Dum autem colliderentur " exercitus fortissimi, fortitudo Brittannorum dissipata est, quia Deus " spreverat illos, et facta est victoria patens, et acquisierunt duces præ" dicti regiones non paucas, et per eos fortitudo Certici terribilis facta " est, pertransiitque terram in fortitudine gravi."

Compare this with 1 Macc. VI. 39.

their kindred with Cerdic, and as an introduction to subsequent notices of their proceedings.

"At early dawn the commanders of the Britons arrayed "their ranks against them very beautifully, according to the "tactics of war; and when part on the hills, and part in the "valley advanced cautiously, and according to prearranged "plan, the rising sun appeared, and his rays were reflected "from their gilded shields, and the hills shone with them, "and the air was filled with splendour, and the Saxons were "greatly afraid, and drew near to battle. But when the "brave armies engaged, the might of the Britons was scat-"tered, for God had cast them off, and the victory was de-"cisive, and the aforesaid chieftains gained regions not a "few, and by their aid the might of Cerdic became terrible, "and he passed through the land in great strength."

Thus the sixth year after A.D. 487, *i.e.* A.D. 492, was marked by the arrival of a large auxiliary force, and by a great battle afterwards,—a battle for which great preparations had been made, not the result of a hasty gathering of the Britons to oppose the small band of Stuf and Wihtgar; and the coincidence of the date, together with what is said of the might of the Britons being scattered, because God had cast them off, indicating a decisive victory, clearly establishes its identity with the battle of Camlann.

It appears from the description of this battle, that the British forces were drawn up to the westward of those of the Saxons, and this would really be the case; for Layamon's testimony, and local tradition, that it was fought near Camelford in Cornwall, have been confirmed by discoveries of bones and armour in the neighbourhood; and Arthur's castle of Tintagel is to the westward of the river Camel. So, on the morning of the battle, the rising sun would reveal to Modred's forces, encamped on the opposite bank of this river, those of Arthur occupying the valley and the hills, between it and the sea. The possession of Tintagel would be one of Modred's objects; it had been his residence whilst he was regent; it was now in Arthur's hands, and had victory declared in his favour, it would have been the place of his retirement, rather than Glastonbury; it was doubtless what Boece calls his camp, which fell into the hands of his enemies, after the battle.

There is a statement in the notes to "Excerpta e Chronicis "Scocie" that Modred's allies were Cerdic, and Eugenius, King of the Scots. This agrees, with regard to the former, with what we are told elsewhere of his alliance with Modred; and taking this in connection with the passage above cited, we may believe that he brought to Modred's assistance all the forces he could command, including the recently arrived band of Stuf and Wihtgar. Elaes who fell in this battle may have been his father Elesa. Etbrict or Olbrict may have been Ida's great grandfather Æthelberht. Ælle perhaps fell in this battle, for he must have been engaged in it, and Henry of Huntingdon continues:[29]—

"About this time died Ælle, King of the South Saxons, "who was supreme lord of all the kings and chieftains of the "Angles, and Cissa his son reigned after him."

With regard to Eugenius, Fordun, Boece, and Buchanan also mention him, as king of the Scots at this time, and Modred's ally; but they interpolate his name in the series of the kings of Scotland, in order to reconcile their statements with the false chronology by which they are fettered; for the Duan, the earliest authority for this succession, shows that there was no king of this name in Scotland during the sixth century. The series in the Duan commences with Loarn, whose ten years' reign ended probably in A.D. 502,[30] and this

---

[29] "Circa hoc tempus obiit Ælle, rex Australium Saxonum, qui "omnia jura regni Anglorum, reges scilicet et proceres, in ditione suâ "tenebat. Regnavitque post eum Cissa filius ejus."

[30] It was subsequent to A.D. 501, for in that year Muircheartach, who murdered him, was in Ireland, but it cannot have been much later. According to the Duan, the succession of the kings of Scotland, between his death and the accession of Aodhan, A.D. 570, was—Feargus 27 years,

Eugenius may have been his immediate predecessor, and have fallen in this battle, with the rest of the leaders of the Picts and Scots.

In the Life of Merlin, Taliesin is represented as saying,[31] that Arthur was received at Glastonbury with great honour by Queen Morgen, who examined his wound, and gave hopes of his recovery. These hopes, however, were disappointed. After lingering for some time, Arthur perceived that his end was approaching, committed the kingdom into the hands of Constantine, and died A. D. 493, (May 21, according to Rosse).

An ancient sepulchre, intended by those who were interested in the search, to prove itself the sepulchre of Arthur, was opened in A. D. 1189,[32] in the cemetery at Glastonbury. There was on the one hand a superstition that he was not dead, and on the other a tradition that he was buried at Glastonbury; it was the policy of Henry II. to establish the

---

Domhangart 5, Comhgall 24, Gabhran 2, Conall 15; and this gives four years more than the interval between these dates; but by making Conall's reign 10; *i. e.* 2×5, (the number of years assigned to him by Fordun, Boece, and Buchanan), instead of 3×5, (as it is in the Duan), we obtain the sum of their reigns, very nearly coincident with the interval between these limits. If, then, we date the death of Loarn in A. D. 502, the succession will be as follows:—A. D. 502 Feargus, 529 Domhangart, 534 Comhgall, 558 Gabhran, 560 Conall, 570 Aodhan; and there is no room for the reigns of Eugenius, Constantine, and Eugenius, which Fordun, Boece, and Buchanan interpolate in this series.

31 "Illuc, post bellum Camblani, vulnere læsum
"Duximus Arcturum, nos conducente Barintho,
"Æquora cui fuerant et cœli sidera nota.
"Hoc rectore ratis, cum principe venimus illuc,
"Et nos quo decuit Morgen suscepit honore,
"Inque suis thalamis posuit super aurea regem
"Strata, manuque sibi detexit vulnus honestâ,
"Inspexitque diu; tandem redire salutem
"Posse sibi dixit, si secum tempore longo
"Esset, et ipsius vellet medicamine fungi.
"Gaudentes igitur regem commisimus illi,
"Et dedimus ventis redeundo vela secundis." L. 930-941.

32 The last year of Henry II, and most probably the first of Abbot Henry de Soilly, under whom the search was made.

truth of the latter; and a search was ordered to be made, in a spot which was sure to be crowned with success by the discovery of an interment. It was recognized as a sepulchre, indeed distinctly marked as such by the pyramids, (tapering pillar-stones), one at either end,—objects of curious interest, on account of their venerable antiquity; and William of Malmsbury, thirty years before, (at a time when no suspicion that Arthur was buried there, existed at Glastonbury), had recorded his belief, that the bodies of those whose names were written on the monuments, were contained in stone coffins within. To prove that this was the sepulchre of Arthur, nothing more was necessary than to forge an inscription, which might impose on the credulity of the twelfth century, but which the archæological science of the nineteenth must condemn. The cross of lead, which served to identify the remains of Arthur and his queen is lost, but a representation of it has been preserved, sufficient to show, that its form and character were precisely such as were usual in the twelfth century, such as those, discovered in the coffins of Prior Aylmer (who died A.D. 1137), and of Archbishop Theobald (who died A.D. 1161), and in the cemetery of Bouteilles near Dieppe, present. The pyramids appear to have resembled the Bewcastle and Ruthwell monuments; their age is determined, by the names of King Centwine and Bishop Hedde,[33]

[33] It was twenty-six feet high and had inscribed on it these names, and two others, Bregored and Beorward. Centwin became King of the West Saxons, and Hedde Bishop of Winchester, in A.D. 676; the former became a monk in A.D. 685, the latter died in A.D. 705. Bregored was an abbot of Glastonbury, (but not in the times of the Britons, as William of Malmsbury concluded from his name, for it is clearly Saxon), and Beorward may be the abbot Beornwald who attested a charter of Ine in A.D. 704. The larger pyramid, twenty-eight feet high, which stood at the head of the grave, is said to have been in a very ruinous condition, and the only intelligible words in the inscriptions upon it, (as given by William of Malmsbury), are the names of Wulfred and Eanfled. The discovery of these trunk-coffins at Glastonbury, has not been noticed by Mr. Wright, in his account of the similar discoveries at Gristhorpe, Beverley, Driffield,

inscribed on the smaller one, to have been the close of the seventh, or the beginning of the eighth century; and as the skeletons of a man and a woman were found in coffins hollowed out of the trunks of oak-trees, it is probable that they were those of Wulfred and Eanfled, whose names occur in the inscription on the larger one.

The Brut says that Guennuuar fled to Caerleon, after Modred's first defeat. However, she was with Arthur at the time of the battle of Camlann, for Boece says, (and his statement appears to be worthy of credit, because he accounts for her subsequent history, of which the Brut tells us nothing), that she was taken after the battle, and conveyed by the Picts to Dunbar, that she lived there during the remainder of her life, and that she was buried at Meigle in Angus, where her monument was distinguished, in his days, amongst the many ancient sepulchral memorials which existed there, and still exist.

---

and Selby, (Gent. Mag. 1857, vol. ii. p. 114), nor by Mr. Wylie in his paper on the Oberflacht graves, (Archæologia, vol. xxxvi. p. 129), but deserves to be mentioned, in connection with them.

CHAPTER XVI.

The Reigns of Constantine, A. D. 493; *Conan,* 495; *Vortipore,* 496; *Maglocun,* 500; *Caredig,* 502; *and Muircheartach Mac Erc,* 506 *to* 513.

IF my theory as to the original compiler of the Brut be correct, his authority is most valuable with regard to the circumstances of Arthur's two campaigns in Gaul, and his short residence in Britain during the interval between them. Of these, as a young noble of the court of Hoel, he may have been an eye-witness, and they are detailed with greater minuteness than those of any other event in the history. This minuteness of detail is wanting in the narrative of Arthur's struggle with Modred; and now his interest in the affairs of Britain ceases, and he passes hastily over the events of the five following reigns.

The conclusion of Henry of Huntingdon's notice of the battle of Camlann,—"The might of Cerdic became terrible, "and he passed through the land in great strength,"—indicates a continuation of the war; and the Life of Merlin[1]

---

[1] "Illico Modredi duo nati regna volentes
"Subdere quisque sibi, cœperunt bella movere,
"Alternâque suos prosternere cæde propinquos.
"Deinde nepos regis dux Constantinus in illos
"Acriter insurgens, populos laniavit et urbes,
"Prostratisque simul crudeli morte duobus,
"Jura dedit populo, regni diademate sumpto." L. 1125-1131.

informs us, that the war was continued by the two sons of Modred, but that they were eventually defeated by Constantine, and together put to a cruel death. The Brut says, that after their defeat, the Saxons fled with one of them to London, where he was killed, and buried in a monastery, and that the other fled to Winchester, and was slain there in the church of Amphibalus, (the Abbot), before the high altar.

Here Boece's statement, relative to the marriage of Modred about A. D. 470, is confirmed, for he must have been married about that time, to have had sons old enough at this to compete with Constantine for a kingdom, and S. Gildas, (as we shall see), tells us that they were already famous warriors.

He was at this time resident at Glastonbury. The feelings which the murder of his brother had excited more than twenty years before, and which he had endeavoured to subdue, had been revived by Arthur's perfidy towards Modred; and now these sacrilegious murders provoked him to write his famous letter of reproof, to Constantine and other princes of Britain. This is a most important document, inasmuch as three of these princes whom he addresses, as reigning cotemporaneously with Constantine, are named in the Brut as his successors; the Brut is therefore entirely independent of it, and receives from it incidental support; and when we read the introductory passages, with the aid of the history, as we have gathered it from other sources, we see in them strong internal evidence that its author,—however severely, (as having had the advantage of an education in Gaul), he may have spoken of the barbarism of the Picts and Scots in his History,—was himself either a Pict or Scot, attached to Modred's interest.

Thus when he says,[2]—

"Britain has kings, but they are tyrants; she has judges,

---

[2] "Reges habet Britannia sed tyrannos; judices habet sed impios; " sæpe prædantes et concutientes, sed innocentes; vindicantes et patro- " cinantes, sed reos et latrones; quamplurimas conjuges habentes sed

"but they are unjust ones; often plundering and invading, "but the innocent; avenging and patronizing only criminals "and robbers; having many wives, but harlots and adul- "teresses; often swearing, but perjuring themselves; making "promises, but almost immediately breaking them; warring, "but prosecuting civil and unjust wars; strenuously indeed "pursuing thieves throughout the land, and not only loving, "but rewarding, the robbers who sit with them at table,"— we are reminded of Arthur's unprovoked invasion of Gaul on Hoel's behalf, and of his wars with the Picts and Scots in Britain; of his vigorous resistance to the encroachments of the Saxons, and his liberality towards his allies and supporters; and of his violation of the treaty with the family of Loth. Grief for his brother's death occasioned S. Gildas to destroy what he had written about Arthur's early successes, and to withhold his name in his History, even when he had occasion to speak of one of these successes; and in the epistle, although he evidently alludes to him when he styles Cuneglas[3] "the driver of the chariot which carried the bear," it is but to express his detestation of his memory.

His notice of the murder of the sons of Modred, enables us to understand more clearly the brief statements in the Life of Merlin and the Brut:[4]—

"scorta et adulteras" (vel 'scortantes et adulterantes'); "crebro jurantes "sed perjurantes; voventes, et continuo propemodum mentientes; bel- "ligerantes, sed civilia et injusta bella agentes; per patriam quidem "fures magnopere insectantes, et eos, qui secum ad mensam sedent, "latrones, non solum amantes, sed et munerantes."

[3] "Auriga currus receptaculi ursi."

[4] "Immundæ leænæ Damnoniæ tyrannicus catulus Constantinus. Hoc "anno, post horribile sacramentum juramenti, quo se devinxit, nequa- "quam dolos civibus, Deo primum jureque jurando, sanctorum demum "choris et Genitrice comitantibus fretis, facturum, in duorum venerandis "matrum sinibus, ecclesiæ carnalisque, sub sancto abbate" (vel 'sancti 'abbatis') "Amphibalo, latera regiorum tenerrima puerorum, vel præ- "cordia crudeliter duum, totidemque nutritorum,—quorum brachia ne- "quaquam armis, quæ nullus pene hominum fortius hoc eis tempore "tractabat, sed Deo altarique protenta, in die judicii ad tuæ civitatis

"Constantine, the tyrannic whelp of an unclean lioness of "Damnonia. In this year, after the fearful sacrament of an "oath, by which he bound himself never to practice treachery "against his countrymen, who trusted in God first and the "oath, in company with the choirs of Saints, and the Mother "(of God), he has cruelly torn with his wicked sword and "spear, for teeth, the tender sides or hearts of two royal "youths, and of their fosterers, in the venerable embrace of "their two mothers, the church and their carnal mother, "under the holy Abbot Amphibalus, amongst the holy altars "themselves, as I have said, so that their cloaks, purple with "coagulated gore, touched the seat of the heavenly sacrifice; "whose arms stretched forth, not with weapons, which scarce "any one in this time handled more bravely than they, but "to God and the altar, will hang up the venerable trophies "of their patience and faith, in the day of judgment, at the "gates of Thy city, O Christ."

This is a strictly cotemporary notice, written in the very year of the murder, and therefore of great value. Although the presence of their mother and of their guardians is mentioned, it states expressly that the youths were warriors, inferior in valour to none of their cotemporaries; it alludes to an oath, taken by Constantine, to keep peace with them, of which the Brut says nothing; and it appears to represent the murders as having been perpetrated in the same place, the monastery of the Abbot Amphibalus,—in this respect differing from the Brut, but agreeing with the statement in the Life of Merlin.

"portas, Christe, veneranda patientiæ ac fidei sua vexilla suspendent,— "inter ipsa, ut dixi, sacrosancta altaria, nefando ense hastâque pro dentibus laceravit, ita ut sacrificii cœlestis sedem purpurea ac si coagulati "cruoris pallia attingerent."

"Sub sancto abbate Amphibalo" is the reading of Polidore Vergil's MS., and I prefer it to "sub sancti abbatis Amphibalo" of the Cambridge MS., as agreeing better with the Brut.

In the third year of his reign, A.D. 495, Constantine was slain by Conan. In the Life of Merlin,[5] this is said to have occurred in warfare; and with this notice, which speaks of Conan as still living, its history of these British princes ends.

Conan is stated in the Brut, to have been prompt and spirited in war, but the murderer of an uncle and two cousins whose right to the crown was nearer than his own. S. Gildas accuses him of murders, fornications, and adulteries, and reminds him of the untimely death of his parents and brethren. He died in the second year of his reign, A.D. 496.

Vortipore, his successor, (according to Geoffrey and the Book of Basingwerk, but not noticed by Walter), is said to have reigned four years, and to have suppressed an insurrection of the Saxons, who were aided by a large body of their countrymen from Germany.

This seems to be the battle of which Henry of Huntingdon speaks, as fought in the seventy-first year of the coming of the Angles, A.D. 498:[6]—

"The kingdom of Wessex begins in the seventy-first year "of the coming of the Angles—which kingdom in process of "time subdued all the other kingdoms, and obtained the "monarchy of all Britain. For in that year the bravest of "the Britons made war against Cerdic at Cerdicesford; and "their leaders fought bravely and obstinately on either side,

---

5 "Nec cum pace fuit, quoniam cognatus in illum
"Prælia dira movens violavit cuncta Conanus;
"Proripuitque sibi regiones, rege perempto,
"Quas nunc debiliter nec cum ratione gubernat." L. 1132-1136.

6 "Regnum Westsexe incipit anno adventus Anglorum LXXI—quod "scilicet regnum cætera omnia sibi processu temporum subjugavit, et "monarchiam totius Brittanniæ obtinuit. Certic regnavit XVII annis in "Westsexe: inierant namque bellum fortissimi Brittannorum contra "eum apud Certicesford in eodem anno; perstiteruntque duces eorum "magnanimiter et proterve ex utrâque parte, donec, declinante jam die "ad vesperum, Saxones victoriam obtinuerunt; et facta est plaga magna "in die illâ super incolas Albion; atrocior vero multo fuisset, nisi sol "occidens prohiberet. Ampliatum est autem nomen Certici, et divul-"gata est fama bellorum ejus et Kinrici filii sui per universam terram. "Ab illâ quippe die incepit regnum Westsaxonum."

" until, when the day was declining towards evening, the " Saxons obtained the victory; and there was a great scourge " on that day on the inhabitants of Albion; but it would " have been much more severe had not the setting sun hin- " dered it. So the name of Cerdic was magnified, and the " fame of his wars, and those of Cyneric his son, was spread " abroad throughout the land. Indeed from that day began " the kingdom of the West Saxons."

Severe as the slaughter is said to have been, from the statement that the victory was not so complete as it might have been, we may infer that it was a drawn battle, so that either side might claim the victory. However, from this year the foundation of the West Saxon kingdom is dated; this is the last date in the Chronological Notes; this probably is the original conclusion of the history, from which Henry of Huntingdon has hitherto derived his materials, and we hear no more of the computation from the coming of the Angles. The West Saxon kingdom is said to have begun in this year, because, although Cerdic had been twenty-four years in Britain, up to this time he had owned the supremacy of Ælle, and his son Cissa. Such is clearly the meaning of Henry of Huntingdon's authority, for after the notice of the supremacy of Ælle, and the accession of Cissa, quoted above, he continues, with reference to the South Saxon dynasty:[7]—

" But in process of time they were greatly reduced, until " they became subject to other kings:"—

and then follows this notice of the rise of the West Saxon kingdom.

S. Gildas calls Vortipore the wicked son of a good king. He was, probably, the degenerate offspring of Ambrosius, to whom he alludes in his History. Besides the crimes with which he taxes Conan, he accuses him of incest with his own daughter.

---

[7] " At in processu temporum valde minorati sunt, donec in aliorum " jura regum transierunt."

Malgo or Maglocun succeeded him. The Brut and S. Gildas are agreed as to his character; he was sagacious, bold, and war-like, was taller in stature, and possessed more influence than the other kings of Britain; but was addicted to the sin of Sodom.[8] S. Gildas says, that in his youth he had rebelled against and oppressed the king his uncle; that after he had attained the object of his ambition he was impelled by remorse of conscience to embrace the monastic state, but abandoned it after a time and married; that he rejected his wife for the sake of another, the wife of his nephew, whom he publicly espoused, after the murder of her husband and his own wife.

His expedition against his uncle appears to be mentioned in the Life of S. Paternus, where it is said, that Mailgun, King of the Northern Britons, led an army into the territories of the Southern Britons, and gained a victory over them. On his return he was guilty of an outrage on the saint, but being afterwards afflicted with sickness and blindness, he confessed his fault, begged pardon, and recovered. It is not unlikely that his embracing the monastic profession was the consequence of this repentance.

He is said to have been the first successor of Arthur who exacted tribute from the six countries which Arthur had subdued, Ireland, Isoland, Scotland, Orkney, and Norway. He died of the yellow plague[9] in a monastery, ten years after the

[8] The later Malgo, who has been confounded with this, was a person of very different character.

[9] We learn, from the lives of S. David, S. Theliau, and S. Paternus, that there was a visitation of the yellow plague, many years previous to the date which is marked in the Annals of Cambria and Tighearnach.

S. David was born about A.D. 462; S. Theliau was his fellow pupil in the school of Paulens, a disciple of S. Germanus; S. Paternus came with a colony of monks from Armorica, and was founding monasteries in Cardiganshire, when his adventure with Mailgun occurred. Those three made a pilgrimage to Jerusalem together, and on their return they found the yellow plague raging. This, therefore, was earlier than the synod of Brevi, which is the next event recorded in the Life of S. David, and which is generally dated A.D. 512.

battle of Camlann, (according to the Annals of Cambria), *i. e.* in A. D. 502.

It is possible that Vortipore did not enjoy the sovereignty, but reigned cotemporaneously with Maglocun; and that the succession was, as Walter gives it, Constantine, Conan, and Maglocun, all nephews of Arthur; for a prophetic passage in the Life of Merlin[10] speaks of the nephews of the "Boar of "Cornwall" as laying snares for one another, and gaining the throne by murder; and their successor (Caredig) is said to have been the fourth of the series. If so, the sovereignty of Maglocun would commence in A. D. 496.

If the genealogy which is given later in the Brut[11] be genuine, it will agree very well with the date here determined for Maglocun's death, A. D. 502. His great grandson Iago fell in the battle of Chester, A. D. 617, Cadvan his son died soon after, and Cadwallo his son was killed in the battle of Heavenfield, A. D. 634. The interval between this date and A. D. 502 gives twenty-six years for a generation; whilst the interval between it and A. D. 551 gives not quite seventeen.

Caredig succeeded Maglocun. On account of disputes with his kindred he became unpopular amongst the Britons; and the Saxons, aware how little hold he possessed on the affections of his subjects, sent to Ireland for Garmund, a

---

10 "Cornubiensis apri conturbant quæque nepotes
"Insidias sibimet ponentes, ense nephando
"Interimunt sese, nec regno jure potiri
"Expectare volunt, regni diademate rapto.
"Illis quartus erit, crudelior asperiorque." L. 586-590.

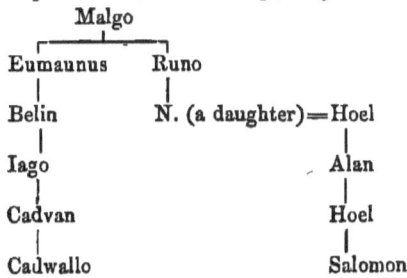

11 Malgo

Eumaunus — Runo

Eumaunus | Belin | Iago | Cadvan | Cadwallo

Runo | N. (a daughter)=Hoel | Alan | Hoel | Salomon

King of Africa, who had come thither with a fleet, and invited him to invade Britain. He came accordingly with three hundred ships.

This was the person who was destined to complete the conquest of Britain. Layamon, whencesoever he derived them, gives the fullest details of his history. There was, he says, a powerful king in Africa, named Anster, who had two sons Garmund and Gerion. At his death, he left his kingdom to Garmund, who handed it over to his brother, saying he would win a kingdom with his sword, collected a large force of adventurers from different countries, embarked in a career of piracy, subdued all the islands in his course, visited Ireland, and came at last to Southampton. Six chieftains in the North, of Hencgest's kindred, hearing of his coming, sent an invitation to him, and he proceeded to Northumbria by sea, and formed a league with them.

There were at this time, as we shall see in the sequel, connections of Hencgest in the North; indeed, from what is related of Garmund's distributing the kingdoms, it is not unlikely that these chieftains were the founders of the Anglo-Saxon royal dynasties; and in the poem of Beowulf, the scenes of which are certainly laid in Northumbria,—in the very district in which Garmondsway moor, (about six miles from Durham), preserves the remembrance of a chieftain of this name,—a Garmund is mentioned incidentally, as one who was well known to Northumbrian tradition.

Garmund and his Northumbrian allies marched against Caredig, whose subjects now flocked to his standard, defeated him and put him to flight.

The date of this war, I believe, was A. D. 506; for Cerdic, in whose territory Garmund landed, would of course be engaged in it, and Henry of Huntingdon's next notice belongs to this year:[12]—

[12] "Certic et Kinric filius ejus, anno nono regni ejus, pugnaverunt "iterum contra Britannos apud Certicesford, et facta est strages magna "ex utrâque parte."

"Cerdic and Cyneric his son, in the ninth year of his "reign, fought again with the Britons, at Cerdicesford, and "there was great slaughter on either side."

It was not however at Cerdicesford, but at Cerdicesleage, (as it is in the Saxon Chronicle), that this battle was fought. In the South there is no place which will answer to this name, but in the Central districts there are two Charleys, one in Staffordshire, and one in Leicestershire, and I give the preference to the latter, because there is a place called Battle Flat in the neighbourhood; and Garendon, also in the neighbourhood, may have derived its name from Garmund—Garmundes-dún. Other circumstances, which will be noticed in the sequel, confirm this conjecture.

Caredig fled to Cirencester, and Garmund followed, and besieged him there, whilst he continued to ravage the country. At this time he was joined by a force of two thousand Franks led by Isembard, (or Imbert), who had been dispossessed of his territory by his uncle Louis, (Chlodovech), and had fled to save his life; and who now engaged to assist him in this war, on condition that he should accompany him to Gaul, after its conclusion, and assist him in return to recover his kingdom.

Now, although we do not find the name of Isembard in the history of the Franks at this period, the circumstances of his story are in exact accordance with what we actually find recorded therein. At this very time, the policy of Chlodovech was to destroy all the kings of the Franks, and the foundations of the empire he bequeathed to his children were laid in their blood. Sigibert, Chloderic, Chararic, Ragnachar, Ragnamer, and Richar, with many others, fell victims to his treachery; so that, when he hypocritically complained that he was left without kindred, in order to learn if any yet survived, not one could be found. Others doubtless had escaped, and Isembard may have been one of them.

Garmund, (according to Layamon), invested Cirencester

with a circuit of five castles. These may still be traced; there are irregular entrenchments at Trewsbury to the south-west, at Ranbury to the south-east, and at Bibury to the north-east; and Bagendon to the north, and Pinbury to the north-west, (the names of which indicate the former existence of something of the same kind), complete the circuit of twenty-two miles—five forts at an average distance of four miles and a-half from each other, and of four from Cirencester.

The city was taken at length by a stratagem; nutshells filled with combustibles were attached to the wings of sparrows, and fire was thus communicated to the thatch of the buildings.[13] Caredig sallied forth to give battle to his enemies, but was defeated and driven beyond the Severn into Wales.

Gaimar, in a short, and evidently distinct narrative, confirms this part of the story. Omitting all mention of Garmund, he says, that Cirencester was set on fire by sparrows, through the negligence of the Britons, whilst Cerdic was besieging it, and then that the Saxons took the city, and drove the Britons beyond the Severn. This notice is valuable, as evidence that Cerdic was associated with Garmund in this war.[14]

Layamon says it was never known what became of Caredig; that a messenger came to Garmund with intelligence that he was in Ireland, preparing to renew the contest; but that no one ever knew the issue of this threat. A clue to the mystery of his disappearance is supplied by a story which will be noticed presently; but Layamon's record of a rumour, which reached the ears of Garmund, but was not verified by

---

[13] A similar story is told of Harold Hardrada in the eleventh century.

[14] The taking of Cirencester by these chiefs is not to be confounded with the later capture of the same place by Ceawlin, A.D. 576, which Gaimar mentions also, in its proper place. Walter writes Caer Vyddau (*i. e.* Silchester) for Cirencester. In the Life of Merlin it is Kaer Keii (*i. e.* Cirencester).

the event, has at least a character of verisimilitude about it. It is exceedingly improbable that such a circumstance could have been invented; the original chronicler of a mere rumour must have lived very near to the time of the events with which it was connected.

After this, Garmund overran the whole country, and did not desist until he had entirely subdued it; destroying the cities, wasting the country, murdering even the clergy and husbandmen, and forcing the rest to flee whithersoever they could for safety.

Here the original Brut, the work (as I conceive) of S. Albinus, ends. The words which follow are evidently the valedictory address of the author, evidently the effusion of a cotemporary, deploring the vices and misfortunes of the Britons; and he speaks of them not as his own countrymen, but as of another nation.

"Alas! Britons, is it nothing strange that ye are thus "humbled? Your ancestors subdued other nations in former "ages, and ye now have fallen so low, as not to be able to "defend your own country from foreigners. Repent, un-"happy Britons, according to your misdeeds, and acknow-"ledge the truth of the words of the Gospel, that a kingdom "divided against itself cannot stand. For it is thus that the "disunion of the Britons destroyed their country, and there-"fore the Pagans inherit it."

Having completed the conquest of Britain, Garmund went to London, assembled there the Saxon chiefs, apportioned to them the conquered provinces, and departed. For a long time after this the Britons made no attempts to recover what they had lost; even that part of the island, which still remained in their hands, being divided into three principalities, between which there were frequent civil wars. The Saxons also are said to have had three (or five) kings, constantly occupied in war, either with the Britons, or with one another.

This is exactly accordant with what Henry of Huntingdon

says, immediately after his notice of the battle of Cerdicesleage:[15]—

"At that time came many, and frequently, from Germany, "and occupied East Anglia and Mercia, but they were not "yet subjected to one king. Many chieftains occupied the "provinces in turns, whence there were innumerable wars, "but the chieftains are nameless, because they were many."

Garmund abandoned his British conquests in order to fulfil his promise to Isembart, the proper sequel to which is contained in one MS. of Wace,[16] in a narrative which is confirmed by a passage in the Life of Merlin,[17] and by Giraldus Cambrensis; to the effect, that they sailed from the Humber to the Somme, and there disembarked, and that Chlodovech, hearing of their arrival, hastened to give them battle, and defeated and slew them at S. Valery.[18]

---

[15] "Ea tempestate venerunt multi et sæpe de Germaniâ, et occupa-"verunt East Angle et Merce; sed necdum sub uno rege redacti erant. "Plures autem proceres certatim regiones occupabant, unde innumera-"bilia bella fiebant; proceres vero, quia multi erant, nomine carent."

[16] Bibliothèque Impériale, MSS. du Roi 7515 3. 3.

[17] "Illis quartus erit crudelior asperiorque.
"Hunc lupus æquoreus debellans vincet, et ultra
"Sabrinam victum per barbara regna fugabit.
"Idem Kaer Keii circumdabit obsidione,
"Passeribusque domos et mœnia trudet ad imum,
"Classe petet Gallos, sed telo regis obibit." L. 590-595.

[18] One or two French chronicles combine this story with the history of the Danish invasion of France and Belgium in A.D. 880, and say that Guaramund or Guormund fell in the battle of Sancourt, in A.D. 881. But Guthrun or Gorm, whom they identify with Guormund, died in England in A.D. 890, and in the best French authorities for the events of this war, the cotemporary Chronicles of S. Vedast and Regino, there is no notice of such a person. On the contrary, it appears that the leaders of the Danish force, which sailed from Fulham to Ghent in A.D. 880, ravaged the districts between the Scheldt and the Somme in the following year, and were defeated at Sancourt, were Godfrid and Sigefrid. Under A.D. 882, the Chronicle of S. Vedast contains a notice, which may account for the introduction of Garmund's name in connection with these events. After he had concluded a treaty with Hæsten, on the Loire, Louis III. pursued the daughter of one Garmund, and on attempting to enter her

The date, A.D. 506, which I have assigned to this war of Garmund and Caredig, (by a collation of the Brut with Henry of Huntingdon), will exactly allow for Muircheartach Mac Erc the seven years' reign in Britain, which is given to him in the Legend of S. Cairnech in the Book of Ballymote. The story is as follows:—

Sarran assumed the sovereignty of Britain, and established his power over the Saxons and the Picts. He had married Babona (or Pompa), daughter of Loarn king of the Scots, and had issue by her S. Cairnech, S. Ronan, S. Brecan, and Luirig. He afterwards married her sister Erc, who eloped with Muiredhach, and was the mother of four sons, Muircheartach, Fearadhach, Tighearnach, and Maian. After victory and triumph he died in the house of Martin. Luirig succeeded him and extended his power over the Saxons; but, having forcibly built a fort within the monastery of his brother S. Cairnech, he was slain by Muircheartach, who was at that time an exile in Britain, for having slain some monks in Ireland, and his grandfather Loarn in Scotland, in A.D. 502. Muircheartach succeeded him, and enjoyed for seven years the sovereignty of Britain, Caithness, Orkney, and the Saxon land. He took to wife the widow of Luirig, after many battles with the king of France, and had by her Constantine, and three other sons. The Franks and Saxons made war upon him, but he destroyed their country and cities after a long contest. He then went to Ireland, and established his kingdom there, and the power and strength of Britain were destroyed after him.

Now Muircheartach figures in the Irish annals from A.D. 482 to 501, and he became King of Ireland in A.D. 513. His seven years' reign in Britain, therefore, must have com-

---

father's house, to which she had fled, received the injuries which caused his death.

Gaimar, unsupported by any respectable authority, introduces Garmund into his narrative of the Danish wars in England, A.D. 879.

menced in A. D. 506; and this story accounts for his appearance in Britain as an exile, by saying, that he was banished from Ireland for the murder of the Crossans, and from Scotland for the murder of Loarn. The interval of twelve years in his Irish history will exactly allow for what is here related of him in Britain; and I am satisfied that Sarran, and his son Luirig, are no other than Maglocun and Caredig.

The circumstances of the early history of Maglocun,[19] his repudiating his wife for the sake of another, the wife of his nephew, his victorious career, and death in a monastery, almost exactly correspond with Sarran's union with two sisters, his victorious reign and death in a monastery, (either dedicated to S. Martin, or following his rule). Maglocun had a son called Rhun, and Sarran a son called Ronan.

Luirig, which the editors of the Irish version of the History of the Britons justly regard as corrupted,[20] may well stand for the name of Caredig; for it is remarkable that a very similar mis-spelling occurs, in the case of the name of the father of the earlier S. Cairnech or Carantoc, which was also Caredig, but is written Luiteic by MacFirbis. The injustice towards his brother, of which Luirig is accused, may have been one of those disputes with his kindred, which (according to the Brut) made Caredig unpopular amongst the Britons; and it is a very remarkable coincidence, that Muircheartach, already an exile in Britain, should commence his reign exactly at the time of Caredig's disappearance. We are also told, that Muircheartach fought with the king of the Franks, to gain possession of his daughter, the widow of Luirig; and then that the Franks and Saxons made war upon him; and here we have another coincidence with the story in

---

[19] Maglocun and other similar words are rather surnames, (as in the instance of Tuathal Maelgarbh), than names; and this person may have been called Sarran, as another who figures later in the history was called Peredur.

[20] The MSS. of this version abound in corruptions of proper names.

the Brut, which associates Franks with the Saxons in the war which was not concluded by Caredig's defeat. It is by no means unlikely that Caredig's wife should have fallen into the hands of the Frank prince Isembard; the only circumstance that excites surprise, though not impossible, is that she should be said to have been his daughter.

This story is important in another respect. It enables us to form a probable conjecture, relative to a matter which has hitherto baffled the ingenuity of every investigator of the history of this period, the identity of the Constantine, whose conversion is recorded in the Annals of Cambria, Ulster, and Tighearnach. I believe him to have been the son of Muircheartach, by the widow of Caredig.

He could not have been the son of Cador, who was killed by Conan; and yet Boece relates of that Constantine, what evidently belongs to the history of this; saying, that Jurmirik, a Saxon chief, came with a fleet to Britain, gained an easy victory over him, and drove him into Wales; that he, finding his life there insecure, fled into Ireland, and lived with his wife and children for some years unknown, subsisting on alms; that afterwards, when he became known, he was persuaded by some monks to receive the tonsure in their monastery, and lived a devout life therein for some years; and that eventually he was slain by the Scots, and venerated as a martyr. In the Life of S. David, we read of a Constantine who left his kingdom, was received into S. David's monastery, spent a long time in servitude there, but at length departed into a distant country, and founded a monastery. The lessons for the feast of S. Constantine, in the Aberdeen breviary, say, that he abdicated the throne, retired to Ireland, became miller to a monastery in which he was afterwards ordained priest, accompanied S. Columba to Scotland, A.D. 565, preached the Gospel in Cantyre, and then suffered martyrdom, A.D. 576. Fordun mentions him as a king of Cornwall, who abdicated the throne, accompanied S. Columba, evangelized the Picts of Cantyre, suffered martyrdom, and was buried in the monastery which he had founded, at Govan on the Clyde.

The son of Muircheartach is the only person to whom all these statements can apply. Born probably in A. D. 507, and driven from Ireland by Tuathal Maelgarbh, (after Muircheartach's death, in A. D. 534), he might attempt to gain a footing in Cornwall, and be repulsed, as Boece says, by Eormenric, who was then reigning in Britain, over a territory far more extensive, than that which afterwards owned the authority of his son. S. David's monastery afforded him shelter for a time, and his leaving it is accounted for by Boece's statement, that he found his life insecure in Wales. In Ireland obscurity would be his only safety, for he would be an object of suspicion to the reigning king. The Annals of Cambria place his conversion, (*i. e.* his monastic profession), in the year 145, which, (according to the date of the battle of Camlann and some others), would correspond to A. D. 544; and this date will agree exactly with those of his departure to Scotland A. D. 565, and his death A. D. 576.[21]

[21] A similar difference appears in the date of the death of S. David, in these Annals. It is placed under the year which answers to A. D. 601, and forty-five years deducted from this will give A. D. 556, which, although later than the generally received date, is at any rate nearer to the truth than A. D. 601, and may possibly be the truth itself.

CHAPTER XVII.

Recapitulation; the Lay of Havelok.

THE computation from the coming of the Angles ceases with the establishment of the West Saxon kingdom, in the seventy-first year, A.D. 498. This appears to have been the original limit of the authority which Henry of Huntingdon followed, for after this date he adopts another computation, that of the regnal years of the West Saxon kings. This, too, is the proper limit of the present inquiry, and it only remains for us briefly to consider, what are its results.

According to the system of chronology which we have adopted,—in which, taking in good faith the Saxon and British annals, and giving in their due succession the events they respectively record, we have only corrected the former in accordance with a date supplied by the earliest authority, for the coming of the Angles, A.D. 428, and the latter, in accordance with a date given by other authorities, for Arthur's accession, A.D. 467,—we have seen, as the events of these years have passed in review before us, how all anachronisms, —involved in the system which is based upon the dates in the Saxon Chronicle and the Annals of Cambria,—have disappeared one after another; every successive event has fallen into its proper place; the Saxon Chronicle and the Brut have been proved accordant; and the result is a perfectly connected and consistent history, such as has never yet been expected, vindicating the truth of our early historians, and showing that authentic materials formed the substance of their Chronicles.

According to this system alone, the first coming of S. Germanus, of which the date is certain, falls within the reign of Vortigern, and the place of the Alleluia victory, which certainly belongs to his first sojourn in Britain, is fixed; his second coming coincides with the time of Vortigern's death, and both the first and the second with the expeditions of Ambrosius, thus vindicating what is said of him in the History of the Britons, and the Life of S. Dubricius; the forty-fourth year of the coming of the Angles, the date of the siege of Bath, is also the fifth of Arthur's reign; Arthur's war with Hueil in Anglesey is followed in due course by his reconciliation with S. Gildas; Cerdic's arrival occurs at a time when Arthur was absent from Britain, and Arthur's cession of certain districts to him proves to have been a measure necessary for the security of his own kingdom, preparatory to his Norwegian expedition; the story of this expedition is in perfect accordance with the chronological data supplied by two distinct stories of Havelok; his first Gallic campaign appears to have been undertaken at the very time when Odoacer, who would certainly have repelled and chastised such an invasion, was engaged in his struggle with Theodoric, and in the first year of the struggle; his transactions in Burgundy and projected invasion of Italy, are singularly in accordance with the history of Burgundy at the time; S. Dubricius, who is said to have presided at the festivities of Caerleon, was actually Archbishop of the see at the time, when (according to this system) it must have been celebrated, but not at the date which the usual chronology would give; Cerdic's decisive victory over the Britons, in the sixty-fifth year of the coming of the Angles, corresponds with the battle of Camlann, in which one authority informs us that he was engaged; the time of Garmund's war, in alliance with a nephew of Chlodovech, and with Cerdic, agrees with that of Chlodovech's reign, and of Cerdic's victory at Cerdicesleage; and lastly the story of Muircheartach's seven years' reign, commencing from the time of that victory, and ending A.D. 513, supplies, as it were, the key-stone of the whole structure.

It is evident that a system of chronology, founded on dates, not arbitrarily assigned, but deduced from authorities as trustworthy as any that we have, and confirmed by others; a system which brings so many distinct authorities into harmony, removing all anachronisms, and giving us in their place so remarkable a chain of coincidences as this; a system which enables us to discover a foundation of historic truth, in stories which have hitherto been looked upon as mere romances; a system which guides us through the maze, as it has hitherto seemed, of the history of the fifth century; must be true. One difficulty, however, will naturally occur to the reader; how is this system to be reconciled with the West Saxon annals of the sixth century? This is easily removed. To the end of the reign of Cerdic, I still follow Henry of Huntingdon, dating successive events according to the years of his reign. Thus, in his thirteenth year, A. D. 510, he conquered the Isle of Wight; in A.D. 514, he committed the government thereof to his nephews Stuf and Wihtgar. He reigned seventeen or eighteen years, so that his death must be dated A.D. 515 or 516. The accession of Cyneric who reigned twenty-six years and died A.D. 560, must be dated A.D. 534; so that we have an interval to account for of about nineteen years.

Now it appears, from the oldest statements of the West Saxon genealogy, that this Cyneric was not the son of Cerdic, who accompanied him to Britain, in A. D. 474, but his grandson, the son of Creoda. Either, therefore, the first Cyneric may have reigned during this interval, and his name have been confounded with that of the second; or Creoda may have succeeded Cerdic, and the annals of his reign have been lost, because they were not marked by any victories, (the only events which the Chroniclers of those days thought worth recording). So, in the history of Kent, the reign of Ossa is lost, and his name, like that of Creoda, known to us only from the genealogies. We may remark, however, as some confirmation of this mention of the name of Creoda, that there was certainly a Creoda connected with the West Saxon kingdom; for the Codex Diplomaticus gives us Crudansceat[1] near Bentley in Hampshire, Creodanhyl[2] near Alton, not far from the last, Creodantreow,[3] certainly in Hampshire, (the place where Egberht assembled his army preparatory to his expedition against the Britons in A. D. 825), Criddanwyl[4] (now Crudwell) near Malmsbury in Wiltshire, and Crydanbricg[5] (now Curbridge) near Witney in Oxfordshire. The only other places in England that bear this name are in Staffordshire, Warwickshire, and Worcestershire, where of course, (although they may indicate Creoda's presence during Garmund's war), the later Mercian Creoda may claim them. Independently of these, we have nearly as many traces of Creoda within the limits of the West Saxon kingdom, as we have of his father Cerdic, although his name, like those of Cissa, Ossa, Eormenric, and other princes of his time, has all but disappeared from the pages of history; whilst but one trace is to be found of a Cyneric, either his brother or his son, Cynerices gemæro[6] near Upton in Wiltshire.

---

[1] Cod. Diplom. 1093. [2] Ib. 1035, and 1070. [3] Ib. 1033, and 1035.
[4] Ib. 271, 329, and 817. [5] Ib. 1201. [6] Ib. 468.

If now we examine the story of Havelok, we shall find, in the chronological indications it contains, a confirmation of our theory, which thus connects, by a reign of nineteen years, our chronology of the fifth century with that of the sixth.

Peter Langtoft testifies, that the traditions of this Havelok were rife in Lincolnshire in his day, though he could not find his story in writing; but Gaimar, about two centuries before, had published it at full length; and there is a separate Lay of Havelok appended to the Arundel MS. of Gaimar, and an English version in a MS. at Oxford. In the French versions we are told, that he was the son of a king of Denmark named Gunter, who was slain by Arthur; that Grim, one of his father's thanes, fled with him, an unconscious infant, to Britain, and settled at Grimsby; that he was brought up in ignorance of his real parentage, and, when he had attained to manhood, placed as a servant in the kitchen of a king named Æthelsige,[7] whose dominions extended from the Humber to Rutland, and whose residence appears to have been at Lincoln. Cotemporary with Æthelsige was a king named Earconberht,[8] who reigned, the story says, in the country which is now called Northfolce; whose dominions are represented as extending from Holland to Colchester (or Leicester); who had married Orwen, a sister of Æthelsige, and had by her Earconhild,[9] whom at his death he committed to the care of her uncle, with a charge to marry her to some prince of acknowledged bravery. He died at Tiedfort,[10] (or Teford), and Orwen died soon after him in Lincolnshire. Æthelsige, hoping to gain undisputed possession of Earconberht's kingdom, gave his niece in marriage to his servant Havelok, who had already, in the humble situation which he filled, displayed all the qualities which

[7] Edelsi in the MSS.

[8] Ekenbright in the Lay of Havelok, Achebriht in the earliest MS. of Gaimar, Edelbrict in the others.

[9] Argentille in the MSS.

[10] Tetford in Lincolnshire.

befitted his royal birth. A dream led to inquiries on her part as to his real origin, and, to satisfy her, he took her to Grimsby, where the secret was revealed to them by Grim. Havelok then sailed to Denmark, which was still governed by Odulf, (or Adulf), the brother of Æscil, who had received it from Arthur, after Gunter's death. There he was recognized by Sygar, one of his father's thanes, with whose aid he gathered an army, defeated Odulf, and recovered his paternal dominions. He reigned in Denmark for four years, then collected a fleet, returned to England, landed at Carlefleur,[11] defeated Æthelsige in a battle at Tetford, obtained the kingdom of Earconberht, and shortly afterwards, on the decease of Æthelsige, his kingdom also. He reigned for twenty years. After his death, these kingdoms were separated; Gaine[12] apparently ruling Lindsey, and Burghard Northfolce. Wasing, another king of the same race, made war upon them; Gaine fled before him, and acquired the epithet of Coward on that account; but Burghard sought the aid of Cyneric and Ceawlin, and with them defeated and slew him.

Now, if we suppose that twenty years elapsed from the time that Havelok was brought to Britain, an unconscious infant, to that of his marriage, this term added to A. D. 487, when his father was slain, will bring us to A. D. 507, for the date of his expedition to Denmark, and recovery of his father's kingdom; four years more, the duration of his reign in Denmark, will bring us to A. D. 511,[13] for the time of his return to England; and twenty years more, the duration of his reign in England, to A. D. 531, for the time of his death. Thus three years only, of the reigns of Gaine and Burghard, are all that are required to bring us within the reign of Cyneric, A. D. 534 to 560; and it must be remembered, that the first

---

[11] Possibly Saltfleet. [12] Whose name we have at Gainsborough.

[13] The very time when the conquest of Britain was completed, and Henry of Huntingdon speaks of a fresh influx of the Teutonic tribes.

term, of twenty years of the life of Havelok, is set down at the lowest probable estimate.

Thus these forty-four (or forty-seven) years connect our chronology of the fifth with that of the sixth century; and this story affords an additional confirmation of the truth of our system, and in particular of the conjecture, that a reign of about nineteen years intervened between those of Cerdic and Cyneric; whereas it is evident, that according to the usual computation, forty-four years after Arthur's Norwegian expedition, (even supposing that it were possible according to that computation), would carry the date of Havelok's death twenty years beyond that of Cyneric's.

For the limits of Earconberht's kingdom, the variations in the MSS. give us the alternative of Leicester and Colchester, and I prefer the former, which would make his dominions coterminous with those of Æthelsige, as throughout the story they appear to have been; and Leicester is afterwards mentioned in connection with Burghard. By Northfolce, then, we must understand Holland and parts of Northamptonshire and Leicestershire. Tetford in Lincolnshire was the place where Earconberht died, and Havelok gained his victory.

Thus we have attained in great measure the object proposed at the outset of this inquiry, and by a careful collation of the authorities we possess, have gathered therefrom a clear, connected, and consistent history of the eventful fifth century; the period of Britain's emancipation from the Roman yoke, vigorous struggle for independence, and eventual subjugation by the Saxons. We have fixed positively the date of the great advent, and have shown how the struggle was continued, and when completed.

THE END.

CHISWICK PRESS:—PRINTED BY WHITTINGHAM AND WILKINS,
TOOKS COURT, CHANCERY LANE.

www.ingramcontent.com/pod-product-compliance
Lightning Source LLC
Chambersburg PA
CBHW032015220426
43664CB00006B/249
* 9 7 8 3 3 3 7 0 9 1 4 5 3 *